Carpatho-Ukraine in the Twentieth Century

Carpatho-Ukraine in the Twentieth Century
A Political and Legal History

Vincent Shandor

Distributed by Harvard University Press
for the
Ukrainian Research Institute, Harvard University

Printed in Canada by Best Book Manufacturers
Jacket Design by Jennie Bush, Designworks

This volume represents an important new direction for the publications program of the Harvard Ukrainian Research Institute as it begins to publish the memoirs and analyses of outstanding individuals who have significantly contributed to Ukrainian history. We are pleased that we can begin this new effort with Dr. Shandor's work. The editorial board would like to thank Mr. Raymond Smith, whose work editing the text was invaluable. Mr. Benjamin Szporluk diligently keyboarded the text. Ms. Mary Foster Richards assisted with the final proofing and indexed the text. Ms. Jennie Bush of Designworks designed the jacket and binding stampings.

The Harvard Ukrainian Research Institute was established in 1973 as an integral part of Harvard University. It supports research associates and visiting scholars who are engaged in projects concerned with all aspects of Ukrainian studies. The Institute also works in close cooperation with the Committee on Ukrainian Studies, which supervises and coordinates the teaching of Ukrainian history, language, and literature at Harvard University.

This Work Is Dedicated
to the Shining Memory
of Ivan Shandor

✳

Ця книжка присвячена
світлій пам'яті
Івана Шандора

Vincent Shandor

Contents

Editor's Note

Raymond Smith

The release of Dr. Vincent Shandor's *Carpatho-Ukraine in the Twenti-eth Century* represents a significant scholarly occasion: the publication of the political memoirs of a still-living author who was an important government official in pre-World War II Central Europe. While there were a profusion of such political memoirs published after the war, it is only a rare confluence of events that makes possible the publication of this book as the twentieth century draws to a close. At thirty years old in 1937, Shandor was a newly trained lawyer and economist invested with unusually important responsibilities for a man of such relatively young age. At ninety years old in 1997, he is an elder statesman blessed with a productive capacity and an agility of mind rare at any age.

During the Cold War years, Dr. Shandor published numerous schol-arly articles on Carpatho-Ukraine, and the 1990s have seen the publica-tion of two books by him in Ukrainian. The first, a companion volume to this work, entitled *Transcarpathia: A Historical-Legal Essay from the Ninth Century to 1920,* was published in 1992, while the first volume of his *Reminiscences: Carpatho-Ukraine, 1938–1939,* appeared in 1996. While Shandor worked on the present volume throughout the Cold War, it was only after the tectonic shifts caused by the collapse of the Soviet Union in 1991 that he drew together all the disparate pieces of this book. The finished product is a synthetic work—political memoir, scholarly analysis, and patriotic manifesto.

The Life of Vincent Shandor

Views based strongly in Ukrainian patriotism are entirely consistent with the life and history of Vincent Shandor. He was born on October 12, 1907 in the village of Baranintsi, a few miles from the Carpatho-Ukrainian capital of Uzhhorod, into a family of five children which self-identified as Ruthenian-Ukrainians. Of these five children, two went on to receive university degrees, two went on to become teachers, and the fifth was an agronomist. His father, a plowman, was elected *starosta,* or head of the village, under both Hungarian and Czechoslovak rule and belonged to the Christian Peasant Party headed by Msgr. Avhustyn Voloshyn.

During World War I, a soldier named Yulian Bebeshko, a prisoner of war from the Russian army, lived with the Shandor family and

worked in their household. The family soon discovered that they understood the language spoken by Bebeshko and other prisoners from
eastern Ukraine far better than the language spoken by those from
Moscow and other Russian regions. As Shandor relates the story, it was
these prisoners who enabled the local Ruthenians to "perceive their
linguistic and historical closeness to those who were from Ukraine. The
prisoners were the first to talk openly about Ukraine, its history, traditions, and culture." The Ukrainian songs they learned "from the captured Russian Army soldiers of Ukrainian origin gave a strong impulse
to the self-identification of Ruthenians from Transcarpathia, spurring
national revival and development." After World War I, Shandor's father became politicized as a Ukrainian nationalist. In January 1919, the
elder Shandor took part in a Congress in Khust that endorsed the
unification of Carpatho-Ukraine with the rest of Ukraine, one of several political acts which provoked an angry response from local Hungarian officials. Shortly thereafter, however, the region became part of
the new Czechoslovak state.

Shandor himself graduated from secondary schools in Uzhhorod and
Mukachevo, beginning work at the Podkarpatskyi Bank in Uzhhorod in
1927. He recalls that during this period, Carpatho-Ukraine was steadily
"de-Magyarized" as the influence of Hungary began to wane. From
1928 to 1930, he served in the armed forces in Uzhhorod, at that time
studying Latin in order to be able to enter law school. From 1930 to
1935, he studied law at Charles (Karlový) University in Prague, obtaining his doctorate in law in 1939. During the tumultuous decade of 1935
to 1945, Shandor was manager of the regional branch of the Zemská
Banka in the Slovak capital city of Bratislava. For the crucial years
1938 to 1939, Shandor was named the representative of the Khust-
based Carpatho-Ukrainian Government to the Czechoslovak Federal
Government in Prague, charged in part with negotiating Carpatho-
Ukrainian autonomy. One major project was to secure the symbolically
important right to use Ukrainian as the official language of government
in Carpatho-Ukraine—and then to oversee the translation of technical
legal materials and, when necessary, to develop appropriate Ukrainian-
language terminology. Shandor also had responsibility for budgetary
matters for the financially strapped Carpatho-Ukrainian government,
which had few sources of revenue beyond timber and salt exports.
Drawing on his background in banking, he negotiated several loans
from Prague and also managed trade contracts.

With the invasion of Carpatho-Ukraine by the Soviet Red Army at the close of World War II, Shandor was forced to flee to Germany. There he entered the Political Science Department at the Goethe University of Frankfort. With the financial assistance of an uncle from Pittsburgh, Shandor secured a Czechoslovak visa for himself, his wife Oksana, and their son. After briefly taking a job in the U.S. in a tin factory, Shandor became Director of the Secretariat of the Pan-American Ukrainian Conference, where he worked from 1948 to 1961. At the same time, he also helped found the New York office of the Ukrainian Congress Committee and undertook further study in political science at Columbia University, from 1953 to 1954. In 1959, he began work as an economic researcher at the General Secretariat of the United Nations. From 1961 until his retirement in 1977, Shandor analyzed politics and economics in the Communist world for the U.S. Department of the Treasury. Even after his retirement he continued to research and write, and also served from 1985 to 1989 as Vice-Premier of the Government of the Ukrainian National Republic in exile.

Carpatho-Ukraine in the Twentieth Century *as a Scholary Work*

Carpatho-Ukraine in the Twentieth Century is imbued with a crystalline traditionalist view of Carpatho-Ukrainian nationalism that eschews the current vogue for viewing nations as "imagined communities." Dr. Shandor's perspective on the "Ukrainian question" in Carpatho-Ukrainian history is so strong and organic that it has little need of elaborate justifications: he and his compatriots know themselves to be Ukrainians and have demonstrated this knowledge by repeatedly and openly casting their lot with a Ukrainian national identity. In matters of law, Dr. Shandor is firmly positivist and, as befits a legal scholar of his generation, firmly rejects the neo-realist school of international law that grew up in this country (around Yale Law School) after World War II. His application of international law, it should also be noted, is timebound. One of his major points of reference are traditional principles of Roman Law, which form the basis of European jurisprudence. Notable in this regard is his rejection of the application of the doctrine of *terra nullius,* or the concept that land which does not have an established sovereign becomes "no man's land" and thus open to be claimed by others. Part of his rejection of this concept with regard to Carpatho-Ukraine is rooted in Roman Law and part in such Wilsonian concepts as the right to national self-determination and to territorial inviolability, precepts of positivist international law, which were very much in the minds of the "small nations" of Europe during the interwar period.

* * *

Although—like many of his compatriots who were forced by Communism into political exile—he was not able to live in Carpatho-Ukraine for half a century, Vincent Shandor has remained deeply committed to the causes, first, of Carpatho-Ukrainian inclusion as part of the larger Ukrainian nation-state and, second, of self-determination for that nation-state. *Carpatho-Ukraine in the Twentieth Century*, published at the start of the tenth decade of his life, represents an important intellectual legacy to future generations of Carpatho-Ukrainians in particular, and, indeed, to all those interested in the reborn Ukrainian state.

Abbreviations

AKPR   Arkhyv Kantseliariï Prezydenta Respubliky [Archives of the Office of the President of the Republic]

AMZS   Arkhyv Ministerstva zakordonnykh sprav [Archives of the Ministry of Foreign Affairs]

AMZV   Archiv Ministerstva zahranicnych věci [Archives of the Ministry of Foreign Affairs]

ANRR   Amerikans'ka narodna rada rusiniv [The American National Council of Ruthenians]

ČSR   Československá republika [Czecho-Slovak Republic]

KSUT   Kul'turnyi soiuz ukraïns'kykh trudiashchykh [Cultural Union of Ukrainian Laborers]

Külmst.   Külügyminisztérium. Orszagos leveltar. Hungary [State Archives of the Ministry of Foreign Affairs Of Hungary]

OL   Orszagos Leveltar. Magyarország [State Archives of the Republic of Hungary]

PDMF   Polska Rzeczpospolita Ludowa—Ministerstwo spraw zagranicznych [Polish People's Republic—Ministry of Foreign Affairs]

PUN   Provid ukraïns'kykh natsionalistiv [Leadership of Ukrainian Nationalists]

RGADA   Rossiiskii gosudarstvennyi arkhiv drevnikh aktov [Central State Archives of Ancient Documents]

RNK   Revoluční narodní komitét [Revolutionary National Committee]

RNP   Revoluční narodní parlament [Revolutionary National Parliament]

Sb. zák. a n.   Sbírka zákonů a nařízení [Collection of Laws and Decrees]

SEC   State Economic Council (Prague) [Ukr. Derzhavna hospodars'ka rada]

SOS   Stráž Obrany Státu [Guardian of the Defense of the State]

TOPMR   Tiskový Odbor Presidia Ministerské Rady, Praha [Press Agency of the Presidium of the Ministerial Council, Prague]

TsRNR   Tsentral'na rus'ka narodna rada [Central Ruthenian National Council]

UNA   Ukraïns'ka natsional'na armiia [Ukrainian National Army]

UNO   Ukraïns'ke natsional'ne ob'iednnania [Ukrainian National Union]

UNR   Ukraïns'ka narodna rada [Ukrainian National Council]

UNRP   Ukraïns'ka narodna rada Priashivshchyny [Ukrainian National Council of the Priashiv Region]

UPA   Ukraïns'ka povstancha armiia [Ukrainian Insurgent Army]

UZIS   Uchenye zapiski Instituta slavianovedeniia, Moskva [Scientific Notes of the Institute of Slavonic Studies, Moscow]

ZODA   Zakarpats'kyi oblasnyi derzhavnyi arkhyv [State Archives of the Transcarpathian Region]

Preface

Owing to the historical developments of political conditions, the territory of the state of Ukraine has over long periods of time been under foreign occupation. As a result, each occupying power invariably attached to the territory of Ukraine it ruled a name that best reflected its domination, political demands, and goals.

The name of the part of Ukraine and its population under study here, Carpatho-Ukraine and Ruthenian-Ukrainians respectively, clearly points to their common national and historical past with Kyivan Rus'-Ruthenia, which eventually adopted the name Ukraine.

Under Hungarian occupation up to the end of World War I, this territory was referred to as "Uhorska Rus" or Hungarian Ruthenia. The name was applied to the territory that at the time encompassed thirteen *zhupy* or districts, reaching deeply into what is today considered Hungary proper and in which lived "Ruthenians" (i.e., Ukrainians). This designation was in use both in literary works as well as in political documents and therefore indicates not only a geographic area but also gives it a juridical, political connotation.

From 1919 to 1939, this territory constituted a part of the then newly established state of Czecho-Slovakia and was officially accorded the name "Podkarpatská Rus" or Subcarpathian Ruthenia. Subsequently, for a brief period of time—from October 1938 to March 1939—the government of the province adopted the name of Carpatho-Ukraine, which was formally legalized by an act of the Soim (Diet) on March 15, 1939. Throughout this work, we shall refer to this territory as Carpatho-Ukraine except where it is cited differently in documents or quotations.

Also to simplify matters, we shall use the hyphenated name Czecho-Slovakia instead of Czechoslovakia again except in documents and quotations. It should be pointed out here that the English spelling *Czechoslovakia* or the Czech and Slovak *Československo* was used from the inception of the republic until October 1938 and then for a number of years after World War II. The hyphenated version of the spelling denotes the federative structure of the republic from October 1938 to March 1939 and then again from 1968 to the proclamation of full independence by Slovakia.

Proper names of persons used in the Ukrainian language are translit-
erated into English phonetically, as is common in their later writings in
the West, but may appear in different spellings in citations, depending
on what original language may have been used. Thus, for instance, the
name of Carpatho-Ukraine's prime minister and later president may
appear as Voloshyn or Vološin or simply Volosin (from Ukrainian,
Czech, and Hungarian languages). Place-names have been transliter-
ated according to the standards of Harvard's Ukrainian Research Institute.

Part of the territory under discussion had been ceded to Slovakia and
Romania to be administered temporarily by them until a final solution
of the borders was to be found. Thus, the Priashiv (Prešov) Region fell
to Slovakia after the formation of the republic and is still being administered by Slovakia, while the Maramorosh Region was ceded to Romania. Moreover, a part of the territory in which Ruthenian Greek-
Catholics lived remained within the confines of Hungary. In this study,
the territories of Priashiv and Maramorosh Region, together with
Carpatho-Ukraine proper, are referred to as Transcarpathia. In 1944,
Carpatho-Ukraine proper was joined to the Ukrainian SSR and designated as the Transcarpathian Oblast or Region.

In this work, I availed myself, aside from other sources, of my own
notes taken during the short-lived federation union, along with a part of
official government materials gleaned from the archives of the Office
of the Representation of the Carpatho-Ukrainian government in
Prague. In 1939, I transferred the major portion of these archives to the
Museum of the Liberation Struggle of Ukraine in Prague. However, the
building which housed the Museum was bombed in April 1945, and I
could not salvage any archival materials from the debris when I arrived
at the site in May 1945.

Also, I utilized for this work a number of interviews recorded on
audio tapes, many letters received from participants in the building of
our state, as well as previously published works in several foreign
languages on topics relating to my subject that have appeared in a
rather impressive number.

I must admit and am conscious of the fact that this work bears a
pioneering character. My intention was to systematize the available
material and project it in a certain historical perspective, according it a
national and political image along the lines of the concept underscoring
Transcarpathia's union with a Ukrainian state. This historical concept
and aspiration was viewed as state treason by the various foreign

occupiers of the individual Ukrainian lands and assiduously combatted by them. A profound and thorough analysis of the problem of Transcarpathia's belonging to the Czecho-Slovak Republic is yet to be thoroughly explored as are the many-faceted fields of its statehood to be individually analyzed.

I would find it most gratifying should this work prove to have contributed to a correct understanding of Transcarpathia's historical and juridical past as well as of its age-old aspirations to have Kyiv as its state capital.

I wish to express my sincerest thanks to those who have made this work of mine possible. My thanks go to my wife Oksana for her help in reading the manuscript of this work and for her patience and devotion which she has so unflinchingly displayed over the many years of its preparation.

I also wish to express my appreciation and gratitude to Father Dr. Atanas Pekar, OSBM, and Oleh Lashchenko for their invaluable advice after reading the manuscript.

I am especially grateful to Imre Kardashinetz for his translation of this work, his invaluable remarks, constructive critique, professional advice, and great help. I further wish to thank my uncle Ivan Petrus, my son Bohdan and his wife Maria, my late son Ivan's wife Lydia, Ing. V. Kachurovsky, and V. Stelen for their moral and financial support for the translation. I am also grateful to the Executive Board of the Carpathian Alliance, Inc., my countrymen, and people of good will who have made my work possible. Finally, I would like to thank Raymond Smith, who edited the manuscript, and Robert De Lossa, who oversaw the publishing process, for their help and scholarly comradeship.

This book required a full seven years of almost uninterrupted research work for which I am grateful to Almighty God for having blessed me with good health, the necessary stamina, and longevity of life to complete this work.

I dedicate this work to the memory of my son Ivan, who died tragically at far too early an age.

Vincent Shandor
October 1997

Carpatho-Ukraine in the Twentieth Century

PART I

The Interwar Years, 1918–1938

CHAPTER ONE

The Unification of Carpatho-Ukraine with Czechoslovakia

Action Taken by Ruthenian Americans

Toward the end of World War I, the subjugated peoples of the Austro-Hungarian Empire began to raise their voices for their national and cultural rights. Some of them, for instance, the Czechs, Slovaks, Romanians, and Croats, already had their political representatives abroad who engaged in activities designed to promote the idea of liberation and statehood for their respective peoples. Such activity was possible only abroad, for within the Austro-Hungarian Empire it was tantamount to high treason and, in the event of war, punishable by death.

In the United States, there lived a community of some 200,000 Carpatho-Ruthenians dispersed throughout a number of states who at the beginning of 1918 began to show interest in the political future of their Old Country. The government of Hungary combatted all manifestations of national life among the Ruthenians both at home and in America as well. In order to more effectively combat such manifestations, Hungary resorted to a stratagem which branded professions of Ukrainian national adherence as "pro-Russian Slavophilism" or "Slavic peril" and associating them with political movements in Russia and the "Russian" peril. Offering an example of the methods and means Hungary used in its struggle against the aspirations of Ruthenians and Slovaks residing in the United States is a document, titled Ministerial Communication No. 393, directed February 4, 1907 by the Hungarian Minister of Religion and Instruction to the Cardinal Prince Primate, Archbishop of Esztergom, in reference to the spiritual case of Hungarians who had emigrated to America.

The Hungarian government pointed out that Slavophilism was spreading among Ruthenians in America and that this could become

dangerous for Hungary once the Ruthenians returned home. It, therefore, proposed the following counteractions:

> ... the Government with the hearty cooperation of the *Congregatio
> de Propaganda Fide* and of the Bishop of Eperjes [i.e., Priashiv—
> V.Sh] contemplates shortly sending at its own expense zealous
> priests from Eperjes to take charge of the Mission. Furthermore, a
> concordat of principles has been concluded between Propaganda Fide
> and the Hungarian government looking forward to the appointment
> of an Apostolic Delegate at Washington, likewise at the expense of
> the Hungarian Government, to keep the Ruthenians in America under
> surveillance in the interest of their spiritual guidance. From the point
> of view of the internal politics of Hungary, this proves to be consider-
> ably more important than the question of the organization of the
> Ruthenians.

The Hungarian consul in Pittsburgh advised his government not to
allow priests with Slavic leanings to go to America. The Hungarian
government proposed to create and dispatch a special commission to
America consisting of the bishops of Košice, Nitra, Banská Bistrica,
Spiš, and Rožňava. The government would gladly defray the costs of
such a commission. The official copy of this document bears the signature of Komlóssy, Officer of the Ministerial Bureau.

United States government agencies drew attention to the fact that a
foreign country was using police-espionage methods against American
residents, frequently also American citizens. They were incensed:

> It has been known for years that the Government in Buda-Pest has
> been subsidizing newspapers in this country printed in Magyar, Slo-
> vak and Ruthenian to inculcate in their readers the sentiment of
> Magyar patriotism. It was also equally well known that certain
> Austro-Hungarian consular agents in the East were under special
> instructions to report to Buda-Pest on the so-called Panslav propa-
> ganda among the Hungarian Slavonians.

> But it was a surprise and a revelation both, when on the publication of
> this ministerial order it was learned that the Government proposes to
> extend its net of espionage over the thresholds of American priests,
> hiring "well-meaning priests" to use the language of the order for the
> purpose of spying on the "Panslav sympathizing priests."

> This order will set many a man thinking. Why is the Hungarian
> Government taking all these unusual and expensive measures? Why
> does it propose to keep the Slovaks and Ruthenians in the United
> States under surveillance, any more than [to turn] the Magyars, Ger-
> mans and Croats into detective bureaus and the parishes of Magyar

priests into houses of espionage? Why maintain here, in the pay of the Hungarian Government, visitants who stir up trouble among our Greek-Catholics, discouraging them from American citizenship? And why, above all, support a number of reptilian sheets that disseminate dangerous ideas among our foreign population? Let Mr. Komlóssy answer these questions, if he can.

What the Hungarian Government should do, instead of devising means how to save the Slovaks and Ruthenians in America to "their faith and country," would be to better their lot at home, to protect them from the violence and the rapacity of government officials. It is true that the Slovaks and Ruthenians make poor Magyar patriots and that on coming to the United States they learn to hate the tyrants who oppressed them in their ancient homes. But when and where did cruelty beget gratitude?[1]

Presented above is almost the entire text of these important documents issued by the Hungarian and American governments. It is gratifying to learn that the U.S. government had taken such a determined stand in defense of the rights of Ruthenians and Slovaks not only in the United States, but also of those at home. The Hungarian statistics of 1910 claim that some 70 to 90 percent of the population in Carpatho-Ukraine was illiterate.[2] It is, therefore, all the more astonishing that a powerful state such as Hungary should have considered these "illiterate" Ruthenians, who travelled to the United States in order to earn money for their daily bread, as so dangerous that they felt compelled to organize an espionage network against them. This act apparently was dictated by the Hungarian Government's bad conscience. As regards the 1910 statistics, its falsity is evident in the fact that Hungarian officials registered everyone as illiterate who could not read or write in Hungarian even if they had command of their own native language.[3]

In the early years of World War I, the Ruthenian Americans did not show any noticeable uniform, centrally organized political movement. It was not until after America had entered the war in 1917, and particularly in 1918, that the first signs of such a movement became evident. Under the leadership of Dr. Gregory Zhatkovych, Ruthenian Americans in 1918 entered into negotiations with Prof. Tomaš G. Masaryk, chairman of the Czechoslovak Liberation Council Abroad, with a view to preparing the groundwork for uniting their homeland with Czechoslovakia. But because of the war, it was impossible for the Ruthenian

Americans to establish contact with leading political figures in their
Old Country.

In order to render the negotiations more efficacious, an American
National Council of Ruthenians (Amerikans'ka Narodna Rada
Rusiniv—ANRR) was formed under Dr. Gregory Zhatkovych's chair-
manship on October 23, 1918. This was accepted into membership of
the Mid-European Democratic Union of which Masaryk was president.
In his capacity as a representative of Carpatho-Ruthenians,
Zhatkovych, together with representatives of eleven other nations,
signed the "Declaration of Common Aims of the Independent Mid-
European Nations" in Philadelphia. During his stay in Philadelphia,
Zhatkovych and five other members of the American National Council
of Ruthenians devoted their efforts to negotiations with Masaryk concerning a federation of Carpatho-Ruthenia with Czechoslovakia. No
formal agreement, however, was signed at the end of the negotiations.[4]

The American National Council of Ruthenians (ANRR) presented
its territorial and political demands in the form of a resolution to
Masaryk which read as follows:

> That the Uhro-Ruthenians with the broadest autonomous rights as a
> state, on a federative basis, be united with the Czechoslovak Demo-
> cratic Republic, provided that attached to our land are all the original
> Uhro-Ruthenian counties: Szepes, Sáros, Zemplén, Abauj, Borsód,
> Ung, Ungocsa, Bereg, and Maramorosh.[5]

Zhatkovych presented the resolution to Masaryk, who welcomed it
with gratification being pleased that the issue of federation was making
headway. Replying to Zhatkovych's inquiry about the possibility of a
federation between the Ruthenians and the newly created Czechoslovak state as well as the future frontiers, Masaryk said, "If the
Ruthenians decide to join with the Czechoslovak Republic, they shall
constitute a fully autonomous state." As for the frontiers, he declared
that "the frontiers will be so determined that the Ruthenians will be
satisfied."[6] Unfortunately, this latter promise was not kept, a circumstance that gave rise to political tension between the representatives of
the Ruthenians-Ukrainians and the Czechoslovak government.

The territorial demands embodied in the aforementioned resolution
were fully justified in that they referred to areas in Hungary originally
inhabited by Ruthenians although in some of the counties they did not
constitute a majority. In subsequent negotiations with Zhatkovych,

Masaryk cautioned that the idea of unification with Czechoslovakia could be construed and objected to as that of only the American Council of Ruthenians itself. It was, therefore, agreed to hold a plebiscite among Ruthenian Americans in the Greek-Catholic (i.e., Uniate) parishes which, indeed, did take place in Scranton, Pennsylvania, on November 12, 1918. The outcome of the plebiscite was as follows:

Table 1[7]

For union with:

Czechoslovakia	67%
Ukraine	28%
Hungary	less than 1%
Russia	less than 1%
Galicia	less than 1%
For full independence:	2%

Several conclusions may be drawn from the results of the plebiscite. First, since less than one percent voted for union with Russia, the Hungarian government's accusations that the Ruthenians were imbued with Russian Slavophilism were groundless and spiteful. Second, it should be pointed out that despite the all-out efforts of the Hungarian government to Magyarize the Ruthenians only less than one percent voted for union with Hungary. Thus, the outcome was a reflection of the attitude of the Ruthenians-Ukrainians toward Hungary, a fact that has not lost its actuality to this day.

Originally, Carpatho-Ukraine did not figure in Masaryk's liberation program or, for that matter, in that of the Czechoslovak National Council. At the beginning of May 1918, Masaryk arrived in the United States where he met with representatives of united Yugoslavia, and of Romania, all Czechoslovakia's future allies. He realized that Carpatho-Ukraine would be of monumental strategic importance for Czechoslovakia in a configuration of alliance with these states. From this initial friendship there later arose the Little Entente, namely the alliance of Czechoslovakia, Yugoslavia, and Romania. Territorial access to Romania was possible only through Carpatho-Ukraine. This realization probably was what had prompted Masaryk while in the United States to conclude a unification of Carpatho-Ukraine with Czechoslovakia without giving thought to what the Ruthenians at home might desire in regard to their political future.

In order to make their voice count in support of the idea of unifying the homeland with Czechoslovakia at the Peace Conference, ANRR representatives Zhatkovych and Yuliy Gardosh left for Paris. On February 17, 1919 they were received by Col. Edward Manel House, who in the absence of President Woodrow Wilson headed the American Mission and, on April 24, met with André Tardieu, a member of the French Mission. They discussed the problem of Carpathian Ruthenians with the two distinguished diplomats and presented to them all the decisions hitherto passed as well as other relevant documents. Zhatkovych reported on these discussions to Beneš in a letter.

By then the Czechoslovak Government had dispatched Dr. Anton Beskyd to Paris as its delegate representing the Priashiv National Council, of which he was head, and as well as Carpathian Ruthenians.[8] While in Paris, Zhatkovych, Gardosh, and Beskyd formed the so-called Ruthenian Commission that was supposed to "represent all Ruthenians."[9] On March 15, 1919, Zhatkovych arrived in Uzhhorod, where he submitted a report on his actions up to date. Early in May, the Central Ruthenian National Council (TsRNR—Tsentral'na rus'ka narodna rada), which was created from the various local councils, approved Zhatkovych's report, endorsed all of the agreements he concluded with Masaryk and Beneš, and decided to appoint Zhatkovych as "Organizing Minister of the Ruthenian State," authorizing him to continue negotiations with President Masaryk and the government of Czechoslovakia as well as with foreign diplomats.[10] It was only at this point that he was invested with full negotiating powers by the TsRNR; he had not possessed such full powers while in Paris and thus lacked the legal basis at the time in forming the Ruthenian Commission with Beskyd.

Development of Events in Carpatho-Ukraine

By the end of October 1918, Austria-Hungary was nearing its demise. Emperor Charles had abdicated as Emperor of Austria, but retained the title of King of Hungary. He set up in Hungary a liberal government headed by Count Mihály Károlyi, whose task it was to save Hungary from total disintegration. It was to this end that the Hungarian Parliament, on its own initiative, adopted Law No. X which provided for broad autonomy powers, including ownership rights over territory, to the Ruthenian province to be henceforth known as *Rus'ka Kraina* or "Ruthenian Land."

The Law evoked a sharp reaction among the Ruthenians, inasmuch as only four counties (Ung, Bereg, Ugocsa, and Maramorosh) were to be included in the *Rus'ka Kraina*. The Ruthenian-inhabited counties of Zemplin, Šaroš, and Spiš were promised to the Slovaks by the Hungarian Minister of National Affairs, Oszkár Jászi, a historian and statesman. The Hungarian press also protested, although not for the same reason: it vehemently opposed the endowing the Ruthenians with autonomy rights. Having had disappointing experiences with promises of the Hungarian government in the past, the Ruthenians demanded international guarantees of their autonomous rights from the Peace Conference. In response, the Hungarian Ministerial Council declared that, "regarding this matter, it cannot do anything since it has no diplomatic relations with the Entente countries."[11]

Ignoring Law No. X, local national councils began to crop up throughout Carpatho-Ukraine, such as in the Maramorosh area, Svaliava, and Stara Liubovna, as well as among students at the University of Budapest, all of whom declared themselves in favor of a union with Ukraine. Of particular historical importance in this respect was the convocation of the All-National Congress in Khust on January 21, 1919 at which 420 delegates from the entire territory of Carpatho-Ukraine resolved to join with Ukraine. To implement this decision, it was necessary that the Ukrainian Army occupy the territory of Carpatho-Ukraine. This, however, was not to come to pass since the Ukrainian National Republic was not in a position to extend any military assistance: Galicia (Western Ukraine) was locked in a war with Poland while Eastern Ukraine grappled with the Russian/Bolshevik invaders. Two representatives of the Ruthenian Council for Maramorosh county, Stepan Klochurak and Maj. Evhen Puza, arrived in Stanyslaviv, then the seat of the government of the Western Ukrainian National Republic in Galicia, where they solemnly proclaimed at a meeting of the parliament that Carpatho-Ukraine wished to belong to the Ukrainian state. The parliament took the declaration into consideration under resounding applause and accepted the two guests into membership of the local Ukrainian National Council (UNR).[12]

Another country that coveted Carpatho-Ukraine was Romania. Its cavalry units staged forays into the territory, once reaching as far as the immediate vicinity of Uzhhorod. The political scene in Central-Eastern Europe was changing with lightning speed. Insufficient contacts with the outside world inevitably led to a shortage of badly needed information. What the situation was like at the time was eloquently described to this author by Rev. Avhustyn Voloshyn much later, during his premiership. This eminent political figure in Carpatho-Ukraine at the time had this to say:

> We had to seek some realistic solution to our problem once we no longer wished to remain in union with Hungary. But our Ukrainian solution was impossible to materialize as in those days military might was the decisive factor everywhere, and we did not possess this might. We knew very little about the Czechs as a people, but then the only feasible solution to our quandry was to join our destiny with that of a Slavic people.

At the beginning of January 1919, a special delegation consisting of Msgr. Voloshyn, Pavlo Legeza, and Irynei Kondratovych, was dispatched by the Uzhhorod National Council to Budapest with the express purpose of meeting with the Czechoslovak ambassador, Dr. Milan Hodža, and submitting to him a request for Czech troops to occupy the territory of Carpatho-Ukraine. The Czech troops then entered Uzhhorod on January 12 which, undoubtedly, influenced the final decision to join the land to Czechoslovakia.[13] The railroad line in the southern part of the city of Uzhhorod leading north to Uzhok served as the demarcation line, thus leaving the area south of the city still under Hungarian administration.

Carpatho-Ukraine also figured in discussions conducted at the Peace Conference in Paris that dealt with the problem of Ukrainian statehood, the latter issue being vehemently challenged by tsarist Russian and Polish diplomats. The proposal regarding Ukrainian statehood submitted to the Peace Conference read as follows:

> 1. That there be established a Ukrainian state, provided Ukrainian nationalism is strong enough to justify that decision;
>
> 2. It is recommended that Eastern Galicia be included in the Ukrainian state, if the state is strong; otherwise, in Poland as a self govern-

ing province, guaranteed the right to determine its allegiance at a later date. If at the time of decision by the Peace Conference the Ukraine should give evidence of vitality, the disputed belt [Galicia—V. Sh.] should be assigned to it because in that region the Ukrainians outnumber the poles two to one.

3. It is recommended that the Crimea be given to the Ukraine.[14]

And as for Carpatho-Ukraine proper, the following recommendations by the same commission were submitted at the Peace Conference:

It is undesirable that the Ruthenians of Eastern Hungary should continue under Hungarian rule. They have suffered particularly from Magyar oppression which has led to intense hatred of Hungarian Government and to a strong movement of emigration. Union with Ukraine, which might lead to incorporation within a future Russia, is opposed by many Ruthenians. It is certainly undesirable that Russia should never extend across the Carpathians down to the Hungarian Plain. The physical weakness of Ruthenia and the political incapacity of its inhabitants seem to forbid a complete independent state.[15]

In light of such developments of events, the Ruthenian Central National Council (TsRNR) unanimously decided on May 15, 1919 to annex Carpatho-Ukraine to Czechoslovakia and to this end adopted relevant decisions concerning the autonomy of the land and its boundaries. Point 2 of the resolutions states that, "the boundary will be drawn so as the officially dispatched representative of the Ruthenian State and of the Czechoslovak Republic should determine."[16] Such a stipulation contained in the resolutions corresponded fully with the agreements earlier achieved by Zhatkovych with Masaryk and Beneš. The formulation of the boundaries was worded in the resolutions thus:

The borderline facing Romania shall be determined by the Peace Conference; facing Hungary, the boundary has been established at the Peace Conference and shall extend to a point where it meets the western border of the Szikszói district; along the western and northern border of this Szikszói district up to the river Hernad; thence along Hernad to the confluence of the river Torys (Tarcza), then proceed north of Torys to a point where the river crosses the border of the Spiš and Šariš districts, and from here along the southern border of the Hethari district (and Lubloi's western border), the Lubloi district in the Spiš country up to Popradremete.[17]

On May 23, 1919, a delegation of 112 members of the TsRNR arrived in Prague to forward to President Masaryk its decision, a protocol dated May 8 which contained its conception of the juridicial status of Carpatho-Ukraine as a state. It was hoped that this plan would demonstate and officially confirm the province's union with Czechoslovakia. All throughout the more than sixty some odd years, materials have been published in Czechoslovakia, including the Czechoslovak Socialist Republic (ČSSR), that point out that President Masaryk had declined to answer questions posed to him by the delegation, noting that he "regarded them as his private guests and not official representatives of the entire people."[18] Masaryk's refusal to answer the questions is, however, more than odd, considering the fact that he had previously talked with Zhatkovych regarding the demands of Carpatho-Ukrainians and was familiar with them. To declare that it was not in his competence to decide anything on Carpatho-Ukraine's status within the Czechoslovak Republic and that, therefore, he could not receive the delegation as representatives of the Carpatho-Ukrainian people but merely as his guests cannot be viewed as a statesmanlike gesture.[19] It should be further noted that such a remark on the part of Masaryk seemed incongruous in legal terms, since, although the the Constitution of the Republic had not yet been adopted at the time, even in its absence Masaryk was elected president of Czechoslovakia with certain prerogatives that were later included in Article 64 of the Constitution. One may conjecture that what prompted Masaryk's statement was his inclination to impute a more important role in the matter of the union to Ruthenian Americans rather than to the representatives of the province, the TsRNR and its 112 delegates. Or, perhaps, his attitude may also have been influenced by the fact that originally Carpatho-Ukraine had declared itself for union with Ukraine rather than Czechoslovakia. Yet strangely enough, there seems to have been a congruence of opinion between his argument and that of the Hungarians in this respect, for the latter also claimed that the matter of union with Czechoslovakia was the doing of the Ruthenian Americns. A Hungarian author writes that, "as we may see, the peace dictate is actually based on the Scranton resolution just as it is on the decision of the St. Germain Treaty."[20]

On the first anniversary of the founding of Czechoslovakia, October 28, 1919, the Czechoslovak Parliament invited President Masaryk to deliver a speech. In his lengthy memorial speech on this solemn occasion, Masaryk reviewed the achievements of his foreign policy during the war and gave a comprehensive survey of important political events affecting the state in 1919. However, he failed to make any mention of the TsRNR and the Protocol he had received regarding the unification of Carpatho-Ukraine with Czechoslovakia.[21]

The Slavic People's Party, a Slovak group founded by Rev. Andrei Hlinka which consistently opposed the government, demanded that the Czechoslovak government fulfill the Pittsburgh Agreement signed on May 30, 1919, to which also Masaryk had appended his signature. Masaryk told them that the decision to form Czechoslovakia was left to the legitimate representatives of Czechs and Slovaks. This was because for the "Czechs and Slovaks attending the convention in Pittsburgh were well aware of the fact that they as American citizens did not possess the right to decide on matters concerning the formation of a Czechoslovak state."[22] Such reasoning could also have been applied to the decision of the Ruthenian Americans, for among them were also American citizens. What is more, the first governor of Sub-carpathian Ruthenia, Dr. G. Zhatkovych, was an American citizen.

Dr. Milan Hodža, chairman of the Foreign Commission of the House of Deputies, spoke in a similar vein but in a rather offensive tone about the Ruthenian delegation: "The Ruthenian Delegation, which we have welcomed here, does not at all represent the Ruthenian people. It was proper for us to welcome them as we had, but in regard of pragmatic politics we must realize that their intelligentsia is composed largely of priests, a few administrative officials, and some teachers. All of them are from under the Hungarian regime and against us."[23]

And even later, as minister of education, Dr. Hodža was known for his antipathy towards the Ruthenians-Ukrainians. Ironically, Hodža, himself a Slovak, had also lived under Hungarian rule. The difference, however, was that during the war he was a military censor in the Austro-Hungarian Army, and thus apparently he was trusted. Masaryk's son Jan, later ambassador to London, was also an officer in the Austro-Hungarian Army.[24]

Until World War I, Hodža was a frequent contributer of articles to the Slovak press, particularly the *Slovenský týždennik* (*Slovak Weekly*), in which he often voiced his views in defense of the rights of the Ruthenians, calling them brothers. On December 18, 1918, he approached 22 representatives of the Ruthenian National Council from the Uzhhorod, Bereg, and Maramorosh counties. In his report to the Ministry of Foreign Affairs, Hodža said of the Council's members that they "categorically demand to be separated from the Hungarian state and are for unification with Ukraine or, if this were not feasible, then with the Czechoslovak state."[25]

In February 1919, Beneš drew up an updated memorandum for members of the Peace Conference and pertinent commissions in which he featured statistical data and stated that the boundary between Carpatho-Ukraine and Slovakia ran along the river Uzh. He included also a map showing the territory of Carpatho-Ukraine and areas inhabited by Ruthenians. However, the area north of Priashiv, although inhabited by Ruthenians in compact masses, was marked as inhabited by "Czechoslovaks." The map further designated the area south of Priashiv and vicinity, predominantly inhabited by Magyarized Ruthenians, also as being inhabited by "Czechoslovaks." After considering the recommendation that the river Uzh (Ung) ought to constitute the borderline, members of the Commission that were later to act on matters on border settlement adopted it, since it had originated with Beneš, the head of the Czechoslovak Mission to the Peace Conference.

Such an arbitrary move on the part of Beneš was at variance with all previous agreements and understandings Zhatkovych had reached with Masaryk and Beneš and in contradiction to the authorizations given Beneš by TsRNR, which formally and legally went into effect only after the Protocol had been presented in Prague on May 23, 1919.[26] At the same time that the Beneš information memorandum was being considered, the publication *La Republique Tchecoslovaque* appeared in February 1919 in Paris, published by Louise Weiss, with a foreword penned by Beneš. The publication made no mention of Carpatho-Ukraine, but a map included in the publication showed the boundary between Slovakia and Carpatho-Ukraine as lying on the river Uzh.[27] Louise Weiss was at the time publisher of *l'Europe Nouvelle* and for almost twenty years she received annual "subsidies" from the Ministry of Foreign Affairs in Prague (i.e., from Beneš), in the amount of 30,000 French francs which at the time equalled 40,000 Czechoslovak *koruny*. In 1930, the sum was increased to 100,000 francs. Her co-workers received 47,000 francs through her separately.[28]

Prof. Masaryk had published an article in *The Bohemian Review*—the official press organ of the Bohemian (Czech) National Alliance of

America—entitled "The Future Status of Bohemia" (vol. 1, no. 3 [April 1917]). At this point, Masaryk himself was not yet clear in his views about the configuration, state system, and the borders of his future state. In his article, he advanced several possible forms for the future state system, including a monarchic one, linked to the Russian tsarist dynasty. Attached to the article was a map depicting rough contours of the Czech lands and of Slovakia, without Carpatho-Ukraine, that was to serve as the territorial basis of the future Czechoslovak state. The map likewise did not include other areas that were later incorporated into the republic, for instance, the cities of Karlový Varý (Karlsbad), Liberec (Reichenberg), and others. Instead, the borders of Slovakia in the East were moved up to the city of Uzhhorod (i.e., up to the river Uzh), just as Beneš had marked it on the map intended for the Peace Conference.

Until 1917, both Masaryk and Beneš could rightly consider the land of the Ruthenian as Hungarian and thus enemy territory. But then they did not foresee it becoming a political entity within the framework of the newly established Czechoslovak Republic after the war. Later on, however, in 1918, when Masaryk began negotiations with Ruthenian Americans regarding unification of the land with Czechoslovakia, the land of the Ruthenians ceased to be for him a hostile Austro-Hungarian territory, particularly since the Ruthenians had been accepted as members into the Mid-European Union of which Masaryk was head.[29] Because members of the said Union were formally on a war footing with Austro-Hungary, the Ruthenians were considered to have enjoyed the same political status as the Czechs and Slovaks. Consequently, Masaryk and Beneš were obliged to revise their initial incorrect and unfriendly attitude regarding the borders of the Carpathian Ruthenians, but this they had not done. In 1917, neither Masaryk nor Beneš had full powers to make such important decisions; therefore, their premature action, undertaken by Beneš at the Peace Conference regarding the border on the river Uzh, was an arbitrary act, prepared and carried out illegally, without the consent of the population and in contravention of agreements concluded with Zhatkovych. As such, this act violates the principles and customs of International Law as well as the principle of the right of self-determination.

During Zhatkovych's talks with Masaryk and Beneš, the two statesmen were in agreement with his attitude and proposals, but did not want to commit themselves in writing, allegedly because there was a congruence of views between them anyway. Nor did they make any public statements regarding the western border of Carpatho-Ukraine. Beneš began to speak out openly to Carpatho-Ukraine's disadvantage only after having made the necessary preparations at the Peace Conference and only after having been given full powers by the TsRNR in May 1918. As he himself admitted to me, Zhatkovych had boundless confidence in these men that only came to harm the cause he had so fervently championed as well as his own prestige in the eyes of his countrymen, following his resignation from the post of governor and return to the United States. In another discussion with this author in Pittsburgh in 1952, Zhatkovych exclaimed embitteredly, "The Czechs have deceived us."

At Paris, Beneš told the members of the Boundary Commission that he would want the Peace Conference to resolve the problem of the boundary between Carpatho-Ukraine and Slovakia. In so doing, Beneš managed to have this problem resolved in accordance with his own wishes, but passed the responsibility on to the Peace Conference. By invoking the Conference's authority and decision, he was able to block Zhatkovych. Moreover, this move was intended to curry favor with the Slovaks. However, it backfired and Beneš became one of the most hated Czech politicians in the eyes of the Slovaks.

Having set the stage, Beneš was now free to inform Masaryk by telegram in July 1919 that, "the Peace Conference itself will establish the final boundary between Czechoslovakia and Subcarpathian Ruthenia."[30] Zhatkovych learned about the telegram from Masaryk himself in Prague. He immediately left for Paris, where Beneš informed him about the reasons for the "unexpected" decision of the Peace Conference, noting that the "Peace Conference changed its stance and now wishes for its own reasons to draw the borders of Subcarpathian Ruthenia as short as possible."[31] In this connection, Beneš warned Zhatkovych that any protest on the part of the Ruthenians would be futile, and then added that the "Peace Conference intends to place the Slovak-Ruthenian boundary on the river Uzh."[32]

Zhatkovych vigorously protested against this, declaring that the main reason for the union with Czechoslovakia was that, "the Ruthenians would not be divided into two or more parts."[33] At the end of the discussion, Zhatkovych and Beneš agreed that the Peace Conference would establish the boundary but only as a temporary one. In response to Zhatkovych's question whether the Peace Conference would honor this agreement, Beneš replied, "I promise you that the Peace Conference will do what we have agreed upon, but should it not, then I promise not to sign the conditions of the Peace Treaty."[34] This was typical of Beneš' style of "double-dealing" in politics in which he excelled right at the outset of our common life with the Czechs and Slovaks. He had secured just the kind of a solution he had himself contrived and wished and had propogated in the press and among members of the various commissions of the Peace Conference.

The question of the boundary between Carpatho-Ukraine and Slovakia was strictly an internal affair between Czechoslovakia and Carpathian Ukrainians, not an international problem and thus not within the competence of the Peace Conference to resolve. As a full-fledged representative, Zhatkovych had conducted talks with the government of Czechoslovakia and not with the Slovaks. Only these two principals were entitled to deal with the problem of boundaries as had been agreed upon between them. The Peace Conference's competence lay in dealing with the boundaries of Czechoslovakia, Yugoslavia, and Romania but not with boundaries within the states.

Zhatkovych was in a position to verify the reason for the "change of attitude" of the Peace Conference. As he has told this author, one of the secretaries of President Wilson was his schoolmate and it was through him that he was able to gain access to the United States Mission. However, Zhatkovych did not take advantage of this opportunity, for he believed without reservation in Beneš and Masaryk and was not sufficiently versed in the workings of international politics.

Instead of unifying the territory of the Ruthenians into a single whole, Beneš arbitrarily and unlawfully divided it. He left to Hungary the historical territory inhabited by Greek-Catholic Ruthenians, placed the Priashiv Region under temporary administration of Slovakia, which continues to this day, and ceded part of the Maramorosh county along with the city of Maramorosh Siget to Romania. The organ of the then Prime Minister Dr. Karel Kramář, *Národní Listy* (*National Newspaper*), published in Prague, carried in its April 10, 1919 issue an article in which the following reference was made to the Maramorosh county: "Although the city of Maramorosh Siget and its surroundings are inhabited predominantly by Ruthenians, it will be ceded to Romania as a gift of our government." The statement speaks for itself.

Only four counties were incorporated into Carpatho-Ukraine: the Uzh, Ugocsa, Bereg, and Maramorosh counties, although the remainder of the Ruthenian territories also could have been incorporated as had been done in the case of other subjugated peoples that received their ethnic territories from Hungary on the same international and legal grounds that were embodied in the St. Germain Treaty.

The best example of the distribution of the Ruthenian population in Hungary is given by the ancient Ruthenian diocese of Mukachevo (Munkács, Mukachiv), once a single diocese, whose Ruthenian Greek-Catholics lived in 13 *comitats* (counties) in Hungary. The first assault of a forced Magyarization in the 19th and beginning of the 20th century was delivered at this very same Mukachevo Diocese, considered the national and religious bulwark of the Ruthenians, by repeated divisions of its jurisdiction. Thus, for instance, in 1818 the Priashiv Eparchy (diocese) was created out of 194 parishes, now subjected to Slovakization, in 1823 72 parishes were ceded to the Romanian Diocese in Velyky Varadyn (Nagyvárad), in 1853 an additional 94 parishes were detached from the Mukachevo Diocese and assigned to the Szalosujvár (Geda) Diocese in Romania, in 1912 the Hajdudorog Diocese was formed with 72 parishes, presently completely Magyarized. After the frontier between Czechoslovakia and Hungary had been established in the aftermath of World War I, an Apostolic Exarchate was formed in Miskolc out of 26 Ruthenian parishes, now also Magyarized. All of the aforementioned parishes and dioceses were originally Ruthenian-Ukrainian but later separated from their religious and national center and denationalized by constant divisions. The population, of course, remained in the territories ceded to the new dioceses.[35] The denationalization policy in Slovakia also affected over 160 Ruthenian-Ukrainian schools between 1870 and 1900.[36] It should be noted here that according to the Hungarian staistics of 1900, there were 1,841,272 Greek-Catholics in union with Rome. They represented 10.93 percent of the total population of Hungary.[37] The figures given on the number of Ruthenians living in Hungary at the time are approximately correct. To better visualize the situation, the statistics below show the growth of the Hungarian nation at the expense of non-Hungarians over a period of time of less than two hundred years:

Table 2[38]

Year	Total Population	percent Magyars	percent Non-Magyars
1787	8,003,000	29.0	71.0
1840	12,807,000	38.1	61.9
1850	11,364,000	44.0	56.0
1869	13,579,000	44.4	55.6
1880	13,750,000	46.6	53.4
1890	15,003,000	48.5	51.5
1900	16,772,000	51.4	48.6
1910	18,265,000	53.1	46.9

It is no small wonder then that the Norwegian writer and poet Björson saw it fitting to describe the denationalization policy of Hungary as the "biggest industry of Hungary."[39]

What the documents of the Peace Conference reveal is as follows:

On May 15, 1919, the Commission on Czechoslovak Affairs at the Peace Conference held a meeting to discuss the "Eventual Government of Ruthenians in Hungary." Protocol No. 12 of the session reads as follows: "Beneš insisted that the delimination between Slovakia and Ruthenia should be imposed by the Peace Conference, in order to avoid all disputes."

Laroche (France) replied that the Commission had already made the following motion concerning the delimination: Leaving the junction point of the frontiers of Hungary, the Ruthenian territory and Czechoslovak 2 kilometers east of Csap and in a northerly direction, the frontier between Czechoslovak and Ruthenian territory was determined:

A north-east line generally parallel to the Csap-Ungvár-Perecseny railway, The line of the ridge between the Ung and the Latoricza basins through point 978, 992 then toward the north, Rejoining the principal chain of the Carpathians at a point situated approximately:

22' 53' east of Greenwich

48' 56' north.

This point is the point of junction of the frontiers of Galicia, the Ruthenian territory of Czechoslovakia."

Beneš recognized that the line is perfectly exact.

Laroche (France) remarked that only a proposal of the Commission should be confirmed by the Supreme Council.

The Chairman believed it should be indicated in the report that Beneš recognized the correctness of the lines.[40]

The chairman of the Commission, Harold Nicolson of Britain, was asked by the Commission to present a report on Carpatho-Ukraine to the Council of Five and to stress that the Commission's decision fully coincided with Beneš' position. Thus, Beneš was assured that the matter of the boundary between Carpatho-Ukraine and Slovakia would be settled in accordance with his wish and that there would be nobody else to exact a change of this decision.

The Peace Conference initiated certain inquiries into the conduct of the Central Powers toward their subjugated peoples. Britain's representative Nicolson was so much affected by the findings of the research that he leveled a severe criticism for which the Hungarians have not forgiven him to this day. He stated, "I confess that I regarded, and still regard, the Turanian tribe with acute distaste. Like their cousins the Turks, they had destroyed much and created nothing. Buda-Pest was a false city devoid of any autochtonous reality. For centuries the Magyars had oppressed their subject nationalities."[41]

With regard to the boundary of Carpatho-Ukraine with Romania, Beneš acted in like manner and established it as a temporary one that persists to this day. The demarcation line between Carpatho-Ukraine and Romania ran some 4 kilometers west of the Maramorosh Siget-Yablonsky Pass. Thus, some 2,000 sq. km of Ukrainian territory was cleaved away and attached to Romania. This is how Beneš was "uniting" the Ruthenians in Czechoslovakia.[42]

In his message to the National Assembly, President Masaryk noted in December 1918 that the Carpathian Ruthenians had through their representatives in America expressed the wish for union with the Czechoslovak Republic. He apparently had in mind the agreement with Zhatkovych, for people had not yet decided about its fate. The delegation of the Ukrainian National Republic at the Peace Conference protested against the union of Carpatho-Ukraine with Czechoslovakia. Invoking the resolution adopted at the Khust Congress on January 21, 1919, which decided in favor of union with Ukraine, the deputy head of the delegation demanded that the Peace Conference:

> 1. Demand of the Czech government to withdraw its military forces from Carpatho-Ukraine.
>
> 2. Send a special neutral commission to Carpatho-Ukraine with a view to ascertaining the true opinions of the Ruthenians as to which country they would wish to belong.

3. Undertake the initiative of conducting negotiations regarding the boundary between Slovakia and Carpatho-Ukraine.[43]

The issue of the boundary between Carpatho-Ukraine and Slovakia was to remain acute for some time to come in the relations between Uzhhorod, Prague, and Paris. The Central Ruthenian National Council (TsRNR) in Uzhhorod sent a letter on July 1, 1919 to Beneš and Kramář in Paris in an effort to find a realistic, feasible and correct solution to the problem. Apart from its territorial claims and guarantees of rights for the national minorities, the TsRNR stated in its letter: "Should the Peace [in the original "peaceful"—V.Sh.] Conference leave the solution of the Slovak-Ruthenian territory to the Czechoslovak Government, the presidium of the TsRNR would then demand that a plebiscite be held on this question in the historical territory of Carpathian Ruthenia."[44] The demand for a plebiscite was an indication of the faith in victory and unequivocal proof of the correctness of TsRNR's demands.

Beneš paid no heed to the aforementioned letter. He continued to act behind the scenes, demanding from the Peace Conference that it not draw up the final boundaries, but only temporary ones, insisting further on the line "from the city of Csap northward along the river Uzh to Uzhhorod and to continue northward to the Carpathians."[45]

All memoranda and proposals concerning Carpatho-Ukraine submitted to the Peace Conference were prepared by Beneš alone without the participation of representatives of the Ruthenians and in outright contravention of the agreements he had with them. He wrote thus about the matter: "Our demands are accepted by the Conference without fail, even with sympathy. There are no objections of any consequence to our official demands presented at the Conference, neither by the Englishmen, nor by the French, Americans or Italians. We may, therefore, assert with certainty that our program is triumphant." For the Council of Ten and the Commission on Czechoslovak Affairs created by it, Beneš formulated a program which he himself had drawn up in the form of eleven *Memoirs,* including that on the "Problems of Ruthenians of Hungary."[46] Thus, the placing of the Priashiv Region under the temporary administration of Slovakia and of the Maramorosh County under that of Romania was the work of Beneš alone.

The fact that the Priashiv and Maramorosh regions were placed under temporary administration of Slovakia and Romania respectively clearly suggested that it was an act intended to dispose of an alien, i.e. Ukrainian territory. On the basis of the sources cited regarding the establishment of temporary boundaries between Slovakia and Carpatho-Ukraine on one hand and between Romania and Carpatho-Ukraine on the other, it may be deduced that:

1. The Czechoslovak government officials had decided on the matter long before they received the necessary full powers from representatives of the Carpathian Ruthenians-Ukrainians.

2. Members of the Czechoslovak government violated the agreements with Zhatkovych as well as the resolutions of the TsRNR in Uzhhorod, particularly those relating to the boundaries of Carpatho-Ukraine and its territorial integrity, not being legally authorized to change the boundaries of the land.

3. The right of self-determination of the Carpathian Ukrainians recognized by the Peace Conference was violated.

4. The norms of International Law governing the right to conclude international agreements concerning Carpatho-Ukraine were violated, inasmuch as all was done without the participation of Carpathian Ruthenians and even against their will.

Thanks to his skillful and apt maneuvering, Beneš managed to exact a change in the once favorable attitude of the Peace Conference toward the integrity of the entire Ruthenian land and its autonomy, thereby succeeding in misleading the whole Conference. Thus, the Peace Conference's decision to cede parts of the territory was carried out on a false legal basis. In such cases, Roman Law has a dictum that may well be applied here: *Quod ab initio vitiosum est, tracta temporis convalescere non potest*—"What has started out as erroneous cannot become right even with the passage of time."

In this connection, it may be pointed out here that Beskyd, who visited Paris on several occasions as a supposed "representative" of Carpathian Ruthenians and himself hailed from the territory ceded to Slovakia by Beneš, was not a member of any commission and did not participate in meetings, the Czechoslovak government used him merely as a figurehead in order to fortify Beneš' stance, while the actual decisionmaker was Beneš himself.

The St. Germain-en-Laye Treaty and the
Constitution of the Czechoslovak Republic

By force of the peace treaty concluded between the victorious Principal Allied and Associated Powers and the Czechoslovak Republic in St. Germain-en-Laye on September 10, 1919, Subcarpathian Ruthenia was joined to Czechoslovakia. The provisions of the Peace Treaty, including Articles 10–13, relating to guarantees of autonomous rights and thereby constituted the basis for a juridicially legal intrastate relationship between Carpatho-Ukraine and the Czechoslovak Republic. The pertinent articles to this effect read as follows:

Part II, Article 10

Czechoslovakia agrees to constitute the Ruthenian territory south of the Carpathians within frontiers delimited by the Principal Allied and Associated Powers as an autonomous unit within the Czechoslovak State, and to accord to it the fullest degree of self-government compatible with the unity of the Czechoslovak State.

Article 11

The country of the Ruthenians south of the Carpathians shall possess a special Diet. This Diet shall enjoy legislative powers in all linguistic, scholastic, and religious questions, in matters of local administration, and in other questions which the laws of the Czechoslovak Republic may attribute to it. The governor of the country of the Ruthenians, who shall be appointed by the President of the Czechoslovak Republic, shall be responsible to the Ruthenian Diet.

Article 12

Czechoslovakia agrees that officials in the country of the Ruthenians will be chosen as far as possible from the inhabitants of this territory.

Article 13

Czechoslovakia guarantees to the territory of the Ruthenians equitable representation in the legislative assembly of the Czechoslovak Republic, to which assembly it will send deputies elected according to the constitution of the Czechoslovak Republic. These deputies will not, however, have the right of voting in the Czechoslovak Parliament upon legislative questions such as those attributed to the Ruthenian Diet.

In compliance with the obligation undertaken, the aforementioned provisions of the Treaty were incorporated into the Constitution of Czechoslovakia, but in a somewhat altered form. The Constitution of the Republic was embodied in the official *Sbírka zákonů a nařízení* (Collection of Laws and Decrees; henceforth to be referred to as *Sb. zák. a n.*) on February 29, 1920 under No. 121. The League of Nations took it upon itself to guarantee the implementation of the autonomy. In accordance with the Constitution of the Czechoslovak Republic, the international accords or parts there of that were published in the *Sb. zák. a n.* assume all the attributes of the Law of the Land. They cannot be rescinded by regular diplomatic act, as is customary in international agreements, but only in an appropriate manner and form by the new law, in the given case by a qualified three-fifth majority (Article 33 of the Constitution).

The Constitution's guarantees of autonomy became a powerful legal weapon in the hands of the Ruthenians-Ukrainians, for now one could not label their struggle for it as irridentist or anti-state. However, between the provisions of the St. Germain Treaty and the Constitutional Charter concerning the autonomy there were significant divergencies as well as erroneous interpretation thereof. We would like to draw attention to the more important discrepancies among these. The provisions of the St. Germain Treaty on autonomy were embodied in the Constitutional Charter under Section I, paragraph 3 and read as follows:

> 1. The territories of the Czechoslovak Republic shall form a united and indivisible unit, the frontiers of which may be altered only by Constitutional Law (paragraph of the introductory law).
>
> 2. The autonomous territory of Subcarpathian Ruthenia, which shall receive the widest measure of autonomy compatible with the unity of the Czechoslovak Republic, shall be an integral part of this unit by the terms of its voluntary unification as declared in the Treaty between the Principal and Allied Powers and the Czechoslovak Republic concluded in St. Germain-en-Laye on September 10, 1919.
>
> 3. This diet shall legislate in linguistic, educational and religious matters, in matters of domestic administration and in such other matters as may be assigned to it by the laws of the Czechoslovak Republic. Laws enacted by this Diet, and signed by the President of the Republic, shall be published in a separate series and shall be counter-signed by the Governor on Subcarpathian Ruthenia.
>
> 4. Subcarpathian Ruthenia shall be represented in Parliament by Deputies and Senators elected according to the general suffrage law of the Czechoslovak Republic.

5. The head of Subcarpathian Ruthenia shall be a Governor, appointed by the President of the Czechoslovak Republic on the recomendation of the Government, and shall be responsible also to the Diet of Subcarpathian Ruthenia.

6. Public officials in Subcarpathian Ruthenia shall be, insofar as possible, selected from the population of Subcarpathian Ruthenia.

7. Details as to the right of suffrage and eligibility to the Diet shall be defined by special legislation.

8. The law enacted by the Parliament defining the frontiers of Subcarpathian Ruthenia shall form part of the Constitutional Charter.

In the provisions of the Constitutional Charter there is a noticeable tendency to decrease the powers of the Governor and to weaken the legislative power of the Carpatho-Ukrainian Diet. Clearly, the St. Germain Treaty was not to resolve all the legal problems arising from the unification of Carpatho-Ukraine with the Czechoslovak Republic, but left the field wide open for future agreements between the two parties. However, some fundamental principles of the Treaty were flagrantly violated by the state's Constitution. For instance, paragraph 5 states the following: "The head of Ruthenia shall be a Governor, appointed by the President of the Czechoslovak Republic on the recommendation of the Government, and he shall be responsible *also* to the Diet of Ruthenia."

There are two basic deviations from the provisions of the St. Germain Treaty. First, the Peace Treaty clearly states that the Governor of Subcarpathian Ruthenia shall be appointed by the President of the State but does not stipulate that this should take place upon the "recommendation of the Government," i.e., of *the central government in Prague.* This is a deviation because the St. Germain Treaty mentions nothing about the central government but does indicate that the governer is responsible to the *Soim* (Diet) of Carpatho-Ukraine. The involvement of the central government strips the governor of much autonomy, making him nothing more than a high state official, whom the Prague government could replace at any time. This state of affairs changed the entire meaning of the peace treaty about the "fullest degree of self-government compatible with the unity of the State."

The second deviation is the insertion of the word "also," which alters the concept of the St. Germain Treaty concerning the powers and responsibilities of the Governor. The Peace Treaty clearly stipulates that the Governor "shall be responsible to the Ruthenian Diet." The insertion of the word "*also*" relegated his responsibility to the Diet to one of secondary importance, for in the modified provision in the Constitution, the Governor is responsible to the President of the State, a passage lacking in the Peace Treaty, and only then also to the Diet. These two changes in the Constitution signify a gross violation of the basic precepts of the St. Germain Treaty which Czechoslovakia accepted and undertook to fulfill.

Even such an evident restriction of the Governor's rights and powers did not seem to please the Prague government. An ordinance issued by the Government on April 20, 1920, No. 121, Para. 3, vested the entire civilian power in Carpatho-Ukraine in the hands of the Vice-Governor thereby divesting Governor Zhatkovych of all his executive powers, much to his displeasure. In spite of this, Zhatkovych further sought to establish the constitutionally legal relations in Carpatho-Ukraine called for in the St. Germain Treaty and agreements between President Masaryk and Minister Beneš. Yet, after all his efforts in the matter of autonomy did not produce the desired results, Zhatkovych, after ten months of governorship, tendered his resignation to President Masaryk, on March 16, 1921. The Government did not immediately accept his resignation and did not even notify the President of it, but rather assumed a waiting position in the hope that there might still be some negotiations forthcoming. Then, on April 22, Prime Minister Ján Černý convoked a meeting of the province's political parties, that lasted a full week, having invited even representatives of Hungarian political parties with which the Government had heretofore never consulted in affairs pertaining to Carpatho-Ukraine. This move was, undoubtedly, designed to paralyze the Ukrainian national influence with which Zhatkovych himself sympathized. It was this stance of his that engendered enmity toward him among those Czech political parties which sided with the Russophile cultural orientation in Carpatho-Ukraine, notably among them the ruling Agrarian Party, and others. It was not until May 16, 1921 that President Masaryk accepted Zhatkovych's resignation.[47]

In the Prague Parliamentary Senate, Sen. V. Klofáč severely censured Zhatkovych, decrying his activity as "anti-state and anti-constitutional."[48] Klofáč went so far as to even call Zhatkovych a "Magyarone" or Magyarophile although he well knew that Hungarians hated

Zhatkovych.[49] Klofač's ill-advised outbursts were completely out of order inasmuch as Zhatkovych was an initiator and the most avid enthusiast for the unification of Carpatho-Ukraine with Czechoslovakia.

Such a biased and, to a certain degree, anti-constitutional attitude of the ruling Czech political parties with respect to Carpatho-Ukraine generated resentment among nationally conscious Ruthenians-Ukrainians. The Czech administration viewed the expression of such resentment as irridentist or anti-state activity, which it was not, since Carpatho-Ukraine was constitutionally entitled to autonomy. In the wake of such unfounded accusations, many Ukrainians were automatically removed from the state-building process in the republic.

In connection with the aforementioned statement made by Klofáč against Zhatkovych, we consider it appropriate to recall a passage in his article written after the severance of the Sudetanland from the ČSR in 1938. Klofáč then wrote:

> National Socialism emerged in our midst. Here we were forming it in the course of forty years; it accomplished much in our conditions but could not become as decisive a force as it did in Germany. We ought not only catch up with Germany and its national socialism, but also outstrip it. In practice, national socialism in Germany actually outstripped us. It wields power and does not serve the oppressors. We must reject everyone who babbles like a child about the not-too-distant time when all would be returned to us that we had forever lost in October. Being in Central Europe, we must give a model example of coexistence between Slavs and Germans which is all the more easier since we are often related by blood. The father of my mother was a full-blooded German from Pohled near Německý Brod.[50]

We do not believe that the cited passage from Klofáč's article did in any way contribute creatively to the building of Czechoslovakia as a state.

Zhatkovych's disillusionment and disenchantment with the evolving situation in the republic with regard to Carpatho-Ukraine were given profound expression in his speech at a farewell banquet in his honor in Uzhhorod in which he, among other things, said the following:"I have promised my people, in conformity with the honestly concluded agreements, that its entire territory south of the Carpathian Mountains will be a fullfledged self-ruling unit within the framework of the Czechoslovak Republic and that the Carpathian Ruthenians will be the sole masters of their small native land. Unfortunately, however, I must openly and honestly admit that this promise has not yet been fulfilled through no fault of mine."[51]

Having returned to the United States, Zhatkovych presented a report on the situation in Carpatho-Ukraine to a Congress of Ruthenians held in Pittsburgh. The participating Ruthenians then dispatched a memorandum to the Czechoslovak Government in which they pointedly stated, "if the Ruthenians are mature enough to join the ČSR, then they are surely mature enough for autonomy."

Meanwhile, however, the issue of autonomy was not by any means subdued with Zhatkovych's resignation. On the contrary, American Ruthenians and representatives of other Ukrainian lands insistently launched protests to the League of Nations in Geneva. In 1928 such a protest was forwarded by Dr. E. Petrushevych from Paris as head of the Ukrainian National Council of Galicia with which a three-member committee of the League of Nations was to concern itself. The findings of the committee was that the protest was justified. Consequently, the League of Nations demanded that Czechoslovakia state the reasons why it had so far not fulfilled its international obligations. Beneš replied that the "enforcement of the autonomy in Subcarpathian Ruthenia could open the way for the proliferation of communism in this land." The committee refused to recognize these reasons as satisfactory and therefore required that the League of Nations insist on the execution of the autonomy.[52]

In view of the attitude assumed by the Czechoslovak Government, the further development of relations between Carpatho-Ukraine and the Czechoslovak Republic did not revolve around the issue of autonomy but rather around the issue of how to attain a more strongly centralized state.

The author of the Constitution was my university professor Dr. Jiří Hoetzl. During our seminar exercises, I used to point out the erroneousness of the interpretation of the territorial integrity or inalienability of Carpatho-Ukraine. I esposed the idea that the voluntary joining of Carpatho-Ukraine as a foreign territory to the Czechoslovak Republic and the endowing it with the broadest autonomous rights did not yet constitute a legal title that would interpret it as an integral part of the state. Autonomous state-juridicial units or territories with a different status within the framework of a state are in a certain respect historically or nationally alien territories which by force of the given political conditions, as in the case of Carpatho-Ukraine, unite with foreign countries.[53]

Consequently, and by the same token, Carpatho-Ukraine as an autonomous part of the ČSR was not and could not have been viewed as an integral part of the country merely on the basis of the unification act alone. The St. Germain international agreement concerning the unification and the act of territorial integrity in the state are two different legal acts. Hence, for Carpatho-Ukraine to constitute an integral part of the ČSR, it was necessary to obtain the assent of the former's Diet as was the case of the Czech territories mentioned above. But Carpatho-Ukraine did not adopt any such decision.

The Pragmatic Sanction was adopted also by Hungary's Parliament through a law promulgated in 1723, which was incorporated into the laws of the state. This act signified Hungary's renunciation of its state's independence. Moreover, it was on this juridicial basis that the 1867 Austro-Hungarian "Ausgleich"or Compromise Act was promulgated forming the new Dual Monarchy. It also entailed provisions for the "integrality and indivisibility of the empire's parts."[54]

Thus, Carpatho-Ukraine did not constitute an integral part of either the ČSR or Hungary since in both instances it was a territory of foreign nationality and there were no juridical foundation to be one. The basic difference between the St. Germain agreement and the Constitution arose only because the Carpathian Ukrainians were not represented at the drawing up and the promulgation of the Constitution. Czechoslovakia's independence was proclaimed on October 28, 1919. The Revolutionary National Committee (RNK) in Prague, which was composed of representatives of political parties, was later expanded to include various civic, cultural, and church organizations and to declare itself Revolutionary National Parliament (RNP). Ultimately, the RNP boasted 270 members, including fifty-five Slovaks. The Carpatho-Ukrainians were not represented in the RNP at all. Its first meeting was held at the historic building of the Czech Crown's Assembly in Prague on November 14, 1918.[55]

The final draft of the ČSR Constitution was adopted unanimously by the RNP but not by a parliament elected by the peoples of the republic or with the participation of representatives of Carpatho-Ukraine, although the parliamentary elections in Czechoslovakia took place two

months after the promulgation of the Constitution. The absence of
Carpatho-Ukrainians afforded an opportunity for Czechoslovak gov-
ernment officials to arbitrarily modify the provisions of the St.
Germain Treaty that were entered into the state's Constitution.

Given the contemporary political conditions of life in Czechoslovakia, we believe that all juridical and practical elements were at hand
then to invite representatives of Carpatho-Ukraine to participate in the
work of the RNP. This was all the more possible since on May 23, 1919
a delegation of the Central Ruthenian National Council submitted a
memorandum in Prague concerning the unification of the land with the
ČSR, whereas the Constitution was not promulgated until February 29,
1920 and internal matters of the state were well regulated. Moreover,
the TsRNR was a revolutionary body representing Carpatho-Ukraine
just as the RNP represented Czechoslovakia so that there were no
divergences between them, neither from the point of view of law nor
with regard to competencies. The Carpatho-Ukrainians' participation
in the preparation and promulgation of the final draft of the Constitution was predicated on two facts. First, this was a new territory joining
a state with whose people it had never had any legal or historical ties,
except for a brief period of time under Hungarian King Mátias Corvin
during the fifteenth century. Second was the matter of guaranteeing
autonomous rights ensured by the St. Germain Treaty.

According to the text of the minutes of a session held by the Commission on Czechoslovak Affairs in Paris on May 15, 1919, No. 12, the
Commission's Chairman Laroche of France asked Beneš, "whether an
article specifying the special regime granted to Ruthenia, the same as in
the draft Treaty, should not be incorporated into the constitution. Beneš
declared that it should be done; he added that the constitution even of
Czechoslovakia would be debated in the presence of and with the
delegates from Ruthenia."[56] The document cited here refutes the argument of those Czech publicists, scientists, and politicians, who maintain that Czechoslovakia did not obligate itself to insert the provisions
of the St. Germain Treaty concerning the autonomy of Carpatho-
Ukraine into the state's Constitution as well as of those who assert that
Czechoslovakia was not obliged to invite representatives of Carpatho-
Ukraine to participate in the drawing up of the final version of the
State's Constitution.

Notes

[1] "Hungary Exposed: Secret documents reveal the plotting of the Government in the United States; American Slovaks and Ruthenians 'The Irish of Hungary' to be the Victims" [Pamphlet] (New York, 1907).

[2] Paul R. Magocsi, *The Shaping of a National Identity* (Cambridge, Massachusetts, 1978), p. 169.

[3] Hans Ballreich, *Karpatorussland* (Heidelberg, 1938), p. 86.

[4] Joseph Danko, "Plebiscite of Carpatho-Ruthenians in the United States." *Annals of the Ukrainian Academy of Arts and Sciences in the USA* (New York) vol. 11 (1/2) 1964–1968 (31–32): 188–89.

[5] G. J. Zhatkovich, *Otkrytoe-Exposé* (Homestead, PA: Undated), p. 3 (Hereafter cited as Exposé); See also, Ivan Vanat, *Narysy novitnoï istoriï ukraïntsiv Skhidnoï Slovachchyny,* vol. 1 (1918-1938) (Priashiv: Slovak Pedagogical Publisher in Bratislava, Department of Ukrainian Literature in Priashiv, n.d.), p. 55; Archive of the Ministry of Foreign Affairs (AMZV) PA, No. 5124; Archives of the Chancellery of the President of the Republic (AKPR) PA, III-13.

[6] *Exposé,* p. 2.

[7] *Exposé,* p. 3(1). The Carpathian Ruthenians of the Eastern Orthodox Faith did not participate in the plebiscite.

[8] On November 6, 1918, the Ruthenian National Council was formed in Stara Liubovna, Priashiv (Prešov) Region, headed by Rev. Emylian Nevytsky, which drew up a manifesto favoring a union with Ukraine. The Council expanded its activities to include the counties of Spiš, Abouj, Zemplin, and Šariš and, on November 19, moved its headquarters to Priashiv. However, it was at this new location that Dr. Anton Beskyd, together with Galician Muscophiles Dr. Andrei Gagatko and Dmitry Vyslotsky, and further assisted by the Czechoslovak police and gendarmerie, broke up Rev. Nevytsky's council and formed his own, which declared itself in favor of union with Czechoslovakia. Shortly thereafter, the Czechoslovak Government designated Beskyd as representative of the Ruthenians to the Peace Conference in Paris. See Zygmund Zawadowski, Ruś Podkarpacka i jej stanowisko prawno-polityczne (Warsaw, 1931), p. 13. In Paris, Beskyd conducted himself as the satellite of the Czechoslovak Foreign Minister Eduard Beneš, carrying out Beneš' policies. For acquitting himself "successfully" of his functions in Paris, Beskyd was appointed governor of Subcarpathian Ruthenia in 1923. Until 1918, Beskyd had been a member of the Hungarian Parliament in Budapest, but did not belong to any caucus composed of Slavic deputies. What is more, in 1916, he declined to intercede in favor of retaining the Cyrillic alphabet in Carpatho-Ukraine, which the Hungarian government had painstakingly sought to expunge.

9   *Exposé,* p. 8.

10   Ibid., p. 7.

11   Rev. Avhustyn Voloshyn, Spomyny (Uzhhorod, 1923), p. 54.

12   Lonhyn Tsehelsky, *Vid legendy do pravdy* (New York-Philadelphia: Bulava Publishers, 1960), p. 230.

13   Msgr. Voloshyn, *op. cit.,* pp. 54–55. *See also,* Ladislav Fajták, *Národnodemokratická revolúcia na Východnom Slovensku roku 1918* (Bratislava, 1973), p. 101.

14   David Hunter Miller, *My Diary at the Conference of Paris with Documents* (New York, 1925), p. 227.

15   Ibid., p. 231.

16   *Exposé,* pp. 7–8.

17   Ibid., 8.

18   Ivan Krempa, *Za internacionálnu jednotu revolúčneho hnutia v Československu* (Bratislava: Nakladateľstvo Pravda, 1975), p. 57.

19   Vanat, *op. cit.,* p. 94; Archives of the Office of the President of the Republic, PR III/17; Archives of the Ministry of Foreign Affairs, PR, No. 5151; *Golos Russkogo Naroda* 31 May 1919.

20   Balogh-Beéry László, *A rutén autonomia* (Pécs, 1937), p. 16.

21   *Národní Shromáždění Republiky Československé,* vydalo Předsednictvo Poslanecké Sněmovny a Předsednictvo Senátu (Prague, 1928), p. 101.

22   Ferdinand Peroutka, *Budování státu,* vol. 3 (Prague, 1936), p. 1584.

23   Krempa, *op. cit.,* p. 57, quoting the Stenographic Record of the meeting of the Foreign Commission of the House of Deputies of Czechoslovakia, dated the afternoon of June 4, 1919.

24   Konstantin Čulen, *Po Svatoplukovi druhá naša hlava* (Cleveland, 1947), p. 60.

25   Ladislav Fajták, *op. cit.* p.92; See also, AMZV, 24/1918, Československá likvidačná komísia.

26   This was the reason why Beneš did not dateline his memorandum submitted to the Peace Conference in February.

27   Zawadowski, *op. cit.,* p. 10.

28   Dr. Rudolf Urban, *Tajné fondy III. sekce* (Prague: Archives of the Ministry of Foreign Affairs of the Czechoslovak Republic, 1943), p. 40.

29   T. G. Masaryk, *Svitova revoliutsiia za viiny i u viini* (Lviv, 1930), p. 248. [A translation from the original Czech.]

30   *Exposé,* p. 10.

[31] Ibid.

[32] Ibid., p. 11.

[33] Ibid.; See also, Darás Gábor, *A rutén kérdés tegnap és ma* (Budapest, 1938), p. 37.

[34] *Exposé,* p. 11.

[35] Rev. Athanasius Pekar, OSBM, *The Bishops of the Eparchy of Mukachevo with Historical Outlines* (Pittsburg, 1979), p. 31.

[36] Rev. A. Voloshyn, *op. cit.,* p. 46.

[37] N. Wickham Steed, *A Short History of Austria-Hungary and Poland* (London, 1914), p. 160; *See also,* Viator Scotus, Racial Problems in Hungary (London, 1908), p. 205.

[38] Czechoslovak Consulate General, *The Racial Minorities in Hungary and Czechoslovakia* (Prague, 1922), p. 6.

[39] Ibid.

[40] National Archives, Washington, D.C. Microfilm, No. 820,181.21201/12.

[41] Harold Nicolson, *Peace Making* (New York, 1965), p. 34.

[42] Alois Hora, *Karpatská Rus a hranice našeho státu* (Prague 1919), p. 5.

[43] I. Vanat, *op. cit.,* p. 98; *See also,* Archiv Ministerstva zahraničních věcí, Nos. 4962 and 4963. Dr. A. Beskyd inveighed against the demands of the Ukrainian delegation, alleging that the Carpathian Ruthenians were a branch of the Russian people and had nothing in common with the Ukrainian national political movement.

[44] Vanat, *op. cit.,* pp. 98–99. *See also,* Archiv ministerstva zahraničních věcí, PA. No. 5114.

[45] Vanat, *op. cit.,* p. 100. *See also,* Archives of the Office of the President of the Republic, Prague, PR, I/23.

[46] As quoted by Ferdinand Peroutka, *op. cit.,* p. 590.

[47] Ivan Krempa, *op. cit.,* pp. 351–53. Cited also in Krempa's work are the following sources: Prager Tagblatt, No. 48 of February 26, 1921; the Prague *Tribuna* of April 5, 1921; *Venkov* of May 1 and 12, 1921; Dr. Zhatkovych, *Exposé;* Archiv Kanceláře prezidenta Republiky—AKPR-T, 97/12; AKPR-PR 346/21 of May 4, 1921; as well as others.

[48] Peroutka, *op. cit.,* p. 2463.

[49] Ibid., p. 2464.

[50] Miloslav Brouček, *Československá tragedie* (Germany-New York, 1956), p. 154; See also, České Slovo 20 November 1938.

[51] Peroutka, *op. cit.,* p. 2467.

[52] *Družina* (Prague) 9(23) 2 June 1928. *Družina* was the organ of the Czechoslovak legionnaires.

[53] As for the legal aspect of the matter, we shall take a page out of Czech history. The Czech King Ludvík, who was also crowned King of Hungary, fell in the battle against the Turks at Mohács Hungary, in 1526, leaving no heir. As the Turkish armies swept into the Hungarian plains, confusion and panic spread among the people in Bohemia. In order to save the country from the impending Turkish onslaught, the Czech parliament decided to petition Austrian Crown Prince Ferdinand Habsburg to become king of Bohemia. Ferdinand accepted the invitation, and shortly thereafter was also crowned king of Hungary. The new king ushered in the reign of the Habsburgs in Bohemia which continued until 1918.

Later, Austrian Emperor and King of Bohemia Karl VI, father of Maria Theresa, issued in 1713 his "Pragmatic Sanction" introducing the centralization of the state and declaring the Habsburg Empire indivisible and hereditary even down the women's lineage. Thus, it became mandatory also for the Czech, Moravian, and Silesian parliaments, which adopted this law in 1721, as other European countries did later on. Even in centralized countries, however, it became inescapably evident that such decisions could no longer be contigent on the will of the emperor but also required the assent of the legal representatives of the country.

[54] Miklós Szinai and László Szücs, *Horthy Miklós titkos iratai,* 3d ed. (Budapest, 1965), p. 19.

[55] *Národní Shromáždění Republiky Československé* (Prague, 1928), p. 19.

[56] National Archives, Washington, D.C., Microfilm No. 820. 181.21201/12.

CHAPTER TWO

The Revisionist Movement in Hungary

Connected with the outbreak of World War I was the question of who was responsible for it. The Paris Peace Conference imputed it to Austria-Hungary and its ally Germany. Although official documents of many countries have since been published on the matter, which to some degree tend to mitigate their record of responsibility for the war, they did not absolve them of the blame itself. The diplomatic activities of other countries, such as, for instance, Russia, are equally to blame for the outbreak of the war.

When the provisional parliament in Petrograd discussed the reasons and causes of the war, Russian Foreign Minister Sergei D. Sazonov mentioned the "Ukrainian idea" as one of the most important. It follows that Russia regarded the national and political development of the Ukrainians in Galicia as an assault on the unity of the Russian empire.[1]

Austro-Hungary was a multinational state with ten different major nationalities inhabiting it, but the State Council which decided for the war in 1914 consisted of two Hungarians, a Pole, a Croat, and only one German.[2] The question of fault or blame for the war was appropriately answered by the French historian Fabre-Luce when he said, "By their actions Germany and Austria made the war possible, the Triple Entente by their actions made it inevitable."[3]

The Trianon Treaty was prepared without the participation of Hungary and, when finalized, handed over to it for signing on June 4, 1920. Already in its introduction, the Treaty stated that the world war, "came into being as a result of the declaration of war by the imperial and royal government of Austria-Hungary on Serbia on July 28, 1914 and of the hostility on the part of its ally Germany." Hungary recognized the accusations for the eruption of the war in conformity with chapter 161 of the treaty which at the same time made it and its allies "responsible for all the damages, the caused misery and the casualties sustained by the citizens of the Allied and Associated States, due to the war imposed upon them by Austro-Hungary and its allies."[4] Count Albert Apponyi, an experienced politician, who headed the Hungarian delegation to the Peace Conference, sought to forestall the dismemberment of Hungary, saying that "the dismemberment of Hungary is incompatible with the idea of the reconstruction of Europe and the consolidation of European conditions."[5]

In his memorandum and speeches at the Peace Conference, Apponyi also sought to refute the question of fault, which had weighed heavily on Austro-Hungary since the beginning of the war. As early as 1914, the historian Seton Watson formulated his view, subsequently adopted by the Peace Conference, as follows: "The Magyar oligarchy which already had its back against the wall, realized that the moment for action had come. Its reactionary ideas of racial dominance found a leader—fanatical iron-handed—personally equally brave and honest, but politically quite immune from all scruples, in Count Stephan Tisza, the Hungarian Premier. The murder [of Crown Prince Ferdinand—V. Sh.] provided a splendid pretext for aggression."[6] Seton Watson belonged to a group closely cooperating with Masaryk, who skillfully utilized this formulation of war fault during his talks with representatives of the Entente.

Annoying as the issue of guilt was, it was not Hungary's major problem, for it opened avenues for legal and political discussions. Incomparably more painful was the problem of minority nationalities, which all declared their unequivocal desire to withdraw from Hungary. Hungarian allegations that the Peace Conference was to blame for the dismemberment of Hungary do not correspond to fact. Hungary collapsed as a result of the withdrawal in 1918–1919 of its bonded people, hence long before the Trianon Treaty was signed in the wake of an international and legal basis, which at the time became the moving force in the politics of the victorious Entente, namely on the historical right of nations, the national principle, and the right of self-determination.

Hungarian political literature consciously kept silent on these fundamental principles of the right of individual peoples or simply did not recognize them. Hungarians demanded that these territories be returned to them, but overlooked the desire of the peoples who inhabit these territories and to whom they belonged, invoking instead the Medieval principle of *terra nullius* ("no-man's-land"), which was in force when territories belonged to dynasties.

In his New Year's radio message to the population of Carpatho-Ukraine in 1940, Hungary's Prime Minister Count Pál Teleki posed this question: "And what was the case of Subcarpathia? It was such that Czechoslovakia was left with one colonial dominion and, because Czechoslovakia ceased to exist, it became a "no-man's-land." He proceeded to say that "Hungarian *honvéd*s [i.e., soldiers—V. Sh.] occupied this 'no-man's-land' in March 1939."[7] Teleki "forgot" to mention how many *honvéd*s lost their lives in the campaign against the "no-man's-land," which defended its territory and the young Carpatho-Ukrainian statehood against these very same *honvéd*s. By coming up with the concept of "no-man's-land," Teleki sought to obliterate all preceding international and constitutional acts, including the proclamation of independence, which after World War I normalized the legal and political life of Carpatho-Ukraine. Indeed, he sought to erase Carpatho-Ukraine from history altogether.

Seton Watson, who was well conversant with the history of Hungary, stated that the era of the Middle Ages came to a conclusion in Hungary in 1848. From what Hungarian politicians had previously maintained, it would follow that Seton Watson erred in his date; a more appropriate date would be 1918. For instance, as early as 1918, "Esterházy owned twenty-one castles, sixty market towns, and over four hundred villages in Hungary as well as a number of castles and lordships in Austria and a considerable slice, a whole county, of Bavaria."[8] Hungarians well realized that they possessed no legal or historical title to Carpatho-Ukraine and therefore built their dubitable claims on the application of the principle of *terra nullius* descending from the feudal-royal era which in the 20th century is but merely a remnant of those times lacking any legal or historical content.

Hungarians have in the past and even to this day maintain that they have ruled over the peoples subjugated by them justly. Yet the reality was different. For instance, while the Hungarians who constituted half of the population in 1910, and had 413 representatives in the Parliament, the other half of the population composed of minority nationalities had only 8 representatives.[9]

It is true that from among the warring countries, Hungary suffered most in terms of loss of territory and population, but it is also no less a truth that it had ruled over the largest multinational territory. As a result of the Trianon treaty, Hungary lost:

1) 61,6333 sq. kilometers (km) with 3,517,000 inhabitants to Czecho-Slovakia (Slovakia and Carpatho-Ukraine).

2) 103,093 sq. km. with 5,257,000 inhabitants to Romania (Transylvania, and half of the Bánát along with the city of Temesvár).

3) 20,551 sq. km. with 1,509,000 inhabitants to Yugoslavia (the other half of Bácska, Croatia, Bosnia-Herzegovina, Slovenia, and Montenegro).

4) 4,020 sq. km. to Austria (the so-called Burgenland).

5) 589 sq. km. to Poland.[10]

All in all, Hungary lost 68 percent of its pre-war territory with 58 percent of its population.

The problem of certain modifications or supplements in the peace agreements soon became evident even in the minds of the authors. Thus, for instance, this is what President Woodrow Wilson had to say at the plenary session of the Peace Conference: "We know that the conditions of peace will sooner or later have to be revised and amended."[11] From the logic of the agreement itself it follows that consideration of any such amendments or revisions can allude only to certain parts of the treaty whose implementation would not lead to complications among states or endanger the peace. The Hungarians had, even in this case, their own "truth," which they enunciated point-blank: *Mindent vissza*—"Everything back!" These words were to become the pithy slogan of the Hungarian revisionist movement. In an attempt to thwart any move on the part of Hungary that would imperil the peace, established by international agreements, the country's military might was restricted to 35,000 soldiers.[12]

To propagate the idea of revising the Treaty of Trianon in the international arena, Hungary created an organization called the Hungarian Revisionist League (Magyar Revíziós Liga), which opened its offices in the capitals of states that carried political weight. To the Hungarians this cause was of such paramount importance that the entire internal life in the country was subordinated to it—so much so that it was nurtured in schools which taught their children geography according to old maps, instilling in them the idea that the territorial changes after World War I were caused by "lands being stolen" from them. In other words, the Hungarians did not consider the decisions of the Peace Conference as binding upon them and thereby also ignored the expression of the will of those nationalities which detached themselves from Hungary in 1919–1920.

In their revisionist propaganda, Hungarians emphasized that they were defenders of European culture and, therefore, must control the Carpathian Mountains, i.e. Carpatho-Ukraine, so as to successfully carry out this mission. To be more precise: "Times without number the Hungarian nation has saved Europe from the onslaught of barbarian people coming from the East"[13]—even though the Hungarians themselves had come to Europe from Asia.

During the Austro-Hungarian period, the Hungarians endeavored to create a homogeneous Hungarian state at the expense of other nationalities. This they have, however, achieved only after these nationalities seceded from Hungary after the First World War. Having their own, distinctive national state, Hungarian government officials now had the opportunity to institute necessary reforms for the benefit of their own people, a move they previously hesitated to carry out supposedly because of the preponderance of alien nationalities in the country. And yet, they were not prepared to go about implementing the reforms. Instead, Hungarian feudal lords continued to rule the state by virtue of possessing large landed estates and with the help of a corrupt administration. As Oszkár Jászi had put it:

> Though the peace treaty of Trianon made Hungary really a united nation state consisting almost exclusively of a Magyar population, the ruling class eliminated universal suffrage, re-introduced the old corrupt electoral system, and maintained the overwhelming influence of the large estates and the domination of the gentry administration in the counties. The pretext of the nationality danger ceased, but the system of class domination continued. The theory of the "nationality bugbear" was transformed into that of "Jewish bugbear."[14]

Despite the Hungarian national character of the state, the ruling class continued to deny its people the introduction of general suffrage to say nothing of some social or economic amenities. Jászi draws attention also to this circumstance by stating that "it was emphatically asserted that the idea of democracy and of a Magyar nation state are irreconcilable."

The first to come forth with the idea of revisionism was the former Prime Minister Count István Bethlen (1921–1931). Like other statesmen, Bethlen demanded justice for Hungary but also simultaneously denied the same justice to the nationalities whose territories they wished to recover for themselves. In their demands, they propounded the need for plebiscites in these territories as if the will of these nationalities expressed in 1918–1919 was not definitive or sufficient.

In an interview published in *The New York Times* of November 1930, Bethlen expounded the following official position on the problem: "We desire the re-incorporation of those of our former nationals who are Magyar by race, as also the holding of a plebiscite in the former Hungarian territories to ascertain whether certain other nationalities desire to return to union with us or not."[16] Juridically, such a description of incorporation is erroneous with regard to Carpatho-Ukraine, which never was an integral part of Hungary and did not constitute a national state unity.[17] Hungary's juridicial relationship to Carpatho-Ukraine and other lands may be legally defined by the term "occupation."

Hungary wanted to restore everything to its previous state, i.e., to dominate the entire area. This goal was eloquently expressed by no other than the eminent Hungarian politician and framer of the Nationality Law and of the Austro-Hungarian Compromise of 1867, Ferencz Deák (1803–1876): "What violence robs us of, fortune of time and circumstances may restore; but if we ourselves give up our rights, they will be forever and irrevocably lost."[18] With regard to the invasion of Carpatho-Ukraine in 1938–1939, Hungary considered Hitler its "fortune of time," but life proved it to be short-lived, for it was pressed into the services of arbitrariness.

Through its committees representing the Hungarian Revisionist League in foreign countries, Hungary sought to win public opinion for its revisionist goals. It succeeded in winning over the British press magnate, Lord Harold Sidney H. Rothermere, who unequivocally lent his support to Hungary's revisionist propaganda. His first article that appeared in the April 27, 1927 issue of his *Daily Mail* under the title "Justice for Hungary" so deeply moved the Hungarians as to prompt former Minister of Agriculture Dr. Földes to write in the May 16, 1928 issue of the *Pester Lloyd* that "Lord Rothermere by his articles had performed an act similar to that of Luther in attaching his theses to the church door at Wittenberg."[19] For the successor states ČSR, Romania, and Yugoslavia, the revisionist propaganda was caustic not only abroad but also on the home front. In the ČSR, however, the revisionist movement did not prove itself organizationally feasible. In order to defend their interests and to counteract the Hungarian revisionist movement, these three countries concluded a defense pact known as the Little Entente.

Even after they might have learned a lesson from history, such as the Trianon Treaty and World War II, the Hungarians had not relinquished their imperialistic encroachments on their neighbors. In his introduction to a digest of his speeches, the very same Bethlen formulated Hungary's position thus:

> The existence of the Magyar nation today depends on its ability to ensure dominion over the territory which is bounded by the Carpathians and which forms the Danube-Tisza basin. Within the present frontiers of the Hungarian State this nation perishes if timely control is not achieved over those lands without which the country's independent existence is unthinkable.

In his Berlin lectures he quite sincerely admitted that "Territorial revision has always been very difficult, for land which it was necessary to gain by blood and iron cannot be regained by fair words and diplomatic moves."[20]

Notions of this kind were not rare or exceptional; they were shared by the entire ruling strata in Hungary, both political and scientific. A similar attitude was espoused by Professor of Jurisprudence at Debrecen University, V. Haendl, who, "pronounces as a terrible mistake on the part of the Hungarians the fact that nationality questions were not dealt with in time, that the non-Magyar nationalities were not assimilated in time, and he reproaches the Hungarian governments of 1862-1918 with weakness and shortsightedness."[21]

St. Stephen's Crown As State Ideology.

Hungarian historiography justifies the necessity of conquering lands of other peoples on the grounds that Hungary, in its historical development within the boundaries of the Crown of St. Stephen (the symbol of the historic Hungarian kingdom), was the defender of European culture and civilization against the "barbarians" from the East as well as against the Turkish-Tatar plunder in the past as well as defender of Christianity.

For a peaceful coexistence of peoples it is necessary that each and every state or people correctly understands its historical destination and role in the area of its habitation. It is in this direction that Hungarian historiography makes a cardinal mistake by crediting Hungary with an historical role and importance it did not have and was not capable of fulfilling. This argument is advanced solely for the purpose of justifying the expedience of a so-called Greater Hungary to exist, a concept for which Hungarian political and scholarly circles seek to win the support of world political opinion.

The Hungarians tend to emphasize that they are defenders of the "Christian Faith" in Europe. Yet, this too, does not correspond to historical reality, for, to cite an example, the Hungarian public and political opinion supported the Turks in the war between the latter and the Serbs in the second half of the 19th century. Moreover, the Calvinist faith, which accounted for only 20 percent of Hungary's population after the Trianon treaty and was identified with Hungarian chauvinist nationalism, was recognized as the "Hungarian religion" and enlisted in the services of forced Magyarization. No other nation in the Danubian Basin or beyond it, with the exception of Poland, practiced this kind of nationalism blended with religion. Hungary's leading statesmen Horthy, Teleki, Csáki, Darányi, Bethlen, and Tisza, all were of the Calvinist faith.[22]

As far as their Slavic neighbors are concerned, the Hungarians said that they were carrying out a "historical mission," which was predestined to them, namely to wage the struggle against Pan-Slavism. This third "historical task" with which they felt endowed by destiny is but only partially justified, for "after they have intermarried with Slavs throughout a thousand years and by living in close proximity with four Slav nations, they have themselves to a certain extent become 'Slavs racially.'"

In recent times, the Hungarians concerned themselves with delving into the history of their origin in conformity with the "Turanian concept." They have established societies and worked on this problem in an attempt to prove their affinity with the Turks. From the brief outline it may be concluded that Hungary's claims to territories inhabited by other nationalities reveal a purely imperialistic character rather than a historical-defensive trait that Hungarian historiography and propaganda, together with the St. Stephen Crown, continually stresses.[24]

While in exile in Switzerland, the last king of Hungary, Charles, made the necessary preparations for a return to his throne in Hungary which he planned to implement after Hungary had signed a peace treaty. In his letter to Horthy, Charles clarified his position on the problem thus: "As a juridically and constitutionally crowned king, who has not renounced any of his rights and is therefore conscious of all of his duties, I want to participate in the consolidation of the state and its reconstruction."[25] With this aim in mind, Charles showed up in Hungary on two occasions, but was not received and had to leave the country.

In the interwar period, Hungary considered itself a kingdom despite the fact that it had no king. Horthy explained this situation thus:

> Everybody knows that all power in Hungary belongs to the Holy Crown and that only through the act of coronation is it invested in the king. Therefore, the royal castle and the royal estates belong to the Holy Crown and not to the king. It is, therefore, possible to have a kingdom without a king.[26]

Another Hungarian statesman, Count Albert Apponyi, wrote on November 29, 1919:

> In view of the fact that King Charles's rule over Austrian provinces has ended, the Pragmatic Sanction's provisions stating that the eldest son of the king or his closest male relative ascends the throne are now invalid, as a result of which Hungary has now recovered the right to elect its own king after the death or abdication of a king.[27]

However, in practice, this right has never been applied.

The issue of the king was the subject of a lively debate also at a meeting of Parliament on February 16, 1920. The conclusion arrived at was that the "crowned king has not renounced his rights." The National Assembly, as the embodiment of national sovereignty, at the same time passed a resolution to the effect that "relations with Austria as well as our Compromise Act of 1867 have ceased to exist." In actual fact, what happened was that the legislators divested the king of only his executive powers and made arrangements to elect a regent, who was to govern the country until such time as the executive power would be restored to the king.[28]

The Council of Ambassadors of the victorious Entente, which continually functioned in Paris, was of the opinion that a return of the Habsburgs to Austria and Hungary "Would basically pose a threat to peace" and that allies were not prepared to either recognize or tolerate" such a move.[29] "On December 3, 1921, the National Assembly enacted another law, which dethrones the Habsburgs and simultaneously abrogates the Pragmatic Sanction." As the reason given for the law, the legislators maintained categorically that it was passed only as a result of the violation of Hungary's independence.[30]

We have presented a review of the Holy Crown issue and its state-political importance so as to demonstrate that the Ruthenians-Ukrainians as well as the peoples formerly under Hungarian domination have nothing in common with the Holy Crown either historically or juridically speaking and are thus in no way bound by it. It is a specific creation of Hungarian history and of the Hungarian people, but for the non-Magyar peoples it was nothing more than an egregious symbol of economic misery and national and political oppression.

The Munich and Vienna Arbitrations

After the end of World War I, there emerged two distinct cultural movements in Carpatho-Ukraine, the "populist" and the "Muscophile," between which an unremitting struggle was carried on. The Ukrainian populist orientation sprang forth from the nature of the population of the country itself which, though still using the old name of "Rusyny" (Ruthenians), felt organically related to and part of the great Ukrainian nation, a sentiment it had expressed spontaneously in the decisions of the national *radas* (councils) throughout the years of 1918 and 1919. It would be to the point to note that on December 4, 1919 the Czechoslovak Academy of Sciences in Prague recognized this fact.

The Muscophile orientation in Carpatho-Ukraine was artificially foisted upon the population by both Czech and Hungarian officials and politicians who were not sympathetically disposed toward the natural Ukrainian national development. Support for the Muscophiles came from among such Czech political parties as the Agrarian, the National-Socialist (Beneš' party), and the National Democratic Party (Kramář).

On the other hand, however, the Social-Democrats supported the Ukrainian orientation while the Subcarpathian Communists published their newspapers also in the Ukrainian language. Odd as it may seem, Hungary, which in the past had severly persecuted the Carpatho-Ukrainian people for their supposedly "Russian Slavophilism," was now financing the Autonomous Agricultural Union, commonly known as the Kurtiak Party, and the cultural movement of the Muscophile orientation. It was doing this with the express intention of hampering and ruining the sound Ukrainian national movement and thereby diverting the people from their natural national and cultural development.

The Hungarian revisionist propaganda had no influence or sympathizers in the populist-Ukrainian camp. What is more, even among local Hungarians there were no organized pro-revisionist manifestations. Possibly this was so because of a law in the ČSR for the protection of the state whose violation, such as the revisionist political activity, could have lead to prosecution.[31] Moreover, the ethnic Hungarians in Czecho-Slovakia had after a while been able to discern the difference between life in the democratic Czecho-Slovak Republic and in the semi-feudal system of Hungary. It is only from this aspect understandable why the Small Farmers' League in Czecho-Slovakia issued a Manifesto in which the following passage was embodied: "We declare emphatically that in all respects the Magyars in Czechoslovakia enjoy more rights than they ever had in former Hungary or that the citizens of present-day Hungary possess."[32]

To cite another example, Ambassador Montgomery, the United States' representative in Budapest had the following to say in his report to the State Department: "Reliable reports from Upper Hungary indicate that the former Hungarian minority of Czechoslovakia has already suffered some disillusionment as a result of their detachment to Hungary."[33]

In the same report, the Ambassador offers another interesting observation: "No secret has been made of the fact that the Hungarian Free Corps was active in Ruthenia until the Germans ordered them to be withdrawn. Members of the Free Corps have marched through the streets of Budapest during recent weeks, dressed in black boots, black coats, and fur shakos (military caps)."[34] Hungary denied having ordered its subversive units into Carpatho-Ukraine and, instead, imputed their terrorist acts to the Czechs and the local inhabitants discontented with the government.

The Autonomous Agricultural Union, headed by Deputy Ivan Kurtiak, was a local political party with which some Magyarophile elements associated overtly or covertly. Among them were also some Magyarophile priests, who screened themselves behind the name *Russkie* (Russians) and for whom it was at the time not beneficial to openly profess themselves as Magyars or Magyarophiles. It was public knowledge in Carpatho-Ukraine that Kurtiak's party—which after Kurtiak's death in 1930 was headed by Andriy Brody—was receiving money from Hungary. It was undoubtedly a strong political trump-card in Hungary's hands to have a man in its pay who presided over a political party, was a member of the Czechoslovak Parliament and thus protected by immunity from prosecution, pretended to be in public a fighter for the "good of the Carpatho-Russian people," and was able to do Hungary's bidding. Other political parties in Carpatho-Ukraine were by and large branches of Czech parties.

With Hitler's coming to power in January of 1933, Hungary found in him a new partner for its revisionist policy. It subsequently became one of Hitler's most devoted allies, to which several of Horthy's letters to him as well as his official pronouncements testify. Hungarian government circles were so carried away by the prospect of a successful revision of the borders that they completely ignored voices of sound warnings by the opposition in the Parliament. For instance, when the Social-Democratic Deputy Daniel Varnai pointed to the possible and baleful consequences of such a policy, Prime Minister Bethlen reported "The Deputy certified that not a single drop of Hungarian blood flows in his veins."[35]

The occupation of Austria by Germany was a signal for Hungary to activate the issue of revising its borders. At the same time, the political situation in Czecho-Slovakia was becoming critical because of the demands of Germany, Hungary, and even Poland to settle its nationalities problem. So tense was the situation that Czecho-Slovakia felt compelled to mobilize over a million men into the army. The mobilization was carried out in a swift and orderly fashion. The army was motorized and equipped with modern weapons. But all this did not save Czecho-Slovakia from the catastrophe that the dictate of the four powers meeting in Munich (Germany, Britain, France, and Italy) held in store for it.

In accordance with the Munich decision (September 29, 1938), Czecho-Slovakia was obligated to resolve the problem of its Hungarian and Polish minorities. Poland, whose interests were represented in Munich by the Mussolini government, sought to resolve the problem of its rather small Polish minority by sending a 24-hour ultimatum, which Czecho-Slovakia immediately accepted. Poland was very much in a "hurry" to defend the rights of a small Polish group settled in the area around the city of Těšin (Teschen), but did not seem to be in such haste to resolve in a civilized and humane manner a problem closer to home, namely that of over six million Ukrainians of Galicia who were forced to live under Poland for almost twenty years by virtue of the decision of the Council of Ambassadors made in Paris in March 1923.[36] Poland's ultimatum to Czecho-Slovakia aroused the indignation of the civilized world. The French ambassador in Germany, François Poncet, characterized Poland's conduct thus: "Now the Poles were moving into Teschen 'like the ghost who in former centuries crawled about the battlefields to kill and rob the dead and wounded.'"[37] And the English writer John Wheeler-Bennett called Hungary and Poland "jackals."

Although the Vienna Arbitration was not a component part of the Munich Pact, it nevertheless was in some respect its supplement. One of the points of the Munich Pact states the following: "In the additional Declaration the Heads of the Governments of the four Powers declare that the problems of the Polish and Hungarian minorities in Czecho-Slovakia, if not settled within three months by agreement between the respective Governments, shall form the subject of another meeting of the Heads of the Governments of the four Powers here present."[38]

And with respect to the guarantee of the new Czechoslovak borders, the Munich Pact states: "In the annex to the Munich Agreement of September 29, 1938, it is stated that His Majesty's Government in the United Kingdom and the French Government stood by their offer in regard to an international guarantee of the new boundaries of the Czechoslovak State against unprovoked aggression and that the German and Italian Governments would, after the question of the Polish and Hungarian minorities had been settled, for their part give a guarantee to Czecho-Slovakia."[39]

However, in total disregard of its commitment concerning the guarantee of Czechoslovakia's new borders, Germany had no intention of following up on its promise, as the course of further development was to evince. Hitler had already devised other plans with regard to the political future of Czecho-Slovakia, and thereby of Carpatho-Ukraine as well. An inkling of Hitler's true intentions could be gathered from the memorandum sent on February 7, 1939 by Germany's State Secretary Ernst von Weizsaecker to the Hungarian Government:

> It was a considerable time since the British had declared themselves for a frontier guarantee for Czecho-Slovakia. I could also assure the Minister that these British views were of no interest to us. The only frontier guarantee for Czecho-Slovakia that could be effective or of consequence for her was a German one. We had, however, postponed this, as conditions in Czecho-Slovakia had not yet sufficiently calmed down.[40]

As far as the Hungarian minority in Slovakia and Carpatho-Ukraine is concerned, an attempt at settling this matter with Hungary in some agreement was made even before the Vienna Arbitration. To this end, a joint meeting of representatives of Hungary and the ČSR was convoked to Komarno, Slovakia, on October 9, 1938. However, due to the exaggerated territorial demands raised by Hungary, the negotiations eventually broke down completely without achieving any mutual agreement. It may be of interest here to draw attention to a statement made in Komarno by the representative of Carpatho-Ukraine Minister Dr. Edmund Bachynsky, in which he expounded the legal basis for the unification of the land with the ČSR in 1919 and referred to the people's will supporting this act. He further noted the joint protestations of the Ruthenian parliamentary representatives at the Prague Parliament concerning the changing of the previous state status into a federative one, underscoring the fact that the Ruthenians had already determined their fate and now wish to live with the Czechs and Slovaks as equal partners in a federated Czecho-Slovak Republic. He resolutely denounced any attempt to detach or cede any larger city to Hungary.[41]

Following the fiasco of the negotiations in Komarno, Hungary and Poland immediately embarked upon a propaganda calling for a common border with one another. Although Carpatho-Ukraine had never belonged to Poland and never had any historical ties with the Poles, Poland was now determined at all costs to destroy the young Carpatho-

Ukrainian federated state since the latter's mere existence reactivated the demands of six million Ukrainians in Poland for political and autonomous-federative as well as elementary national and cultural rights they have been deprived of. The representatives of Czecho-Slovakia at Komarno—Czechs, Slovaks, and Carpatho-Ukrainians—defended the state and territorial integrity and unity of the Republic in their arguments against the demands of Hungary. However, an unpleasant and unexpected incident occurred which we could not have anticipated even in our wildest dreams.

While the negotiations were going on in Komarno, the Hungarian Ambassador in Warsaw, András Hory, reported to the Hungarian Ministry of Foreign Affairs that, "M. Kobylanski alerted the Polish ambassador in Prague to a statement by Prime Minister Tiso to the effect that the Slovaks would renounce Carpatho-Ukraine in order to keep Bratislava.[42] If we should win this game, then such a sacrifice should be made according to him."[43] Even though Msgr. Tiso sacrificed his life, this act cannot be viewed as anything less than unethical, to say the least.

Carpatho-Ukraine's attitude was clarified by Msgr. Voloshyn in an address delivered in Uzhhorod on October 27, 1938:

> We stand for the inviolability of Carpatho-Ukraine's boundaries as delineated by the National Council. We, therefore, most resolutely reject any plebiscite since Carpatho-Ukraine's belonging has definitively been decided. We are for a federative form of the state of Czechs, Slovaks, and Ukrainians.[44]

Meanwhile, the Czechoslovak foreign minister, Dr. František Chvalkovský, visited Berlin and after his return suggested to the representatives of Slovakia and Carpatho-Ukraine to pay a visit to the German foreign minister, Joachim von Ribbentrop, to discuss the problem of the Hungarian minority. Indeed, Dr. Edmund Bachynsky of Carpatho-Ukraine and Msgr. Jozef Tiso of Slovakia followed the advice. In the meantime the British and French ambassadors, for their part, suggested to Chvalkovský that instead of calling in the four powers to arbitrate the Hungarian problem in Czecho-Slovakia only two of them, namely Germany and Italy, be invited. The suggestion was accepted and so on November 2, 1938 an arbitration commission consisting of German Foreign Minister Ribbentrop and his Italian counterpart Count Galeazzo Ciano convened at the Belvedere Castle in Vienna upon the invitation of the governments of Czecho-Slovakia and Hungary. Czecho-Slovakia was represented by Chvalkovský, Msgr. Voloshyn, and Msgr. Tiso, with accompanying advisors, while Hungary sent its Prime Minister Teleki, Minister Kánya, and some advisors.[45]

In Vienna Hungary did not raise the question of annexing all of Carpatho-Ukraine, although it broached the matter behind-the-scenes, as may be deduced from the statement of Miklós Kozma (former Hungarian Minister of the Interior, later appointed Commissioner of Carpatho-Ukraine) that "the Ruthenian land in political terms is by far of greater value than whatever city or a number of cities taken, the return of which we now demand."[46] However, the Hungarian government conducted secret talks with Dr. Stefan Fentsyk and Msgr. Dr. Jozef Tiso regarding the possible annexation of Carpatho-Ukraine and Slovakia by Hungary, while in its official notes and acts Hungary demanded only that the Slovaks and Ukrainians be given the right to self-determination in the form of a referendum.[47] Apparently, Hungary expected that the outcome of the referendum would be in its favor.

During a meeting with Ribbentrop, Ciano succeeded in prevailing upon the latter to have Uzhhorod, Mukachevo, Berehovo, and Košice ceded to Hungary. In a private talk with Msgr. Voloshyn in Vienna, Ribbentrop offered the explanation that the reason why the region's capital Uzhhorod was ceded to Hungary was that not only that the city's Hungarian inhabitants, but also its Jewish dwellers, who constitued 40.68 percent of the city's population, demanded it.[48]

The decision of the Vienna Arbitration was far beyond any expectations in its harshness. Carpatho-Ukraine lost its capital Uzhhorod and two other important commercial centers, Mukachevo and Berehovo. All in all, Carpatho-Ukraine lost to Hungary 1,586 sq. kilometers with a population of 181,609. Czecho-Slovakia, as a whole, lost to Germany and Hungary as a result of the Munich and Vienna agreements 40,959 sq. km. and almost five million people.[49]

The Vienna Award caused great dismay among the Ukrainians in Carpatho-Ukraine and abroad. Prime Minister Msgr. A. Voloshyn issued a manifesto on this occasion entitled "To the Citizens of Carpatho-Ukraine," in which he denounced the Vienna Award, noting:

> The tearing away of our ancient cities, Uzhhorod, Mukachevo, and
> Berehovo, from Carpatho-Ukraine is a blow to our fatherland. This

heavy blow, which met us, will not shake our will to accomplish that great task which history has destined for us. We have decided to begin the historical task of building up our severed but independent country. God will help us to fulfill our historical task.[50]

At the same time a protest was lodged by Dr. Luka Mishuha, a delegate of the Ukrainian Organization of the United States, who was dispatched to Europe, which claimed that "the Arbitration Commission's decision has inflicted great harm on Carpatho-Ukraine and the entire Ukrainian people. Ukrainian Americans do not recognize this decision and strongly inveigh against it."[51]

France's role in these hapless days and months was undeniably unenviable. However, it embarked upon a road of appeasement that ultimately led to its downfall. France, known as the architect of the Versailles Treaty of 1919 and the dominant figure in matters pertaining to Eastern Europe as well as the author of the *Cordon Sanitaire* concept, during the Munich days brought about the demise of its loyal and well-armed ally, Czecho-Slovakia, in return for which it hoped to secure Hitler's friendship. At Munich, France and Germany seemed to have reconciled their differences to a point that prompted Ribbentrop to sign a document in Paris about the "Good and Peaceful Coexistence" between the two states and to embrace the French Foreign Minister, George Bonnet.[52] There was a time when the French refused to shake hands with the German democrat Gustav Stresseman, head of the People's Party, who was willing to pursue the French policy in Berlin, but now they were not loathe to embrace a representative of Hitler although they were well aware of the political goals and the moral value of all declarations and documents signed by Hitler's and his minister Ribbentrop.

According to the Czechoslovak Constitution, the cession of state territory to another state could take place only with the assent of the Parliament and then only by a qualified majority of its members. Beneš was right in the political sense not to submit the problem of the Sudetenland to the League of Nations, which at that time could have passed a decision favoring Germany and thus given the detachment of this territory an international sanction that would have re-inforced Germany's legal position. Conversely, for its part, Germany failed to submit the issue of annexing the Sudetenland, to the Czechoslovak Parliament for a vote. Pursuant to Paragraph 64 of the Czechoslovak

Constitution, any territorial changes in the state must be approved by a three-fifths majority of the Parliament. Hence, in conformity with the Constitution, the severance of the territories on the basis of the Munich and Vienna decisions was an unconstitutional act.

The Munich and Vienna decisions were formally and legally null and void also because of another consideration, namely because the agreements infringed on the accords by not fulfilling their obligations concerning the guarantees of the borders. Moreover, Germany contravened the Munich Award by setting up by force the Protectorate of Bohemia and Moravia. Hungary, too, violated the Vienna Award by arbitrarily committing military aggression against Carpatho-Ukraine. In International Law the view prevails that if one of the contracting parties neglect to honor the provisions of an accord signed by it, then the other party is entitled to nullify such an agreement. Neither the Munich nor the Vienna Award receive international recognition and, thus, they are today nothing more than ordinary historical acts of a dismal past.

Hungary was not to be content with the acquisition of territories from Czecho-Slovakia. The Vienna Award was but only a good beginning for further acquisitions of lands from its other neighbors. It is clear that politically and practically the Vienna Award vindicated the revisionist movement. There were huge demonstrations throughout the country, particularly in Budapest, extolling Horthy as the "országgyarapító" or "one who has enlarged Hungarian lands" and chanting "Horthy, Hitler, Mussolini." To solemnize the occasion, Horthy saw it fit to ride into Komarno and Košice on a white horse. To show Hitler its gratitude, the Hungarian Government renamed the Köröndi Tér, one of its most beautiful squares in Budapest, after him.

The Vienna Award not only aroused great enthusiasm in Hungary, but also stimulated the revisionist hopes of achieving a common bond with Poland. Apart from the massive demonstrations staged throughout the country in honor of Hitler, Mussolini, and Horthy, the Hungarian press went out of the way to express the country's profound gratitude, recognition, and friendship. Thus, for instance, *Uj Magyarország* (New Hungary) wrote that, first and foremost, Hungary was grateful to the "Führer" for his lion's share in making it possible for Hungary "to celebrate today such a joyous holiday." Another newspaper, the government mouthpiece Függetlenség (*Independence*) extolled the immense role that the "two great friends of Hungary—Germany and Italy" had played in this respect. It assured Führer and Chancellor Hitler that Hungary would never forget that it was he who made it possible to recover the upper-Hungarian territories. The organ of the revisionist movement *Pesti Hirlap* (*The Pest Herald*) wrote: "We think with undying love and attachment of our great three friends—Germany, Italy, and Poland—which were the executors of the will of Providence." The influential *Pester Lloyd* wrote in a similar vein, saying that, "without the might and power of Germany and Hitler's will, the developments could not have advanced that far, for we did not even dare to initiate them."[53]

These exclamations of fidelity, gratitude, and friendship toward Germany sharply contrasted with Hungary's foreign policy only a few years earlier. In March of 1935, for instance, Hungary signed an agreement in Rome with Italy and Austria which was directed against Germany. The agreement's aim was to contain Germany's influence upon Austria and Hungary. Yet Hungary was soon to draw away from its partners in the agreement and side with Germany. It turned out that:

> ... ever since January 1935 personal contacts existed between Horthy and Hitler, contacts that had been taken up in full secrecy. Not even the Hungarian minister in Berlin, Szilárd Masirevich, was kept informed about the negotiations. When, for reasons of prestige, he asked for information about the subject of one of Horthy's letters to Hitler, he was given the answer that "it was the wish of H.S.H. the Regent to impart the contents exclusively to the Führer."[54]

Hitler replied to Horthy with a letter of May 13, 1935 in which he said, "And if Hungary will, out of sheer necessity, also seize every opportunity that offers itself, she may count on my full sympathy."[55] In this connection, it should be recalled that at that time Gyula Gömbös was the first head of government to visit the Nazi leader after his acsession to power.

The state of exaltation and the period of exclamations of recognition and gratitude to Hitler and Mussolini were gradually to wear off, for with the acquisition of the new territory by virtue of the Vienna Award, Hungary was to become fraught with new problems. Czecho-Slovakia was a prospering, orderly democratic state in which the individual nationalities, including the Hungarian, were given legal possibilities to a free life and development. It was no wonder then that the Hungarian minority did not manifest enthusiasm for the prospect of the change of having now to belong to Hungary. On the basis of information received from the Italian ambassador, Dr. Bernardo Attolico, the Polish ambassador in Berlin, Jozef Lipski, with a certain degree of consternation had the following to say in his report to Warsaw: " . . . from Carpathian Ruthenia not a single petition of the population for union with Hungary had been forwarded to the arbitrators."[56] The government machinery and the commissions especially created for this purpose sought to cover up the adverse reaction of the population in the territories ceded to Hungary as the Hungarian troops were occupying them.

Even Hungarian authors, noting their observations made in the reoccupied territories, had to admit that, "the Hungarians fear that they are are more worried and that a more difficult future is awaiting them than they had experienced in their lives under the Czechoslovak Republic."[57] Such sentiments were forthcoming also from the Hungarian border villages in Carpatho-Ukraine and Slovakia. For instance, one read thus: "Stay where you are, do not endeavor to liberate us, we are living better here than you there; first of all, liberate yourselves."[58] And when the Hungarian army entered these territories, there were frequent incidents—mentioned in the report—of Hungarians in Hungarian villages refusing to cooperate with the army. For instance: "In a purely Hungarian village with one thousand inhabitants, the Hungarian army quartermasters were compelled to use force to requisition living quarters for the soldiers."[59] If the ethnic Hungarians in Carpatho-Ukraine and Slovakia were critical of the forcible change of their citizenship, then one can only imagine with what sentiment the Ukrainians greeted the return to the Hungarian feudal system.

On November 5, 1938, Regent Horthy issued a battle order to the army in which he, among other things, stated the following:

> Our Honvéds, liberated from the shackles of Trianon and again reborn after twenty years of waiting, shall cross the borders that we have always considered to be only temporary. You shall enter our highlands, our homeland that has so often been sanctified with the blood of our forebears. Welcome, with dignified love into your hearts, equally each and every inhabitant of the recovered ancient Hungarian soil—Hungarians, Slovaks, Ruthenians, and Germans— all our brothers.[60]

The following day, Horthy issued a "Proclamation" to the "liberated population of the Highlands," in which he said: "Hungarians! You are free again. The love and concern of the Hungarian people are awaiting you. We embrace with love the inhabitants of this territory, the sons of several nationalities, so that they may rejoice with us and partake in the feast of liberation."[61] Expressions of friendliness and love in Horthy's proclamations and other official statements by state officials, however, were at variance with the reality that was created from the outset by Hungarian policy and the army on the reoccupied territories.

During the era of Czecho-Slovakia, Hungary had continuously emphasized through its retainers, including Andriy Brody, head of the Autonomous Agricultural Union, and Rev. Dr. Stefan Fentsyk, head of the fascist "Black Shirts" party, that Czecho-Slovakia was not fulfilling its obligations regarding the autonomy of Carpatho-Ukraine. Yet, when on November 10, 1938 it occupied the cities of Uzhhorod, Mukachevo, and Berehovo with their vicinities, it immediately went about removing all signs in the Ruthenian-Ukrainian language from government buildings and streets and replacing them with Hungarian signs and names.[62] More than that, the Ukrainian cultural society "Prosvita" was banned as were other Ukrainian professional organizations. On the other hand, however, the Muscophile cultural "Dukhnovych Society" was permitted to remain active under the supervision of the state Commissioner Perényi.[63]

The occupation of the three cities and surrounding villages, however, turned out for Hungary to be not only a nationality problem but also a social one, for it caused unemployment. The population's dissatisfaction reached such proportions that it forced the Hungarian government to send its State Secretary Tibor Pataky to deal with the problem.[64] An action initiated by Premier Imredy's wife called the "Hungarians' Aid to Hungarians" was but a drop in the bucket and could not alleviate the situation of general privation or, for that matter, convince the population that the "change of policy [to Hungarians—V. Sh.] would bring social benefits."[65] It may be noted here that in Czecho-Slovakia there was state aid for organized laborers only in the event of unemployment, whereas in Hungary there was none. If we take into consideration the fact that at that time there were some 30,000 unemployed white-collar workers waiting for jobs in the occupied territories, then it becomes clear, as the Hungarian Ambassador in Prague, Wettstein, admitted, why the local Ruthenian-Ukrainian officials, teachers, professors, and others were dismissed from their jobs and became unemployed.[66]

The   Hungarians were astonished to learn after their return to Uzhhorod, Mukachevo, and Berehovo, that the people there were not the same as they had left them twenty years before. During this period of time in a democratic Czecho-Slovakia, the Ukrainian people grew into a national and political force the Hungarians now had to face eye-to-eye. The moral resistance of the Ukrainian population could not be subdued even by the organized "vad magyar nacionálisták" (rabid Hungarian nationalists) who immediately upon the occupation of the newly regained territories resorted to all kinds of terrorist actions with a view toward intimidating the population.[67]

Realizing the strong resistance on the part of the Ukrainian population, with which they did not reckon, the government circles in Budapest set out to seek a solution to the problem. With this in mind, the Hungarian government ordered a draft project of an autonomy for the entirety of Carpatho-Ukraine to be prepared. The plan was then communicated as strictly confidential information to Msgr. Voloshyn in Khust at the beginning of December 1938 with the remark that, "it is still time to accept the Hungarian position."[68] Msgr. Voloshyn, however, declined the proposal and made the information about it public.[69]

The decisiveness displayed by Msgr. Voloshyn and his government in rejecting and combatting the various Hungarian attempts on the life of the young Carpatho-Ukrainian federated part of the Czechoslovak Republic evoked a clear positive reaction within the population and quarters of the central government in Prague. Hungary's conspiracy with Poland against Carpatho-Ukraine, coupled with subversive work and military action in the territory as well as in the international forum, was a flagrant violation of the principles of legality and morality that was rightly denounced by the civilized world.

Notes

[1] Stepan Tomashivsky, *Halychyna, politychno-istorychnyi narys z pryvodu svitovoï viiny*, 2nd ed. (Lviv, 1915) p. 29.

[2] Ibid., p. 56.

[3] Ibid., p. 163.

[4] Jenö Horváth, *Felelöség a világháboruért és a békeszerzödésért* (Budapest, 1939), p.1.

[5] Légrády Brothers, *Justice for Hungary,* third edition (Budapest, 1931), p. 80.

[6] Jenö Horváth, *op. cit.,* p. 6; *See also,* Seton Watson, *The Austro-Serbian Dispute, The Round Table* (London, September 1914).

[7] Loránt Tilkovsky, *Revizió és Nemzetiségpolitika Magyar-országon, 1938-1941* (Budapest: Akademian, 1967).

[8] Edward Crankshaw, *Maria Theresa* (New York, 1969), p. 131.

[9] Jenö Horváth, *A magyar kérdés a XX században* (Budapest, 1939), p. 14; *See also,* R. W. Seton Watson, "The Fall of the Habsburg Empire," *The Listener* (London) 13 (1935): 794–97.

[10] Miklós Horthy, *Emlékirataim,* 2nd ed., (Buenos Aires, 1953), pp. 129–30.

[11] Legrády Brothers, *op. cit.,* p. 78.

[12] Ibid., p. 38.

[13] Ibid., pp. 43–44.

[14] Oscar Jászi, *The Dissolution of the Habsburg Monarchy* (Chicago, 1929), p. 326.

[15] Ibid., p. 326.

[16] Légrády Brothers, *op. cit.,* p. 80.

[17] The contention that "before World War I Carpatho-Ukraine was an integral part of the Hungarian Kingdom" is erroneous and historically at variance with the juridical-political development that Carpatho-Ukraine had underwent.

[18] Count Albert Apponyi, *A Brief Sketch of the Hungarian Constitution and of the Relations Between Austria and Hungary* (Budapest, 1908), p. 8.

[19] Seton Watson, *Treaty Revision and the Hungarian Frontiers* (London, 1934), p. 50.

[20] As quoted by Dr. Kamil Krofta. *See The Substance of Hungarian Revisionism* (Prague, 1934), pp. 10–11.

[21] Ibid., pp. 22-23. For clarity, we should make clear that the ancestral homeland of the Hungarians (Magyars) is the remote area of northern Siberia, a

corner wedged between the Ural Mountains and the Arctic Ocean, which is inhabited by people whom Russian scholars and the Russian government consider to consist of two peoples. They are the Ostiaki and the Voguli, presently occupying what is known as the Ostiaki-Vogulsky National Rayon or district. The administrative center of the Omsk Oblast or province is located at Samarovo, renamed Ostiakovogulsk by the Bolsheviks. They are a woodland people engaged in hunting, fishing, and picking mushrooms and forest berries. They do not till the land; they keep domesticated animals and reindeer. They are short in built, have black or dark-blond hair and, for the most part, are dark-eyed. Their culture is on a rather low level, but they excel in hunting and fishing. Their language, with which Prof. Nestor Korol, became acquainted on his official trips on behalf of the Soviet Ministry of Agriculture in Siberia and the Soviet Far East, is very similar to Hungarian. However, Prof. Korol was not aware of the similarity until after World War II when he met some Hungarians in the West and was able to identify many words he had become familiar with in Siberia. [I tape-recorded an interview with Prof. Korol, a former Moscow University professor, who was a geneticist and had spent a considerable length of time in the area inhabited by these minorities and was able to partially learn their language. The sound tape is in my possession.] Another author has this to say about these minorities and their language: "The most definite Magyar characteristic is language. It is a branch of the great Ugrian stock; its nearest existing congeners being the Ostiak and the Vogul of the Ural range and the banks of the Ob River." (*See* R.G. Latham, *The Nationalities of Europe,* vol. 2 (London: Wm. H. Allen & Co., 1863), p. 394.)

With regard to the question of Hungarian "rights" with regard to Carpatho-Ukraine, let me make clear the precise juridical-political history: Hungary continues to this day to invoke the state-political idea of the Crown of St. Stephen as the basis for its territorial claims to foreign, non-Hungarian countries that it had ruled until the end of World War I. To be sure, the St. Stephen Crown must serve as the source of their claims, as it is the symbol of Greater Hungary. According to Hungarian historiography, this crown was given to King Stephen by Pope Silvester II in a special Bulla with which he was invested as the first Hungarian sovereign. World history accepted this thesis in the form and content presented by Hungarian history. This could have happened only because the background of the crown's history had not been researched for more than seven hundred years.

Actually, the St. Stephen Crown consists of two original parts: the "corona Graeca" (Byzantine), constituting its lower part, and the "corona Latina," its upper part. This fact became known only in 1792, when Emperor Joseph II of Austria was also crowned King of Hungary. On that occasion experts had the opportunity of making a thorough examination of the Crown and deciphering the Greek inscriptions on its lower part.

In 1880, a special commission attached to the Hungarian Academy of Sciences and headed by Arnold Ipolyi, a historian of arts, was called into being to research the genesis of the Crown. The commission published a monograph entitled *History and Description of the Holy Hungarian Crown and the Insignia* (in Hungarian) in Budapest in 1886. Years later, in 1928, with the approval of pertinent state officials, Julius Morávcsik conducted further research of the Crown's history, especially of its lower so-called Byzantine part which features the images of Jesus Christ, the Archangels Michael and Gabriel, and of apostles with inscriptions in the Greek language. The Byzantine part of the Crown was given to King Géza I of Hungary (1074–1077) by the Byzantine Emperor Michael Dukas VII, who reigned from 1071 to 1079. The Byzantine part also displays the inscription "Géza faithful king of Turkia," which obviously implies the Turkish-Turanian racial descent of the Hungarians ("Turkia" was the contemporary name of Hungary). Géza was Emperor Michael Dukas VII's contemporary and probably was crowned with the Byzantine crown. Thus it follows that the Byzantine crown was brought into Hungary in the eleventh century and that King St. Stephen (997–1038) could not possibly have been enthroned with this crown, which presently constitutes the lower part of the presumably original crown.

The upper part, i.e. the Latin crown, features images and names of only eight apostles which fact leads some experts to believe that this crown is not complete. It is not known what the original Latin crown looked like or when and why it was superimposed on the Byzantinian crown. The absence of four apostles is believed to be due to the fact that when the two crowns were being joined together a part of the Latin crown was cut off that happened to bear the likenesses of the now missing four apostles. Hungarian historiography also does not have the answer to whether the upper part, i.e., the Latin crown, is identical with that which was sent by Pope Silvester II. Significant also is the fact that Hungarians continue to use the double-bar Byzantine cross as a "symbol of Hungarian royal power." Hungarian historiography has yet to find the answer to all of the unresolved problems connected with the St. Stephen Crown. As far as the double-bar cross is concerned, it merely presumes that it was introduced most likely by King Béla III (1172–1196), who was educated in Byzantium: "At the Court of Manuel he joined the Orthodox Church and was the first to receive the rank of a *despot* in Byzantium." (Julius Morávcsik, "The Holy Crown of Hungary," *The Hungarian Quarterly* 4(4) Winter 1938/ 39.—N.b., this was published by the Society of the Hungarian Quarterly, President Count Stephen Bethlen.) Emperor Manuel died in 1080.

The then-existing Church structure in Hungary was identical with that of the Church of the Byzantine rite. In conformity with the Szabolcs Synod of 1092 and that of Ostrogom of 1104. For instance, priests at the time in Hungary were allowed to be married just as those in Byzantium. (Gyula Morávcsik, *Bizánc és Magyarország* (Budapest, 1953), p. 64). The influence of the Old Slavonic Church rite in Hungary was so cogent that "a Magyar Archbishop and four or five bishops openly joined the Orthodox communion and willingly crowned Manuel's nominees despite the anathemas of their Catholic brethren." (Steed H. Wicckham, *A Short History of Austria-Hungary and Poland* (London, 1914), p. 70.)

These as-yet unresolved problems attracted the attention of Hungarian historians of the past century, who arrived at the conclusion that the Bulla of Pope Silvester II presenting the Crown to St. Stephen was forged. The historian Dr. János Karácsonyi summed up his findings concerning the Bulla thus: "Silvester's Bulla, which is known under this name to Hungarian historians, stems from a more recent era, namely 1576, and is a 'forged document.'" (Dr. János Karácsonyi, *Szent István király oklevelei és a Szilveszter-Bulla diplomatikai tanulmány* (Budapest, 1891), p. 216.) An analogous opinion was also expressed by the prominent Hungarian historian Armin Vambéry in his book *A magyarság keletkezése és gyarapodása* (Budapest, 1895), p. 249. *See also,* Mihaly Horváth, *A kereszténység elsó százada Magyarorzágon* (Budapest, 1878).

Such historical assertions of Hungarian authors, members of the Hungarian Academy of Sciences, change the previous concept of Hungarian historiography, particularly at its inception stage, and give an idea of the scope and importance of the cultural and religious influence of Byzantium and the Slavs upon Hungary. It is namely this cultural and religious influence of Byzantium, related to the culture of the Ruthenians of Kyivan Ruthenia, that the ruling Hungarian feudal historians assiduously keep silent about or expunge from their works.

[22] Kolarz, *op. cit.,* p. 96.

[23] Ibid., p. 94.

[24] To give an idea of how far this revisionism went: After World War I, Hungary found itself in grave economic straits. Instead of revamping and strengthening the economy of its people and country, as did Austria, Hungary embarked on a large-scale revisionist propaganda campaign in foreign countries. It goes without saying that such an enormous undertaking required huge sums of the state treasury's funds. In order to help the state treasury and to finance the revisionist movement, the Hungarians hit upon the singular idea of forging French francs. Young Hungarian patriots were called upon to exchange the counterfeit francs abroad and to transfer the money thus obtained to the common revisionist movement's fund via Hungarian embassies. The moral or ethical aspects of this affair did not worry them in the least, to say nothing of possible consequences. They pursued but one single goal: to create a revisionist revolt in Europe and to regain and reannex to Hungary the detached territories at all cost.

[25] Miklós Szinai and László Szücs, *op. cit.* (Budapest, 1965), pp. 25–26. Charles's letter to Horthy of 20 May 1920 is cited.

[26] Ibid., p. 139—Horthy's discourse on the kingdom issue delivered in Mezötur during the unveiling of a monument on October 8, 1933.

[27] Ibid., p. 140.

[28] Miklós Horthy, *op. cit.,* p. 124.

[29] Ibid., p. 135.

[30] Idid, p. 149. *See also Das neue Fischer-Lexikon,* 3 Aufgabe "Habsburger," pp. 2439–2440.

[31] I myself was brought to court under this law "For the Protection of the State." The first time was in Uzhhorod in 1930 on charges lodged by the state prosecutor, Dr. Kubiček, at the Land Court and the second time was at the District Court in Uzhhorod on charges of having broken up a meeting held by Drs. Fentsyk and Beskyd in the village of Dovhe near Uzhhorod.

[32] C. J. C. Street, *Slovakia Past and Present* (London, 1928), p. 50.

[33] National Archives, Washington, D.C.: American Legation, Budapest, December 14, 1938; File #760 F. 64/224, p. 2.

[34] Ibid., p. 5.

[35] Elek Karsai, *Stalo sa v Budíne v Šándorovskom paláci (1919–1941)* (Bratislava, 1966), p. 202.

[36] On March 14, 1923, the Conference of Ambassadors in Paris decided to annex Galicia to Poland with the proviso, however, that Poland endow this territory with autonomous rights. Yet the autonomy was never granted despite the fact that the Polish *Sejm* (parliament) had adopted a statute to this effect. Instead, Poland engaged in a campaign of Polonizing the Ukrainian population. For instance, of the 2,417 Ukrainian schools under the Austrian administration there remained only 352 by 1937. (Shevchenko Scientific Society, *Entsiklopedia ukraïnoznavstva, Slovnykova chastyna, zoshyt,* vol. 5, p. 342.)

[37] As quoted by Leonard Mosley, *On Borrowed Time: How World War II Began* (New York: Random House, 1969), p. 84.

[38] U.S. Department of State. *Documents on German Foreign Policy 1918-1945,* Series D, Vol. 2, p. 1016. From the Archives of the German Foreign Ministry, United States Government Printing Office, (Washington, 1949); henceforth referred to as *DGFP*.

[39] Ibid., Series D, Vol. 4, p. 207.

[40] Ibid.

[41] Ádám Magda, *A Müncheni Egyezmény Létrejötte és Magyarország Külpolikája 1936-1938* (Budapest, 1965), p. 760.

[42] Kobylianski was head of the Political Department of the Polish Foreign Ministry during the period 1935 to 1939.

[43] Ádám Magda, *op. cit.,* p. 775.

[44] A. I. Berndt, Stelvertr. Pressechef der Regierung in *Das Archiv* (Berlin, 1938), p. 124.

[45] Ibid., p. 1311.

[46] Akademiia Nauk Ukraïns'koï RSR, *Ukraïns'ko-uhors'ki istorychni zv'iazky* (Kyiv: 1964), pp. 88. *See also,* The State Archives of the Ministry of Foreign Affairs of Hungary, Kozma irathagyaték naplójegyzétek, 1938, X. 10—(Posthumous Notes from Kozma's Diary).

[47] *Ukraïns'ko-uhorski*, p.88—B. Rozsony 34, sz.t.

[48] Vanat, *op. cit.*, p. 41. *See also,* Státní Ústřední Archiv, PMR, 2690, k 4113, "Protokol o schůzi ministerské rady konané 4. listopadu 1938; Akten zur deutschen auswärtigen Politik–ADAP–IV, 99, pp. 106–114.

[49] Ludvik Svoboda, *Cestami života I.* (Prague: 1971), p. 171.

[50] Prime Minister Augustyn Voloshyn, "Do hromadian Karpats'koï Ukraïny," *Natsionalist* (New York) November 16, 1938); quoted by Peter G. Stercho in *Diplomacy of Double Morality. Europe's Crossroads in Carpatho-Ukraine 1919-1939.* (New York, 1971), p. 280.

[51] Yulian Chiminec, "Za kordonom," Ukrainian Press Service, (Vienna, 1939), p. 31.

[52] Ladislav K. Feierabend, *Ve vládách Druhé republiky* (New York, 1961), p. 85.

[53] As quoted by György Ranki, *A Wilhelmstrasse és Magyarország—Német diplomaciai iratok Magyarországról 1933-1944* (Budapest, 1968), p. 323.

[54] As quoted by *The New Hungarian Quarterly* (Budapest) 4(11) July-September 1963: 180. *See also* O. L. Kum, res. pol. 1935-21-51; Miklós Szinai and László Szücs, *Horthy Miklós titkos iratai, harmadik kiadása* (Budapest, 1965), p. 152.

[55] *The New Hungarian Quarterly,* ibid., p. 181; Szinai and Szücs, *op. cit.*, p. 153.

[56] Jozef Lipski, *Diplomat in Berlin 1933-1939* (New York, 1968), p. 459.

[57] Loránd Tilkovszky, *op. cit.*, p. 34. *See also* István Dobi, *Vallomás és türténelem*, vol. 2 (Budapest, 1962), p. 87.

[58] Tilkovszky, ibid. *See also,* Antal Szakács, *Körjegyzö jelentése* (Zajta, October 25, 1938), OL ME Nemzetiségi 0.52 cs.P 17185/1938.

[59] As quoted by Tilkovszky, ibid. *See also, A csendörnyomozó osztály parancsnokság jelentése* (Budapest, November 23, 1938), OL ME Nemzetiségi 0.52 sz. P 17392/1938.

[60] *Pesti Hirlap* November 5, 1938.

[61] *Pesti Hirlap,* November 6, 1938.

[62] Tilkovszky, *op. cit.*, p. 157. *See also* OL ME Nemzetiségi 0.59 cs. L 17660/ 1939.

[63] Ibid., p. 232.

[64] Ibid., p. 44.

[65] Ibid., p. 46.

[66] Ibid., p. 147. *See also,* OL Kum Res Pol 71 cs. 1499/1938.

[67] My mother, returning home from Uzhhorod along the Radvans'ka Street, was pelted with stones by these very rabid Hungarian nationalists, who shouted "éz is egy ukrán anya" (this, too, is a Ukrainian mother). A good Hungarian acquaintance of the family, Lajos Kozár, in whose house she took refuge, upon seeing the blood streaming down her face from a head wound, became enraged and called the police. In his excitement, he exclaimed: "We have not expected such from Hungarians!" In response, the police told him in no uncertain terms to be quiet about the incident or else expect the same thing to happen to him.

[68] Ibid., p. 153. *See also* OL Kum Res. Pol 71 cs 1499/1938: "Az autonomia tervezet, amélyre 1938 dec. 8- szigoruan bizalmas jelentés utal, nem került elö." The planned autonomy, which was communicated in a strictly confidential manner on December 8, 1938, was not implemented.

[69] Ibid., p. 153. *See also,* Kozma levele Ullein-Reviczky Antal külügyi sajtó fönökhöz (Budapest, April 5, 1939), OL Kozma iratok, 27 cs.

PART II

The Period of Federation, 1938–1939

CHAPTER THREE

The Period of the Czecho-Slovak Federation

The demand for the fulfillment of the promised autonomy for Carpatho-Ukraine had turned into a political, permanent issue pursued by the Ruthenians-Ukrainians ever since 1919, when Czecho-Slovakia began to introduce a centralistic state system. The political tension in Czecho-Slovakia, caused by the problem of the Sudeten Germans, also activated the autonomy demands for Slovakia and revived the problem of the Hungarian and Polish national minorities. Thus, matters that seemed to constitute solely internal problems of the Republic inevitably gained international attention and were even more enhanced with the arrival in Czecho-Slovakia of the "honest broker" Lord Viscount Walter Runciman, who was sent by the British government to mediate between the Czecho-Slovak government and the Sudeten Germans.

Ever since the Muscophile faction had deserted the TsRNR in 1919, an unrelenting cultural-national struggle had ensued in Carpatho-Ukraine between the Ukrainian and Muscophile camps. In this struggle, the Muscophile movement received significant moral and material aid from three political sources: Czecho-Slovak, Hungarian, and Polish. Carpatho-Ukraine was the arena in which the interests and influences of these three countries clashed, each of them pursuing its own political aims joining forces with the others particularly against the populist Ukrainian movement by whose growth and power they all felt threatened.

Despite these countervailing interests of the countries neighboring Carpatho-Ukraine, the local population remained calm and loyal to the Republic, as was authoritatively corroborated in a report submitted by the Minister of Agriculture, Dr. J. Zadina, who in September of 1938 visited Carpatho-Ukraine and traveled in the country with its Governor Konstantyn Hrabar. The following month, in October, the latter voluntarily resigned his post and was succeeded by Dr. Ivan Párkányi, a native of Carpatho-Ukraine and Director of the Department for Sub-Carpathian Ruthenian Affairs, attached to the Office of the President of the Republic.

The newly appointed governor issued a manifesto in Uzhhorod on October 16 that was distributed throughout the region. In it he pointed to the existing danger for the state and called on the citizens to remain calm, go on with their work, live in peace, and maintain their loyalty to the Czecho-Slovak Republic.

However, the rapid succession of events rendered the post of the governor out of step with the times. At this point, Carpatho-Ukrainian parliamentary representatives in Prague were demanding the establishment of an autonomous government in which, of course, the post of governor would be superfluous. As a result, Dr. Párkányi resigned on November 4, 1938.

The end of September 1938 was a turning point in the relations between the two national-cultural groups (pro-Ukrainian and pro-Russian) in Carpatho-Ukraine. Representatives of both orientations in the Prague Parliament felt the need for joint political action in the face of the deteriorating situation in the country and in their dealings with the Prague Government, if they were to be successful in achieving the long-promised autonomous status for Carpatho-Ukraine. The move toward a common front was to be enhanced further by the arrival in September of a delegation of American Carpatho-Russians of the Orthodox faith, consisting of Ivan Popp, Rev. Joann Vanchyshyn, and Dr. Aleksei Gerovsky, which was to help the parliamentary representaives of both groups to resolve pressing political problems of the region.[1]

As was to become evident from later sources, the delegation of the American Carpatho-Russians was organized by the Hungarian consul in Cleveland with the aim of preparing the annexation of the region by Hungary.[2] To make this revanchist work on behalf of Hungary more successful among the "American Ruthenians of the Muscophile orientation," the Hungarian Foreign Minister, Kálmán Kánya, transmitted 10,000 dollars to the Hungarian consul in Cleveland (a certain Alexy).[3] It may be justifiably assumed that the appointment of Brody to the post of prime minister of Carpatho-Ukraine may have been the workings of the American Carpatho-Russian delegation.

The joint meeting of the parliamentary representatives of Subcarpathia Ruthenia that followed issued the following declaration:

> The Carpatho-Russian people is represented in the legislative assembly of the Czechoslovak Republic by six deputies and two senators: Dr. Pavel Kossey, Yulian Revay, Andriy Brody, Petro Zhidovsky, Dr. Ivan Pieshchak, Dr. Stefan Fentsyk, Senators Edmund Bachynsky, and Yuliy Földessy. Besides them, there are two deputies and one senator who belong to the ranks of the international communist party.
>
> We, the undersigned, state that Carpathian Ruthenia was joined to the Czechoslovak Republic on the basis of the right of self-determination of our people under the condition that our territory would enjoy the broadest autonomy rights with its own legislative organ and autonomous government, responsible to this legislative body.
>
> We further state that these conditions, contained in the St. Germain Treaty and incorported into the Constitution of the Czechoslovak Republic to this day, in the course of 19 years, have not been fulfilled by the government of the Czechoslovak Republic in spite of the fact that we, representatives of the Russian people, have done everything possible in our might to attain the realization of the rights of our people.
>
> In consideration thereof, we, the representatives of the Russian people, cognizant of our responsibility before the history of our people and wishing to secure its freedom and a better future as well as its very existence on its national territory, hereby declare that our people has never renounced its right to self-determination or the right to govern ourselves and that we demand this right now in this fateful time when the fate not only of Czechoslovakia, but also of our Russian people, is being decided upon.
>
> Prague, September 21, 1938.

Dr. Edmund Bachynsky	Andrey Brody
Dr. Ivan Pieshchak	Yuliy Földessy
Dr. Pavel T. Kossey	Petr Zhidovsky
Dr. Stefan A. Fentsyk	Yulian Revay

At the beginning of October, the mentioned parliamentary representatives met again in order to establish the first autonomous government. At this meeting, they accepted the resolution that in the first autonomous government only members of the Prague Parliament and Senate should participate, thus excluding any other candidates. This was done with the intention of securing success in the government, for the pro-Russian Muscophiles had a predominant majority of deputies here, but in this situation they were not sure that they would achieve political success among their constituents. The Ukrainians, on the other hand, were in the parliament and senate minority, but were confident that their positions would be supported among the people if needed.

In spite of this resolution, Deputy Yulian Revay moved that three members from the Ukrainian and the Pro-Russian Central Councils be invited. The proposal was accepted, and the invitations went out to Msgr. A. Voloshyn with two members from the Ukrainian side, and to Dr. Yosyf Kaminsky with two members from the pro-Russian side. The picture now presented a ratio of 4 pro-Ukrainian members to 10 pro-Russian members.

Meanwhile, the central government underwent a significant change. In accordance with Paragraph 60 of the Constitution, it entrusted Prime Minister Gen. Jan Syrový with the execution of the functions of the President during the absence of the President of the Republic.[4] At the first meeting of his cabinet, he presented also the "real demands of Slovakia and Carpatho-Ukraine in changing the current form of the state." Soon, thereafter, on October 11, 1938, Carpatho-Ukraine was finally granted its own autonomous government as provided for in the Constitution. With this fact, following Slovakia's autonomy a few days earlier, the unitary state of Czecho-Slovakia ceased to exist and was transformed into a federated Czechoslovakia. The following day, the first autonomous government of Carpatho-Ukraine introduced itself to the public at a mass gathering in Uzhhorod in the following composition: Andriy Brody—prime minister; Dr. Edmund Bachynsky, Yulian Revay—ministers; Dr. Stepan Fentsyk, Msgr. Avhustyn Voloshyn, and Dr. Ivan Pieshchak—state secretaries. In connection with the appointment of Carpatho-Ukraine's autonomous government, the Stálý Výbor (Permanent Committee) endorsed on October 12 the proposal of the Central Government in Prague to establish an Appellate Court and a State Prosecutor's Office with their seat in Uzhhorod. At its meeting on November 29, the Constitutional Court confirmed that all instructions of the Permanent Committee were issued in conformity with the Constitution.[5]

The appointment of Brody to the post of prime minister was a great strategic achievement for Hungary, on which it could contrive its political plans and foster its revisionist hope. If heretofore Hungary's revisionist movement was viewed in the political world as a "violator of European peace," it was now for Hungary possible to claim Carpatho-Ukraine "legally." The mode selected to attain this goal was to demand a plebiscite in Carpatho-Ukraine. The demand was to be raised at and through the Ministerial Council in Prague by no other than Andriy Brody himself. Through this political ploy, the Hungarians were convinced they would fully succeed in winning the approval of the population of Carpatho-Ukraine to be joined to Hungary. They could not fail inasmuch as even Fentsyk assured them, and they believed him, that 90 percent of the population would vote for Hungary in such a plebiscite. Moreover, Fentsyk went a step further in assuring the Hungarian ambassador in Prague, János Wettstein, that in the event Czecho-Slovakia was not willing to permit a plebiscite he and his associates would provoke an uprising.[6]

To Hungarian government officials Brody reported under the pseudonym "Bertalan." It was under this name that he was to receive money from Hungary over a period of several years. Hungary did not stint in providing huge sums of money to be used in subversive acts against Carpatho-Ukraine, as Hungary's Foreign Minister Kálmán Kánya (minister 1933–1938) revealed in a telephone conversation with Hungary's Ambassador Wettstein in Prague that for the "leaders of the Ruthenians there is a certain amount of money at their disposal with Petravych."[7] In his telegram messages to Wettstein in Prague, Kánya reminded Bertalan-Brody not to yield, under any circumstances, to Czech promises but to steadfastly demand the plebiscite.[8] The demand for a plebiscite was to be widely propagated in the press.[9]

Simultaneous with this political-diplomatic action, preparations were afoot for military and subversive operations in Carpatho-Ukraine. Hungary's Prime Minister Béla Imrédy charged the former Minister of the Interior, Miklós Kozma, with the task of organizing partisan units, the so-called Szabadcsapatok, for subversive operations. By October 5, Kozma was so advanced in his preparations, carried out in collaboration with the military General Staff, that on that day he was able to dispatch small units of his partisans into Carpatho-Ukraine, where they engaged in sabotage actions using explosives and in preparing for an armed uprising.[10]

Poland, because of its own interests, was more than willing to assist Hungary in its diplomatic and military undertakings aimed against Carpatho-Ukraine. As early as the next day after the formation of the federated government in Carpatho-Ukraine, Hungary's Foreign Minister Kánya notified Poland through its Ambassador in Warsaw András Hory that Hungary had "succeeded in infiltrating 750–800 of its Szabadcsapatok, which would need the help of Poland." Upon completing their tasks, the Hungarian partisans were to cross over into Poland where, as pre-arranged, they were to identify themselves by producing "holy pictures" 6.0 x 3.3 cm in size and with the numbers 40 printed on the reverse side.[11]

According to Kánya's own admission, contained in his *Diary*, the saboteurs stirred up "disturbance and spread death."[12] In his own words, the operation against Carpatho-Ukraine had "developed into a small war."[13] And yet, at the same time, Hungary was blarring to the world about the people of Carpatho-Ukraine having allegedly risen against their government, that there was unrest, etc. Notwithstanding these hostile endeavors on the part of both neighbors, the government of Carpatho-Ukraine, its para-military Organization for the National Defense "Carpathian Sich," and the population conducted a successful defensive operation: calm was maintained throughout the country to the great dismay of the neighbors. Apparently aware of the reality in the province, Kánya on one occasion expressed the wish that it would be good if the local Ruthenians joined the Hungarian partisans—but this was never to occur.

Meanwhile, Hungarian-Polish cooperation intent on destroying the federated Carpatho-Ukrainian state was assuming wider concrete forms. According to a message dispatched by the Hungarian military attaché in Warsaw, the Polish General Staff had announced that "there are now six to eight squads, i.e. over 53 Polish partisans operating in Carpatho-Ukraine and those of them who have blown up a bridge Nyžni Veretsky have already returned."[14] The military unit in which this author had served captured in the town of Perechyn, north of Uzhhorod in November 1938, two Polish officers dressed in civilian clothes who had engaged in sabotage acts.

But Hungary was not to be content even with these large-scale sabotage acts of the General Staffs of both countries. To secure success in its undertakings, Hungary enlisted the aid of Italy. On October 9, 1938, Kánya contacted his Ambassador Frigyes Villani (from 1934 to May 1939) in Rome: "Please bring it to the attention of Minister Ciano that the uprising action in the Ruthenian territory has begun and that it will become more evident tomorrow. This information is being divulged only to the government of Italy. It is possible that tomorrow we shall request immediate delivery of the promised one hundred airplanes."[15] Ambassador Villani lost no time in informing Budapest the following day that Ciano had asked about the "extent of the uprising, says the airplanes are ready for takeoff, considers it expedient to have the Italian pilots obtain Hungarian uniforms from Budapest. He is receiving many telegrams from Carpatho-Ukraine that speak out against the province being joined to Hungary, but he does not ascribe much importance to them."[16]

In the first half of October, the Czecho-Slovak army captured some 300 Hungarian partisans in Carpatho-Ukraine. According to the then existing military laws, they faced death penalty under the circumstances of full mobilization in the country and the imposition of martial law in some areas. Realizing the gravity of the situation for its captured irregulars in Carpatho-Ukraine, the Hungarian government contacted its ambassador in Italy, instructing him to request through the services of Foreign Minister Ciano in Rome "the Vatican to intercede with the Prague government on behalf of the captured insurgents." Msgr. Dominico Tardini immediately took the necessary steps by contacting the papal Nuncio, Ritter, in Prague.[17] The upshot of the action was that Endre Korláth, a senator in the Czecho-Slovak Parliament for his Hungarian political party in Carpatho-Ukraine, dispatched a special telegram to the Ministry of Foreign Affairs in Prague in an effort to save the captured terrorists who were about to be brought before a court-martial in Carpatho-Ukraine invoking "national solidarity."[18]

Czecho-Slovak authorities recorded testimonies of the captured Hungarian terrorists on gramophone records at the prison in Ilava, Slovakia, that were then used in radio broadcasts to refute Hungary's assertions that it was the local populace that was creating the unrest in Carpatho-Ukraine. The terrorists were soon freed upon the intervention of Germany and Italy.[19]

The situation, of course, was quite different than what Hungarian propaganda would have it. An accurate description of the conditions in Carpatho-Ukraine was afforded by the British journalist Alexander Henderson:

> In the district of Slanky [should read Šalanky—V.Sh.] twelve miles
> east of Berehovo, Czecho-Slovak units have captured 297 Hungarian

terrorists, comprising 26 officers, 62 non-commissioned officers, one officer cadet, and 205 soldiers—all reservists of the Hungarian army—and four Czecho-Slovak subjects of Hungarian nationality. It is shown by the documents seized that the activities of the Hungarian terrorists were directed by the General Staff of the War Ministry. Interrogation of the prisoners established the fact that the terrorists had been assembled and instructed at Kisvárda and that they were commanded by Lieutenant-Colonel István Hejás provided with some thirty officers of the Hungarian army of the ranks of lieutenant and captain. In Ruthenia some 2,000 Hungarian terrorists are scattered . . . .They belonged to a so-called "Szabad Csapat"—Volunteer Corps—organization. The men were army reservists called up in the usual way.[20]

It is striking that from among the local Hungarians only four joined the terrorists and not a single Ruthenian, much as Minister Kánya would have wished.

We have cited some incidents of Hungarian and Polish activities aimed at destroying the nascent federated state of Carpatho-Ukrainians. The terrorist detachments of these two states engaged in blowing up bridges, schools, government buildings, disrupting communication lines and killing innocent residents. This notwithstanding, they continued unabashedly to cry out to the world that "disorder" was prevailing in the province. At that time, Poland was oppressing the more than six million Ukrainians, depriving them of the right of having their own schools with Ukrainian as the language of instruction and ruining Ukrainian cultural and economic institutions through the pacification of the area by military units.

To be assured of better results in its determination to liquidate the Carpatho-Ukrainian part of the Czecho-Slovak federation, Hungary did not limit its activities to propaganda and diplomatic moves in the international arena. It contemplated achieving its aims by subverting the province from within. To this end, it enlisted the aid of pro-Hungarian politicians, such as Brody and Fentsyk. Because of Brody's known sentiments and suspected clandestine contacts with Hungarian government officials, Prague had kept him under strict surveillance. Hungarian Ambassador János Wettstein had to admit on one occasion in a report dispatched from Prague that "only at a public steam bath was he able to transmit to him [Brody—V.Sh.] information."[21] And the Czecho-Slovak government was, indeed, in possession of proof concerning Brody's pro-Hungarian activities. Minister of Internal Affairs Jan Černý confirmed that the contents of deliberations of the Ministerial Council were leaked out to the Hungarian Embassy in Prague. On the strength of such evidence, Gen. Jan Syrový, exercising the functions of the President of the Republic, deprived both Brody and Fentsyk of their government positions. Since both were members of the Parliament as well, warrant for arrest had to be signed by the minister of justice. This having occurred, Brody was arrested on October 27, but Fentsyk managed to escape to Hungary, undoubtedly having been forewarned by someone.[22]

Coming as it did shortly after the Munich *Diktat,* the cessation of large tracts of territory to Hungary, and the formation of a truncated Czecho-Slovak Republic, the arrest of Prime Minister Brody was bound to wreak havoc among Hungarian and Polish government circles, dashing their previous plans. Poland blamed Hungary for not being determined enough regarding the invasion of Carpatho-Ukraine and not taking corresponding action. Hungary's excuse was that "it expected an upheaval to break out in Carpatho-Ukraine that would induce the local population to call for international help. However, because of Brody's arrest, this plan, together with his plebiscite idea, failed."[23]

As for the Czech political quarters, they finally realized that it was they themselves who had financed traitors of their own country, people who were undermining the very foundations of its existence. The incidents of Brody's and Fentsyk's high treason convinced them more than previous Ukrainian contentions accusing the Muscophile movement in Carpatho-Ukraine of being financed by Hungary and Poland, which they refused to believe. On the other hand, credit is due to Czecho-Slovak officials who, finally and without further experimentation with the Muscophiles, transferred the political power of the province into the hands of the most competent and meritorious representative of the Ukrainian movement, namely Msgr. Avhustyn Voloshyn. This event occurred so unexpectedly that Msgr. Voloshyn had to be appointed prime minister by Prague over the telephone and that he, in turn, had to be sworn in office likewise over the phone from Uzhhorod to Prague. Another interesting outcome of the change of heart of most of the leading Czech officials and political parties was that they now considered as unwarranted the label of "Ukrainian irredentists," attached to the Ukrainian-populist movement over a period of almost twenty years and erased it from the political vocabulary. The wounds inflicted by it remained, but it was not now the time for settling of accounts. The state-political rebirth of the land strongly unnerved its neighbors, a portent of the danger to its existence. It was thus necessary to divert all attention to and concentrate all efforts on the military and diplomatic defense of the land.

At the end of September 1938, an arbitrated decision was reached by Germany, Italy, Great Britain, and France to transfer the territory occupied by the German national minority of Czecho-Slovakia, the Sudetenland, to Germany. At the same time it was decided that Czecho-Slovakia should resolve the cases of the Polish and Hungarian national minorities within three months. The arbitration was completed on November 2, 1938 in Vienna by decision of Germany and Italy, since Great Britain and France had ceded their mandates to them.

Even this "Vienna Arbitration"—whose authors were intent on undermining the viability of Carpatho-Ukraine, particularly as communications and supplies were concerned—could not break the faith and spirit of the members of the government and of the people in their righteous cause. However, discouraging reports were arriving from occupied territories ceded to Hungary about the cruel treatment of the people by Hungarian gendarmes, dismissals from jobs, liquidation of Ukrainian cultural institutions, schools, and the like. All this only intensified the anti-Hungarian mood of the population which was pointedly characterized in *Lidové Noviny* of October 12, 1938 by Dr. Avhustyn Shtefan, an attorney in Rakhiv and former commissioner for the *Ruška Kraina* appointed by the Hungarian government in 1918:

> Since 1919 much has changed in Subcarpathian Ruthenia. The youth feel Ruthenian and are nationalists. The young generation admits that the Czecho-Slovak state has given the land a lift in every respect. The Czecho-Slovak state has rectified the injustices committed by the Hungarian regime. If the Hungarians love us, as they constantly assert, then let the Pest [Hungarian—V.Sh.] propaganda leave us in peace. We shall not allow ourselves to be prevaricated . . .

Organs of the Agrarian Party in Carpatho-Ukraine *Zemledilska politika* (Minister Dr. Edmund Bachynsky), and the Ukrainian National Union (UNO) *Nova Svoboda* (Minister Yulian Revay) wrote in a similar vein, emphasizing that the Ukrainians of Carpatho-Ukraine will never want to return "into the Hungarian brotherly arms" as it would be tantamount to national death.

At this point in time, still entertaining the idea of marching against the USSR, (i.e., into the Ukrainian SSR), Hitler did not support the Polish-Hungarian actions against Carpatho-Ukraine with regard to attaining a common border. It would be interesting here to refer to a conversation between German Ambassador Otto von Erdmannsdorf (from 1937 to 1941) and Regent Horthy in Budapest during which the former asked whether it was true that some action was contemplated against Carpatho-Ukraine. Horthy replied that the Hungarian troops were preparing to go to the aid of the Ruthenians and to hold the province until its people would express its self-determination. Erdmannsdorf thereupon wanted to know why Hungary had demanded an arbitration if it did not wish to adhere to its decision. If Hungary, he continued, was to interfere in Carpatho-Ukraine's affairs by applying such methods, it could provoke a conflict with Czecho-Slovakia and, in that case, it should not count on Germany's assistance. Horthy suspended the preparations, removed Kálmán Kánya from his post as foreign minister, and appointed in his place István Csáky, whom he immediately dispatched to Hitler with a special letter of greetings in which he stated that "as long he [Horthy—V.Sh.] is at the helm of Hungary, Germany can rely upon Hungary as its most devoted friend."[24]

A few years later, on September 7, 1941, Hitler bestowed upon Horthy for his faithful services "Das Eiserne Ritter Kreuz" (*Hung.*, Vaskereszt lovagkereszt)—the Iron Knights' Cross, personally decorating him with it and embracing him.[25] To show appreciation for this great honor, Hungary was to deliver to Germany certain raw materials indispensable to the German war efforts: "Besides the Transylvanian timber, a large share of the now rapidly increasing production of the Lispe oil-fields the export of which had been valued only at 133,000 *pengö* in 1940, was 18,508,000 in 1941, and 45,476,000 in 1942."[26] Furthermore, the German company "Wintershall A.G. of Berlin had been granted a concession for exploiting oil, methane gas, and minerals on Hungarian soil."[27]

While Hungary sought to regain territories once belonging to the Crown of St. Stephen through diplomacy or outright subversive activities in Carpatho-Ukraine, Poland got involved and carried out destruc-

tive operations against the province for no other reason than fear of the
Ukrainian state-liberation problem, which it viewed as a threat to itself.
Thus, for instance, the Czech newspaper *Lidové Noviny* of October 25,
1938, reporting from Budapest, said that Poland feared that Carpatho-
Ukraine "could become the embryo of a future independent Ukraine"
to be composed of Galicia and Carpatho-Ukraine. It further remarked
that Poland did not feel that Kyiv posed a similar danger to Poland
since the Kyiv government was subordinated to the central government
in Moscow. It sounded strange that the puny Carpatho-Ukrainian federated state should have struck such fear in the heart of the great Polish
state. This fear was to be traced to the fact that the political demands of
the six million Ukrainians living in Poland had not been met.

As a federated state of the Czecho-Slovak Federation, Carpatho-
Ukraine aroused overwhelming enthusiasm among Ukrainians
throughout the world, notably among the six million in Poland. The
Ukrainian nationalist youth of Galicia, ruthlessly persecuted in Poland,
crossed the border into Carpatho-Ukraine *en masse* to offer their services to the young state. Already in October of 1938, following a
solemn Mass celebrated at the Cathedral of St. Yury (George) in Lviv
for Carpatho-Ukraine, a twenty thousand-strong crowd of Ukrainians
gathered outside to protest Hungarian territorial demands on Carpatho-
Ukraine. Ukrainian deputies in the Polish Parliament issued a memorandum to the Polish government with a similar protest, demanding at
the same time the granting of autonomy for the Ukrainians of Galicia. It
must be added that the events in Carpatho-Ukraine found a positive
response also among Ukrainians in Soviet Ukraine as we were later to
learn from Soviet Ukrainian refugees.

Even among the Czechs there were some party functionaries and
politicians who likewise feared the growing Ukrainian national movement in Carpatho-Ukraine. They adamantly fought against it and, by
the same token, were ill-disposed toward the state-liberation aspirations of the Ukrainian nation. For instance, Dr. Hubert Ripka, Beneš'
right hand, even while in emigration after World War II, never used
such one-sided denunciatory pronouncements against the real traitors
of the Czecho-Slovak Republic as he used against the Ukrainians.
There may be one explanation for such a stance on the part of Ripka
and other likeminded authors, namely that, as a rule, their sympathies
lay with the Soviet Union.

During a visit in Prague in January 1939 by members of the Government, Prime Minister Voloshyn revealed to me in confidence that 150 Austrian Jews were living now in Carpatho-Ukraine whom we ought to transfer to a safe country whence they could proceed to Palestine. This action must be carried out, he remarked, in utmost secrecy so as preclude Germany learning about it. He asked whether I could be of assistance in this matter. After both of us examined all the possibilities, I promised to help as much as I could. I assigned the implementation of the undertaking to Dr. V. Oreletsky, our officer for foreign liason in the Representation. Once the necessary information regarding the possibilities was obtained we immediately set out to contact the French and Romanian consulates and successfully carried out the assignment. He recounted this venture in an article that appeared in *Shliakh Peremohy* on March 15, 1970. Around the beginning of March 1939, I received a telegram from Khust from S. Klochurak, Voloshyn's political secretary, asking me to secure a special passport—a semi-diplomatic passport of sorts issued by the Ministry of Foreign Affairs. I filed a petition with the Ministry wherein I asked to forward the passport directly to the addressee in Khust.

The Government of Carpatho-Ukraine in Khust

With the change of the status of Czechoslovakia from a unitary into a federated state of Czecho-Slovakia, effected on the basis of the Constitutional Law promulgated on November 22, 1938, certain fundamental administrative-legal changes had to be implemented in Carpatho-Ukraine as well under the direction of the newly appointed government of Msgr. Voloshyn. This Constitutional Law was the crowning point of the struggle for autonomy that had been conducted since the land was joined to Czecho-Slovakia.

The transfer of administrative power into Ukrainian hands required some regrouping of forces. This could have been accomplished without great difficulties in Uzhhorod, where the government would have had all state facilities at its disposal. However, since the capital city of Uzhhorod was ceded to Hungary, the Ukrainian government found itself in a very distressing situation. In the history of arbitration decisions, the Vienna Arbitration may have been the only one ever to cede the capital city of one land to a foreign country. The cession of two other cities, Mukachevo and Berehovo, exacerbated the government's position, leaving it to establish its new capital in the small city of Khust.

Ukrainians evacuated from the cities lost to Hungary had to part with their cultural and property assets, for which they had labored over a period of many years. The arbitrators, Germany's Ribbentrop and Italy's Ciano, and with them undoubtedly Hungary, expected that Carpatho-Ukraine would fall to its knees, because of the seemingly insurmountable difficulties presented by the loss of its major cities and ask to be united with Hungary. Their hopes, however, did not materialize.

The Herculean task of evacuating government office and state institutions from Uzhhorod to Khust fell to the Czecho-Slovak army, which deserved full recognition and thanks for a well performed operation. It should be recalled here that the evacuation process carried out by the army and civilian authorities was so efficient that it prompted the Hungarian authorities to announce a large monetary award to whoever would hand over to them the evacuation leaders responsible for the evacuation of government and other institutions from the territory ceded to Hungary by the Vienna Arbitration.[28] While the government moved to Khust, other state officials and schools were relocated in other smaller cities and towns.

The new federated state, however, suffered other great inconveniences and shortages. With the loss of its principal cities, Carpatho-Ukraine also lost direct rail and road links with Slovakia and Prague. The main railroad was severed by Hungary so that the nearest town connecting the State with Prague was Priashiv (Prešov) in Slovakia, some 120 miles west of Khust. The town of Perechyn, halfway between Priashiv and Khust, had a narrow road that lead westward. It was dubbed "the lifeline road," since the transportation of people and goods by the army was carried on it and it was temporarily the only direct gateway to the west. It must be said that the Ukrainian population understood the significance of the events unfolding and so maintained exemplary order and was prepared to endure temporary restrictions necessitated by the circumstances. There were no protests or other anti-government activities. On the contrary, the people assisted the government wherever they could.[29] However, at the same time, Budapest Radio was broadcasting daily that the government was hiding from the wrath of the people who had allegedly risen in protest against Voloshyn's government, along with other similar fabrications.

The new Carptho-Ukrainian government's foremost task after the evacuation was to put internal affairs in order and to settle the federated state's finances. The problems arising from the evacuation of Uzhhorod, Mukachevo, and Berehovo were considered predictable ones. But there were also unpredicatable problems with which the government had to cope. These stemmed from the actions of Hungarian and Polish terrorist units which infiltrated the land and created confusion with their attacks. Because of these actions, there was little sympathy for either Hungary or Poland even among adherents of the Muscophile camp. This was particularly so among the young, high-minded students who looked upon the professed pro-Hungarian sentiments of their leaders Andriy Brody, Stefan Fentsyk, Alexander Ilnytsky, Juliy Maryna, and others as a betrayal of their people's national interests. It was only then that they had discovered the double-dealings of their Muscophile leaders that had driven them into the Hungarian embrace. Some among them, such as the poets Andriy Karabelesh, Andriy Patrus, and others, having observed the vitality of the Ukrainian camp and the enthusiasm of the population for their government, had publicly joined the Ukrainian camp.

The evacuation of the chief city of Uzhhorod and the further two cities of Mukachevo and Berehovo was no easy event, especially since in the latter two cities Premier Brody had already succeeded in filling the two top spots with his own people, either Hungarians or Magyarized Ukrainians. The consequences of the evacuation is proof that the Rusyn-Ukrainians mobilized all their forces from all parts of our population, including nationally conscious workers and villagers, who helped with distinction. It must be kept in mind that the Ukrainian intelligentsia itself evacuated.

Thanks to the arduous and devoted work of the government, the intelligentsia, and the nationally conscious peasants and workers, the general stabilization of the state after the evacuation proceeded quickly. Peasants from the Hungarian-occupied territory crossed *en masse* into Carpatho-Ukraine. The Ukrainian peasantry, oppressed under Hungary for many centuries, experienced the contentment of living in its own federated state, being able to participate in its development, and possessing rights. Thus, the Hungarian and Polish terrorist actions were fated to fail.

On November 10, 1938, the Carpatho-Ukrainian government issued a Manifesto to the population in which it outlined its program. It stressed its intention of coming to an agreement in a brotherly manner with the Slovak government regarding the Ruthenians living in the Priashiv Region. It also expressed the need to rid the state of foreign political agents who were spreading fabricated rumors and engaging in subversive activities. Furthermore, the government announced a land reform, the nationalization of land and forest management, and it called for the development of own industry.[30]

At the same time, a delegation of Dutch journalists was visiting Khust in order to get acquainted with the actual conditions in the state. They were particularly interested in what the Hungarian and Polish radio stations were broadcasting. The delegation was just visiting Msgr. Voloshyn when they heard a broadcast from Budapest Radio which falsely claimed that the population of Carpatho-Ukraine had risen in rebellion against its government and that Msgr. Voloshyn had left Khust and was hiding at some unknown place. The journalists from the Netherlands were taken aback and immediately voiced their indignation, condemning Hungary for such conduct and expressing their high esteem for the Carpatho-Ukrainian government and people.

The mendacious Hungarian and Polish propaganda campaign waged against Carpatho-Ukraine had assumed such proportions that it could not help attracting the attention of the foreign press to the falsity of the broadcasts. For instance, *The Daily Express* reported from Berlin that "Berlin was disturbed by Hungary's and Poland's incessant agitation for a common border and the joining of Carpatho-Ukraine to Hungary." In the opinion of German officials, this problem was resolved in Vienna.[31] Significantly, the Polish newspaper *Głos Naroda* was dubious about the value of having a common border once Budapest joined the Berlin-Rome Axis, for then Warsaw would have had to cease conducting its own independent policy.[32] This was a rare but sound Polish voice which, however, Polish political quarters preferred to ignore, being blinded by their hostile anti-Ukrainian attitude.

Meanwhile, the government of Carpatho-Ukraine was able to confirm that false appeals were prepared in Hungary allegedly in the name of many villages and towns in Carpatho-Ukraine demanding a plebiscite and begging to be united with Hungary. Neither village councils, nor notarial offices, nor individual citizens had ever forwarded such appeals to the Hungarian government, Hitler or Mussolini. Dr. Mykola Dolinay, a member of the Ukrainian Delimination Commission, submitted proof in Budapest that no one had sought to be united with Hungary, refuting the allegations contained in the falsified appeals and lodged a protest.[33]

The members of the Carpatho-Ukrainian government also took a stand on the Hungarian-Polish territorial claims. On November 19, 1938, Minister Yulian Revay of the Carpatho-Ukrainian government, in a speech broadcast over the radio, denounced the activities of the traitorous Fentsyk and Brody and rejected as false the charges and contentions spread by hostile parties. Refuting these fabrications, he asserted that "a new era has set in, a new and happy history of our people, which has become a sovereign master on its own Ukrainian soil."[34] And Minister Dr. Edmund Bachynsky, in an interview for the Czech press in Prague, remonstrated with utmost resoluteness against the Hungarian-Polish irredentist tendencies, declaring that Carpatho-Ukraine wished to continue to freely develop within the framework of federated Czecho-Slovakia.[35] Indeed, the Czech press responded favorably to the Carpatho-Ukrainian government's defense of the need for unity of the federated state entity. Thus, for instance, the Czech newspaper *České Slovo* of December 1, 1938, which during the First Republic (the period before federation), was not known for its sympathies toward the Ukrainians, wrote that Msgr. Voloshyn was exerting all efforts to give "his free homeland security. He does not shy away from a struggle with stronger adversaries. In the diligence of this first representative of the Carpatho-Ukrainians, we see the soul of the entire people."[36]

The political tension caused by a vacancy in the presidency of Czecho-Slovakia was somewhat relaxed in the republic with the election of Dr. Emil Hácha to that post on November 30, 1938. There were 313 deputies and senators present in the Parliament for the voting, 272 of whom cast their ballots for Dr. Hácha. The outcome exceeded the three-fifths majority required by the Constitution; 39 ballots were blank.[37] Following the election of Dr. Hácha as president of the Republic, the Carpatho-Ukrainian government tendered its resignation. The President appointed a new Carpatho-Ukrainian government consisting of Msgr. Voloshyn and Yulian Revay as ministers but without the former Minister Bachynsky. Representatives of government, the military, and State Security congratulated Msgr. Voloshyn. Thanking his well-wishers, the Prime Minister replied:

> I believed in our victory, which we have achieved by federating with the Czechs and Slovaks. It was Divine Providence when, in 1919, in spite of the promises given us by the Hungarians, our people joined and shared its fate with that of these brotherly peoples. Within a matter of twenty years, our people rose from the depths of degradation, and now in a federated state has become equal among equals and entirely free.[39]

After the Vienna Arbitration, the nationality composition of Carpatho-Ukraine presented itself as follows:

Ukrainians	413,481	(75.90%)
Jews	65,828	(12.80%)
Hungarians	25,894	(4.75%)
Czechs and Slovaks	17,495	(3.25%)
Germans	8,715	(1.60%)
Poles	78	(0.02%)
Others	13,268	(2.44%)[39]

By a decree issued by the Vatican, the Uzhhorod Bishop, Aleksander Stoyka, was deprived of his jurisdiction over Greek-Catholics in Carpatho-Ukraine and in the whole of Czecho-Slovakia. In his place appointed was an Apostolic Administrator at Khust Dr. Dionisiy Nyarady, Bishop of Križevci, Yugoslavia, who assumed his post in a ceremony attended by members of the Carpatho-Ukrainian Government on December 4, 1938. Thus, Khust also became the residence of a bishop. Rev. Stefan Reshetylo, OSBM (Order of St. Basil the Great), a devoted and meritorious priest of the Greek-Catholic Church and people, was appointed secretary to the Bishop. On March 18, 1939, two days after the occupation of the province by Hungary, Bishop Nyarady was placed under house arrest at his residence in Khust and was not allowed to leave his house or communicate with anybody. The Bishop was to suffer humiliation and degradation at the hands of the Hungarian gendarmerie and other government officials until the Apostolic Nuncio in Budapest, Angelo Rotta, intervened and obtained his and his secretary's release to leave for Rome.[40]

The peaceful development of Carpatho-Ukraine was, however, being hampered by Hungarian and Polish propaganda and terrorist actions conducted on a large scale. in order to assess the situation in Carpatho-Ukraine and to obtain trustworthy information, the secretary of the German Embassy in Prague, Dr. Hamilkar Hofmann, arrived in Khust toward the end of November. During his stay, he had talks with Msgr. Voloshyn and Gen. Oleh Svátek, a divisional commander. On November 28, 1938, the German Chargé d'Affaires in Prague, Andor von Hencke, communicated to Berlin the following from Hofmann's report:

> Complete calm in Carpatho-Ukraine with the exception of attacks by Polish terrorists on the northern frontier, which still continue.
>
> No foundation for reported existence of Carpatho-Ukrainian terrorists. Home defense organization, Sich, is only in elementary stage and not yet in possession of firearms.
>
> Morale among the consciously Ukrainian population is good; they see in Germany a powerful ally who will help them in solving their internal problems.
>
> A plebiscite for union with Hungary would now have only a small chance of success. No sign of food shortage; food supply for the population, according to data from Carpatho-Ukrainian government and the Czech military authorities, almost completely assured for the winter.
>
> Chief economic problem lies in the cutting off by Hungary of transit traffic, which, above all, renders impossible transport into and through the territory of Czecho-Slovakia. Carpatho-Ukraine government regards this as a violation of the Vienna Award.
>
> To sum up: Carpatho-Ukraine is viable, especially if foreign help is available for reconstruction. Prerequisite for this is stability of frontier and also restoration of internal security.[41]

These salient passages from Hofmann's report on his mission are important for a correct assessment of the situation in the land. The strategic value of Carpatho-Ukraine may be gauged by the fact that, notwithstanding the various destructive actions perpetrated by Hungary and Poland, the outside world was interested in entering into economic and political relationship with Carpatho-Ukraine. It is to be regretted that the League of Nations, which in 1920 took upon itself the obligation to guarantee the fulfillment of Carpatho-Ukraine's autonomous rights, or its member states did not intervene in defense of Carpatho-Ukraine's rights.

After the inauguration of the new government, foreign diplomats converged on Khust either to size up the situation there or to establish diplomatic contacts. Thus, the Italian Consul in Bratislava, the Counselor of the Polish Embassy in Prague, Kornicki, and the Polish Consul in Sevliush all paid visits to the Khust Government. Other foreign diplomats expressed the wish to establish their representations in Khust. Romania wished to open its consulate in Khust as did Japan, the latter having sent its Secretary of the Japanese Embassy in Moscow Kataoka to negotiate with the Khust Government. Other foreign diplomats expressed the wish to establish their representations in Khust. The little obscure city of Khust had overnight become an international strategic and political arena in which diplomatic battles of both friendly and not-so-friendly world powers were to be fought.

Before leaving Prague for Khust, a well-known foreign correspondent of The New York Times, Anne O'Hare McCormick, visited the Office of the Government of Carpatho-Ukraine in Prague to inquire about the possibility of driving around the countryside, especially the highlands near Khust even if only by horse-driven wagon, and of being able to talk to the local people. She said she wanted to ascertain whether the Ruthenians-Ukrainians were really behind their government, as claimed, or whether the Hungarians and Poles were right in claiming the contrary. Serving as interpreter for McCormick during her travels in Carpatho-Ukraine was Kalenyk Lysiuk of the United States, who was visiting Khust at the time. In recollecting the travel with McCormick, Lisiuk singled out this episode for attention:

> We were driving a horse-driven wagon from Khust and crossing the river Tisa when I got the urge to tease our driver, a peasant, and asked, "What is this murky little creek, anyway?" Somewhat irritated, the peasant replied, "That's no murky creek but the Tisa." Playing the ignoramus, I continued, "Yes, so much has been written and so many songs composed about the Tisa, and yet it is so murky." Even more irked than before, our driver turned around and retorted with emphasis, "Murky, but ours." When I translated his words to Mrs. McCormick, she remarked, "If we could only love our Mississippi as much, then everything would be all right."

McCormick published several articles about her impressions of Carpatho-Ukraine after its fall. She spoke about Carpatho-Ukraine's struggle and the struggle of the Ukrainian people in general, whereas American diplomat George Kennan showed no interest in the life of the Ukrainian people, nor in its history, nor in its liberation struggles.[42]

In the meantime, Brody was still kept in the Pankrác prison in Prague. On two occasions, the Prague government sounded me out about what the government of Carpatho-Ukraine thought about whether Brody should be kept in prison or be released. As head of the Office of the Government of Carpatho-Ukraine, I conveyed my government's opinion that Brody should be further held in prison. On the other hand, Fentsyk, who had managed to escape to Hungary, was appointed deputy to the Hungarian Parliament in Budapest, where he frequently was able reaffirm his loyalty to Hungary. In fact, according to the Hungarian press, he made a very good impression with a speech delivered on November 28. He tried to curry favor with Hungarian official circles and to squeeze out Brody, with whom he was constantly feuding. Miklós Kozma, then Hungarian Commissioner in the occupied part of Carpatho-Ukraine, later admitted that "Fentsyk's speech was born in my apartment in Uzhhorod."[43]

However, Fentsyk continued to work actively for the "Russian orientation," so much so in fact, that at a rally of his fascistic organization of "Chornorubashniki" (Black Shirts), he had the Tsarist Russian flag hoisted. This, of course, was not to the liking of the Hungarian authorities, which impressed upon him in no uncertain terms that the "Muscophile" game was over. In mid-December, 1938, he convoked a meeting of his supporters to Mukachevko to whom he conceded that there was no longer any possibility to promote the "Russian orientation" in Hungary and that he, therefore, resigned from this activity. He thereafter emigrated to America.[44] Thus ended the "Russian career" of the political operative Fentsyk, whom Hungary, Poland, and Czecho-Slovakia had financially supported for twenty years in Carpatho-Ukraine to hinder and combat the Ukrainian populist movement.

Meanwhile, the Carpatho-Ukrainian government was also preoccupied with the economic situation in the land, giving high priority to securing enough foodstuffs from abroad. To this end, it needed to reconfigure the road and rail communication system that had been interrupted in several places by the cession of territory to Hungary.

However, by the end of 1938, it successfully concluded an agreement with Romanian, Hungarian, and Czecho-Slovak railroad representatives concerning permission to have freight trains cross through the ceded territory. This agreement improved trade relations and secured sufficient supplies of foodstuffs for the population. The so-called "Southern Highway," connecting Priashiv in Slovakia with Khust, was also completed, thereby considerably shortening the motor vehicle transportation route.[45]

Despite the initial difficulties, the transportation system and the supply of necessary products for the population were operating smoothly, largely thanks to the help rendered by the army. According to government reports, the supply of foodstuffs was secured to last until the end of March 1939 and the situation boded well for the following year. [46]

Hungary's expectations that the transportation difficulties could not be overcome and would lead to Carpatho-Ukraine's collapse suffered a great disappointment. By the end of 1938, besides having to set the administration of the land in order, following the evacuation of the ceded territory, and to cope with the economic situation, the government also had to turn its attention to the minorities living in Carpatho-Ukraine and to normalize relations with them. Prime Minister Msgr. Voloshyn was visited by representatives of the Czech, Jewish, and Romanian national minorities, who assured the Premier of their loyalty to and support of the government. Msgr. Voloshyn in turn assured them that his government would continue to exert all effort to see that their rights were honored and that none of them would be wronged. The positive development of these relations undoubtedly strengthened Carpatho-Ukraine's position on the home front as well as abroad. Hungary, however, saw in it an obstacle to attaining its political goal. Hungary's conduct displeased even its Italian friend, Foreign Minister Ciano, who jotted down these words in his diary on January 10, 1939: "The Hungarian attitude is not so good. From the beginning, they tried to sabotage the Vienna Arbitration. This is stupid politics, since it irritates both us and Germany and certainly cannot modify the situation."[47]

The political world continued to be interested in Carpatho-Ukraine, and a number of countries would send their reporters to survey the situation and elicit interviews with government officials. Toward the end of the year, the editor of the *The Times of London,* Maj. MacNeil Moss arrived in Khust as did a representative of the Japanese news agency "Domei." In an interview with the Polish *Kurjer Codzienny,* Minister Revay made it clear that Carpatho-Ukraine was not entertaining any hostile intentions or engaged in any hostile actions against Poland or Hungary with both of whom it wished to live in peace. Revay also said that the Carpathian Sich served as a military training school for Carpatho-Ukrainian youths and was merely an internal educational institution.[48] All along and until the end of 1938, Germany did not favor the idea of a common Polish-Hungarian border or the notion of a possible unification of Slovakia and Hungary. At this juncture, Germany was already hatching plans of influence it would exercise in a future independent Slovakia.[49]

But these were not all the problems the nascent federated state was to face. Of major importance to the Khust government was to improve relations with the Czechs and the Slovaks. These relations were vital because in Slovakia strident centrifugal political voices were increasingly clamoring for an independence that would not bode well for Carpatho-Ukraine. Prime Minister Voloshyn clarified his stand on issues of greatest concern to both the entire federation and the federated State in an interview with *Lidové Noviny* that appeared in the later's New Year's issue. He positively reassessed the co-existence within the Czecho-Slovak Republic over the past twenty years and welcomed the republic's transformation from a unitary state into a federative one in which all three members had become equal partners. He expressed the hope that "we shall, together, pass this new test." He further noted that the Carpathian Ukrainians had lived with the Czechs so closely that he always felt at home in Prague, that the Ukrainians wished to foster their own culture, and he believed the "Ukrainian national idea will come out victorious from the elections."

The world press continued to concern itself with the issue of a Greater Ukraine and the Carpatho-Ukrainian's government's stance on it. The French daily *Le Matin,* for instance, carried in its January 3, 1939 number an interview with Premier Msgr. Voloshyn in which he stated:

> It is certain that the Ukraine in Poland and Soviet Russia is formed by one and the same people and that we have many sympathies for our brethren. But I repeat: this is a problem which concerns the Big

Powers and we are too small to interfere with it actively; it is our first
duty to keep peace in everything that concerns foreign policy with the
Czecho-Slovak federation.[50]

A similarly judicious opinion was also expressed by Minister Revay
in his public speeches. The foreign policy of Czecho-Slovakia was
conducted by the Central Government in Prague, of which the government of Carpatho-Ukraine was a constituent member. The Ukrainian
problem was gaining publicity in the world and mobilizing both friends
and enemies of the Ukrainian liberation idea. In the face of these
developments, it was only natural, justifiable, and expedient for the
government of Carpatho-Ukraine to refrain in its public pronouncements from stepping out of line in the given situation and trying to
achieve what was then politically impossible.

On January 2, 1939, the government of Carpatho-Ukraine convened
in a conference to discuss two very important problems: state finances
and the distribution of administration posts on the higher levels, in view
of the diminished size of the land. The finance question was the most
burning one for the government, for it was dependent on aid from the
Czecho-Slovak federation, an aid which it granted even though it was
itself having difficulties. Czecho-Slovakia, however, had a healthy root
and structure, which did not allow even the general mobilization in
1938 or the political catastrophe that struck it to undermine its economic potential.[51]

The trend toward stabilization in Carpatho-Ukraine attracted the
interest of countries with an abundance of capital. As early as the
beginning of January, a representative of the shoe concern Bata arrived
in Khust to explore the possibilities of exploiting the beauty of the
country for tourism; the Italian manufacturer S. Anaduci arrived to
explore possible production of paper and cellulose from Carpathian
wood; a representative of the Škoda firm was interested in setting up
the necessary enterprises for automobile manufacture. The joint-stock
company Latorytsia moved its headquarters from the occupied
Mukachevko to the town of Svaliava. The interest of foreign compa-
nies in Carpatho-Ukraine was an indication of their confidence in the
viability of the country and its leadership.

During the Ukrainian Christmas holidays (in early January), members of the government as well as leading civic workers set out to tour
the countryside in order to inform their people in person about the work

so far accomplished and the tasks still lying before them and to prepare the land for the elections to the Soim. Msgr. Voloshyn delivered his speech in Sevliush, while Minister Revay spoke in Seredne.[52]

Polish and Hungarian Attitudes towards the Khust Government

In its subversive activities against Carpatho-Ukraine, Poland went so far as to depict, in its diplomatic notes to foreign countries, the government of Msgr. Voloshyn as a Bolshevik one, mentioning even localities where kolkhozes (collective farms) and soviets (councils) were supposed to have been set up.[53] The Polish ambassador in London, Jozef P. Lipski, sought to convince Hitler that Carpatho-Ukraine being a "center of the Communist movement," could not, as an independent or autonomous state within the framework of Czecho-Slovakia, serve as a bridge-head in the struggle against Bolshevism. He, therefore, suggested that a common frontier between Poland and Hungary be established.[54]

Lipski and Foreign Minister Col. Józef Beck were not able to foresee the tragedy that was to befall their own nation at the hands of their ally Hitler. Lipski's assertions that he was a good expert on Germany and its policy proved tragic for Poland. In fact, he considered it to be his diplomatic success, and a guarantee for Poland, to have received Hitler's assurances during talks with him on September 20, 1938 to the effect that in the event of a conflict between Poland and Czecho-Slovakia, Germany would side with the former.[55] With this false sense of security in mind, Poland ventured to mass its troops on the Czecho-Slovak border.

In its overestimation of the strength of its army and its overwhelming and near-absurd self-righteousness, Poland paid little attention to the development of events in Europe. This sense of pride was openly flaunted. For instance, in his talk with the American journalist Robert Parker, Beck is quoted as having said, "You must realize that Poland is one of the world's great powers." And to Parker's inquiry about Danzig, he said: "Confidentially, I can tell you Germany's tanks are made of imitation metal. Hitler is bluffing. He knows perfectly well the great Polish army would be in Berlin in two months if he started anything."[56]

It was only a short time thereafter that events proved Poland's German policy to be pernicious not only toward Carpatho-Ukraine and the Ukrainians in general, but also toward Poland itself. However, it was too late for Poland to learn its lesson.

To round out the picture, it is appropriate to mention a concrete incident that occurred at the Polish Parliament in Warsaw. The Polish parliamentary deputy, Wacław Dudziński, submitted an interpellation to the Parliament in which he pointed to the "continuous agitation in Subcarpathian Ruthenia which poses a serious threat to the peace in the southern parts of the Polish state." As proof of his allegation, he referred to the alleged "creation on November 17, 1938 of a Communist soviet in Velyke Berezne which took over the administration of the entire town." He then claimed that also in the town of Volove (now Mizhhiria), "in the immediate vicinity of the Polish border a Communist soviet was established on September 20 whose members conduct a vehement anti-Polish agitation." Furthermore, according to him, "Communist armed units, under the red banner, are attacking the local residents and during the night of November 22–23 tried to cross the Polish border near the Užok Pass. Such attempts are made daily!" The Deputy demanded in his interpellation the "creation of a common Polish-Hungarian border."[57]

The Christmas peace was disturbed by the most significant border incident up to that time near the city of Mukachevo on January 6, 1939, which provoked a political reaction that the world press immediately registered. Col. Ján Heřman of the General Staff of the Czecho-Slovak Army and commander of the "Stráž Obrany Státu" (*SOS*—or Guardian of the Defense of the State) units along the demarcation line had the following to report about the incident:

> At 3 o'clock in the morning of January 6, 1939, a three-member patrol of our gendarmes was returning down the street near the vineyards to Pidmonastyr. Suddenly, they were fired upon from the opposite Hungarian side of the street. The patrol returned the fire, but one of the gendarmes was wounded. At the nearby intersection, three other members of the permanent guard of SOS were drinking with four Hungarian border guards, celebrating one of the latter's birthday and the forthcoming Ruthenian Christmas holidays. As a result of the exchange of fire in their immediate vicinity, they became alarmed and, in order to prevent the Hungarians from using their weapons against our boys, our soldiers interned them at a nearby tobacco store.

Some 35 of our soldiers came rushing out of the monastery, upon hearing the shooting, and took up battle positions up to the banks of the Latorytsia River. In no time there also appeared three of our armored cars from Kolchyno under the command of First Lieutenant Řiha whose task it was to flush out the Hungarians from their pockets of resistance all the way from Rosvygovo up to the bridge on the Latorytsia, followed by our three squads. Upon hearing the shooting, Captain Maks asked for two squads, which also engaged in the fighting. The Hungarians were pushed back behind the demarcation line, causing alarm in Mukachevo and prompting the Hungarians to advance against our units. On orders of Captain Řiha, artillery units were called in which began to shell Mukachevo. Hit were the theater, a hotel, a movie theater, and other buildings.[58]

In charge of one of the artillery units was Second Lieutenant Udut, who hailed from the town of Chinadiievo.[59] The Hungarians were taken aback during the attack by the fighting skill displayed by the Czecho-Slovak military units, in which many Carpatho-Ukrainians participated. The incident prompted the Hungarian government to "demand in an ultimatum that we surrender to it a tract of territory north of Mukachevo." In the end, they were content with our withdrawal from this territory under condition that only SOS units would remain on the border since there would be no clashes initiated on the Hungarian side. In addition, an investigation commission was created in which Col. Heřman represented Czecho-Slovakia and Col. Andorka represented Hungary. As for the reasons that caused the incident, no agreement could be reached. Hungary demanded reparations for the damage in the amount of 226,000 *pengö* (the pre-World War II currency of Hungary), but finally agreed to 33,000 *pengö,* which Czecho-Slovakia paid out. Col. Andorka is said to have told Col. Heřman that "As a soldier, I must congratulate you on the fighting skill of your soldiers." In the pitched battle, Czecho-Slovakia lost five dead and five soldiers taken prisoner as well as a number of wounded. Hungary acknowledged the death of ten soldiers and four officers. Hungary must have learned its lesson that with its terrorist tricks it could not intimidate either the government, or the army, or the population of Carpatho-Ukraine, and that it would receive a just rebuff. Despite the vigorous Hungarian and Polish propaganda, world opinion leaned toward Carpatho-Ukraine.

By having accepted the decision of the Vienna Arbitration of November 2, 1938, Hungary agreed to honor the demarcation line as the temporary frontier. However, it was just one day later that it breached its obligation and continued to violate the agreement by carrying out nineteen more terrorist acts against Carpatho-Ukraine before 1938 came to an end. In view of the continued terrorist acts, the Czecho-Slovak government lodged a *demarche* in Budapest on January 11, 1939, listing the incidents and identifying them by dates, localities, and casualties.[60]

That Hungary could allow itself to engage in such illegal forays against Czecho-Slovakia in general and Carpatho-Ukraine in particular at this juncture can be explained only by the fact that it was then enjoying Hitler's sympathy.

The subversive actions were to be carried out by the *Rongyos Gárda*, which were organized and commanded by Miklós Rozma, general director of the Hungarian Information Service, immediately after his return to Uzhhorod and Mukachevo from the Vienna Arbitration conference. Poland refused to participate in any joint Hungarian-Polish military ventures in Carpatho-Ukraine, but consented to sending its own irregulars and acting independently in subversive operations in the land. Poland's irregulars were organized and dispatched to Carpatho-Ukraine, carrying out their terrorist attacks in coordination with the Hungarians throughout the whole period. Poland was also to secure Romania's neutrality "even by force of arms."[61]

Through his Rongyos Gárda, Kozma had hoped to stir disturbances among the population that would encompass the entire land. The action was supposed to commence on November 20, 1938, with the Hungarian press to print headlines on the first page reporting that the "Ruthenian National Council is appealing to Hungary to send its troops into Transcarpathia and that Hungary has agreed to fulfill this request and has ordered its troops to invade the land on the morning of the 20th."[62] The commander of the 6th Department of the General Staff, Col. Sándor Homlók, received precisely defined tasks to carry out. The army was to invade Carpatho-Ukraine supposedly to protect the liberty and property of the population and to establish order.

However, the invasion did not take place. The command of the Hungarian Army had a change of heart and at the last minute ordered the military operation shelved by 24 hours, believing the troops needed rest after long marches. Because of this oversight, it transpired that the newspaper *Felvidéki Magyar Hirlap* (The Hungarian Highlands Herald), unaware of the change of plans, carried a frontpage headline in huge bold letters on November 20 that "Transcarpathian Ukraine is asking for help."[63] Kozma entered into his diary the news:

> I read the news and exclaimed: This is a catastrophe! The news that the National Council of Transcarpathian Ukraine called in the Hungarian troops went to press 24 hours too early; something happened that should have not happened until tomorrow. When the Ministry of Foreign Affairs ordered the publication of the news, it did not know that . . . Homlók could not begin action this evening.[64]

The whole action was prepared in utmost secrecy. Only Mussolini was informed about it and, therefore, the oversight was all the more embarassing to the Hungarian government. The German government, on the other hand, reacted to the affair in a special note to be delivered to the Italian Government through Ribbentrop:

> The Führer is of the opinion that the occupation of Transcarpathian Ukraine by the Hungarians would discredit the Axis Powers, to whose arbitration decision Hungary submitted unconditionally three weeks ago. Hungary is playing a dangerous game by intervening by force and, therefore, bears the full responsibility for possible consequences.[65]

To the European political world, such modes of action were not unfamiliar. In March 1938, Germany resorted to similar tactics when the Austrian Nazis asked Hitler for help "on behalf of the people" and got it. Hungary, which declared itself to be "Hitler's most loyal ally," considered it natural for it to avail itself of such methods, forgetting, however, that at this point in time Carpatho-Ukraine was Hitler's trump card which he was not willing to let go of. The political world identified Carpatho-Ukraine with the overall Ukrainian liberation problem, which Hitler kept open on the European political forum.[66]

The American journalist Robert Parker, in an interview with Hungary's Prime Minister Count Pal Teleki in March 1939 asked him,

> . . . whether Germany had agreed to let Hungary take over the Subcarpathic [*sic*] Ukraine or whether it had been done so against Hitler's will. "Frankly," said the Prime Minister, "we were told to go ahead." He smiled and stood up. "It was the price Hitler paid for the right to talk with Stalin. After we took over the Subcarpathic Ukraine, Hitler sent word to Stalin that it was proof Germany no longer had any designs on the Russian Ukraine. Fuehrer stressed that inclusion of the territory in Hungary, abandonment of the Ukraine

militia, and dispersion of the local government showed Russia had nothing to fear from him."[67]

Romanian Foreign Minister Grigore Gafencu's stance was similar:

Obviously, anticipation accounted for the deeper basis in the matter of détente between Moscow and Berlin. For Germany, it was important before military actions to have its back protected. For the Soviet Union, it was the anticipation to divert Hitler from his Ukrainian objectives and to push him into war with the West."[68]

Notes

[1] The delegation did not represent Ruthenian Americans of the Greek Catholic faith, who constituted the overwhelming majority of Ruthenians in the U.S.

[2] Akademiia nauk UkrSSR, *Ukraïns'ko-uhors'ki istorichni zv'iazky* (Kyiv, 1964), p. 83. *See also*, Külmst. Hungary, res. pol. 1940, 10/a t. 148, a.sz.

[3] Ibid., pp. 83–84. *See also*, Külmst. Hungary, sz. 0. 1938. K.7 sz.t.

[4] President Eduard Beneš resigned on October 5, 1938.

[5] *Venkov* November 30, 1938.

[6] Ádám Magda, *Allianz Hitler-Horthy-Mussolini. Dokumente zur ungarischen Aussenpolitik (1933-1944)* (Budapest, 1966), p. 833.

[7] Petravych was the Hungarian consul in Bratislava. Ibid., p. 729.

[8] Ibid.

[9] Ibid., p. 774.

[10] Ibid., p. 755.

[11] Ibid., p. 736

[12] *Ukraïns'ko-uhors'ki*, p. 86; Cf. Külmst. Hungary, Kozma irathagyaték naplójegyzétek, 1938, XI. S. 76, 77, 84.

[13] Ibid., pp. 86–87. *See also*, Külmst. Hungary, Kozma irathagyaték . . . ., 1938, XI. X. 12.]

[14] Ádám Magda, *op.cit.*, p. 868.

[15] Ibid., p. 773.

[16] Ibid., p. 774.

[17] Ibid., p. 804.

[18] Ibid., p. 811.

[19] Loránt Tilkovszky, *Revizió és nemzetiségpolitika Magyarországon 1938-1941* (Budapest, 1967), p. 151; OL kum. Res. Pol. 61, cs. 3265–7–7/1938; OL Filmtár, 11057, doboz, 448678.

[20] Alexander Henderson, *Eyewitness in Czechoslovakia* (London, 1939), pp. 250–51.

[21] Ádám Magda, *op.cit.*, p. 833. On October 17, Yulian Revay warned Foreign Minister Chvalkovsky of Brody's contacts with Hungary, the upshot of which was that the Prague Government prohibited Brody and Voloshyn from making a visit to Budapest where they were to enter into negotiations with the Hungarian Government regarding the borders. *See,* Ivan Vanat, *Narysy novitnoï istoriï Skhidnoï Slovachchyny*, vol. 2 (Priashiv, 1985), p. 37. *See also*, I. I. Pop, *Chekhoslovatsko-vengerskie otnosheniia (1935–1939)* (Moscow, 1972), p. 199; and František Lukeš, *Podivný mír* (Prague, 1968), p. 130.

[22] Dr. Ladislav Feierabend, *Ve vládách Druhé republiky* (New York, 1961), p. 50.

[23] Ádám Magda, *op. cit.,* p. 876.

[24] István Pintér, *Ki volt Horthy Miklós?* (Budapest, 1968), p. 144.

[25] Ibid., p. 177.

[26] C. A. Macartney, *A History of Hungary, 1929–1945,* part 2 (New York, 1957), p. 53.

[27] Ibid.

[28] *A-Zet* January 4, 1939.

[29] As an officer of the Czechoslovak Army, I was assigned to a military unit stationed in Perechyn, Carpatho-Ukraine, during the period of the federation where I was put in charge of arranging transportation service between Priashiv and Khust. As commander of one such military convoy, usually consisting of some 50 military trucks, I noticed in the oncoming dusk that there were some people on the road ahead in the woods near the town of Svaliava. Since at this time Polish and Hungarian terrorists were roaming the countryside, I issued an order putting the soldiers on heightened alert. However, as the convoy reached the spot where people seemed to be milling about, it turned out that there were eight peasant women busy filling in the potholes in the road with sharp shards of stone. Confounded, I asked one of them in a typically military fashion what they were doing. "We are filling in the potholes," she replied. And upon asking her who had instructed them to do so, the woman replied without hesitation, "Nobody." "Then why are you doing this work?" "How else would you be able to bring us food if the road had holes in it?" was her simple, sincere answer. I was touched.

[30] Tiskový Odbor Presidia Ministerské Rady (TOPMR) No. 316 16.XI.1938.

[31] TOPMR No. 322. *See also, Národní Osvobození* of November 24, 1938.

[32] *Nova Svoboda* January 25, 1939.

[33] TOPMR No. 332 of November 22, 1938.

[34] TOPMR, No. 320 of November 20, 1938.

[35] TOPMR, No. 330 of November 30, 1938.

[36] TOPMR, No. 331 of December 1, 1938.

[37] TOPMR No. 331; *Venkov* of December 1, 1938.

[38] TOPMR No. 333; *Venkov* of December 3, 1938.

[39] *České Slovo* December 4, 1938; TOPMR No. 334 of December 4, 1938.

[40] For more details, see Avhustyn Shtefan's article entitled "The Dolorous Path of the Late Bishop Nyarady" in *Ameryka* (Philadelphia) Easter 1977.

[41] Documents of German Foreign Policy (hereafter: DGFP), Series D, Vol. 4, 1951, pp. 170–71.

[42] My reaction to Kennan is published in *The Ukrainian Quarterly* (New York) 26(3–4) 1970: 15–18 and in *Suchasnist* (Munich) September 1971.

[43] Tilkovszky, *op. cit.,* p. 229.

[44] TOPMR, No. 356 of December 25, 1938.

[45] TOPMR No. 351; *Lidové Listy* of December 21, 1938.

[46] From November 14 to December 20, 1938 a total of 3,200 army trucks were employed on the Priashiv-Khust highway, having carried 19,200 metric tons of freight over an aggregate of 1,740,000 kilometers. *See,* TOPMR No. 354; *Lidové Noviny* of December 24, 1938. To these figures should be added the delivery of mail on 12–15 trucks, which transported a total of 26,000 metric tons of postal items and traveled a total of 240,000 kilometers. In the given circumstances and in view of the difficult terrain, this was a great accomplishment.

[47] *The Ciano Diaries 1939–1943* (New York, 1946), p. 9.

[48] *Lidové Noviny,* December 23, 1938.

[49] Ranki György, *Emlékiratok és valóság Magyarország második világháborus szerepéröl* (Budapest, 1964), pp. 141–42.

[50] Dr. Hubert Ripka, *Munich Before and After* (London, 1939), p. 264.

[51] By the end of 1937, the total amount of *koruny* circulating in the country was 6,902 million and by the end of 1938 it rose to 6,950 million *koruny* in a territory now truncated by the Munich Dictate. The gold reserve by the end of 1937 was valued at 2,620 million *koruny* or 36.5%. During the weeks of the mobilization, the value of the domestic currency was 9,608 million and that of the gold reserve 26.5%. But by the end of the year, the gold reserve soared to 33.8% [*Ceské Slovo* January 3, 1939]. As member of the State Economic Council dealing with the allocation of credits to Carpatho-Ukraine, I prepared calculations which showed that the federated State of Bohemia and Moravia was giving Carpatho-Ukraine in general approximately 750,000 *koruny* daily for credits not covered.

[52] *Lidové Noviny* January 6, 1939.

[53] To officially accuse the government of a Catholic monsignor of being Communist was clearly indicative of the degree of hatred which the Polish state—a Catholic one at that—harbored toward Ukrainian state aspirations. In this connection, it may be pointed out that Msgr. Voloshyn, President of Carpatho-Ukraine, was tortured to death in the Moscow Lefortov Prison in 1945. *See,* Augustyn Shtefan, *Avgustyn Voloshyn, Spomyny* (Toronto, 1977), p. 147.

Soon after Germany's capitulation in 1945, the Soviets arrested in Prague Msgr. Voloshyn and his associates Stepan Klochurak, Dr. Mykola Dolynay, Yuriy Perevuznyk, and V. Chaplya and deported them to the Soviet Union. None of them had ever been a Soviet citizen and yet the Soviet Union unlawfully arrested and deported them. This was obviously a flagrant violation of state and international laws, but the free world, including President Beneš, preferred to keep quiet about the affair as it almost always did when injury was inflicted on the Ukrainian nation.

[54] *Ukraïns'ko-uhors'ki,* p. 91. *See also,* Sir Lewis Bernstein Namier, *Diplomatisches Vorspiel, 1938–1939* (Berlin, 1949), p. 57.

[55] Jozef Dánás, *Ludácký separatizmus a Hitlerovské Německo* (Bratislava, 1963), p. 72; *Documents on the Eve of World War II,* Prague, No. 23.

[56] As quoted by Robert Parker, *Headquarters Budapest* (New York-Toronto, 1944), pp. 86–87.

[57] Ministry of Foreign Affairs, Prague, No. 173696/II-I/38 of December 6, 1938. Confidential. *Aide Memoire.* Office of the Government of Carpatho-Ukraine in Prague, No. 315/38.

[58] Colonel of the General Staff Ján Heřman's military report, pp. 5–6.

[59] After the collapse of Carpatho-Ukraine, Udut joined the Slovak Army and participated in the fighting against the Hungarian intruders south of Košice. One night, detachments of the *Rongyos Gárda* (Hungarian volunteers, "Ragtag Guards") terrorists attacked his home near the border, captured, and then killed him.

[60] To mention only some of the incidents listed:

September 3, 1938—attack with grenades and machine gun fire near Kosyno; one Czecho-Slovak soldier killed, 5 wounded.

September 4—repeated attack near Kosyno; one soldier wounded;

November 17—attack against SOS station near Strabičov; one soldier seriously wounded; another attack near Nižný Koropec; one police officer seriously wounded;

December 6—an insidious murder of a gendarme officer committed with a grenade near Goronda;

December 13—attack on a patrol near Verbivtsi; one soldier seriously wounded;

December 24—attack on guards near Baranintsi; one soldier seriously wounded.

[61] *Ukraïns'ko-uhors'ki,* p. 95. *See also,* Külmst. Hungary sz.0 1938, B. Varsó 446 szt.

[62] Ibid., p. 96. *See also,* Külmst. Hungary, Kozma irathagyaték, napló jegyzétek, 1938 XI.21.

[63] Karsai, *Stalo sa v Budíne v Šándorovskom paláci 1919-1941* (Bratislava, 1966), p. 355. *See also,* Külmst. Hungary, ibid.

[64] Karsai, ibid.

[65] *Ukraïns'ko-uhors'ki,* p. 96. *See also,* A.D.A.P. IV.T. Aus dem Archiv des Deutschen Auswärtigen Amtes, p. 138.

[66] At the expense of the Ukrainian problem, Hitler was able to create an opportunity to talk with Stalin that eventually led to the signing of the Molotov-Ribbentrop pact. Already during the initial stage of the preparations for the pact, namely in March 1939, Hungary received Carpatho-Ukraine from Hitler, for which it eventually had to pay dearly, as did Poland.

As early as 1935, Hitler made an offer to Poland that they jointly attack the Soviet Union and occupy Ukraine and Lithuania, through which Poland would gain access to the Black Sea. Poland, however, turned down the proposal, noting that such a war would be conducted on its territory. (Parker, *op. cit.,* pp. 90–91.)

Instead, in 1939, Hitler deftly used the Ukrainian problem in the opposite direction, having concluded an agreement with the Soviet Union aimed against Poland. As already noted, it is this event that the historiographies of Ukraine's neighbors failed to talk about lest the attention of the world be directed to its economic, strategic, and national importance in Central-Eastern Europe.

[67] Ibid.

[68] Grigore Gafencu, *Vorspiel zum Krieg im Osten* (Zurich, 1944), pp. 64–65.

The Carpatho-Ukrainian Government's Representation in Prague

In order to facilitate official business with the central government, the federated states of Slovakia and Carpatho-Ukraine opened representation offices of their respective governments in Prague. The Slovak office was headed by Minister Karol Sidor, while I headed the Ukrainian office. In view of the complexity of business that stemmed from the federated status of the state, as well as of the difficult communication connections with Khust, such an office in Prague was indispensable for Carpatho-Ukraine.

At this time, Prague was the center of attention of the Ukrainian political and cultural world. Ukrainians in Czecho-Slovakia and in the world throughout reacted to the creation of the Carpatho-Ukrainian federated state with great enthusiasm and supported it with all available means. Ukrainian civic and political circles in Prague actively participated in the work of the Representation by providing advice related to a variety of economic, financial, organizational, and other problems emerging from the new needs of the federation. It was because of this circumstance that the office had to see to it that its employees had the necessary professional skill in order to successfully cope with its tasks.

Immediately after the demobilization of the Czecho-Slovak Army at the end of November 1938, I received via the Zemská Banka in Bratislava, at which I was employed, an invitation by telegraph from the government of Carpatho-Ukraine to take over the following day at 10 a.m. the Office of the Government of Carpatho-Ukraine housed in the building of the Ministry of Unification located at 17 Dušní Street in Prague.

On the way from Bratislava to Prague, I pondered plans of my future work, having no clear idea of the scope and demands of the assignment.

I set up a general list of duties which I proceeded to faithfully and systematically implement:

1. To enter into a business-like and friendly contact with the Ukrainian emigration for the purpose of utilizing their experience, advice, and help.

2. To organize a group of Czech friends through whom a better access to Czech official circles could be gained; to prepare and fulfill through them the tasks set before us; to win the confidence of official quarters in Carpatho-Ukraine the idea of Ukrainian statehood in general, and in me personally.

3. To select qualified personnel to the Representation Office conversant with the current problems and expected to perform well.

4. To centralize Carpatho-Ukrainian affairs in the hands of the Representation Office in Prague. (Prior to the Federation there was a bureau for Carpathian Affairs attached to the Presidium of the Ministerial Council.)[1]

The overall atmosphere in the Czech country was rather tense; it was difficult to control the discontent of the population. In November 1938, Czech students of the Department of Philosophy at Charles University in Prague tore down the bust of President Masaryk. This was a cry of desperation in a situation caused not so much by a mistaken foreign policy by the Czecho-Slovak state but rather by the emergence of Hitler's Germany and the expansionist policies in Europe, which Western democracies tolerated.

It was not until Msgr. Avhustyn Voloshyn was appointed prime minister of Carpatho-Ukraine on October 27, 1938, that the Czech attitude toward the Ukraine and the Ukrainian state idea changed. The Czechs finally realized that the so-called Muscophile cultural orientation, which they had supported in Carpatho-Ukraine, had driven them down a dead-end street. In this disconcerting atmosphere, the Ukrainians proved to be the only people with a constructive state-political program that could help salvage the given situation. It is for this reason that the Czechs then turned their attention to the Ukrainians.

In this rather explosive and tense atmosphere the first steps had to be taken in Prague toward building sounder foundations under the common state-federative construction. I was aware of the possibility that a single faulty move on my part or an improper statement of mine supporting or agreeing with Germany's policy would have rendered impossible my task of defending the basic interests of Carpatho-Ukraine in Prague. As the results have shown, I managed successfully to carry out the tasks with the help of my co-workers.

The State Economic Council (SEC)

Because of the changed political situation in the state, the previously approved Czecho-Slovak budget for 1939 could not be applied to the new circumstances. In December 1938, the Prague Parliament conferred full powers on the Central Government to run the country for two years and authorized the President of the Republic to rule by decree or even to change the Constitution, with the exception of Constitutional Law No. 328 that created the federative form of the state.

By virtue of these full powers, the Central Government issued decree No. 384 (*Sb. zák. a n.*) dated December 23, 1938, calling into being the State Economic Council (SEC) attached to the Government Presidium in Prague as an advisory organ of the government of the Czecho-Slovak Republic in economic, social, and financial matters. The SEC's task was to submit reports to the government either on its own initiative or upon the demand of the prime minister and to present proposals concerning economic, social, and financial matters.

The SEC had 65 members appointed by the individual federated governments for three years. The Czechs had 45 members, the Slovaks 15, and the Ukrainians five, including myself. First head of the SEC was Dr. Hodač, who was then succeeded by Jan Baťa at the beginning of January 1939. Because of the distance and poor communication, Msgr. Voloshyn issued a special authorization, contained in a telegram to me, to represent Carpatho-Ukraine in the SEC and also endeavor, among other things, to obtain necessary credits for Carpatho-Ukraine. Slovakia was represented by Anton Mederly, who later became general director of the Slovenská Hypotečná a Komunalná Banka (Slovak Mortgage and Communal Bank) in Bratislava.

Among the SEC responsibilities were also the task of organizing special commissions of specialists and inviting the Czecho-Slovak National Bank, the Export Institute, and others to participate. To all intents and purposes, the SEC was becoming a leading factor in the individual domains of the state's activities. Unfortunately, the time was too short for it to develop its work to full extent.

The SEC was initiated at a meeting in the Senate Building in January 1939. In his opening speech, Chairman Jan Bat'a uttered the following maxim to govern the SEC's activities: "Until now what was done in the state was politically advantageous, but now we shall do what is economically useful." The principle was sound and in keeping with the demands of the time and situation in the country.

In accordance with the Constitutional Law on the federation, each federated part was to have its own regional budget whose revenues were to flow from its own resources. In addition, a central state budget was to be drawn up whose funds were to support common state institutions, such as the armed forces, the foreign policy apparatus, and the like. The national budget of the new Federal Republic of Czecho-Slovakia was to allocate the sum of 3 billion 190 million koruny; the budgets of the individual federated states were as follows: the Czech Lands: 5.9 billion, Slovakia—2.37 billion, and Carpatho-Ukraine—550 million. Contributions of these federated territories to the central state budget amounted to 70% for the Czech lands, 24% for Slovakia, and 6% for Carpatho-Ukraine.

Pursuant to Paragraph 4 of the Constitutional Law No. 328, Carpatho-Ukraine, as part of the state federation, became the sole owner of all the natural resources of state properties on its territory, such as forests, mines, mineral springs, railroads, etc. By virtue of this legal status, the government of Carpatho-Ukraine was entitled to enter independently into trade contacts with foreign countries. The principal products for export were: timber, wine, fruits, and salt. The acreage of the state property in Carpatho-Ukraine amounted to 362,314 hectares (941,756 acres) of land, of which forests accounted for 309,500 hectares (764,460 acres).[2] In order to develop the economic life of Carpatho-Ukraine according to plan, the Carpatho-Ukrainian government had set up its own Economic Council.

To be sure, at this initial stage, Carpatho-Ukraine was not self-sufficient in finances and was, therefore, dependent on the Czech lands for aid. Thanks to Jan Bat'a and his understanding for the federation's problems as well as for the specific problems of Ukrainian statehood, which were also of importance to the Czech people, Carpatho-Ukraine was able to obtain the necessary budget credits from the Czechs. The other person who helped us a great deal in financial and other important matters of state—although he had no direct business with the SEC—

was Dr. Jan Kapras, minister of education and chairman of the Czecho-Slovak National Council and my former professor at Charles University at Prague. Kapras was sympathetic toward our cause in the legislative department and stressed out interests in his speeches and at press conferences. Such a common stand had sound logic, for in the given situation the Czechs had the same political interests as did the Carpatho-Ukrainians, namely to preserve the unity of the truncated Republic, to combat the Hungarian and Polish terrorist actions, to counteract the territorial claims of Hungary, and to prevent the establishment of a common Hungarian-Polish frontier.

No doubt, it was not in the interests of Germany to see a normalization of conditions in Czecho-Slovakia. In fact, since January 1939 Germany's state power was applied in full force to bring about the destruction of Czecho-Slovakia from within.

The "Ukrainian Problem" Censored in Prague

Whenever members of the Carpatho-Ukrainian government came to Prague, their appearance seemed to arouse interest among foreign journalists. The Representation Office held press conferences on its premises in which correspondents of British, American, German, French, Japanese, and other newspapers participated. Their interest was not limited only to the problems of Carpatho-Ukraine. The world press at large was quite interested in the political problems of Ukraine as a whole, an interest taken that could not but alarm Ukraine's enemies. Germany deftly used the Ukrainian question for its own political aims in the form of its so-called Ukrainian propaganda. When Poland was not willing to enter into a certain political modus vivendi arrangement with Germany directed against the Soviet Union, Hitler took advantage of Stalin's offer to open negotiations, at first on economic and subsequently on political matters. The upshot of this development was that as of January 1939 the Ukrainian question in German propaganda was losing its anti-Soviet edge that contributed to the drawing closer of the interests of the two great powers and finally led to the signing of the Molotov-Ribbentrop Pact. The following incident in Prague may serve as an illustrative example reflecting the situation.

In 1938–1939, the Czech newspapers in Prague widely reported on Ukraine and its state-liberation struggle in a very favorable light, as did the majority of the world press. One day, in the first half of February

1939, the editorial offices of the Prague newspapers were gripped with alarm when articles on Ukraine were confiscated. The Representation Office was flooded with telephone calls from the newspapers inquiring about the reason for the confiscation. I immediately set out to visit the pertinent state censorship authorities and make my own inquiry. After a brief talk with a competent official, I. Palivec, the latter placed on the table before me two memoranda in Czech translation, one from Berlin the other from Moscow, and left the room. Having carefully perused the texts of both notes, I was astonished to learn that the contents were strikingly similar. The notes expressed the desire that, in connection with Carpatho-Ukraine, the Czecho-Slovak press refrain from writing about the idea of an independent Ukraine or stress Ukrainian statehood or the importance of Ukraine. These were the first harbingers of reconciliation between Hitler and Stalin.

It was suggested that I submit the same day a written protest to the Ministry of Foreign Affairs, equipped with pertinent argumentation, in the hope that matters would clear up the following day. On leaving the office, the official with whom I had the talk said to me: "I knew you were coming and I wanted you to see these letters." I understood him well. The Czechs were reluctant, and justifiably so, to bear the responsibility for the censorship act and, therefore, wanted us to know what in actual fact had transpired. I followed the advice and submitted a written protest the same day to the Ministry of Foreign Affairs. Surely enough, articles on the Ukrainian question reappeared in the press the following day. There was no recurrence of such censorship in Prague thereafter.

During the period of the Federation, the pro-Russian, Muscophile movement in Carpatho-Ukraine did not show any signs of activity as an organization. Instead, however, a strong Muscophile center of intellectuals and university students was founded in Prague. The group published its journal *Dnevnik,* at first in Russian and later also in Czech supplement. They drew strong financial support from pro-Russian Czech political circles and their spokesman in Parliament, Deputy A. Schwarz. Every move the government of Carpatho-Ukraine made was interpreted by them in a most distorted, inimical, and destructive fashion, so much that in general the Muscophile movement as such began to lose its once prevalent popularity among the Czechs. This new development was fittingly seized up by the newspaper *Národní Politika,* which in its December 8, 1938 issue raised the question

"What Really was the Situation of Russophilism in Subcarpathian Ruthenia?" and proceeded to say that "Russophilism is permeated with Magyarophilism" and had been "introduced by Czech political parties." Summing up its evaluation, the newspaper went on to declare that "Russophilism is harmful for Czecho-Slovakia" and recommended replacing this Russophilism with "love for the good and loyal Ukrainians." It stressed the significance, importance, and strength of the Ukrainian nation, which "is becoming more and more an important factor in the European game."

The pro-Russian *Dnevnik* continually poisoned the atmosphere in Prague. Through my friendly contacts with competent Czechs, I was able to have the publication of this journal stopped for half a year without the right of appeal. In consequence, the group turned for help to the cultural attaché of the Italian Embassy. Prewarned in a timely fashion by our Czech friends not to get involved, the attaché declined to intercede in their behalf. The group then proceeded to form itself into a committee dedicated to the idea of combatting the government of Carpatho-Ukraine. Before the elections to the Soim, it contrived to distribute anti-government placards and leaflets in Carpatho-Ukraine. They were so advanced in their preparations that two of the committee's members were on their way to Khust with the material when they were intercepted by Czech officials in Priashiv, upon our request, and the material confiscated. Thereafter, the committee was never again activated.

Recruiting Workers For Germany

With the cession of territories to Germany, Hungary, and Poland, all three portions of the federation suffered great material losses. However, the evacuation of the population from these territories created a surplus of labor force in the Republic. Although the Czechs harbored justified resentment and hatred toward the Germans, they were forced to transfer a portion of their labor force, notably specialized technicians, to work in Germany under contract for one year. The Slovak and Carpatho-Ukrainian federated states followed suit for the same reason.

On January 15, 1939 a delegation arrived in Prague from Germany for this very purpose. The delegation consisted of Ministerial Counselor Dr. H. Rediger, J. Letsch, and J. Hoetzel. Bohemia was represented by Dr. Jan Vrabec, Slovakia by Y. Kasovic, and Carpatho-Ukraine by myself. According to information released by the government's Social Department in Khust, the number of registered unemployed in Carpatho-Ukraine was 5,087. As agreed, a total of 41,000 workers were to be transferred to Germany from Czecho-Slovakia, of this number Slovakia was to deliver 20,000, Carpatho-Ukraine 4,000, and Bohemia the rest. The exact date of the transportation of these workers was not set. In the meantime, registration and other formalities had to be completed. Their status, wages, and other benefits were the same as for German workers.

In view of the upcoming elections to the Soim, I submitted a request that our workers be given the possibility of casting their absentee votes in Germany. The request was granted in principle, but a separate agreement to this effect was needed.

The agreement with Germany concerning the employment of workers from Carpatho-Ukraine entailed precise provisions regulating injuries, death, and work conditions and allowed the contracting parties to exercise control and care. The costs connected with the issuing of passports and transportation to the German border were to be defrayed by the workers themselves or their state. Germany was to bear the cost of their transportation from the border to their destinations. Negotiations lasted three days and were concluded by a bilateral agreement, which I signed on behalf of the government of Carpatho-Ukraine.

The Czech-Ukrainian Society

The growing interest in the Ukrainian state idea among the Czechs necessarily required that we not only establish and expand our political but our cultural relations as well. To promote such relations, it was planned to create a Czech-Ukrainian Society which would have as its members Czechs favorably disposed toward our cause and Ukrainians living in Bohemia. Since, in the past, the press of Czech political parties frequently attacked Ukrainians, it was necessary, first of all, to pacify the anti-Ukrainian mood created by them and to refute their unfounded allegations and misconceptions through creative cooperation.

It was one of my tasks to organize our sympathizers which I partially managed to carry out soon after my arrival in Prague. With the passage of time and our participation in the federated Czecho-Slovak

Republic's state apparatus, the need for an all-round cooperation became even more compelling. Such cooperation would have been only to our advantage. There was, undoubtedly, a great deal for us to learn about the art of building a state and operating it, and to this end our Czech sympathizers proved to be good and sincere teachers.

By the beginning of January 1939, i.e., before the formation of the Czech-Ukrainian Society, a group of our sympathizers began publishing in Prague a Czech-language weekly *Karpato-Ukrajinská Svoboda*. The weekly comprised eight pages and had a two-page Ukrainian supplement, which was edited by Dr. Volodymyr Zborovsky, a member of the editorial college.

The first issue of the weekly carried an article written by me on the work of Prime Minister Msgr. A. Voloshyn and the policy of his government. The article started:

> When twenty years ago a delegation of the TsNR, led by today's chairman of the government of Carpatho-Ukraine Msgr. Voloshyn, arrived in Prague from Uzhhorod to solemnly declare that the Carpathian land was joining the Czechoslovak Republic, no one expected that this very land that had been brutally repressed by the Hungarian regime would twenty years later become a substantive point of interest in world politics and in the calculations of the world powers.

It then went on to critically analyze the political conditions that emerged in relation to Carpatho-Ukraine over the past twenty years and their pernicious results for the Czecho-Slovak state. The article concluded:

> The Ukrainian population of Transcarpathia is building a new life for itself and, in the words of the chairman of the government, Msgr. Voloshyn, is in favor of state coexistence with Czechs and Slovaks. It is desirable that Czech-Ukrainian relations and co-existence in the federated state be reinforced by mutual trust and goodwill of both peoples. A prerequisite to this end is to learn about one another and to have an understanding for one another. And the task of the press is actually to serve as a transmitter of this rapprochement, which undoubtedly is in the interest of good coexistence for both fraternal Slavic peoples.

The article was favorably received in Prague.

In its third issue, the weekly published an interview of Dr. Zborovsky with Prime Minister Msgr. Voloshyn and a photo picture of the latter. In one of his answers to the number of questions posed to him, the Prime Minister pointed out that "Our little Carpatho-Ukraine is presently the only small part of the great expanse of Ukrainian lands that has its freedom." With regard to the Jews, he stated that the "problem of Jews is an all-state matter. Therefore, we Ukrainians embrace the same attitude as that of the Central Government." He also underscored the need for friendly cooperation and goodwill among all members of the federation. The reaction to the article was positive among official circles.[3]

Many prominent Czech experts contributed to *Karpato-Ukrajinská Svoboda,* among them Jan Brandeis. In the sixth issue of the paper, Brandeis stated the following in his article entitled "The Czechs, Slovaks, and Ukrainians": "In the name of false humanism, Hebrew, Jewish, Gypsy, Russian, Hungarian, and other schools were supported in Carpatho-Ukraine while Ukrainian schools always came to be regarded as irredenta." He further reviewed the overall Ukrainian problem with which a sundry of other problems of economic character, industrial expansion, trade, general welfare, and confidence were related.

The newspaper also carried Ukrainian-language courses for the benefit of the Czechs. On the whole, the newspaper was well edited, contained a welter of informative material on Ukrainian issues, and correctly interpreted the Ukrainian problem in Czecho-Slovakia and the world at large. Consequently, in mid-January of 1939, when the constituent meeting of the Czech-Ukrainian Society was convoked, the organization already boasted an unofficial press organ. For its part, the Ukrainian National Council in Khust delegated to the Society myself and five others. The Czech representation consisted of, apart from the already above-mentioned Czech friends of ours, also university professors and journalists as well as persons active in the economic and political walks of life. However, the entire load of work rested on my shoulders for the simple reason that I maintained a permanent residence in Prague.

An *ad hoc* committee was preparing the statutes of the Society and its work plan. Great prospects were opening up for the society which, in the given circumstances, were needed and beneficial to our political and cultural work in Prague.[4]

As these examples of planned arrangements may suggest, life in the federation offered us immense possibilities and the much needed experience as well as the opportunity for a wide-scope activity in the affairs of state. Regrettably, however, the development of political events in Europe and the world took a turn to our great disadvantage, destroying everything along its way.

Trade Agreements

The mountains and woods of Carpatho-Ukraine and their exceptional beauty enjoyed European fame already during the Austro-Hungarian era. At that time, they were owned by the state. However, no provision concerning the transfer of this property to the region's ownership was incorporated either in the Saint-Germain Treaty, by which the land was joined to Czecho-Slovakia, or into the Constitution, which guaranteed the region's autonomy. This was in spite of the fact that such a demand was submitted by Dr. G. Zhatkovych, as he himself had later revealed to me. As a result, after Hungary, Czecho-Slovakia became the heir-owner of the entire land property in Carpatho-Ukraine. It was not until the promulgation of the Constitutional Law of November 1938, No. 328, that this right of ownership was accorded the Carpatho-Ukrainian government.

Upon the recommendation of the Ministry of Economics in Khust, trade negotiations were initiated in Prague regarding the export of timber to Hungary and Germany in which I first participated but was later replaced by Dr. Adalbert Geletka, advisor on economic matters at the Prague Representation. Germany was interested in purchasing railroad ties, and that in great quantities, while Hungary prefered timber for firewood.

During the First Republic, management of the woods was under the control of the state, which set a quota on the number of trees to be felled and the yearly quantity earmarked for export. Under the Second Republic, this right was accorded the individual regions of the Federation. In Prague we concluded only a preliminary agreement inasmuch as the demands submitted by Hungary and Germany required that we first explore the production capability of our sawmills, the problem of delivery and other issues that were impossible to work out in Prague. At that time, our railroad communication was severely impaired as a result of the Vienna Award, which severed our railroad network in favor of Hungary. Our condition for the delivery of timber was that Hungary allow a free transit by rail for both our export and for us through the territory detached from Carpatho-Ukraine—to which it agreed in principle. Other difficulties cropped up as well, such as the matter of payments. We needed ready cash to pay our trading partners for their goods: machinery from Germany, agricultural products from Hungary which could have been purchased from Romania at lower prices. The further conduct of the negotiations was moved to the Ministry of Economics in Khust.

The "Dredoma" firm in Bratislava, Slovakia was in charge of managing the forest industry, tree-cutting and selling. Through Dredoma, the state established a system governing the cutting of various sorts of trees for Carpatho-Ukraine and Slovakia. As in many other institutions during the First Republic, Carpatho-Ukraine was not represented, for instance, in Všeobecný Pensijný Ústav (the General Pension Institution) at all or only to a negligible degree, mostly because we ourselves failed to attend to these matters at the right time. Had we known, dozens of our secondary commercial school graduates could have had good jobs and acquired experience at the ratio of 1:4 in relation to the Slovaks. Instead, after graduation, they almost to a man took up jobs as substitute teachers. True, as nationally conscious citizens, they undoubtedly performed valuable cultural services but lost the opportunity to work in their originally intended professions.[5]

On January 21, 1939, the negotiator M. Babota, a banking specialist, together with the representative of Carpatho-Ukraine in Slovakia, Yuliy Husnay, paid a visit to the Dredoma firm in Bratislava. In the course of the talks, Babota suggested that, if their cooperation were to be successful, the Carpatho-Ukrainians ought to be proportionally represented in Dredoma. He further said that all producers and exporters in Carpatho-Ukraine had been organized in a single union. The union would send its representatives to Dredoma to represent the interests of the entire land rather than, as heretofore, only the interests of their respective firms. As for Dredoma, it would represent the export of lumber only before foreign buyers and would set uniform prices for all exporters. The entire export contingent for all sorts of wood was to be divided between Slovakia and Carpatho-Ukraine immediately following the signing of a trade agreement.

Even before the talks with Babota took place, Dredoma had arbitrarily communicated to the Ministry of Agriculture in Prague its demands regarding the quantity and species of trees slated to be exported to Hungary in 1939 for the sum of 172 million *koruny*. Of this sum, Dredoma alloted only 55 million to Carpatho-Ukraine.

At the end of January 1939, inter-ministerial meetings took place in Prague concerning the planned trade agreement with Hungary. Upon learning of the Slovak action, I strongly protested against such an arbitrarily set quota as well as against Slovak conduct in general. The Czechs gave us full support. The quota for the clearing of forest trees and export was subsequently changed in our favor. We agreed with the Czechs that in the event that it would be impossible to come to some constructive understanding with the Slovaks in Dredoma, we would act in this matter completely on our own. The Ministry of Economics in Khust informed Dredoma that in the future we would be represented by V. Tegze as the nominal head, Ministerial Counselor Voda, university lecturer J. Folka, a representative of the Khust Ministry of Economics, and a junior official. Babota was intent on securing for this post a capable young man, who would expertly master the problem of forestry and the means and forms of trade.

In Prague we found ourselves in a somewhat awkward situation when we were told by our Czech partners that they had received news from Khust about our government having placed 22 forest engineers at the disposal of the Czech government. We tried to explain this act somehow, but I am not sure we were able to convince them. It was under such circumstances that we had to set about drawing up a trade agreement with Hungary. Yet, the improper behavior of the Slovaks at Dredoma notwithstanding, all of us were for the retention of the organizational *status quo* in view of the fact that the Hungarians were already making efforts to freely purchase wood and thus undercut our fixed prices and dictate their own. We had to make sure that we would retain, at all cost, the right to set the prices for wood. We transferred further conduct of the negotiations.

The federative-state status of the region placed our government in the role of an autonomous state entity not only in the formal-legal sense but also as one assuming the full responsibility for the welfare of the land and its population. In addition to the normal difficulties accompanying the outset of every new undertaking in the affairs of state, we also had to experience the disadvantage of having had a disrupted communication system and lost our three major cities with prosperous surrounding villages because of the Vienna Arbitration. The problem of supplying the populace with food became a serious one for the government.

Along with some of the certain actions, handled by me through the services of the State Economics Council since its inception and the Central Union of Czech Cooperatives, our government initiated active trade ties with Romania. On February 18–20, 1939, an inter-ministerial conference was held at the building of the Ministry of Foreign Affairs in Prague dealing with the matter of concluding a trade agreement with Romania. I represented the government of Carpatho-Ukraine. The majority of the conference participants were of the opinion that, in view of the diminished state territory, the total amount in the agreement with Romania ought not exceed the sum of 120 million *koruny* for the current year of which 10 million would go to Carpatho-Ukraine. The Khust Ministry of Economics conveyed to me in Prague a list of requirements for 1939:

> 1) 2,500 freight cars of corn, of which Romania could supply 1,500 to 2,000 carloads;
>
> 2) 600–700 freight cars of seed oil, of which Romania could supply 500 carloads; and
>
> 3) Gasoline and processed oil—retain the current quantity.

On February 24, 1939, a Romanian delegation, composed of representatives of the Romanian National Bank, the Ministry of Foreign Affairs, and the Ministry of Trade and Economics, arrived in Prague. After three days of talks, agreement was reached and accepted concerning the trade issue. What remained to be agreed upon was a special account, contingents, and preferential duty. From Romania we obtained corn at a price lower than that offered by Hungary. In the course of the negotiations, the Romanian representatives drew our attention to the fact that Hungarians had tried to dissuade them from concluding a trade agreement with us, alleging that a "vigorous propaganda campaign was going on in Carpatho-Ukraine against Romania for Bukovina."

Banking and Finance Problems

During the period of Carpatho-Ukraine federation within Czecho-Slovakia, Carpatho- Ukrainians were able to score impressive strides in their national-cultural endeavors, but could not boast equivalent success in the sphere of economic development. Czech, Slovak, and Hungarian banks founded their branches in Carpatho-Ukraine, such as the Agrarian Bank, the Tatra Bank, the Slovak Bank, the Bank of the Czecho-Slovak Legion, the Danube Bank, and others. All of them were profit-oriented trade institutions, which charged high interest rates.

In order to make it easier for our population to obtain lower-rate interest loans, branches of the Městská Spořitelna (City Savings Bank in Prague) were established during the First Republic in four cities of Carpatho-Ukraine: Uzhhorod, Mukachevo, Khust, and Berehovo. This institution was a special finance company covered by city guarantees instead of by the joint-stock capital of commercial banks. Although these savings banks were run on the commercial principle of private banks, their chief goal was not to achieve profit, but rather to provide a certain kind of service, making regulated credits available to the population. They were not subject to control by the Ministry of Finances as were all other commercial banks, but rather to the Ministry of Internal Affairs.

With the change of the state system in Czecho-Slovakia into a federative one, it became necessary for us to change our entire system of finances, including the takeover of the aforementioned branches of Městská Spořitelna. In order to carry out this task, the Městká Spořitelna headquarters in Prague gave its employee Vasyl Kachurovsky a paid leave of absence so that he could also work for the Representation of Carpatho-Ukraine in Prague in the capacity of consultant in financial-economic matters. Our tasks connected with the reorganization of our finances were quite complex for, as already mentioned, we were attached to many Czech, Slovak, and Hungarian banks and had to take them over and found our own bank that would suit our state needs.

Czecho-Slovakia had inherited from Austria a well-organized savings bank system run by the state post office. This post office-savings bank was to become the only state finance institution in Czecho-Slovakia. Through it, the Czech Ministry of Finances apportioned its budget funds. The post office-savings bank had its branches in Brno and Bratislava, but none in Carpatho-Ukraine. Hence, we could not make it independent of its Prague central office during the period of the federated republic as the Slovaks had done. What we needed was to create a monetary establishment which could manage state budget funds. To this end, it was necessary to found a regional bank, i.e., a bank covered by a guarantee of the state through which state loans could be issued.

To study this problem, the Prague Representation directed Vasyl Kachurovsky to the central postal Savings Bank in Prague. Kachurovsky researched there for two weeks and subsequently spent some time at the legal department of the Zemská Banka in Prague to study our monetary problem. At both places he found understanding, willingness, and good will on the part of the officials to help with advice on administrative and legal matters toward the establishment of our separate Zemská Banka. It may be noted here that the Zemská Banka in Prague had opened its branch in Uzhhorod in 1937, but was forced to evacuate to Bratislava at the beginning of November 1938 in the wake of the Vienna Arbitration.

Our newly founded Zemská Banka was also to take over all four branches of the Městká Spořitelna in Carpatho-Ukraine or rather to supervise the liquidation of their assets in the cities of Uzhhorod, Mukachevo, and Berehovo which were ceded to Hungary. By their structure, these financial institutions in our land fell into the category of institutions covered by guarantee of the Carpatho-Ukrainian federated state. In order to take over all other branches of Czech, Slovak, and Hungarian banks, it was necessary to set up a different financial institution of ours and to regulate this problem through a separate law.

During the First Republic, the devlopment of our banking system, represented by Podkarpatský Bank in Uzhhorod, fell initially under the influence of Czech capital, namely of the Banka Československých Legií (Bank of Czecho-Slovak Legions) in Prague. It thus came to pass, that by 1938 Czech capital played a dominant role in Carpatho-Ukraine's banking system, with Slovak and Hungarian capital playing a lesser role. Because of the chronic lack of hard cash, the system of commercial banks had to operate on a short-term credit basis with an extremely high interest rate (12–14%) and could not exert a positive influence upon the economic development of the land. Conversely, the situation with the Zemská Banka in Bratislava, at which I was also employed, was different. It had at its disposal a great deal of capital and issued long-term loans, communal loans, melioration loans, and the like at low interest rates (5–7%).

The Czecho-Slovak National Bank had branches in Uzhhorod and Mukachevo. It regulated and controlled the state's currency. There were several Carpatho-Ukrainians employed at the bank, who had a good banking experience and whose services we now wished to enlist. Two of them, A. Geletka and V. Bora, were allowed to leave in order to join the staff of the Representation as consultants.

The decision of the Vienna Arbitration wreaked considerable chaos also in the banking system of Carpatho-Ukraine in particular and in the financial operations in general. For this reason, to set up a viable system of banks required immediate and prompt action. During the period of the federation, the Czechoslovenská Národní Banka (Czecho-Slovak National Bank) established its branch in Khust. The intentions of the Zemská Banka, evacuated from Uzhhorod to Bratislava in which were deposited Carpatho-Ukraine's regional funds, were not known to us. At the behest of the Ministry of Economics in Khust, I was called upon to enter into negotiations with the management of the Zemská Banka in Prague concerning its former branch in Uzhhorod. In my new capacity as representative of the Carpatho-Ukrainian government, the management of my bank showed me a sympathetic attitude towards our needs. At a joint meeting, I proposed the following notions for review and opinions:

1. That the bank management supply the Representation with a list of deposits and loans of its Uzhhorod branch.

2. Whether it plans to continue its banking operations in Carpatho-Ukraine from its seat in Bratislava or whether it intends to open a branch in Khust.

3. How large is the deposit which the Zemská Banka received at the time of opening of its branch in Uzhhorod?

4. In the event it was planning to open a branch in Khust, whether it would be willing, and under what conditions, to transfer its banking operations to a similar financial institution of ours in Carpatho-Ukraine.

5. Whether the management is engaged in any negotiations with Hungary regarding capital investments and loans from the annexed territory.

The Zemská Banka in Prague sent me at the Representation's office the following abstract of deposits and loans from their Uzhhorod branch for November 30, 1938 (the sums are rounded up to the thousand). In deposits on bank books were 2,568,000 *koruny*. In deposits in current accounts received were 24,504,000, of which the Regional Fund of Carpatho-Ukraine amounted to 11,997,000.[6] Corporate and private loans totalled 33,731,000, of which sum 15,199,000 went to the annexed territory and 18,532,000 to the territory of Carpatho-Ukraine.

As is evident from the brief review, the Uzhhorod branch had at its disposal a rather considerable amount of capital, considering our conditions. What we were interested in was to have the bank or the Ministry of Finances in Prague free for us the twelve million *koruny* of the regional funds and to resolve at the earliest possible time the problem of the Zemská Banka's branch in Carpatho-Ukraine.

I sent a report of the negotiations, together with my remarks, to the Ministry of Economics in Khust for further action. On February 26, 1939, I received from the Ministry a directive to resume the negotiations with the management of the Zemská Banka which I did. Meanwhile, the management conducted negotiations with Hungary, but upon the suggestion of the Prague Ministry of Finances it decided to leave the matter of further negotiating to the Government of Carpatho-Ukraine. The reason for this change of heart is not known to me.

In the course of our continued talks, the Zemská Banka came around to concurring with the result of the negotiations the Carpatho-Ukrainian government had conducted with Hungary concerning the problem of finances on our territory annexed by the latter. It also agreed to help us organize our regional branch of the Zemská Banka. However, all came to naught when the development of events precipitated the collapse of the federated republic following Slovakia's declaration of independence. We fell victim to Hungarian military aggression, and the Slovaks took over the Zemská Banka branch in Bratislava, changing its name to Slovenská Hypotečná a Komunalná Banka (Slovak Mortgage and Communal Bank). I remained there as an employee. On its behalf, I conducted in 1940 negotiations with representatives of Hungary, Poland, and Germany to regulate the matter of property, bank accounts, court and orphan money as well as a number of other financial problems in connection with the cession of territories to Hungary, Poland, Germany, and the formation of the Protectorate of Bohemia and Moravia.

The negotiations were carried out at the Regional Court building in Bratislava.[7] All financial transactions, including the deposits at the Uzhhorod branch of Zemská Banka which was in the state of liquidation, were settled by the Slovak Mortgage and Communal Bank by way of a clearing procedure through Budapest-Berlin-Prague and Bratislava.

Relief Activities

Defeats in foreign policy of great empires, or even of small states, inevitably lead to the same result, namely to a forced exit from the political stage. Despite the various international formulas about the rights of nations, to which the world readily pays homage, life has taught us that right in politics goes only as far as its power reaches. This rule applies, above all, to the captive nations in their liberation struggle.

March 16, 1939 was my last day in office as a representative of the Carpatho-Ukrainian Government in Prague. Before noon of that day, I submitted a letter to the General Staff of the German Army concerning the release from the Czecho-Slovak Army of our soldiers and their transportation to Carpatho-Ukraine. I also called on the minister of Social Care, Vladislav Klumpar, and handed him a memorandum requesting that his Ministry assign 10 million *koruny* for the needs of our refugees. Klumpar replied that the possibility of allocating a considerable amount of money for the needs of our refugees existed as long as the Germans had not taken over the government, but in order that the money be actually transferred the signature of our minister was required.

Minister S. Klochurak was in Priashiv at the time. I immediately contacted him by telephone and informed him of my talk with Klumpar, urging him to come to Prague as soon as possible. However, Klochurak said that he could not now come to Prague inasmuch as he was in the process of winding up some urgent business. The next two days I called him three times. He finally did show up in Prague and both of us paid a visit to Klumpar. But as Klumpar informed us, he could no longer be of help to us since the Germans held all the reins of government in their hands.

On March 17, an emissary of the government of the Protectorate of Bohemia and Moravia—which had been created by Germany on March 15—appeared at the office of the Representation with a letter demanding that I turn over my official automobile to him. I informed my chauffer Josef Skála about his new assignment. When bidding me farewell, Skála emotionally remarked that for twenty years he had driven officials from various Czech ministries, but that "the time I spent with you at the Ukrainian government belongs to the best of my life." My official car was then assigned to Reich Protector Baron Constantin von Neurath.

On March 20, I received another visitor. This time it was a colonel of the Czecho-Slovak Army, Drgáč, who arrived with members of the police and two Germans dressed in civilian clothes and handed me a letter from the German Protectorate authorities demanding the transfer of the premises and archives of the Representation to him. While I officially relinquished the office, I categorically refused to hand over the archives to him. At this time there happened to be present in the office our students and citizens, who were able to help us move to our new location. Drgáč and the police forbade us to carry the archives out of the building and thus created a rather unpleasant and tense atmosphere. To avoid a possible outbreak of confrontation and clash, I suggested to Drgáč that we seal the archives, sign our names to them, and later open them jointly. He agreed and gave his word as an officer to abide by our joint decision. However, when I later returned to open the archives with him, I found to my dismay that the seal and signatures were tampered with. I drew his attention to this fact, causing him to blush and say that it was not he who had opened the materials. My archives were scrutinized, but I am sure that the Germans could not have found in them anything of interest to them.

The Representation moved to a three-room apartment at 14 Bartolomejská Street, where we officiated as the Relief Committee of the Representation since refugees from Carpatho-Ukraine were beginning to pour in. The refugees were largely people who had bad memories of the behavior of Hungarian gendarmes in Carpatho-Ukraine during World War I and were aware of what was waiting for them under Hungarian occupation. Among them were some sick persons, children, and elderly people who needed our help. Moreover, some of them met with accidents while in Prague. Thus, for instance, a certain School Inspector Polyansky was hit by a car while crossing a street and had to be taken to a hospital. X-rays, treatment, and other care had to be paid for, but no funds were available.[8]

Every day required some new relief action. I received the following telegram from Snina, Priashiv district:

> Five hundred Sich members have emigrated to Slovakia. They are at Kamenica nad Cirokou camp. Most are male and female students of the Commerce Academy. There are sick and wounded among them. Intercede immediately with the German Embassy not to return us back. Immediate help is needed. Commandmant of the district— Captain Klymenko.

The Hungarians had demanded the extradition of our refugees and therefore prompt action was of utmost urgency. I did not deem it necessary to appeal to the Germans, for the Slovak state was its own master and it was there, in Bratislava, where I was able to resolve over the phone the problem quickly and successfully. I turned to my army friends, Minister Matúš Černák and Dr. J. Terlanda. In a telephone conversation with them, I laid out the whole problem and the potential danger of the refugees being extradited to Hungary and asked them to do everything in their power to help. Both responded favorably and agreed to extend the needed aid which they did. I transmitted one thousand *koruny* for the refugees.

More and more refugees began to pour in. We registered them, wrote down reports on their escape, and helped wherever we could. I applied for aid to the Young Men's and Young Women's Christian Associations (YMCA and YWCA), and the Salvation Army, all of whom showed understanding and proceeded to help out. I provided free board and lodging for the initial wave of refugees. However, when the influx of people became too high—there were over 650 registered—it became necessary to pay for their support. Initial help came from the Czech Red Cross, but since the latter had already been taken over by the Germans, the Czechs advised me to turn to the Germans—which I did.

In Prague, the German Red Cross set up kitchen stands in the streets from which they doled out food and, while doing so, ironically played the tune "Why Shouldn't We Rejoice," an aria from Smetana's opera *The Bartered Bride*. The Germans recorded the entire action on film, obviously for propaganda reasons. They promised me, too, to provide food supplies. Our people were to report to a place near the Veletržní Palác, located at quite a distance from the center of the city. When I inquired about the address of the building where our people were supposed to report, one German retorted that the Red Cross was not a hotel and people would be consuming their food in the street. On hearing such a remark, I replied that I would not allow our people to eat in the street and be exposed to ridicule. I sardonically thanked him for his kindness and willingness to help. "Does it mean that you are turning down what I am giving you?" he asked, raising his voice. "No, I cannot accept your offer in the form you are presenting it," was my unruffled reply. "I can have you arrested, you know," threatened the German. "Yes, I know that you are in the position to do so, but you cannot make my people eat in the street." With that we terminated our conversation.

The League of Ukrainian Women in Prague operated its own eating establishment, to which I was able to send some of our people for food. The meals were given on credit, for which I signed a promisory note in the amount of 1,800 *koruny* made payable to Mrs. Zinaida Mirna, head of the League. However, when our credit was exhausted, she informed me that no further meals could be given out without payment. I fully understood her, for I was cognizant of the fact that the League women themselves were not in the position to extend credit beyond their means, particularly in view of our hopeless situation. I was then compelled to turn to my Czech friend Dr. Rudolf Sokol, who helped me a great deal when dealing with Czech quarters during the Representation's operations. He understood my predicament and within a matter of two hours handed me 17,500 *koruny* that saved the situation.

At the end of April, one of our professors in Prague received a gift of $2,000 from Ukrainian organizations in the United States for the Relief Committee. We were able to pay off all of our debts. The 5,000 *koruny* I had borrowed I returned privately and, when I was leaving for Bratislava in June 1939, I officially and in writing handed over our ledgers to Stepan Klochurak, who had been nominated a minister of Carpatho-Ukraine, together with a bank book in the amount of 36,800 *koruny*. As Klochurak later apprised me, he had changed the Relief Committee into the Liquidation Commission of the Government of Carpatho-Ukraine in Prague. Although at times we had to struggle hard to overcome very difficult and even unpleasant situations, in the final analysis we in the Relief Committee were exceedingly pleased to hear expressions of gratitude and recognition from our citizens who benefited from our aid.

Notes

[1] The same day, an inter-ministries conference was convoked in Prague concerning the matter of publishing all laws and directives pertaining to Carpatho-Ukraine in the Ukrainian language to be incorporated into the official *Sbírka zákonů a nařízení* (hereafter, *Sb. zák. a n.*) of the Federal Republic. Participating in the conference were two representatives from each ministry and from the legislative department of the Presidium of the Ministerial Council, altogether 20 persons. The meeting was chaired by Minister Dr. Jiří Havelka, who in his opening address immediately assumed a negative stance toward the subject matter. However, after a heated discussion that lasted almost four hours, most of the participants leaned toward the argument presented by me and passed a corresponding resolution. By this decision, all previous statutes concerning publication in the official law digest were necessarily amended and, therefore, also required the approval of the Central Government, which was obtained on December 30, 1939 [*Sb. zák. a n.* No. 392.] For a detailed report on the conference, see articles by V. Shandor in the newspaper *Narodna volya* 17 and 24 March 1977 and April 14, 1977.

The Central Government's first decree was published in the official law digest on January 10, 1939, the last on March 2, 1939. In the course of two months, 59 decrees and other official documents appeared in the Ukrainian language, some of them extending to several pages in number. This was the result of the assiduous efforts performed by the Representation Office in which the translations were being done. The work proceeded very smoothly, there was no recall or complaint from either side. The translations were executed by Dr. Osyp Matkovsky, a jurist.

[2] Chmelář, Josef, et al. eds., *Podkarpatská Rus, Obraz poměrů přírodních, hospodářských, politických, církevních, jazykových a osvětových* (Prague, 1923), pp. 67–68.

[3] *Karpato-Ukrajinská Svoboda* (Prague) 20 January 1939 (3).

[4] To take one example, Jiří Weyr offered to arrange for me, at his own expense, a diplomatic reception for members of the Carpatho-Ukrainian government to be held at his castle in Kosmonosy near Prague sometime in May 1939. Our government was given a free hand to invite, at its discretion, one hundred persons from the diplomatic and international communities to the reception, while Weyr himself would invite certain guests from among the Czecho-Slovak political, economic, and financial circles. We immediately set out to draw up a program for the event, including a list of guests and artistic performers from among Czechs and Ukrainians.

[5] For the sake of illustration and comparison, I would like to refer to statistical data on the quantity of timber cut in Carpatho-Ukraine and Slovakia in 1937 and 1938 and their respective prices:

1937

Carpatho-Ukraine	86,243,000 cubic meters	25,847,000 *koruny*
Slovakia	95,039,000 cubic meters	30,044,000 *koruny*

1938

Carpatho-Ukraine	133,811,000 cubic meters	31,583,000 *koruny*
Slovakia	154,557,000 cubic meters	41,862,000 *koruny*

[6] Emissive loans were granted on the basis of long-term debtor notes, especially to institutions.

[7] Germany's representative began to raise excessive pretentious and unfounded demands and, when I inveighed against them, he banged his fist on the table—presumably with the intention of intimidating us. I calmly replied that a fist in international negotiations was not a proper argument. His face turned red, but he did not utter a word in response.

[8] My private savings in the amount of some 35 thousand *koruny* had been exhausted with paying the salaries of the employees and for expenses incurred by the Representation since the funds promised by the government in Khust had never arrived in Prague. Khust continued to indulge in its isolationist mode of thinking to the very end, and in this lay a certain degree of its administration's weakness. In order to attend to the needs of the relief action, I had to borrow privately five thousand *koruny* from my friend V. Bora. The money, however, was only enough to defray the initial expenses.

CHAPTER FIVE

Crisis in Carpatho-Ukraine

Appointment of Gen. Lev Prchala as minister in Khust

According to Czecho-Slovakia's Constitutional Law No. 328 of 1938, Carpatho-Ukraine was entitled to have three ministerial posts in its government. After Dr. Emil Hácha's election as president of Czecho-Slovakia on November 30, 1938, one of the ministers, namely Dr. Edmund Bachynsky, was not reappointed minister in the Carpatho-Ukrainian Government, thus leaving the latter with only two ministers. From November 30, 1938 until January 17, 1939 (when Gen. Lev Prchala was appointed minister), there were several Ukrainian candidates under consideration for the post. The Government's first choice was Stepan Klochurak. However, when some people in Khust opposed Klochurak's candidacy for party or personal reasons, the Government then proposed the following three candidates: Klochurak, Avhustyn Shtefan, and P. Kalyniuk. The Prague Government was to select one of the three, but the move was blocked by a delegation from Khust consisting of Fedir Revay, head of the Ukrainian National Union (UNO), Andriy Voron, general secretary, and Dr. Stepan Rosokha, member of the Carpathian Sich Supreme Command who submitted their own candidacy to Prague.

The appearance in Prague of this delegation cannot be viewed as useful or contributing to the building of a state. The delegation showed up at the Office of the Representation, but went about making its own arbitrary arrangements without consulting the representative of the Government on any matter. It convoked a political meeting of the Ukrainian community in Prague without first notifying the police authorities, thereby compelling the police headquarters to ban the meeting at the last minute. Later on, officials of the Ministry of Internal

Affairs justified their action by pointing out that the banning of the meeting was necessary in view of the general conduct of the delegation's members. All three members were known in Khust for their avid anti-Czech statements. While in Prague, Fedir Revay introduced himself everywhere as "Vůdce" Revay, from the Czech word for "Leader." Rosokha, for his part, appeared in his Sich uniform at various government offices bearing a dagger with a swastika dangling from his belt. One can only imagine what the Czechs may have thought and how they interpreted such incongruous manners. Moreover, he also showed up at his erstwhile student dormitory which evoked great indignation among Czech students. Obviously, such conduct could not have helped but to cast a shadow upon our land and people.[1]

In our relations with the Czechs, we had to realize that the capitulation of Prague to Berlin regarding the Sudetenland considerably exacerbated their anti-Hitler sentiments, and they came to view any symbol of German hegemony as an act aimed against them and hostile toward their state interests. From the point of view of our interests, the appearance of this delegation in Prague was absolutely unnecessary.

The amicable relations of Carpathian Ukrainians with Czechs suffered a corrosive blow by the above-mentioned appointment on January 17, 1939 of Gen. Lev Prchala as minister in Carpatho-Ukraine's government. This was a fateful error on the part of the Czechs, who could not understand that they were no longer masters in Carpatho-Ukraine. At the time of his appointment, Gen. L. Prchala was army commander in Bratislava.

Gen. Prchala was known for his sympathies for the anti-government Hlinka Slovak National Party and its Guard, groups founded by Rev. Andrei Hlinka and later led by Msgr. Jozef Tiso. Consequently, the Central Government considered it imperative that he be removed from Slovakia altogether and without delay.[2] This was a gross political mistake on the Czech Government, which was settling its own political accounts at our expense and failed to take Carpatho-Ukraine's interests into consideration. Gen. Prchala was an opponent of Beneš and an unequivocal sympathizer of Poland, which conducted subversive activities against Carpatho-Ukraine with all possible means at its disposal.[3]

Only Msgr. Voloshyn (without Minister Revay) attended the meeting of the Ministerial Council in Prague on January 17, 1939. After the meeting, Msgr. Voloshyn stopped by at our Representation office and said to me: "We have a third minister!" In reply to my question as to who it was, he answered, "Try and guess!" I began to enumerate a number of possible Ukrainian candidates, but did not guess. Whereupon, Msgr. Voloshyn noted: "General Prchala." I immediately countered with a question, "And you agreed?" "The Czechs pounced upon me, so what was I to do?" was his answer. I voiced the opinion that this would not augur well for us since Gen. Prchala did not have political trust in our society. If, I continued, the Czechs wanted to appoint a Czech for whatever reasons, then they should have selected, for instance, Gen. Oleh Svátek or Jaromír Nečas against whom there would be no such objections as against Prchala. We both set out to analyze the problem. The end result of our talk was that we dispatched a telegram from my office to Gen. Lev Prchala, signed by Msgr. Voloshyn as prime minister, expressing the hope that he would renounce his appointment as minister in the Carpatho-Ukrainian Government in view of the constitutional law and anticipated unfavorable reaction on the part of our citizenry. The Czech capital's press viewed the appointment positively and received it with great satisfaction. *Lidové Noviny,* for instance, remarked that by appointing Gen. Prchala it wanted to express appreciation to the Army for the great help it had given Carpatho-Ukraine during the evacuation of the areas ceded to Hungary by the Vienna Arbitration. Indeed, we recognized with gratitude the aid extended to us by the Army, but we did not believe that such aid warranted the right to circumvent the Constitutional Law concerning the personnel composition of government. The appointment of Gen. Prchala as minister touched a very sensitive psychological chord in Carpatho-Ukraine that resounded loudly throughout our land.[4]

When later on I was to ask Prof. Kapras, minister of education, about the actual circumstances that led to the appointment of Gen. Prchala as minister, he replied that Msgr. Prime Minister Voloshyn gave his consent to it. But I pointed out that Msgr. Voloshyn had opposed and even voiced a protest against the appointment. Kapras agreed that Msgr. Voloshyn had opposed the appointment, but noted that in the end he concurred. Subsequently, certain circles in Khust demanded that Msgr. Voloshyn tender his resignation which he, however, declined.

Only the official government archives in Prague can tell what actually transpired. In a conversation with Revay years later in New York, the latter confirmed the story that Msgr. Voloshyn had concurred in the naming of Gen. Prchala as minister. I then asked him. "The Czech Government must have certainly also asked you about Prchala, so I would be interested in knowing what your attitude was." Revay replied with a smile, "I dispatched a protest." However, he did not say to whom.

On January 21, Prime Minister Msgr. Voloshyn and Minister Revay privately received Gen. Prchala—not as minister but as a general—and, according to press accounts, carried on an hour-and-a-half talk with him on problems faced by Carpatho-Ukraine. Meanwhile, a wave of protests against Gen. Prchala and his appointment swept Carpatho-Ukraine. The government found itself in a precarious situation, for although, on the one hand, it had the Constitutional Law on its side, on the other hand it was financially dependent on Czech credits which, in keeping with the very same Constitutional Law, the Czechs were not obliged to extend to us. The protest rallies soon turned into generally anti-Czech demonstrations throughout the land, frequently exploited by political demagogy—and that even at the expense of our government. It seems strange to us and even beyond comprehension why such protest rallies were not as exasperating and truculent and with so much bile directed against so dangerous an enemy of our statehood and nation as was Hungary but rather against Prague and the Czechs in general. An outside observer could not fail to note that there were active and behind-the-scenes forces of a third foreign power involved in these public rallies. For instance, two agents of Poland and one agent of Hungary were captured in the Staff of the Carpathian Sich. Minister Stepan Klochurak, asked to advise in this connection, recommended that they be court-martialed. The German Consul in Khust, Hamilkar Hofmann, stated that "the prisoners are under protection of the German goverment," took them out by car and handed them over to the Hungarians.

As for the Government of Carpatho-Ukraine, it committed the mistake of not having from the outset explained the true state of affairs as well as our situation and appealed to the population to exercise restraint, thereby making it possible for the tirade against Prchala to be turned into a campaign with a strongly anti-Czech content. In the further course of developments, our Government came to terms with reality, participated in talks with Gen. Prchala in Prague and Khust, jointly discussed and resolved certain problems, and jointly affixed their signatures to laws and decrees so that all those strident protest rallies, even those that took on massive forms, did not change the essence of the matter. As in other countries, so also in Carpatho-Ukraine there were foreign agents, who craftily exploited every manifestation of discontent in order to create confusion. The times in which we then lived required of us to be cautious in our national protests and utterances at rallies. But while *raison d'état* dictated caution to us, we did not always seem to follow it. We veered away from the principle that state affairs are resolved in government bureaus and not at rallies. Granted, we had the right and reason to protest, but not in harsh, impetuous forms and with such results that were undermining the integrity of the federation.

Sometime in the first half of February 1939, I received a telephone call at my office in the Representation from an adjutant of Gen. Prchala who wanted to borrow my official car for the General. I readily agreed, and for the next three days my chauffeur Josef Skála drove Gen. Prchala around. It was from Skála that I had learned that his usual passengers were two Poles, one by the name of Sławiński, who had just arrived from Poland for some secret meetings. Other passengers were Gen. Jiří Syrový, Gen. Prchala, Dr. Jiří Havelka and Polish Ambassador Kazimierz Papée. Skála further disclosed that he had driven his passengers to the Central Government's Prime Minister Rudolf Beran. He also overheard a talk in the car about a political and military alliance to be concluded between Czecho-Slovakia and Poland and about Carpatho-Ukraine being ceded to Poland. Moreover, the Czechs were to transfer their weapons arsenal to Poland. Such an alliance was to strengthen the defense capability of Czecho-Slovakia and Poland in the event of a military clash with Germany.

Skála's information seemed strange and improbable. It was difficult to accept the notion that somebody in the Czech ruling circles would have contemplated relinquishing Carpatho-Ukraine and forging an anti-German alliance at this juncture. After eliciting details from Skála, I was satisfied that they bore out his stories. Just to be doubly certain, I called on Dr. Fiala, chief of the Police Presidium, who confirmed that the two Poles mentioned by Skála, Sławiński and Stepniewski, had been here on some secret mission, but that his office knew nothing more about it. I also turned to Jiří Weyr, who asked his friend Dr. Josef

Kliment, secretary of President Hácha, to divulge whatever else he knew about the incident that would be of interest to me. Kliment promptly informed Prime Minister Beran who was quite dismayed at learning that the information about the negotiations with the Poles had somehow leaked out and landed in the hands of unauthorized persons. This was the reason Beran decided to remove me from the Representation Office, and did so when he appointed S. Klochurak minister.[5] Having heard nothing more about the matter, I informed members of our government about the incident, which, however, was soon forgotten.

In 1971, the president of Czechoslovakia, Gen. Ludvík Svoboda published a book in which he related the incident thus:

> Ministers Kliment, Havelka, and Prime Minister Beran himself sought understanding with Poland. Their plan called for ceding Subcarpathian Ruthenia to Poland and forging a federation with Poland. In conformity with such intentions, it was then that Gen. Prchala was sent to Subcarpathian Ruthenia.

Gen. Svoboda elaborated further, "the Polish government seized this agrarian [Agrarian Party—V. Sh] initiative and sent its secret envoys, Stepniewski and Sławiński, to Prague who negotiated with government officials and prepared a written statement on the negotiations." Participating on the Czech side in the negotiations were six generals, led by Prime Minister Syrový. In part, the memorandum states that "in view of the impending war, only an immediate joining of Polish and Czecho-Slovak forces and with the help of the Czech army, its rich resources, and the strategic situation of the Moravia-Slovak area can Poland survive." This whole affair, however, fell through, for Poland's President Ignacy Moscicki declined all attempts of the Western powers to draw Poland into an anti-German front.[6]

As a result of the territorial truncation of Czecho-Slovakia in 1938, Carpatho-Ukraine lost its original strategic importance as a bridge between Czecho-Slovakia and the republic's Little Entente allies Romania and Yugoslavia. To preserve the Czecho-Slovak Federation, albeit now truncated and weakened, was the Czechs' last hope to save the country's statehood. They were alarmed by the intensified anti-Czech and anti-state demonstrations and slogans manifested at massive protest rallies in Carpatho-Ukraine, viewing them as aimed at disintegrating the federation from within.

At this very same time, a similar peril to the federation's unity was emanating especially from radical Slovak politicians who had made a commitment to Hitler that they would strive toward the proclamation of a fully independent Slovakia. A group of Czech members of the Government in Prague believed and subsequently decided that, in order to save the unity of the federation for the Czechs and Slovaks, they would cede Carpatho-Ukraine to Poland. Some members of the Slovak Government also embraced this concept, notable among them was Karol Sidor, who was in a way a proponent of Polish interests in Prague.

We do not know when and who conceived the idea of a Czecho-Slovak-Polish alliance. Until the end of 1938, Germany did not favor the policy of a common Hungarian-Polish border, a fact that disturbed both Poland and Hungary. Poland viewed such an alliance as an opportunity to liquidate Carpatho-Ukraine in conjunction with Czecho-Slovakia, but in its own way. It attached great significance to this. Conversely, by emphasizing Poland's goals, Czecho-Slovakia hoped to influence Slovak politicians to put a stop to the movement advocating the declaration of full independence for Slovakia. Thus, the preservation of the unity of the Czecho-Slovak federation was to be attained at the expense of Carpatho-Ukraine, namely by its liquidation. It now becomes clear why Sidor, who was favorably disposed toward the idea of an alliance, declined Germany's proposal that he proclaim Slovakia's independence. Instead, Sidor officially accepted President Hácha's offer appointing him prime minister of Slovakia at 10 p. m. on March 11, 1938.[7]

Thus, when on March 12 the news spread throughout Slovakia that Hitler was planning to take Bratislava by military force, Sidor then "was cooperating with Generals Vojta Hugo and Zák on military countermeasures."[8]

The Slovak radio broadcasting station in Vienna under Foreign Minister Dr. Ferdinand Ďurčanský's direction unflinchingly espoused the idea of declaring a full independence for Slovakia. As may be deduced from the above, Sidor was of a different opinion, for which the radio branded him "traitor."[9]

The German State Secretary, Wilhelm G. Keppler, who conducted the negotiations with the Slovaks and Sidor concerning the matter of proclaiming Slovak independence, reported to Hitler on the course of the talks, saying that "Sidor is Prague's soldier." Given the realities of those days, the intention to form an alliance between Poland and

Czecho-Slovakia was quite a courageous step. In my opinion, Carpatho-Ukraine, and along with it the overall Ukrainian issue at that time, played a decisive role in Hitler's political plans. Hitler was trying to decide whether he should deliver his first blow at the East or at the West. I believe that given the contemporary constellation of political forces in Europe, the matter of alliance had no realistic prospects of materializing, inasmuch as Germany would never have allowed it.

Hitler kept postponing the settlement of the problem of a common Polish-Hungarian border and by so doing led Hungary to understand that it could obtain Carpatho-Ukraine only by the grace of his will. Such a policy caused Poland quite some concern that in turn affected Polish-Hungarian relations. Poland came around to viewing this tactical move of Hitler's as a danger to itself and, as a result, embraced the notion that it would take upon itself unilaterally settling the thorny problem of Carpatho-Ukraine. Poland accused Hungary of indecisiveness, saying that it was becoming a tool of Germany's policy, and that Poland could not expect to benefit from it.

In January 1939, a certain Prof. Grabski held a lecture on the theme of "The Issue of a Common Polish-Hungarian Border," in which he argued that Hungary would do nothing in this matter against the will of Germany and concluded by saying that, "should the need arise, Poland would liquidate Subcarpathian Ruthenia as a hotbed of activities imperiling the unity of Poland. The only dignified resolution of this problem, worthy of a great state, would be to openly and boldly annex Subcarpathian Ruthenia to Poland."[10]

At the time when the Pole Sławiński and his associates were in Prague, Minister Sidor was visiting Warsaw. This coincidence allows one to make the deduction that Sidor's talks in Warsaw were conducted on the same problem as those in Prague. As a sympathizer of Poland, Sidor was not to entertain a benevolent attitude toward Carpatho-Ukraine. A federation of Slovakia with Poland was more in consonance with his political concept than one with the Czechs. Already as a diplomatic representative of Slovakia at the Vatican during World War II, Sidor engaged in spreading the idea among leading Slovak politicians that after the war Slovakia ought to belong to a federative Polish-Slovak state system.[11]

In January 1939, the emissaries of Hitler and Stalin were already engulfed in talks of detente along economic and political lines and, as a result, the problem of Carpatho-Ukraine and the related problem of a common Polish-Hungarian border were no longer of compelling interest to Hitler. By ceding Carpatho-Ukraine to Hungary, Hitler satisfied both Stalin and Poland, relieving both of them of the dangerous specter of the Ukrainian problem.

Enemy Operations in Carpatho-Ukraine

The Munich and Vienna dictates to Hitler were no more than a respite in his policy aimed at completely destroying Czecho-Slovakia. At the secret meeting convened at the artillery school of Juterborg on May 30, 1938, Hitler told his generals: "It is my unalterable will to smash (*zerschlagen*) Czecho-Slovakia by military action in the near future." He issued a general order fixing October 1, 1938 as the deadline for putting "Operation Green" into effect.[12]

In order to avoid the need of interfering militarily, Hitler saw it "morally" more effective to disintegrate Czecho-Slovakia from within and then to occupy it. With this in mind, in January 1939 he summoned Reinhard Heydrich, deputy chief of the Gestapo, and his leading agents to a highly secretive meeting at which he commissioned them to carry out whatever subversive activity was necessary within Czecho-Slovakia, which they lost no time in executing by starting with Slovakia and Carpatho-Ukraine. The date for the liquidation of Czecho-Slovakia was set for mid-March. By now Slovakia already had Hitler's promise that, in the event it proclaimed its full independence, he would take it under his aegis. Carpatho-Ukraine never received such a commitment from Hitler and, therefore, the matter of breaking up Czecho-Slovakia was to have quite different consequences for the Slovaks than for the Ukrainians.

To any rational political observer at that time it became clear that without guarantees and support from some great power neither Slovakia nor Carpatho-Ukraine could survive as fully independent states. Those Ukrainian circles, including the Organization of Ukrainian Nationalists, that frequently stressed the need to declare full independence, should have been cognizant of this factual state of affairs.[13]

The problem of Carpatho-Ukraine figured in Germany's economic-expansionist designs and was closely linked to the overall Ukrainian political problem and therefore its solution was to determine in which direction Hitler would deliver his first assault—against the East or the West. Hitler preferred to go along with Poland against the Soviet Union, but Poland declined his proposal. At the beginning of 1939, he finally decided to go to war against Poland, but for this he needed an agreement with Stalin so that he could turn against the West, a move that fully suited Soviet interests. One of the preconditions of an agreement between the partners was that Hitler jettison the idea of an independent Ukraine and liquidate Carpatho-Ukraine, which would have also meant the liquidation of the Czecho-Slovak state. Hitler was convinced that this *modus operandi* would furnish him unassailable moral arguments absolving Germany of any responsibility for Czecho-Slovakia's disintegration and placing responsiblity on its own peoples, thereby implying they themselves brought about its collapse.

Stepan Klochurak, in a letter dated June 22, 1971 to me, said that such an attempt was contemplated also within the Government of Carpatho-Ukraine. He stated that after his return from a visit to Berlin, Minister Revay relayed the piece of information that "should we declare Carpatho-Ukraine's independence and detach ourselves from Czecho-Slovakia, the German Government would then immediately grant Carpatho-Ukraine a loan in the amount of 10 million German marks. And in order to attract German capital investments, the Government of Carpatho-Ukraine would sell "Latorytsia," (i.e. Count Schoenborn Buchheim's entire estate) to Hermann Göring. Should we undertake this, Germany would be prepared to support Carpatho-Ukraine."[14] "Latorytsia" was a firm with a brewery, large forests, and a wood alcohol distillery in Svaliava, Carpatho-Ukraine, which was owned by Germans but could not be sold without the consent of the Carpatho-Ukrainian goverment.

Klochurak further revealed that, Msgr. Voloshyn, as chairman, and all those present at this meeting unanimously opposed the proposal, protested against it, and asked Msgr. Prime Minister Voloshyn to delete the issue from the agenda. The Prime Minister fulfilled the request, and the matter was dropped from the discussions. Revay did not state with whom he had discussed the matter in Berlin. But in the light of sources now known to us, such a guarantee given Revay could not have emanated from policy-making echelons of the German Government, for by then the fate of Carpatho-Ukraine had already been determined in favor of Hungary, which also was in the interests of the Soviet Union.

However, the government of Carpatho-Ukraine continued to profess its adherence to the federative principles of our Czecho-Slovak statehood, for this was the only viable political solution at the time.

Meanwhile, the process of liquidating the federated Czecho-Slovak republic from within took on some concrete forms also in Carpatho-Ukraine. A group of youthful, albeit meritorious men in the Supreme Command of the Sich, without experience in matters of state, had fallen under the influence of forces inimical to us, and, in their gullibility and naiveté, were preparing to conspire against their own Government. The conspiracy had no support among the population and would have ended in a fiasco. An account of this incident is presented here in an abridged form as it was conveyed to this author by members of the Government and persons close to it.

Concerning the conspiracy against the Government, Dr. Volodymyr Komarynsky provided the following information in writing, asserting that he could attest to it under oath:

> In February 1939, Antonín Doležal, a lieutenant colonel in the infantry, came to my office and told me that he had something very interesting to show me. I recall that he was commander of the SOS and that his attitude toward the Ukrainian Transcarpathia was always sympathetic. He opened his attaché, from which he drew out a used carbon paper sheet. I read the text on it by holding it against the window glass and the mirror. It was typed on a Ukrainian typewriter, and the hand-written signatures were also in Ukrainian. Since the text was brief, I was able to read it several times and, therefore, the impression and the content of it was so unexpected that it etched in my memory. It read as follows: "After proper and thorough deliberations, it was decided to remove such persons: Prime Minister Msgr. Voloshyn, Minister Yu. Revay, Second Lt. Yurko Biley, Dr. V. Komarynsky, Second Lt. Stepan Vayda." I cannot recall with certainty all other names, but I do remember that I counted 17 names in all. That disgraceful document was signed by 7 persons. First among them was Evhen Voliansky, who was commander of the security department of the Supreme Command of the Carpathian Sich, whose real name was Evhen Vretsona and who recently passed away in Switzerland. Others were: Dr. Stepan Rosokha, Ivan Roman, and Msgr. Dr. Voloshyn's private secretary [Ivan Rohach—V. Sh.]. Two other signatures appeared on the document, one which belonged to a member of the Supreme Command who arrived here under the pseudonym Ivan Chorný. Doležal told me that one of his men had

found the carbon paper among other trash in a waste basket in room
no. 17 of the Sich Hotel (Koruna) in Khust.[15]

In the course of the discussion with Dr. Komarynsky, Doležal assured
the latter that he would keep an eye on further developments and,
should the need arise, he "would act." Dr. Komarynsky turned the
carbon paper over to the chief of police, Yurko Biley, who already
knew about the conspiracy.

Discussing this affair with Yulian Revay, I was told the following:

> It is true that a plot was being hatched against the Government. One
> night in February 1939, I think it was on the 17th or 18th at around
> 1:30 A.M., the Khust Police Chief, Yu. Biley, came to my house
> accompanied by Kleist Werner, an editor of the *Voelkischer
> Beobachter,* and had this to say to me: Kleist, as a German, had
> learned about the secret meeting of a group of members of the
> Supreme Command of the Carpathian Sich held at the Sich Hotel
> whose aim it was to prepare the overthrow of the Government, i.e., to
> arrest members of the Government and some 15 other leading per-
> sonalities, themselves take over the reins of government, and then
> declare full independence. A list of names of those who were to be
> removed was prepared. Kleist, as our friend, had notified Biley of this
> incident and for this reason came to me. Present at the meeting were
> some Galician members of the Supreme Command of the Sich as
> were our Rosokha, Roman, Rohach. [The three "Rs'," as Revay
> referred to them—V.Sh.] We immediately reinforced security guards
> around Msgr. Voloshyn, me, and the others. It was obvious that this
> was a German intelligence intrigue. The following day, Biley talked
> to the Galicians in the Supreme Command and threatened them with
> extradiction to Poland if they did not desist from such nonsensical
> behavior. Msgr. Voloshyn had a talk with Rosokha and Rochach—
> Roman was not present—in which he told them that by such an act
> they were breaking up the republic and abetting our enemies. Two
> days after this incident, Kleist was recalled from Khust.[16]

Germany's march toward a "New Europe" captivated the minds of
contemporary statesmen, political parties, and individual peoples who
considered themselves participants in the campaign. It was then quite
natural that a drive to participate in this campaign had not bypassed us
either, not least because at that time much had been written in the
German and world press about the Ukrainian problem in general and
Carpatho-Ukraine, in particular. However, some people, notably those
advocating full independence for Carpatho-Ukraine, however, went so
far as to adopt some outward German symbols, such as the raising of

the arm in salutation and other forms and methods of behavior, convinced that they themselves were also participants in the grand ideological movement for a "New Europe." Yet, in reality, they were only small pawns allowing themselves to be exploited in the name of the Ukrainian cause but not to the advantage of Ukrainian interests.

They did not realize that every subjugated or quasi-free people should build its existence on the roots of its own national, political, and historical traditions rather than appropriate as its own the forms and methods of ruling peoples, particularly dictatorial rulers, that would jeopardize any effort to organize its own force for statehood.

If these people were not able to use good judgment in understanding where the interest of Germany ended and where the interest of our statehood lay then they should have not been allowed to occupy leading positions or should have been removed from them in time. For us, this is a sad incident from which, however, the lesson may be learned that in filling influential posts, the government should be cautious in making the right selection of people. At the behest of the Government, First Lt. Stepan Vayda, chief of state security, investigated the plot. In accord with Yu. Revay's suggestion, the Government refrained from further inquiries into the matter in order to prevent it from leaking out to our ill-intentioned neighbors.

From published materials, it has become evident that Capt. Riko Yariy was instrumental in arousing such pro-German sentiments in Carpatho-Ukraine.[17] A researcher of the Ukrainian nationalist movement has the following to say about Riko Yariy: "Today the matter is clear. Riko Yariy was doing Germany's bidding. Germany was interested in a peaceful liquidation of Carpatho-Ukraine."[18]

Knysh's revelations regarding Riko Yariy's activities provide a key to understanding the multifarious German operations directed against the state interests of Carpatho-Ukraine. It may not be erroneous to say that Riko Yariy was the motivating force behind the plot, that he contrived needless tensions between us and the Czechs, and that he colluded with some commanders of the Carpathian Sich to foster his pro-German policy that was later to drive poorly armed Sich members to perish in battles against Czech heavy machine guns and tanks. He was in command of those foreign agents who were apprehended at the Supreme Command of the Sich, but there were others who were not caught. On the world scene many experienced statesmen and even

whole nations found themselves ensnared by Hitlerite Germany's political image. A wave of intrigues and subversions did not spare either
Carpatho-Ukraine or the Ukrainian cause.

Elections to the Soim

In the federated Czecho-Slovakia, it was necessary to carry out a
reform of the electoral system and political parties, particularly as
regards their programs and numbers. Each of the three federated states
was to hold its own elections independently.

In accordance with Chapter V of the Constitutional Act No. 328 of
November 22, 1938 of the *Sbírka zákonů a nařízení (Sb. zák. a n.)* the
elections to the first Soim of Carpatho-Ukraine were to be held within
five months from the day of the Act's publication. In conformity with
this constitutional-legal provision of the Act, the Ministry of Internal
Affairs in Khust issued a decree over Msgr. Voloshyn's signature
setting the date for the elections to the Soim for February 12, 1939.[19] At
the same time, the following decree, also signed by Msgr. Voloshyn as
prime minister and minister of internal affairs, was issued: "The Ministry of Internal Affairs, on the basis of Article 8.3, the ordinance of the
Czecho-Slovak Government of December 23, 1938 Act No. 355 of the
Sb. zák. a n. with the supplement ordinance of the Government of the
Czecho-Slovak Republic of January 13, 1939, No. 4 of the *Sb. zák. a n.,*
declares:

> The Government of Carpatho-Ukraine (Subcarpathian Ruthenia)—
> proceeding from its concern for public peace and order and from the
> fact that the activity of political parties existing in Carpatho-Ukraine
> (Subcarpathian Ruthenia), whose operations have been suspended,
> endangers public (state) security—has decided to dissolve all those
> political parties that had operated prior to the above-cited ordinance
> of the Czecho-Slovak Government. The consequences of the dissolu-
> tion of the political parties in keeping with Art. II of the cited law,
> went into effect immediately after the announcement of the law. The
> assets of the dissolved political parties, which were confiscated, will
> be liquidated and the remainder diverted to the state treasury.

In connection with the above, another ordinance of the Government
was promulgated, also over the same signature, stating that the "Government of Carpatho-Ukraine gave permission to form a political party
under the name of the Ukrainian National Union.[20]

I learned about the dissolution of political parties from the Czech press on the morning of the following day and immediately called up Minister Revay to state my opinion that this was a big mistake, for the dissolution of all political parties in the manner that it was executed would at the same time exclude all deputies and senators of Carpatho-Ukraine from both Chambers of the Prague Parliament. Astonished by such a denouement of the matter, Revay noted that it was not written in the order. "It isn't in the order," I answered him, "but that conclusion follows from the logic of the order itself, because non-existent political parties cannot have their representatives in the Parliament or the Senate. Thus, by this order they were excluded from the Prague Parliament and Senate, including you."

The following day, I received an order from my Government in Khust to try to rectify this deplorable oversight in Prague. I turned to my professor of constitutional law at the Charles University, Dr. Vladimir Vavřínek, with whom I thoroughly reviewed the possibilities of correcting the error. The Khust ordinance was so badly formulated that it precluded any possibility of interpreting it according to our wishes and needs. In the end, Prof. Vavřínek could do nothing more than say that correction was impossible.

I was reluctant to call on Dr. Havelka, President Hácha's right hand and secretary of the Supreme Administration Court which was to finally resolve this issue, because of his negative attitude toward us. However, I did send my Czech friends over to him who, too, were told that it was impossible to rectify the matter.

Nothing could be done to change the situation even when the Carpatho-Ukrainian Government issued a follow-up ordinance on February 6, 1939 in which it altered its previous decision regarding the dissolution of political parties by stating that it did not apply to the Agrarian, Social-Democratic, Christian National, and National Socialist Parties (the latter of which bore no similarity to "National Socialism" in Germany).[21] The Mandating Senate of the Supreme Administration Court of Czecho-Slovakia, at its meeting on February 7, decided that five deputies and three senators forfeited their mandates as a result of the Carpatho-Ukrainian Government's ordinance of January 16, 1939 concerning the dissolution of political parties. Dr. Zeiss, chairman of the Mandating Senate, argued that the decision was taken in view of the fact that the follow-up ordinance in the given case could not nullify the preceeding one and reactivate the political parties, for the ban applied to all political parties that existed actively on the territory of Carpatho-Ukraine at the time. As a result, Carpatho-Ukraine was no longer represented in the Chambers of the Prague Parliament.

The dissolution of the political parties also had as a consequence the condition that the aforementioned deputies and senators could not be elected to the House of Deputies or Senate for the next three years. In this connection, the Supreme Administration Court was also to concern itself with the problem of Revay's election to the Soim of Carpatho-Ukraine.

During the First Czecho-Slovak Republic, twenty or more political parties went to the polls in Carpatho-Ukraine, but under the new conditions this phenomenon was no longer justified by either political expedience or logic. For this reason, the Ukrainian National Council, its head Prime Minister Msgr. Voloshyn and Acting Head Minister Revay, organized on January 24, 1939 a new political representation—the Ukrainian National Union (UNO), with Fedir Revay as its president. The very same day the leadership of UNO decided that *Nova Svoboda* was henceforth to become the new organization's press organ.[22] In conformity with the Carpatho-Ukrainian Government's decree on elections, the Election Act opened the way also to other public organizations to participate in elections, provided they had met certain conditions required by law.

The elections to the Soim aroused general interest in the political world but displeasure and perhaps some fear in Hungary and Poland. It was generally assumed that the coming elections would be a kind of national plebiscite in which the people themselves would decide their own future and would make known their stand on the Hungarian-Polish aspirations for a common border. One deputy was to be elected for every 20 thousand inhabitants, 32 in all. The candidates were selected by the members of government and leadership UNO according to former political party membership, but non-party candidates also appeared on the list.

In perusing the names of candidates to the Soim, their territorial distribution, and their places of domicile given on the list, I have come to the conclusion that the UNO leadership, in selecting the candidates, was guided by party, personal, and even family considerations rather than by state expedience. Under the provisions of the Vienna Award, three of the most important cities with Ukrainian-inhabited vicinities (Uzhhorod, Mukachevo, and Berehovo) were detached from Carpatho-Ukraine. We continued to consider these territories as ours and, therefore, for national political and even international legal reasons it was indispensable to have elected deputies as representatives of these territories in the Soim of Carpatho-Ukraine. This, to our regret, however, did not come to be. UNO's leadership did not grasp the enormity and gravity of such a political claim.

Such neglect on our part could have been interpreted in the political world as our recognition of the cession of those territories which, obviously, was never the intention of the government. A spokesman for these territories in our Soim would have carried great political weight. Hungary apparently was more astute in this respect, for it lost no time in appointing Fentsyk, Brody, and others members of Parliament whence they were able to appear in the political arena and wage a struggle in favor of Hungary and against Carpatho-Ukraine and its government.

Representatives of the individual nationality groups in Carpatho-Ukraine, such as Czechs, Romanians, Jews, and Germans, had officially declared their loyalty to and support of the official slate of candidates in the elections. According to the Czech newspaper *Lidové Noviny* (8 February 1939), even a larger portion of Hungarians were expected to vote for the official slate.

The elections took place on February 12 and demonstrated a very impressive national and state consciousness. They were conducted in a most orderly fashion, which did not escape the attention of even the foreign press. It, indeed, turned out to be a plebiscite but not the kind Hungary would have expected. Of the 284,365 eligible voters, 243,557 cast their ballots for and 19,645 against the list of candidates. Thus, some 93% voted for the official slate.[23]

Lidové Noviny noted on February 14 that the elections had taken place in an orderly fashion and that they, at the same time, provided an answer to all pro-Hungarian slogans calling upon the Ukrainian people to change their present state citizenship. Moreover, it said, the elections demonstrated the faith the people had in their Ukrainian Government and the Czecho-Slovak Republic. *Nova Svoboda* of February 14, 1939 in Khust carried an editorial by Msgr. Voloshyn in which he remarked that after the elections, Carpatho-Ukraine would no longer be the object of international disputes. The German newspaper close to Marshal Göring, *Nationalzeitung* (Berlin) pointed out that there were signs of reconciliation between the Ukrainians and Czechs.

In the first half of February 1939, we already knew about the promises made by the Slovaks in Berlin to exert all effort to proclaim Slovakia's full independence. This meant the breaking up of the federation, placing Carpatho-Ukraine in a very distressing situation. It was, therefore, in the interests of our state, as in the interests of the entire federation to eliminate the antagonism between the Ukrainians and the Czechs. In order to achieve this goal, Msgr. Voloshyn, as minister of internal affairs, issued a decree against slandering of Czech officials in Carpatho-Ukraine and exhorted both sides to show goodwill and to act in concert and tolerance.[24]

The elections also proved to be an important turning point in the psychology of our population. They infused in our people the feeling of self-confidence, of their power and right, and the feeling of becoming master of their own land—a feeling that had been denied them for many centuries. This feeling was all the more striking since it had emerged within the very same Carpathian Ruthenian people for whom the feudal Hungarian system before World War I was preparing to sound the death knell as a national entity. Despite the hostile propaganda and subversive acts, this most consistent branch of our people demonstrated its stalwartness in forming its state and proclaiming itself to being an integral part of the Ukrainian nation.

Such a transformation within our people was possible because in the period between the two world wars it belonged to a democratic Czecho-Slovakia, where the people enjoyed the possibility of developing culturally and politically. Such a possibility had not existed for the Ruthenians-Ukrainians in Hungary for many centuries. Among those who had harbored suspicions as to the Ukrainian national and state character of Carpatho-Ukraine, the results of the elections ought to have allayed their fears and given them a clear answer.

In the strained foreign political situation, fostered by Hungarian and Polish propaganda, the elections acted as a soothing factor both within and without the country. The fact alone that during the elections there were some 20 foreign journalists on hand should provide proof enough for the great interest the elections had aroused in the political world.

Their presence was looked upon not only as a routine pursuit of their professional duties, but also as an indication of the interest the great powers had in obtaining important information on the strength of the Ukrainian national movement in the population, which strength enemies presented to the world in a distorted and false light.

It was the unanimous consensus of the foreign journalists that the elections were held in an exemplary order without any coercion or intimidation. Indeed, they were a kind of plebiscite through which the people themselves, mindful of their own sad experience in the past, gave a resounding rebuttal to Hungarian efforts to return the land to Hungary.

The press in the capital of Czecho-Slovakia welcomed the elections as a great success for the all-state unity. The fact that there was but only one single slate of candidates did not in any way obscure the *sui generis* democratic character of the elections, for the voter had the possibility of voicing his opposition to the list of candidates by casting his vote against it, as was the case in the village of Iza near Khust where only 390 votes were cast for and 1,109 against the slate.[25] And in Khust itself, 6,208 were registered in favor of the official list while 2,182 voted against it.[26]

The Carpatho-Ukrainian Government utilized the results of the elections in the international forum. Revay, in an interview granted to *Voelkischer Beobachter,* had the following to say:

> These elections mean much more than ordinary provincial elections do. Inimical propaganda has been working against us over a period of several months, alleging that the population would have nothing to do with Ukrainian self-government. As is known, the plebiscite idea had originated with another party. Today, this plebiscite had taken place and its outcome is most impressive.[27]

In Prague, Minister Revay announced to the Czech press that the Soim would convene within a month. The elections testified to the Ukrainian character of the land. Of the 380 villages, 196 hoisted white flags signifying that at least 93% of the electorate had voted for the official slate. In reference to financial matters, Minister Revay declared that our budget for 1939 showed we needed 310,488,909 *koruny,* while state revenues amounted only to 96,604,000 *koruny.* The Government was facing the problem filling the gap.[28] This sum did not include monies for investments.

During his visit to Berlin on January 16, 1939, the Hungarian Minister of Foreign Affairs, Count István Csáky, made every effort to forestall the implementation of elections in Carpatho-Ukraine. He was conscious of the fact that the people of this territory would declare their opposition to the Hungarian-Polish demands for a common border. Csáky even stated that the government of Hungary was prepared to secure for Germany a free transit through Carpatho-Ukraine to Romania (previously, Hungary declined such a German demand) and to give it a blank check in meeting all its desires regarding the Carpathian Germans.[29]

But Hitler continued to advise Hungary to be patient. As was later revealed in diplomatic papers, Hitler had by this time already altered his intention of attacking the Soviet Union. In his political speech delivered to the Reichstag on January 30, 1939, he no longer assailed Communism and the Soviet Union which signified a change in Germany's policy. Polish Ambassador to Germany, Józef Lipski, in his report dated January 23, described the change in Germany's policy thus: "The Chancellor allegedly denied rumors circulated by the foreign press about his alleged plans for the Greater Ukraine. A seeming result from what was said by the German side was that in the future the Ukrainian problem at any rate could not be solved without Poland's participation."[30]

On January 25–27, Ribbentrop paid an official visit to Warsaw. Hitler's present stance on the Ukrainian question fully satisfied Poland, but in its anti-Ukrainian stand it was not capable of perceiving the peril for it from Germany. On February 5, Soviet Commissar (Minister) of Foreign Affairs Maxim Litvinov informed the Czecho-Slovak ambassador in Moscow, Zdeněk Fierlinger, that the Soviet Union was establishing trade relations with Germany, Poland, and Italy.[31]

By now Hitler had decided to use the issue of Carpatho-Ukraine and the overall Ukrainian problem in general, which he previously held up to scare the Soviet Union and Poland, to institute friendly trade and political conditions with the Soviet Union. However, this was also a death sentence passed on Poland. Although Germany was not yet publicly showing any signs of misgivings or outright animosity toward the constitutional stabilization of political conditions in Carpatho-Ukraine, it was, however, engaged through its agents in fostering rebellion in the land and working toward the disintegration and breaking up of the federation. Before handing over Carpatho-Ukraine to Hungary, Germany, along with Hungary, obstructed the convoking of the Soim in order thus to preclude the constitutional formalization and consolidation of the election results.

Culmination of the Crisis

Long before the Munich *Diktat,* Hitler deemed it necessary to inform Great Britain of his political designs regarding Austria and Czecho-Slovakia. As early as August 3, 1938, in a conversation with British Ambassador Sir Neville Henderson in Berlin, Hitler declared, "In the event that unrest should erupt in Austria and Czechoslovakia, Germany would not be neutral but would intervene with the swiftness of lightning."[32]

In order to create for himself a "legal claim" for such a lightning-swift intervention, Hitler called Heydrich and other chief officials of the Secret Service to a conference at which he gave the following secret orders:

> The policy of Germany demands that the Czechoslovak Republic be broken up and destroyed within the next few months—if necessary by force of arms. To prepare and facilitate the moves against Czechoslovakia, it appears expedient to support and stimulate the endeavours of the Slovaks in their movement for autonomy. After that it will be quite easy for Germany to deal with the remaining Czech portion of the Republic.[33]

As well,

> Hitler set the middle of March as the date for the occupation of Czecho-Slovakia. The collapse of the Czecho-Slovak Republic was to be brought about by an open revolt of the Slovak government as well as by the Hungarian occupation of Carpatho-Ukraine. After brief hesitation, Hitler abandoned the plan of using it as a nucleus for a Greater Ukrainian state.[34]

The Hungarians, too, were to be apprised along the same lines. In the Danubian States, this was not realized until the beginning of January, when Józef Beck, the Polish Foreign Minister, saw Hitler in Berlin: "after this visit it was generally assumed that the Ukrainian question had been shelved [and a decision made] not to support the Ukrainian movement for an independent State."[35] This, then, is how the fate of

Carpatho-Ukraine and that of the whole Czecho-Slovak Republic was decided.

The question of Slovakia's independence was explicitly laid down on the table by Deputy Prime Minister Vojtech Tuka and Foreign Minister Ďurčanský when they visited Berlin on February 12, 1939 and pledged to get Slovakia to proclaim full independence and thereby effect the break-up of the republic.

Adressing Hitler as "Mein Führer," Tuka told him: "I lay the destiny of my people in your hands, my Führer: my people await their complete liberation by you." In reply, Hitler declared that if Slovakia declared its independence, he would immediately take over the guarantee for its borders.[36] I learned about this pledge of the Slovak ministers given in Berlin later while visiting Dr. Dobrovodský, director of the Representation Office of the Slovak Government in Prague. Carpatho-Ukraine was not a party to this political game.

In its declarations and press announcements, the Carpatho-Ukrainian Government, and Msgr. Voloshyn in particular, had constantly emphasized the necessity and political expedience of living together in the federated republic of Czecho-Slovakia. In spite of and contrary to this stance of the government, the tendency was evolving within the party ranks of the UNO to declare the full independence of Carpatho-Ukraine, this introduced a certain degree of disorientation. A similar movement for full independence of Carpatho-Ukraine was also afoot among some of the Ukrainian Americans. But all these manifestations for independence did not carry a government imprimatur as in the case of Slovakia. Taking into consideration the political situation then prevailing in Central Europe, and the policy of our neighbors, the preservation of the federation was the only realistically possible solution for Carpatho-Ukraine.

By the beginning of March, the crisis evolving from the developments in Slovakia was reaching its climax, compelling the Czechs to take more radical steps to master it. Certain anti-Ukrainian circles in the Prague Central Government decided to use this opportunity to liquidate or at least to paralyze the Ukrainian movement in Carpatho-Ukraine. This attitude on the part of leading Czech politicians toward Carpatho-Ukraine explains why President Hácha met, without consulting us, with former Prime Minister Andriy Brody, whom the Czechs themselves had arrested in October 27, of 1938 for high treason. The purpose of the meeting was "to deliberate about the possibility of liberating the Ruthenians." Brody, who was preparing to leave for Hungary, advised Hácha to "dissolve the Ukrainian national committees (*Nationalausschusse*), to curtail the influence of émigré organizations in America on the Ukrainian national movement, and to nominate a government cabinet composed of experts."[37] Msgr. Voloshyn enjoyed full confidence among the Czech members of the central government and so it is therefore incomprehensible why President Hácha could have committed such a politically unwise and irresponsible move.

Realizing that he could not settle the problem through the commission, Rudolph Beran summoned a meeting of the Ministerial Council for March 9 in the hope that he would still be able to save the unity of the republic. Although Msgr. Tiso accepted the invitation to attend the meeting, he did not show up. Only Karol Sidor and Pavel Teplanský arrived.

Now armed with irrefutable proof of the negotiations between the Slovak government and Germany, President Hácha, on Beran's recommendation, dissolved the Slovak government during the night of March 9–10 and replaced it with a provisional administration that was to act until the appointment of a constitutional government. The Czecho-Slovak Army was given orders relevant to the situation.[38] A trip of Minister Yulian Revay to Berlin was planned for the beginning of March. On his way there, he made a stopover in Prague on Monday, March 6, where I informed him about the latest developments in the capital, namely that Slovakia very soon would proclaim its full independence—a development that could put us in a very precarious situation. If this should come to pass, I told him that we would have to be prepared militarily and politically and to proclaim our own independence but only after Slovakia had done so, so as not to draw upon ourselves the blame for the disintegration of the Republic. Revay did not seem to share my critical analysis of the situation and remarked that the situation did not look that acute. His doubt about the reliability of my information may have been induced by the fact that he was to embark on a trip to Berlin on March 6 to participate in trade negotiations.

Revay was to be given a similar account of the internal political situation by Beran at a meeting held in the building of the Ministerial Council. An interesting episode transpired during his talks with Beran.

The latter handed over to him a letter, which Revay stuck in his pocket. When bidding farewell, Beran reminded him to read the letter. As it turned out, the letter was from President Hácha dismissing Revay from his post as minister. Fearing, for some reason, that he might be arrested, Revay did not return to the Office of the Representation but instead called me on the telephone from the Parliament building, expressing his fear of arrest and then admitting that "your information was correct and is of immense importance. Therefore, go to Khust without delay and relate it to Msgr. Voloshyn." For his part, Revay left for Vienna on a passport issued by the Police Headquarters in Khust bearing the name Ivan Petrovych. By the afternoon the following day I was already in Khust.

At the railroad station in Khust a pleasant surprise awaited me. Some 25 people welcomed me with a bouquet of flowers and a hospitable speech by Avgustyn Lavryshyn, a prominent official of the soccer team SK Rusj, as "our chancellor from Prague." I then immediately headed for the office of Prime Minister Msgr. Voloshyn to whom I gave an exhaustive account of the real state of affairs in Prague. The conversation revolved around the pivotal point of my report, namely the new situation that would emerge if Slovakia were to proclaim full independence. I pointed out to him that an attack by Hungary was to be expected and that we ought to be prepared for such an eventuality. In this connection, I addressed myself to the following priorities:

1. To proclaim our state independence only after Slovakia's so as not to saddle us, in the eyes of history, with the blame for breaking up the Republic.

2. To assess whether we were militarily prepared in the event of a Hungarian military incursion.

3. To be prepared, should such an incursion occur, to evacuate our government and people to Prague and to transfer a certain amount of funds from our state treasury for its operations in Prague.

In the deliberations concerning the proclamation of independence, attention was focused on the likely scope and outcome of such a Hungarian attack and what effect our resistance could have against it. Not knowing, of course, what turn further events would take and not being able to tell whether the Soim would convene in Khust at all, we agreed that in such an event, and because of the limited time, we ought to consider the possibility of executing the proclamation of Carpatho-Ukraine's independence by our Government.

Msgr. Voloshyn added: "It would be a tragedy if the Hungarians were to render the proclamation of our full independence impossible." This point was agreed upon in the sense discussed above but with the realization that all would be contingent on the further course of events. Depending on the circumstances, the Government would issue appropriate directives. I drew attention to the need for proclaiming our independence immediately after that of Slovakia's in order to avoid creating a *vacuum juris* or legal void that would follow the collapse of the Czecho-Slovak Republic in such a case. Not to do so would indicate our unpreparedness for such events.

In response to my further question as to whether we were militarily prepared to stand up against Hungarian military aggression, the Prime Minister, after some deliberation, replied that we were. I did not feel that I should go into further discussion on this issue, assuming that all had been taken care of in this respect and that there must have been some agreement between the Government of Carpatho-Ukraine and the Czecho-Slovak military. After the fall of Carpatho-Ukraine, I still could not find an explanation for Msgr. Voloshyn's assurance that we were militarily prepared. It was not until later, in exile, that I had learned from Father Sevastian Sabol, OSBM, one of Msgr. Voloshyn's closest advisors, that Sabol had been commissioned twice to journey on a secret mission to meet Gen. Oleh Svátek in Svaliava, then commander of the Czecho-Slovak military forces stationed in Carpatho-Ukraine, and inquire of him about the military defense of the land. Gen. Svátek both times gave him the assurance to be conveyed to Msgr. Voloshyn. The situation in the meantime, however, had changed when Gen. Lev Prchala took over the command of the army.

With regard to the matter of transferring state funds to Prague, Msgr. Voloshyn referred me to the head of the financial department Serhiy Yefremov. After the audience with the Prime Minister, I immediately paid a visit to the financial department, where I recounted the talk I had had with Msgr. Voloshyn. However, I was told that "the government had no money and, therefore, none could be transferred to Prague." Msgr. Voloshyn considered the information I had imparted to him as being of such importance that it warranted sharing it with some others, and to this end he asked Prof. A. Shtefan, head of the Department of Education, to

convoke a meeting of Soim deputies present in Khust and some citizens
to whom I was to relate the information about the events in Prague.

On March 8, President Hácha, upon Msgr. Voloshyn's recommendation, appointed Stepan Klochurak to replace Revay. In his platform
speech over the Prague radio, Klochurak had this to say among other
things:

> Today, after the electoral victory, we are facing three cardinal prob-
> lems in the state life of Carpatho-Ukraine that have to be resolved:
> raising the economic standard of the land, introducing a system gov-
> erning the securing of jobs, and, finally, establishing order and peace
> in the land. As for the matter of the budget of Carpatho-Ukraine, our
> Government has already taken care of it, having arrived at an agree-
> ment with the Central Government that it will amount to 305 million
> koruny not including private credits for anticipated investments.

He further declared that "We want a tranquil and peaceful atmosphere
for our daily constructive work in Carpatho-Ukraine. Under no
condition will we tolerate any manifestation of national and social
extremism."[39]

On the morning of March 9, I returned to Prague, where at the
Wilson Railroad Station I was met by one of my confidants, who
informed me that late in the evening of the day before Minister
Klochurak had given instructions over the phone to the newly appointed state secretary, Dr. Yuriy Perevuznyk, to immediately carry out
personnel changes in the editorial board of *Nova Svoboda*, organ of the
UNO, as well as in the Carpathian Sich, and had also asked Msgr.
Voloshyn to lend his support to these moves. Msgr. Voloshyn had
already earlier planned to take measures to introduce changes in the
government apparatus but because of the serious crisis in Czecho-
Slovakia and the tense atmosphere in Carpatho-Ukraine, I felt that such
a rash and drastic move at this point in time was not advisable, in fact,
risky. In order to avert what I believed would become a dangerous
situation, I had to get in touch with Msgr. Voloshyn and Dr.
Perevuznyk by telephone which was no easy task. Only after my staff
was able to convince the telephone exchange operator of my identity
and get me an official emergency telephone connection from a telephone booth at the Wilson Railroad Station did I contact both men.
Having informed Msgr. Voloshyn of the latest events in Prague, I asked
him to temporarily refrain from executing Klochurak's recommendations because of the internal crisis in the Republic and the chaos that

would follow in our land. Msgr. Voloshyn agreed, but insisted on implementing the changes after the Soim convened and held its first session. I gave Dr. Perevuznyk the same information. Years later, Dr. Perevuznyk, whom I had not known personally, conveyed to me his sincere thanks for the good piece of advice at a time which, as he himself said, "could have really created chaos."

The month of March 1939 was designated by Hitler as the date for the complete liquidation of the already truncated Czecho-Slovakia and in turn also amounting to the sealed fate of Carpatho-Ukraine. Hitler made it clear to Hungary's Foreign Minister Csáky, during the latter's visit to Berlin on January 16, 1939, that he was no longer interested in Carpatho-Ukraine. Such a revelation pleased Hungarian government quarters to no end. Csáky went on to insist on thwarting the holding of elections to the Carpatho-Ukrainian Soim, but Hitler countered by advising Hungary to wait and refrain from any actions on its own.[40] Hungary could gain Carpatho-Ukraine only if Hitler so willed it, and for this reason Hungary became politically indebted to Germany. After March 9, compromise between the Czechs and Slovaks became impossible, since Slovakia had already openly and officially begun talks with Germany about declaring independence.

On March 13, the Hungarian ambassador in Berlin, Döme Sztojay, flew to Budapest where, together with the German ambassador, Otto von Erdmannsdorff, he called on Regent Horthy and handed him and his government a message given to him by Hitler which stated that "the break up of Czechoslovakia was imminent." "He had decided to recognize the independence of Slovakia, but out of friendship would hold up for twenty-four hours his decision whether to grant similar recognition to Voloshin in Ruthenia."[41] However, it no way does it seem likely that such an answer was actually made by Hitler, who by that time was already in negotiations with Stalin and did not support an independent Ukraine.[42]

The news evoked great enthusiasm in Hungary's government circles. In order to carry out the military occupation of Carpatho-Ukraine, Gen. Henrik Werth, chief of staff of the Hungarian armed forces, demanded he be given a week to prepare his forces for the action, reckoning with the possibility of resistance by the Czecho-Slovak army. However, the Germans insisted on immediate military action.[43]

Regent Miklós Horthy's first expression of joy over this generous gift was contained in a letter sent to Hitler. Hungarian as well as foreign historians and foreign diplomats sympathizing with the Hungarians prefer not to mention this letter of gratitude in their works. Nowadays it is not a commendable idea to admit to have entered into an alliance and friendship with Hitler and to link one's political triumphs with him.

The text of the letter reads as follows:

> The Regent of Hungary to the Führer and Chancellor!
>
> Budapest, March 13, 1939
>
> YOUR EXCELLENCY! Heartfelt thanks. I cannot express how happy I am, for this headwater region [*Quellgebiet*] is, in fact, for Hungary—I dislike using big words—*a vital question* [italics in the original—V.Sh.].
>
> Notwithstanding that our recruits have been serving but 5 weeks, we are tackling the matter with enthusiasm. The plans are already laid. On Thursday the 16th of this month a frontier incident will take place, to be followed on Saturday by the big thrust.
>
> I shall never forget this proof of friendship and Your Excellency can at all times ever rely steadfastly [*felsenfest*] on my gratitude.
>
> Horthy

This letter was handwritten in German by Horthy on his Regent's personal stationery.[42]

Unfortunately, there have been instances of falsifying historical reality by Hungarian government circles, thus engendering the fallacious opinion that the Hungarians had allegedly occupied Carpatho-Ukraine against Hitler's will. They have managed to introduce such false contentions even into the reports of foreign ambassadors. Indeed, U.S. Ambassador to Budapest John Flournoy Montgomery also seemed to have fallen victim to this artifice when he described the occupation of Carpatho-Ukraine:

> With Slovakia independent and Bohemia a German Protectorate, Carpatho-Ruthenia was a derelict. Hitler had promised it repeatedly to Hungary, but apparently had no intention of keeping his promise. Not only were the Czech garrisons kept there, but when they were withdrawn as a result of Hungarian ultimatum to the Czechs, it became a no-man's land full of German and Hungarian agents, until the Hungarian army went in and took possession. The occupation of Ruthenia, now part of the Soviet Union, was carried out without the knowledge and counsel of Germany and very much against her wishes.[43]

Hungary's Prime Minister Count Pál Teleki, too, subscribed to the "no-man's land" theory when in his speeches after the occupation insinuated the impression that the land did not have a master of its own. Carpatho-Ukraine, in general, was the subject of the St. Germain international agreement in 1918–1920, but in 1938–1939 it became an international, world problem and center of attention in various state cabinets and military staffs and as such making it possible for the Ukrainian people to play an appropriate role. Thus, the appellation of being a no-man's land is not a political argument.

To quote Ambassador Montgomery further:

> The occupation of Ruthenia, now part of the Soviet Union, was carried out without the knowledge and counsel of Germany and very much against her wishes. It was Poland which urged the establishment of a common Hungarian-Polish frontier, in order to prevent the German army, which entered Slovakia, from moving far east into the back of endangered Poland and establishing direct contact across Ruthenia with Rumania.[44]

This thesis, too, is unfounded and even poorly contrived, for Germany attacked Poland from the territory of Slovakia and, therefore, had assumed protection over the latter. Already since April 1939, the German army had been building and widening roads in Slovakia leading toward Poland, constructing new bridges, and so forth. The reason for such heightened activity of the German military in Slovakia was clear to everyone but the Polish foreign minister, Col. Józef Beck and Polish diplomats who, in their ecstasy over the fall of Carpatho-Ukraine and their common border with Hungary, were blinded to the doom of Poland that was being prepared by the Germans.

Perhaps the best proof of the error of Ambassador Montgomery's thesis, which, after all, had been handed to him by the Hungarians, may be gleaned from the confidential letter Csáky had sent to his ambassador in Berlin, Döme Stojay, on March 3, 1939. In it, Csáky asked him to forward the letter in an appropriate form to Wilhelmstrasse. The last paragraph of the letter read: "Your Excellency may want to assure Wilhelmstrasse that in the event of Carpatho-Ukraine's annexation, the communication desires of German with regard to Eastern Europe will be to the fullest extent [*weitestgehend*] honored."[45] Hungary was willing to take into consideration also the technical side of the problem, such as the building of roads, supply of needed materials, etc.

Since geography comes into play here, one has to conclude that in its confidential letter Hungary was placing its communications network at the disposal of Germany directed eastward, namely against Poland, with which it was actually striving to have a common border. This, however, did not prevent Hungarian diplomacy and later Hungarian authors from spreading the legend that allegedly "the problem of Ruthenia's restitution to Hungary was a Polish problem and involved Poland's military security."[46] Author Stephen Kertész sought to present the pro-German policy of Hungary in an innocent manner, as though Hungarian politicians cooperating with Germany were forced to do so by some coincidental convergence of circumstances and not because of their own pro-German sentiments.

Lest this argument sound unfounded regarding the relationship between Hungary and Germany, note the following quotation from Regent Horthy's letter to Hitler of May 7, 1943 in which he clearly states his attitude. He writes: "There is no other country that would have pledged to produce as many work hours for the German military effort as has Hungary." And further: "To talk of defeatism in the Hungarian government or of its wish to prepare Hungary to step out of the Axis Powers' alliance is, as evidenced from the said, wholly preposterous."[47]

Horthy concludes his letter thus:

> Your excellency. In these fateful hours, you have Hungary's and its government's full confidence, which this land through its conduct in the past and present and also in the future can rightly claim. Hungary is Germany's oldest friend, indeed, also its most faithful. Even without a written alliance agreement, Hungary has always been, out of conviction, for closest cooperation with Germany and has since fulfilled all of its obligations with sincerity and frequently at the cost of neglecting its own interests.[48]

These quotations are from Horthy's letter to Hitler dated May 7, 1943, which was a time when the contours of German military failures on all battlefields were becoming even more pronounced. Nonetheless, Horthy's letter is replete with expressions of sincere loyalty and forthright combatant solidarity. Hitler had done a great deal of good for Hungary's revisionist policy and that country's territorial aggrandizement, thereby considerably enhancing Regent Horthy's stature in the eyes of his homeland. And yet, it is difficult to understand how Horthy could harshly condemn and criticize Hitler in front of the American ambassador in Budapest, Montgomery, on January 12, 1939, at a time of a months-long Hungarian-German honeymoon. It seems obvious that this was merely a way of finding an alibi "just in case." To illustrate the incident more clearly, we shall quote excerpts from a strictly confidential report written by Ambassador Montgomery to the U.S. Secretary of State. Following a luncheon tendered by the Papal Nuncio in honor of the Regent, the Regent engaged Mr. Montgomery and the British Minister in a joint conversation for a considerable length of time. Montgomery subsequently reported:

> The Regent volunteered that Hitler was a madman and that Germany was bringing the world to chaos; that Germany was fomenting anti-Hungarian opinion in Ruthenia to prepare the way for Germany's expansion in that direction, and that a deep-laid German plot existed which had found expression at Munkacs (Mukachevo) . . .
>
> That country had educated Ruthenians in Germany and sent them back to their country as paid agents to foment anti-Hungarian opinion and to prepare the way for Germany's expansion in that direction.[49]
>
> Germany, asserted the Regent, would be insane to use Ruthenia as a base for further operations against Russia because even were it to succeed, it would serve to unite the Russians and also as a basis for building up a Slav empire; which in turn would destroy Germany.
>
> I asked if His Highness thought Hungary would remain neutral in the event of war, to which he answered that as long as he had the breath of life he would keep Hungary neutral.
>
> The Hungarian Jew Law, he said, was inhuman and he would not permit it to be made effective in its present form. It would serve the purpose of getting rid of many Jews who had come to Hungary in recent years, and prevent further Jewish immigration. In this sense it was a threat and it was a good thing to have the public consider that the bill might be made effective, but he had consideration for the patriotic Jews long resident in the country who had helped to make it prosperous and who were as much Hungarians as was he, and he would not permit them to be deprived of their livelihood.[50]

In the light of the cited documents as well as of other pronouncements of loyalty Horthy had made to Hitler, it is safe to conclude that Horthy's talks with the ambassadors of the U.S. and England were contrived to distract the attention of both countries from Hungary's pro-German policy. He used the occasion to deliberately level false accusations against the "Ruthenians," whom Germany supposedly had trained as agents in an anti-Hungarian spirit. During the entire period of the war, however, there were only three students from Carpatho-Ukraine in Berlin, one of whom was from the U.S. At that time, Horthy knew that Carpatho-Ukraine was sure to fall to the Hungarians and that the people would fight, especially the youth. Precisely because of the youth, he inflated the numbers and presented them to the ambassadors as being specially trained by German agents of Hitler.

Similar poorly thought-out and fictitious stories, coupled with various accusations, have been concocted by enemies of the Ukrainian cause to turn world opinion against the Ukrainians by trying to impute to them pro-Hitlerite sentiments, others anti-Jewish, still others pro-Communist feelings, depending on what suits whom. A people without its own state has difficulty in defending its truth against various charges voiced by representatives of inimical states who have at their disposal the necessary media. It is vastly more difficult to defend the truth than to fabricate new untruths.

Hungary's professions of fidelity and loyalty to Hitlerite Germany were to affect also economic matters. In connection with Horthy's visit to Germany on April 16, 1943, the Ministry of Foreign Affairs in Budapest prepared a "Note" bearing the same date in whose chapter entitled "A Political Review" the following was stated:

> True to our traditional policy and true to our close friendship toward the Axis Powers, we have not hesitated to participate in this struggle. We are fighting together for a new Europe which is called to ensure for us all a just order. Since the outset of the hostilities, Hungary has placed all its economic might at the disposal of the Axis Powers. In the past four years, 90% of our exports was shipped to the markets of the Axis Powers or countries.[51]

It is also worth noting an interview of Prime Minister Teleki before his trip to Berlin in April 1939. In it, Teleki points to the course of events that unfolded in Carpatho-Ukraine from the fall of 1938 to the spring of 1939, and in this connection declared:

> It is thanks to the close cooperation between Germany and Hungary within the framework of the Axis policy, which each Hungarian government has supported over the years, that such changes could have been brought about. The events of the past months coincide, also from the Hungarian standpoint, with the glorious feats of Adolf Hitler, the leader and chancellor of the Reich.[52]

World literature abounds in similar incorrect accounts that harm the Ukrainian cause. Not infrequently, even positive achievments attained by Ukrainians in their liberation struggle for statehood are consciously glossed over or are presented in a distorted, negative interpretation. However, Ukrainians are also to blame for not having utilized the opportunities available to them in the free world to properly inform the international, political, and government communities about their cause.[53]

Notes

[1] The information presented here is in reply to the following assertion: "An editorial of *Nastup*, the official organ of 'Carpathian Sitch,' edited by Dr. Stepan Rosokha, strongly criticized those elements in Carpatho-Ukraine who became blind Germanophiles after Germany had saved Carpatho-Ukraine at the Vienna Arbitration conference and then again in November 1938 from Hungarian occupation. The editorial expressed its dissatisfaction about the fact that some of these people saw in Hitler a greater Ukrainian than in themselves or in any other Ukrainian out of their forty-five million . . . " [Italics by Stercho]. (Peter G. Stercho, *Diplomacy of Double Morality* (New York, 1971), pp. 321–22.)

[2] Feierabend, *Ve vládách Druhé republiky* (New York, 1961) pp. 110–11. *See also,* Jorg K. Hoensch, *Die Slovakei und Hitlers Ostpolitik* (Köln-Graz, 1965), p. 219; *Geheimakten Prag* 17713; Hencke Nr. 1 vom 21, Januar 1939 and das Konsulat in Pressburg und Staatssekretaer 76261 von Schleinitz Nr. 27, Januar 1939.

[3] J. I. Pop, *Chekhoslovatsko-vengerskie otnosheniia, 1935–1939* (Moscow, 1972), p. 23. A further note about Gen. Prchala, who made the following interesting observation in connection with Beneš' election as President of Czechoslovakia: "After Dr. Beneš was elected president, I was coming out of the Vladislav Hall in the Prague Castle when I suddenly caught sound of a familiar voice exclaiming exuberantly: 'We succeeded.' I was right, it was the Soviet Ambassador, Aleksandrovsky. These Russian words opened my eyes." (Quotation from Gen. Lev Prchala, "Novy most," *České Listy* 5 (February 9, 1953), published by the Czech National Council in London.)

[4] This author received a telephone call from the Khust Sich Headquarters asking me to inform them about the exact date of Gen. Prchala's arrival in Khust, since the Sich Supreme Command would want to intern him. I tried to dissuade them from such an action, contending that Gen. Prchala, who is also commander of the Czechoslovak Army in Carpatho-Ukraine, would not arrive in Khust alone and that the military would not tolerate someone to intern their general. Yet I complied with their wish, which was not all that easy a task to fulfill, and sent them a telegram that read: "Sister left, will stop over in the Tatra Mountains for two days, and then return home Friday evening." Fortunately, the threatened action did not take place.

[5] One of the conditions for naming Klochurak minister was that he "recall Shandor from Prague," which Klochurak immediately set out to accomplish.

[6] Ludvík Svoboda, *Cestami života*, vol. 1 (Prague, 1971), pp. 264–65. *See also,* Ján Kren, *Do Emigrace: buržoazní zahraniční odboj, 1938–1939* (Prague, 1963), p. 151. As president of the state, Gen. Svoboda had access to all confidential files and resources, of which he availed himself. During the First Republic, Gen. Svoboda served as an officer in the 36th Infantry Regi-

ment in Uzhhorod, while Gen. Prchala was his divisional commander. Later, in the Prague Parliament, Gen. Prchala's great supporter was Deputy Schwartz, an ardent enemy of Ukrainians. Prchala and Svoboda parted ways politically in Poland, where they emerged as immigrants after the occupation of Czecho-Slovakia by Hitler in March of 1939. Gen. Svoboda writes in his book that the Poles welcomed Gen. Prchala with open arms. Another Czecho-Slovak statesman, Zdeněk Fierlinger, also makes mention of Gen. Prchala, stating that "Gen. Prchala came to Poland on its passport and was transported across the border to Warsaw in a car," and proceeds to say that "the Poles accorded him all possible comfort. Apparently, they had some plans in mind with regard to him." (Zdeněk Fierlinger, *Ve službách ČSR. Paméti z druhého zabraničního odboje*, vol. 1, (Prague, 1951), p. 246). After the fall of Poland, Gen. Svoboda went to the USSR, and Gen. Prchala to England—thus their ways separated.

[7] Karol Sidor, *Moje poznámky k historickým dňom* (Middletown, Pa., 1971), pp. 121–23.

[8] Svoboda, *op. cit.*, p. 202.

[9] Štefan Parker, *Protifašistický odboj na Východnom Slovensku* (Košice, 1974), p. 24.

[10] Stefan Faro, "Zakarpatská Ukrajina v politických kalkuláciach ústredných štátov v období od Mnichova po marec 1939," *Slovanské Študia Slovanské študia* (Bratislava) 9 Historia 1971: 68.

[11] Joseph Staško, *Slovensko po druhej svetovej vojne, Aprilova dohoda 1946–47* (Cambridge, Ontario, 1977), p. 34.

[12] Louis L. Snyder, *The War—A Concise History 1939–1945* (New York, 1960), p. 55.

[13] Appeal of the Organization of Ukrainian Nationalists—The Land's Executive Board of Transcarpathian Ukraine, *Postii* August 1938.

[14] Quotation by Klochurak, *pers. comm.* in a letter to the author dated June 22, 1971.

[15] Personal letter from Dr. V. Komarynsky letter to the author dated January 28, 1978.

[16] From V. Shandor's diary about the conversation with Yulian Revay on January 25, 1974. The author learned about the conspiracy from the Czechs in Prague around the 20th of February 1939. For more on the conspiracy, see *Nash Holos* 12(9) September 1980 and also 13(2) February 1981 as well as 13(3) and 13(5) of March and May 1981 respectively. *See also,* Calendar *Svitlo* (Light), Toronto, Ont., Canada, 1974; Ivan Sarvadii, *Zmova proty uriadu Karpats'koï Ukraïny* (Chicago, 1984), pp. 8–12.

[17] Riko Yariy, a German, served as an officer in the Austro-Hungarian Army. He established contact with the Ukrainian nationalist movement after World War I and was able to win the confidence of its leaders.

[18] Zynovii Knysh, *Rozbrat. Spohady i materialy do rozkolu OUN u 1940–1941 rokakh.* (Toronto, January 1960), p. 303.

[19] *Nova Svoboda* 21 January 1939.

[20] *Nova Svoboda* 22 January 1939.

[21] The headquarters of these parties were located in Bohemia. However, they were politically active also in Carpatho-Ukraine so that their members here could be elected deputies and senators to the Prague Parliament.

[22] *Nova Svoboda* 26 January 1939.

[23] Tiskový Odbor Presidia Ministerské Rady report of February 14, 1939 (TOPMR).

[24] *České Slovo* 14 February 1939.

[25] *Polední List* (Prague) 13 February 1939.

[26] Ibid. *See also,* TOPMR, No. 44 of February 13, 1939.

[27] Cited from TOPMR, No. 46, of February 15, 1939. *See also, České Slovo* 15 February 15 1939.

[28] TOPMR, No. 48, of February 17, 1939. *See also, Lidové Noviny* of February 17, 1939.

[29] Loránt Tilkovszky, *Revizió és nemzetiségpolitika Magyarországon 1938-1941.* (Budapest, 1967), p. 158.

[30] Józef Lipski, *Diplomat in Berlin 1933–1939* (New York, 1968) p. 484.

[31] Svoboda, *op. cit.,* p. 185.

[32] Dánás, *Ludacký separatismus a Hitlerovské Německo* (Bratislava, 1963), p. 30. *See also,* Archiv Ministerstva Zahraničných Věcí, telegram No. 177/200/38/AMZV *and, Nové dokumenty k historii Mníchova* (Bratislava, 1958).

[33] Walter Schellenberg, *The Schellenberg Memoirs,* edited and translated by Louis Hagen (London: 1956), p. 56. *See also, Slavic Review* December 1973: 748.

[34] Erich Kordt, Wahn und Wirklichkeit. *Die Aussenpolitik des Dritten Reiches—Versuch einer Darstellung* (Stuttgart: 1948), pp. 143–44.

[35] *The Hungarian Quarterly* (Budapest) 4(1) Spring 1939: 172–73.

[36] DGFP, pp. 210–11. *See also,* S. Harrison Thomson, *Czechoslovakia in European History* (Hamden, Conn., 1965), p. 403.

[37] Jörg K. Hoensch, *Der ungarische Revisionismus und Zerschlagung der Tschechoslovakei* (Tübingen, 1967), p.253. *See also,* PDMF; Papee, No. 51 of March 4, 1939, No. P. III. 119/21/Gn.

[38] Feirabend, *op. cit.,* pp. 144–45.

[39] From the text of the speech in the possession of the author.

[40] Tilkovszky, *op. cit.,* p. 158. *See also,* Hungarian Embassy in Berlin, *Weizsäcker feljegyzése ill. a berlini magyar követség jegyzéke* (Berlin: February 7, 1939) OL Filmtár, Box 11586, 51758, 51759–60.

[41] C. A. Macartney, *A History of Hungary 1929–1945,* part 1 (New York, 1957), p. 336.

[42] On February 13–14, 1939, Hitler had promised the delegation from Slovakia in Berlin that inasmuch as Slovakia would declare full state independence, then he was prepared in turn to provide a full guarantee of its borders. The Slovaks attained full independence through their politics in Slovakia and Prague. In a letter to Horthy, Hitler mentions Slovakia, which he had recognized, but there is no mention that "out of friendship [Hitler] would hold up for twenty-four hours his decisions whether to grant similar recognition to Voloshyn in Ruthenia."

Such a state of affairs leads me to the thought that this insertion about friendship might have been put in by Sztojay himself, as an ill-witted gesture, when he gave the information to the press, and in this way both strike at the Ukrainians, towards whom Hitler was expressing his "friendly attention" in the face of such an important decision.

In his substantial political speech of January 30, 1939 in the Reichstag, Hitler already was not attacking Stalin or Communism, as he had been in his previous speeches. Listening to this speech, it was clear to me that there were serious negotiations of a political or economic nature ongoing between him and Stalin. In this speech, Hitler made it clear that the Ukrainian question was not in his political program. Equally, he made a similar statement for Poland regarding the Ukrainian question, by which he satisfied Foreign Minister Beck and the Ambassador of Poland in Berlin.

Thus, it was generally clear in Europe that through such a type of pronouncement, that Hitler was negative in his attitude toward the case of Ukraine. For that reason, analyzing this speech by Hitler about the Ukrainian cause, it is impossible that he would have torpedoed his own politics—thereby undermining his negotiations with Stalin—by making that kind of a speech to aid Voloshyn or "Ruthenia" (i.e., Ukraine). The Chief of Staff of the Hungarian Army demanded the several days that were necessary to prepare the army, and got the answer from Germany.

[43] DGFP, Series D. Vol. IV, p. 240.

[42] Ibid., p. 241. Slovak author Jozef A. Mikuš gives this letter a historically erroneous interpretation when he states that the area referred to in the letter was Slovakia. As early as February 1939, Hitler promised Dr. Tuka and Karamzin to guarantee the borders of Slovakia if they declared full independence for Slovakia—which indeed, had come to pass. Therefore, this letter has no political or logical connection with the territorial problem affecting Slovakia and Hungary, but rather exclusively with that of Carpatho-Ukraine. (Jozef A. Mikuš, *Slovakia, A Political History – 1918–1950* (Milwaukee, 1963), pp. 76–77.)

[43] John Flournoy Montgomery, *Hungary—the Unwilling Satellite* (New York, 1947), pp. 122–23.

[44] Ibid., p. 123.

[45] Ádám Magda, *Allianz Hitler-Horthy-Mussolini* (Budapest, 1966), p. 215.

[46] Stephen D. Kertész, *Diplomacy in a Whirlpool* (Notre Dame, 1953), p. 39.

[47] Ádám, Allianz , *op. cit.,* pp. 354–55.

[48] Ibid., p. 356.

[49] On the basis of confirmed information obtained by this author, there were at this time only three students from Carpatho-Ukraine in Germany, all of whom were studying in Berlin and were in their second semester at the local university.

[50] National Archives, Washington, D.C.: Legation of the United States of America, Budapest, January 12, 1939, file 762.64/133, p. 1–4.

[51] Ádám, *op. cit.,* p. 335.

[52] As quoted by Elek Karsai, *Stálo sa v Budíne v Šándorovskom paláci 1919-1941.* Bratislava, p. 404.

[53] In 1953, a six-week course in international politics was held at the American University in Washington, D.C., which was attended by several hundred people from various countries of the world. At this course, Dr. Geza Teleki, son of former Hungarian Prime Minister Pál Teleki, delivered a lecture on "The Geopolitics of Central-Eastern Europe." The speaker gave a rather correct presentation of the political and other problems in this area. During the discussion period, I asked him, "What was the reason that the Hungarian government had deemed it necessary in 1939 to launch a military attack against Carpatho-Ukraine?" Teleki went into profound details in explaining the aforementioned theory and added that the government of Carpatho-Ukraine concluded an agreement. I asked him with whom it concluded an agreement? "Of course, with Hitler," was the reply. I then introduced myself as the Carpatho-Ukraine's government's representative in Prague, remarking that if any such agreement had been signed, I would have definitely known about it. I went on to assure the speaker that the government of Carpatho-Ukraine had never concluded any agreement with Hitler and, what is more, no member of this government had ever been received by Hitler in audience. In support of his argument, I read Horthy's letter of appreciation sent to Hitler, thereby refuting the speaker's unfounded statement and political deductions. The audience reacted with applause and expression of satisfaction. On this note, the discussion ended. After the incident, Prof. E. Burr, director of these courses, had this to say to me: "Teleki will never again lecture here."

CHAPTER SIX

The Army and the Carpathian Sich

In the period of the Federated Republic of Czecho-Slovakia, the army was all-national and was subordinated to the Ministry of National Defense in Prague, just as under the First Republic. The commander-in-chief of the 12th Division in Carpatho-Ukraine was Brig. Gen. Oleh Svátek, who was executed by the Germans in October 1941. Chief of Staff until January 9, 1939 was Lt. Col. Lang of the Generals' Staff, followed by Lt. Col. Fischer also of the Generals' Staff, with headquarters in Svaliava. Gen. Svátek, as many other Czech officers, were favorably disposed toward Carpatho-Ukraine and its government. Upon his appointment as minister of the Carpatho-Ukrainian government, Army Gen. Lev Prchala also took over the command of the army from Gen. Svátek, which strongly enhanced Prchala's personal stature.

At the end of 1938, young Ukrainians from Galicia and other parts of Europe, especially leading activists of the Organization of Ukrainian Nationalists (OUN), began arriving in Khust to help the young Ukrainian state stave off the intrigues plotted against it by its hostile neighbors Hungary and Poland. Most of these young people had been in Polish prisons for their patriotism and now felt the need to participate in the building of the Carpatho-Ukrainian state, for which they deserve recognition and appreciation.

With the change of the political status of Carpatho-Ukraine into a federated state, the position and role of Ukrainians in the state also changed. From a national opposition during the First Republic, the Ukrainians now became a leading and constructive state-oriented factor obliged to act on behalf of the state and on their own responsibility. Yet some Carpathian public personalities in leading positions in Khust failed to realize this changed role in a federated Czecho-Slovakia, while some of our brethren from Galicia simply misunderstood it.

A supreme command of the Carpathian Sich (the paramilitary arm of the OUN, cf. pp. 72, 89 above) was created in Khust in whose activity our Galician brethren also participated. They brought with them not only fervent patriotism, but also the expertise in the forms and methods of conspiratorial work they had acquired in their struggle against Poland, which they put to use also in Carpatho-Ukraine. Ignorant of the local conditions and bent on applying their own mode of operations, they failed to take into consideration our political achievements made to date and to understand the state federative system of Czecho-Slovakia or our participation in it. They began to introduce uncompromising new revolutionary methods, which did not always conform to our political interests or, at times, to our state needs either. The times did not allow for uncompromising or revolutionary slogans to resolve our state problems, but rather called for constructive work directed toward a goal, implemented on an all-national scale, and regulated by the government with each member of the society doing his part in the effort.

Within a short time after the formation of the Supreme Command of the Carpathian Sich, there were already visible signs pointing to the existence in it of a secretive group of commanders or officers who operated under assumed names and began to unnecessarily propagate their own political line. In 1938 and 1939, the Organization of Ukrainian Nationalists (OUN), headed by the Leadership of Ukrainian Nationalists (PUN), was organizationally and politically the most powerful Ukrainian organization in the Free World. They exerted their greatest influence upon the youth, particularly in Galicia, and secured for themselves a dominant position in the rank and file as well as the leading echelons of the Carpathian Sich. To this end, a "Special Staff of PUN for Transcarpathian Affairs" was formed including Riko Yariy (foreign policy), Yaroslav Baranovsky (organizational matters and internal policy), and O. Chemerynsky (press and information). Military affairs did not belong to the purview of this Staff, remaining as they were the competence of the OUN Military Staff, subordinated to the officer in charge of military affairs of PUN, Gen. Mykola Kaspustiansky. Transcarpathian affairs were the competence of Lt. Mykhailo Kolodzinsky and liason officer between the Sich Staff for Transcarpathian affairs and the Military Staff was Capt. Riko Yariy. A separate staff of PUN formally and in actual fact became engaged in operations in Carpatho-Ukraine in February 1938 in the capacity of a "coordinating institution" in which the policies of PUN's various departments were synchronized.[1] The Creation of such an institution back in February 1938 was still expedient, but its activities in Carpatho-Ukraine during the federated statehood with a Ukrainian government at the helm is quite a different matter. As a result, PUN had wielded a decisive influence upon the leadership of the Sich and had thus assumed full responsibility.

It presented the demand for a full state independence of Carpatho-Ukraine: "the Delegation, together with the entire [nationally] conscious population of Carpatho-Ukraine subscribes to the stand of full state independence for Carpatho-Ukraine, as the core of the Greater Ukrainian State. It is to this end that we are working abroad, it is to this end that the ground is being prepared in the homeland."[2] Subsequent to the Vienna Arbitration on Nov. 2, 1938, the delegation was disbanded.[3]

In its Appeal and official announcement, the Organization of Ukrainian Nationalists referred to Carpatho-Ukraine as the nucleus or core of a united Ukrainian State:

> The great time is coming close. Transcarpathia must be an independent Ukrainian State! It must become the nucleus of a single, great, independent, and united Ukrainian State from Poprad and the Tatra Mountains and extend as far as the Caspian Sea and the Caucasus Mountains. It should be of greatest honor to us to become this nucleus. We shall take pride in being the first, indeed we, to initiate the restoration of the Ukrainian State.[4]

The authors of the "Appeal" and its concept proceeded from the premise that the then political constellation of forces in Europe then existing was indeed conducive to such a development in the cause for Ukrainian statehood and liberation. Germany, at this point in time, was the only force in Europe that, true to its long-standing doctrine of *Drang nach Osten,* was capable of unleashing a military campaign in the East. After all, Hitler himself had been preparing the ground for such a military intervention, of which he gave ample evidence in his speeches up to the end of 1938.

Furthermore, a critical analysis of Germany's policy with regard to the Ukrainian struggle and liberation, of Hitler's utterances, and mainly of his book *Mein Kampf* did not give cause for such unqualified optimism about Ukrainian statehood. German propaganda was permeated with references to the rich Ukraine, as a terrain inviting Germany's territorial expansionism and economic exploitation for its so-called "Lebensraum," but never as an independent Ukrainian state entity. Yet, all this notwithstanding, Germany succeeded in arousing world interest (particularly French and British) in Ukraine and its struggle for statehood and liberation. Hence, up to the end of 1938, Germany was holding two Ukrainian political trump cards in its hands: both Britain and France, which hoped that Hitler would direct his first offensive moves to the East rather than towards them in the West.

From January 1939 on, it was to become more and more evident that Germany's policy was leaning toward a rapprochment with the USSR preceded namely by Hitler's plan to liquidate Czecho-Slovakia and, by the same token, also Carpatho-Ukraine. It is obvious that Ukrainian political circles had no control whatsoever over Germany's policy or over German military and political quarters that were calling attention to the importance of Ukraine in an eventual clash with the USSR and were favoring a German positive attitude toward it.[5]

The Ukrainians may be likened to astronomers, who follow the course of celestial bodies but do not possess the power to influence it. By taking the stand they did, leading members of the OUN were in their pronouncements transgressing the boundaries of the then existing federal status of Carpatho-Ukraine, and their presentation of the problem in this respect ran contrary to the Government's policy, thereby contributing to the formation of centrifugal forces in the state. Both Ukrainian members of the cabinet emphasized in their public announcements our wishes for a united Ukrainian state, but simultaneously pointed out that the problem of Ukraine in general depended on the great powers for its resolution rather than on our own frail resources.

Jurisdiction over conducting the foreign policy of the federated Czecho-Slovakia came within the purview of the Ministry of Foreign Affairs in Prague, on whose decisions the Government of Carpatho-Ukraine also could exert influence as a member of the Central Government. There was, therefore, no need or legal reasons for the Separate Staff to conduct foreign or domestic policies. The internal policy of the land lay in the competence of Prime Minister Msgr. Voloshyn, as minister of internal affairs. Such political practice evoked distrust in Khust and Prague toward the Supreme Command of the Carpathian

Sich and its activity. Party exclusiveness, introduced and nourished by and within the Supreme Command of the Sich, did not allow expert, professional people of other political persuasions to participate in it. For the struggle of the Ukrainian nation toward a united state, this practice evinced one of the fundamental political shortcomings of the party-oriented nationalist movement, for it excluded from participation patriotic, albeit non-party nationalists, and other Ukrainian elements to the detriment of the liberation cause itself.

The last commander of the National Defense of Carpatho-Ukraine, Col. Vasyl Fylonovych, had this to say in the matter:

> The then managers of the organization of national defense of Carpatho-Ukraine put their own grouping above everything else, above the people, above the nation, thereby causing the people of Transcarpathia to suffer a defeat and leaving behind a lesson to be learned in the future. The matter of forming an army was taken over by people with no professional military training, without experience, without any qualifications, and, finally, without the slightest idea about it.[6]

A similar answer was given by Col. Ihnat Stefaniv and Gen. Omelianovych-Pavlenko.

Col. Fylonovych leveled his critical remarks, first and foremost, against four Transcarpathian members of the Sich Supreme Command: Dmytro Klympush, Ivan Roman, Ivan Rohach, and Stepan Rosokha who, as natives of the region, had a decisive say in the Supreme Command and who, due to their ignorance of military affairs and their improper style of operations, brought about the dismal state in which the Sich had found itself. Col. Fylonovych made it a point to stress that his critical remarks about the aforementioned persons were made only in regard to the question of military professionalism, adding that "these statements of mine are in no way to be interpreted as detracting from these people their patriotism, or loyalty to the ideas of nationalism."[7]

Carpathian members of the Sich Supreme Command demanded for themselves such functions in the state system that were beyond their competence and for which the Sich was not prepared. The chief of press and propaganda in Khust viewed the matter thus: "A so-called Second Department of the Sich Command was set up, which arrogated to itself the right to remove persons they deemed undesirable by resorting to beatings and threats so that our Chief of Police Yurko Biley was compelled to intervene on several occasions."[8] At some time in January 1939, three Carpathian members of the Supreme Command (Roman, Rohach, and Rosokha),[9] without Klympush, called on Komarynsky and asked him to accompany them to Msgr. Voloshyn. Komarynsky went. They put before the prime minister the demand that the Carpathian Government "place 1,200 Czech gendarmes at Prague's disposal and replace them with members of the Sich." Komarynsky's proposal was, however, to attach one Sich member to each gendarmerie station for training. The Sich leaders agreed, but demanded that a Sich member be placed in command of the post. Komarynsky tried to make them realize that a gendarme has to undergo a required and quite exacting training and, therefore, the gendarmerie cannot afford to allow into its ranks people without such training—an argument with which Msgr. Voloshyn totally agreed.[10] Obviously, the replacement of the gendarmerie with Sich members never came to pass, a fact which displeased the Carpathian members of the Supreme Command of the Sich who viewed this as their Government's weakness toward the Czechs.

Some of the Supreme Command's actions caused the Administration headaches. Thus, for instance, the odd situation developed that Dr. V. Komarynsky, as chief of press, felt himself compelled to confiscate their articles in the UNO organ *Nova Svoboda* as well as leaflets, handbills, and the like. The Administration was conducting a struggle against the Hungarian-Polish policy concerning a common border and thus could not take upon itself the responsibility for all kinds of "underground" and unconventional activities that were not under the control of the Government and that frequently were conducted by persons using aliases. Our Galician brethrens usually used assumed names in order to protect their identity from Polish authorities in the event of repressions against them. Poland was swamping the Central Government in Prague with protest notes, which harped on the improperly conducted anti-Polish actions in our midst that Poland used to justify its own inimical actions against Carpatho-Ukraine and underscore the need for a common border with Hungary. We, of course, fully shared the anti-Polish sentiment of our Galician brethren, since Poland and its diplomacy caused great harm also to us, and yet Carpatho-Ukraine was not the terrain to settle such accounts with Poland. Our anti-Polish actions should have been well thought-out and conducted at a proper government level.

Msgr. Voloshyn, to whom many foreign and our own complaints were directed, repeatedly invited the Sich commander, Klympush, to talk with him on the matter of the need of setting the Supreme Command of the Sich in some order. However, Klympush could say nothing, but that "he cannot manage it."[11]

In December 1938, Vasyl Bora—official of the Czecho-Slovak National Bank assigned to the Representation of the Carpatho-Ukrainian Government in Prague—handed over to me the assignment he had received from the Sich Supreme Command to represent in Bohemia the Sich's interests because, as a civilian, he could not fulfill such a role. In the presence of a representative of the society of Ukrainian Engineers in Prague M. Yaremyn (the engineers were willing to purchase for the Sich some 100 complete uniforms), I met twice with an officer of the General Staff in Prague and achieved the following agreement:

> 1) The Army was willing to provide the Sich with military training, including handling of light weapons, such as machine guns, grenades, and mortars. A non-comissioned officer aspirant, Ivan Sarvadiy (a native of Khust), was assigned to carry out the basic training for infantry soldiers.[12]

> 2) The Czechs had in Carpatho-Ukraine four thousand members of the so-called Home Guard, an auxiliary civilian guard which was to defend law and order in the state in the event of an emergency and assist the army. However, after the transformation of the republic into a federative state system, it was disbanded. The Army was willing to turn over to the Sich four thousand rifles, cots, and its entire inventory. Upon completion of this transaction, we were to enter into negotiations concerning further possibilities of training. It was anticipated that the Government of Carpatho-Ukraine would see to it that the problem of the Sich would be properly dealt with in concurrence with the Ministry of Defense in Prague.

I reported on these negotiations and the agreement in a letter to the Supreme Command and asked them to notify me what their stand was and what other assignments they would like me to carry out. However, I did not receive any answer either to my letter or to my repeated inquiries. For that matter, neither did V. Kachurovsky when he was in Khust. I was thus unable to continue the negotiations. As a result, we had wasted three months during which the Sich could have received proper training in handling light weapons and give quite a different display of action, both militarily and organizationally, in its resistance to the Hungarian incursion in the critical days of March. This would have saved many lives at the same time. From the point of view of the interests of the state, such negligence called for punishment.

One late evening in February—it was far after 9 o'clock—Minister Dr. Havelka, Chief of Staff of President Hácha's office, invited me to immediately come to the Hradčany Castle (Seat of President of the Republic). Having arrived there, I found Minister Havelka quite perturbed. He abruptly reproached me, saying that my Government in Khust was not able to control matters, that it was too soft, and that it allowed certain things to happen that "we shall not tolerate." When I inquired as to what "certain things" he was referring to, he replied: "An officer in uniform was walking down a street in Khust and was talking in Czech. A uniformed Sich member accosted him and hit him in the face, saying on Ukrainian land, one should speak in Ukrainian." It was the first time I had heard about such an incident. When I asked what the officer did, Havelka replied: "Nothing." In our continued conversation, I tried to convince Havelka that such incidents are usually provoked by the intrigues of our common enemies, who pit us one against the other. One can imagine what effect such irresponsible and inane behavior may have had upon the Army.

On another occasion, now in March and also late in the evening, Havelka again asked me to come to the President's office. Here I was told that at the Supreme Command of the Sich Dr. Vasyl Fryshchyn, professor at the Ukrainian Gymnasium (a secondary school/high school) in Velyky Bychkiv was beaten unconsciousness and suffered a broken rib. And again, this incident was blamed on our Government. Having possessed no information about the incident, I ascribed it to personal settling of accounts. I must admit here that such visits to the President's office did not belong to the more pleasant ones. After the appointment of Gen. Prchala as minister, Carpatho-Ukraine became the arena of unfettered anti-Czech demonstrations. In retrospect half a century later, it may be fair to draw the conclusion that these anti-Czech demonstrations did not bring about a resolution of the problems besetting our relationship with the Czechs but, on the contrary, strained them even more. Demonstrations are necessary and purposeful when they speak out against violations of rights, but one cannot concur with demagogic declarations that merely fanned hatred in the people against the Czechs, rocked the foundations of the state federation, and offered our malevolent opponents in the Central Government an opportunity to act against us in league with Poland.

People in leading political positions, such as Fedir Revay, head of the Ukrainian National Council, openly called for hand-to-hand fights with the Czechs and even for an uprising. Rohach, Msgr. Voloshyn's secretary, in an unusually acerbic article in *Nova Svoboda* on March 9, 1939 directed against the Czechs, went so far as to say that "We are waiting to see whether the Czech political megalomaniacs—imperialists—will compel us to exclaim: It is all the same whether it is Czech, Polish or Hungarian slavery for us, but we shall not tolerate degradation."

These kinds of outbursts by far overstepped the boundaries of a constructive statesmanship criticism or demonstration, for it amounted to an outright call for a general rebellion at a time most critical for us. Prime Minister Msgr. Voloshyn himself opposed such an unrestrained and unnecessarily provocative general manifestation of hatred for the Czechs. Undoubtedly, it is no easy task to control people's passions and therefore one should not fan them to uncontrollable extents, as they no longer prove to serve the interests of the state. Although leading personalities imbued with such uncompromising tendencies were in the minority, their voices cast a shadow upon the entire land.

The effects of the anti-Czech manifestations proved most disturbing to the representative of the Carpatho-Ukrainian Government in Prague when he had to face officials of the Central Government or Czech civic quarters among whom there were also friends of ours. Our vociferous patriots in Khust neglected to realize that in Prague I, as Revay once put it, "had to extricate budgetary credits" for us, which the Czechs were not constitutionally required to grant, and to secure food supplies for our population for which we were also dependent on Prague to a great extent. It goes without saying that such harsh behavior could not help establishing the kind of favorable atmosphere in Prague we were in such dire need of—even among Czechs who were amicably disposed toward us. What is more, such behavior was not becoming of our state, considering that both Carpatho-Ukraine and Ukrainians in general were being closely observed by foreign countries.

From the very outset of the formation of the federated state system, signs of initial difficulties were becoming more and more evident to us as well as to the Czechs regarding our relations with the latter. Such a development under given circumstances was understandable but had to be overcome with time. Certain political circles in Prague demonstrated an attitude toward us that was to a large degree conditioned by their intrinsic Muscophile and anti-Ukrainian sentiments. It was difficult for these politicians to accept the fact that Ukrainians had become a definitive state factor forming and developing their own power. Some members of the Czecho-Slovak Government in Prague, instead of consolidating their own internal forces in the state, accomodated Poland's desires and endeavored to restrict and even obliterate Ukrainian aspirations. Thus, as a first step in this direction, they contemplated liquidating the Carpathian Sich, to which end they issued appropriate directives to Gen. Prchala.[13] Since Carpatho-Ukraine was part of the state federation, there was no ground to present its problems in such a way as to have them run contrary to the interests of the land and to weaken the unity of the federation. These Czech politicians harbored the illusion that they could procure Poland's sympathy at the expense of the Ukrainians.

What should have been done was not to disband the Sich, but rather to institute essential reforms, accord the organization a legal basis, raise its status to that of a para-military corps led by competent leaders, and to turn it into an organ of the state. This, however, should and could have been accomplished by the Government of Carpatho-Ukraine as early as November or December 1938. Because of the fact that the Sich had only a statutory basis and was not legalized by government decree or separate law, as was the case with the Hlinka Guard in Slovakia, the Central Government and Gen. Prchala were prepared to issue an administrative order to disband the Sich. It was with this intention in mind that on March 7 President Hácha reappointed Gen. Prchala minister of Carpatho-Ukraine's cabinet and, on the basis of the Constitutional Law (paragraph 72, No. 121 of February 29, 1920) assigned him the portfolio of minister of internal affairs.

It should be noted that the Carpathian Sich guardsmen were also needed in villages to combat Hungarian or Polish diversionary activities that began as early as October 1938. However, without an appropriate specification of its tasks, the Supreme Command of the Sich "meddled in everything, wanted to be present everywhere, have a say in everything, and resolve all problems ... This was Carpatho-Ukraine's second cabinet and because being the second, it wreaked chaos and confusion."[14] It was this kind of activity on the part of the Sich that gave Prague and our enemies a trump card to undertake some actions against the Government of Carpatho-Ukraine and against the Sich itself.

> The Sich Command continuously demanded weapons, but did not find understanding for its demands not only within Czech military circles, but not even in the Carpatho-Ukrainian Government, or among members of the Ukrainian National Council, or later in the Ukrainian National Union. It had at its disposal several dozen revolvers and perhaps three automatic pistols. Besides, it acquired a certain number of Czech weapons by breaking into a warehouse arsenal of the Czech gendarmerie located close to the government building in Khust.[15]

Had the Government taken the necessary steps to regulate Sich activities and oversee it properly, there would not have been the need for such arbitrary actions to obtain weapons on the part of the Sich, for its functions would have been restricted by government decree and in full agreement with the requirements of the land's internal security. Indeed, two hundred Sich members, dispatched to assist the Army in certain military undertakings, were engaged in staving off Polish diversionists with weapons received from the Army and with the latter's consent. The matter of arming any organization was left to the discretion of the individual federated state under agreement with the Prague Ministry of National Defense, whose representative in Carpatho-Ukraine and Army commander in the province was Gen. Svátek. Since appointing Gen. Lev Prchala as minister, it probably would not have proved possible to resolve with him the matter of arming the Sich at the time, since his task was to accomplish just the opposite.

Sich members from the highland villages were eminently familiar with the topography of the forests and, therefore, their cooperation with the army engendered good results. It was these successfully conducted joint actions against terrorist subversive groups that spoke in our favor at home and abroad more convincingly than vocal shouts or inappropriately prepared anti-Polish leaflets, which the government had to confiscate. There were high-ranking Czech officers in the army in Khust who were favorably disposed toward the Ukrainian cause as well as a considerable number of young Carpatho-Ukrainian officers out of whose ranks a friendly group could have been formed for mutual cooperation. However, people in the Supreme Command did not seem to sense the need for such cooperation, they did not understand it, nor did they wish it. There, indeed, was necessity to organize our Czech friends, as I did in Prague, and utilize their help instead of pitting them against ourselves with hollow demagogic slogans.

Even during the federation era, the army in Carpatho-Ukraine was a stabilizing factor and in its hands lay the military defense of the land. As long as Gen. Svátek was the commander in chief, there were no major problems or differences. A change set in only when Gen. Prchala was appointed minister, which we correctly interpreted as Czech interference in our state rights. This fatal step of the Czech Government in Prague was what poisoned the relationship between the Czechs and the Ukrainians and, what is more, gave our enemies abroad an opportunity to gloat over the discord. And as for the Government of Carpatho-Ukraine, it committed an oversight by allowing the Sich, from the very beginning, to develop on its own terms under the leadership of patriotic but inexperienced people unprepared for handling military affairs who, these shortcomings notwithstanding, appointed themselves commanders.

Only in the light of all this is it possible to explain why foreign agents were able to infiltrate the Supreme Command of the Carpathian Sich and, as events have shown, successfully execute their pernicious work. In a letter of October 1, 1975, Klochurak informed me that the army had apprehended two Polish and one Hungarian agent in the Supreme Command. Gen. Svátek, Gen. Prchala's deputy, had asked Klochurak what they were to do with the prisoners. His answer was simple: to turn them over to the military tribunal. But the German Consul General in Khust, Dr. Hamilkar Hofmann, called on the army headquarters in Khust and declared that the three detainees were under the protection of the German Government. On recommendation of the Consul, the three were released the very same day and extradited to Hungary. The problem concerning foreign agents had reached such dimensions that Msgr. Voloshyn had to declare a full-scale war against them. However, the time was too short to bring the action to a successful completion.

Availing itself of the aforementioned methods of work, the Supreme Command turned itself into a sort of conspiratorial exclusive body that provoked displeasure in government circles. Responsible for this state of affairs were, in the first place, members of the Supreme Command, namely D. Klympush, I. Roman, S. Rosoliha, and I. Rohach. Because of their overestimation of themselves and their display of exclusiveness, they were not capable of understanding their role and properly performing it in the process of building a state. The Carpathian Sich commanders, as the aforementioned Sarvadiy has stated, had completely neglected the Sich's military training. Typical, from the military point of view, is Roman's statement that "I do not take orders either from Prague or Voloshyn, only from the Sich Supreme Command." Recall that he himself was in the Command![16]

One of our basic political tasks at the time was to organize our own internal force, in which the Sich could also have played a role had it been established on an appropriate organizational and professional foundation. The formation of our own force in Carpatho-Ukraine disturbed mostly our neighbors, Poland and Hungary, for they combatted in every possible manner the existence of this force and the existence of Ukrainian statehood as well. Our critical remarks directed at some members of the Supreme Command of the Sich do not relate to the Sich as a whole, its rank and file, or individual Sich units in the Field. They were carrying out the orders of their superiors sincerely and honorably, as it behooves soldiers, without questioning the rationale of or need for such orders. Hence, they should not be blamed or made responsible for the unusual deeds of the Supreme Command, such as the tragic clash with the army on the night of March 13–14. The Carpathian Sich, the Ukrainian Scouts, and the Ukrainian youth in general as our national defense force had, during the Hungarian invasion in March, given proof of the highest degree of personal bravery and dedication for which they have earned recognition from the entire nation.

The Supreme Command's organizational matters and behavior were the subject of talks with Revay at the Representation office during his visit in Prague to attend a Ministerial Council meeting. We all tried to impress upon Revay the idea that he should put the Sich in shape organizationally and to take over the command of it, as it was similarly done in Slovakia when Minister Sidor assumed the command over the Hlinka Guard. However, Revay declined our proposal repeatedly.

Agitated anti-Czech hatred was also to blame for the skirmish between the Sich and the Army on the night of March 13–14 in Khust. Msgr. Voloshyn did not know the actual cause of the clash. On the morning of the critical day of March 14, he called me on the phone to inform me of the incident, "Armored cars and tanks are patrolling the government building with guns pointed at the building. I have never seen anything like it and do not know what is going on. There was shooting during the night, and there are dead. Please inquire about this at President's Hácha's office." I was told at the President's office that reports had come in on the clash but that the incident was being investigated. I was given a similar answer over the phone also by the Ministry of National Defense. In a subsequent telephone talk with Dr. Havelka at the President's office, I was told that the Sich had attacked the Army and "was preparing a revolt." Ukrainian materials that have so far been published by the Supreme Command quarters maintain just the opposite—that the Army attacked the Sich. Thus, the question still remains open as to who first opened fire; mutual recriminations did not resolve the problem.

The clash between the army and the Sich was also for Msgr. Voloshyn a serious blow, for it was he who had continuously emphasized the need for amiable co-existence with the peoples of the federation, the Czechs and Slovaks. In the light of the development of political events of the time, it was only through such coexistence that he envisioned the possibility and guarantee of a national and state life for Carpatho-Ukraine. Whenever he visited Prague, Msgr. Voloshyn stayed at the Representation Office and held long discussions with me in which he decried any manifestation of exclusiveness. In all his political activities, he constantly espoused the idea of concentration of authority without which, he believed, affairs of the state could not be run.

In connection with the armed clash between the army and the Sich, history still owes us answers to the following questions: Was the clash a defensive measure of the Sich against an attack by the army or was it a revolt by the Sich? And who was the first to attack? Regardless of what answers history will furnish us in the future, there is reason to believe that the clash took place with the participation of German and other foreign agents provacateurs. It was Germany's plan to break up the Republic from within, and for this purpose special agents were dispatched to Slovakia and Carpatho-Ukraine. In order to shed some light on these problems, below are presented views of competent political figures from among Carpatho-Ukrainian government and Sich Supreme Command circles as well as from Czech military men.

In his letter to me, dated September 1, 1975, Klochurak recounted his conversation in Iasinia with the former commander of the Carpathian Sich, Dmytro Klympush. He wrote:

> On that day, a secret meeting took place on the premises of the Sich guards at which it was resolved to start a battle with the army the very same day and at the same time to remove some members of the Government, notably me [i.e., Klochurak—V. Sh.]. The order went out to the effect that the Sich members were to cease fire only upon a given signal. On the night of the same day, Yu. Perevuznyk appeared at my place, and both of us left during the shooting, heading toward the apartment of Prime Minister Msgr. Voloshyn, barely making it.

Klochurak goes on to say:

> Perevuznyk and I have already learned before that Klympush had left town and that Roman took over the command of the Sich. The latter was now in hiding at Prime Minister Msgr. Voloshyn's place. Msgr. Voloshyn did not know of Roman having taken over the command. I warned Roman that if he did not put a stop to the shooting then we would, for we had learned that the Sich members were waiting for their command to give the signal to cease fire. Msgr. Voloshyn revealed to us that Rohach, too, was hiding in his apartment. As it turned out, he was hiding in a bathroom for a couple of hours. Roman relented and said he would go and give the signal. Perevuznyk went with him. Within ten minutes the battle was over, the shooting had stopped. It was only now evident how many dead lay in the streets and in the Sich barracks.

Some 60 dead were later counted, but the number must have been considerably higher since bodies were found elsewhere as well.

In another letter to me, dated November 17, 1979, Klochurak notes that at that critical time Klympush left Khust for Iasinia under the pretext of being ill, but, as he later admitted, he did not want to take the responsibility for those events.

First Lt. Jozef Parčan, a Slovak friend of the Ukrainians, who was liason officer between the army and the Government of Carpatho-Ukraine and was assigned to this function by the Ministry of National

Defense in Prague, wrote this author a letter dated January 30, 1975, in which he relates the incident thus: "Cooperation between the Government and army was very good as was the supplying of food for the population that the army was engaged in and executed unfailingly and without problems." With regard to the armed clash, Parčan recalls that on the night in question, his orderly came to him and said, "'First Lieutenant, there is shooting!' 'Who is shooting?' I asked. 'The Sich,' was the reply. I jumped out of bed and quickly rushed toward the Government Building. As I was traversing the square around the cathedral, they started shooting at a staff sergeant who was crossing the square ahead of us. He was hit in the leg, but kept on going under the fusillage of fire from the cathedral's tower. They did not shoot at me, perhaps, because they recognized me." Parčan reached the Government Building, as it was called. There was gathered here a detachment of soldiers preparing to attack. He shouted at them, "Do not shoot, I'll take care of everything." "Although I am a friend of the Ukrainians," he went on in his letter, "I frowned at the armed revolt against the Government but, especially, against the army whose member I was." Parčan then rushed into the building, in which at one end of the hallway stood a group of soldiers and at the other facing them a group of Sich members. He walked back and forth from one group to the other, shouting not to shoot. He noticed a soldier being carried out of the building, a sergeant shot in the head. Parčan continues: "You can imagine what the army's reaction must have been to all this." Gen. Prchala also appeared at the scene also, and had a brief talk with Parčan. Tanks were firing, but ultimately the shooting came to a stop.

In another letter to this author, dated March 31, 1975, Parčan continued his narration:

> The army was not prepared for such an eventuality, having had no agents of its own planted in the Sich. It was taken completely by surprise and it was not until after the shooting that it concentrated on the defense and liquidation of the putsch. The putsch must have been prepared according to a plan, but no one could say when or where. Responsible for the clashes between the army and the Sich were mainly agitators and agents from Consul Wojnowitsch's entourage. Everything was over before noon. However, none of the organizers were to be seen around, only the boys [Sich members—V. Sh.], who were surrounded by the military and were facing the prospect of being executed. You can imagine the expression on the faces of these

non-military 17- to 20-year-old boys. They all told me that they were called to Khust to attend driving and mechanics courses, but in the morning were given rifles and told to fight against the soldiers and Czechs.

Two Carpathian members of the Sich Supreme Command, Roman and Rohach, as mentioned, were hiding in Msgr. Voloshyn's apartment during the armed conflict while the third member, Rosokha, claims he was at home asleep and did not hear a thing.[17]

Dr. Stepan Rosokha, member of the Sich Supreme Command, noting that tragic days were looming in the future, describes these events thus:

> On March 13 alarming news was reaching us: Hungarian military units were concentrating along the borders of Carpatho-Ukraine. The Carpathian Sich Staff is working feverishly. In the evening a meeting is being held at the Prime Minister's place. That night, the Prime Minister signs an order directing the gendarmerie command to hand over weapons. The order was complied with. The Sich is preparing to leave for the front. At 5:30 a.m., the Czech army attacks it on orders of Gen. Prchala to disarm it. The Government, gathered at the Premier's home, helplessly observe the Czechs shooting from their machine guns mounted on armored cars, batter and torture the Sich guardsmen whom, spattered with blood, they carried off to prison. Prague is deaf and blind to the Government's telegram and telephone protests. Prchala has military dictatorship in mind. The Sich did not surrender to the Czechs. At 10 o'clock, Prchala capitulated, abandoning the destruction of the Sich. In the end, however, it was the Hungarians who triumphed. They utilized the opportunity created by the Czech-Ukrainian fighting in order to occupy three Ukrainian villages in the Mukachevo region: Pidhoriany, Kolchyno, and Koropets.[18]

With such a sensationalist description, closer to fairy-tale narration than a serious outline of such a momentous event, Rosokha evidences how little he knows about the organization and psychology of an army and the meaning of the word capitulation. As chief commander of the army in Carpatho-Ukraine, Gen. Prchala as a commanding army officer had the power and possibility to at any time stage an overthrow of the Government and disband all organizations, including the Carpathian Sich. He did not do this, for Carpatho-Ukraine belonged to a democratic Czecho-Slovak federation, which possessed a constitution under the provisions of which Gen. Prchala would have been court-martialed for such an act. And, as is common knowledge, military tribunals are no-nonsense affairs. Only those people in the Supreme Command did not recognize either the Constitution or state laws who were preparing a conspiracy against the Government and had precipitated the tragic clash of the Sich with the army but themselves disappeared into hiding.

Another witness to the clash with the army, and former member of the Sich Command, was Liubomyr Hirniak, who wrote that by this imprudent step, the Sich provoked distrust toward itself in the Government, the army, and the public at large.[19] He notes that as early as December 1938, as the Government's representative in Prague, I had written a letter to the Sich Supreme Command, telling them that the army was willing to issue 4,000 rifles and the same number of beds to the Sich and take upon itself the military training of its members. But the Supreme Command did not deign to reply to the letter, accept the army's proposal, or to express any further wishes of its own, as I had requested. Instead, to quote Roman, the Supreme Command "was investigating Shandor." Strangely enough, it did not investigate those Hungarian, German, and Polish agents who were in its own midst.

Hirniak further relates that the Sich was put on alert because of suspicion that the Czech garrison was planning to disarm it: "It was 1 a.m. on March 14, when a group of officers walked out of the aforementioned room of the Sich Restaurant to put the decisions arrived at into effect. Downstairs a detachment of Sich men was already waiting to go and take over the weapons from the gendarmerie's storeroom, for the problem of the land's defense was most acute."[20] Hirniak does not specify what decisions were to be carried out by the group of officers leaving the Sich Restaurant.

Another account of the events comes from the Czech author Ota Holub:

> On the night of March 13–14, the Sich commander's runners were dispatched to people favoring the idea of a Greater Ukraine to tell them that the long-awaited moment had arrived. The armed messengers took off. The police guarding public buildings did not put up any resistance. In the city, they were able to disarm several military patrols. The guard at the military depot had noticed the rebels before they reached the building. He threw himself down and fired. The same day, March 14, a telegram was sent from Khust to the Army Headquarters in Prague saying, "The riot by the Sich has been quelled. Since 9 a.m. calm prevails in Khust, the Sich's resistance has

been broken, and its leader has promised to return the appropriated weapons (some 50 rifles). Some 50 Sich guardsmen have been taken prisoner and disarmed, most of them were Ukrainians from Galicia."[21]

The Sich Supreme Command demanded that the weapons be handed over to its members in order to defend the borders of the land against the Hungarian onslaught. Under normal conditions, this would have been quite a normal step, but in the given situation such conditions did not exist, and the Supreme Command either did not want to or was not capable of reacting. According to candidate officer Sergeant I. Sarvadiy, no one from the Supreme Command attended the military training he was giving the Sich for three months with the exception of Second Lt. Lopatynsky and Second Lt. I. Kediulych, who appeared once. This fact is indicative of the Supreme Command's disinterest in the military training of its Sich guardsmen. And to transform the Sich into a formation capable of defending the borders of the state, it was indispensable that it be properly trained in the art of warfare. The possibility for this was fully at hand. Prior to and including March 14, the defense of the borders belonged to the competence of the army or rather the units of the SOS, which also was entrusted with the control of armament in the land.

Dr. S. Suliatytsky, as commander of the Sich garrison in Khust, was in the position to directly observe the events of March 13 and 14, and to participate in them. He describes them as follows:

On March 11, 1939, the Sich Supreme Command asked for and received 80 uniformed and armed men. On March 13, at 12:30 a.m., two liason officers from the Supreme Command showed up at the Sich garrison and conveyed the oral order: "The garrison unit should go to the Government Building and take over the weapons there." Sensing the gravity of the situation, since the Supreme Command was asking for help, the garrison with its 80 men and 50 men of its non-commissioned officers' school, moved out to get the weapons. By 2 o'clock in the morning, the situation was as follows: the Government Building was occupied, the police were driven out from the center of town, and the 150 gendarmes were surrounded. Also Gen. Prchala and his guards were isolated in his home near the Government Building. The Khust chief of police, Yuriy Biley, Dr. Oleh Kandyba, now deceased, the commander [Ivan Roman—V. Sh.] called on the garrison chief. They all demanded that further operations be stopped. When the garrison commander expressly reminded them that in this case they would assume full responsibility, they agreed. The garrison complement returned to its quarters. By 6 o'clock, the same day, the Czechs had already pulled out detachments from neighboring posts, attacked all Sich objects in Khust, overran the headquarters of the Sich Supreme Command and the Sich Restaurant, and forced the Sich garrison to withdraw beyond the Tisa River.[22]

It follows from the above that the Sich Supreme Command had been prepared to accomplish a certain goal with its attack on the Government Building. Other authors report that the gendarmerie and police did not put up any resistance. In analyzing, from the military point of view, Dr. Suliatytsky's account of this event, it may further be inferred that it was not the army, but the Sich which first left its premises. At the present moment, however, it is premature to enter into a political or military analysis of the given incident, convinced that time is truth's best friend and will eventually bring to light more evidence on the event and ultimately lead to its accurate clarification. I would, however, wish to point to the irresponsibility, which deserved punishment, of the people in the Sich Supreme Command who engaged their troops in such a military misadventure.

I have dwelt at length on the issue of the clash, providing some critical observations of others, not with the intention of detracting from any given person's patriotism, but rather as these events concern the building of Carpatho-Ukrainian statehood. The rationale of the nation-state calls for a statesmanship-like style and form of work, regardless of personality or party. Anyone involved in the process of its affairs is bound to assume a certain degree of responsibility for it whatever his station.

The defense of Carpatho-Ukraine on March 14–15 could have been quite different. Had the Sich Supreme Command been led by experienced military men, conducted full military training for its members, and created favorable conditions for work, it would not have clashed in such a way with the Army. To date, nobody has stepped forward to reveal the whole truth and take the responsibility for the death of over 120 Sich guardsmen, young idealists devoted to the cause without reservation, who fell victim to the irresponsible acts of some of the members of the Supreme Command.

It is customary for some among us to shift the blame for all of our woes and mistakes onto our enemies. In the course of nineteen years, the Czech administration had done a lot of good for us, but also a lot of harm. Even under the federated Czecho-Slovakia, we had to sense manifestations of distrust and ill-will toward us among some Czech quarters which our government sought to dispel. In the exposition here, I am dealing with these problems and trying to elucidate them. But I wish to add that for the sake of consistency and objectivity in the pursuit of historical truth, it behooves our people to admit also our fault and tell the truth, however unpleasant, about ourselves. An example: The deputy of the supreme commander of the Carpathian Sich, Ivan Roman, in a telephone talk with a high-ranking Czech officer demanded that weapons be turned over to the Sich. When the officer asked, "What do you want them for?" Roman answered, "To fight the Czechs."[23] Obviously, such a statement by a man holding a responsible position dashes all good intentions and engenders mutual distrust. People with such an attitude toward the general problems of the homeland should not be in the leadership of any state organization.

As already pointed out, a Special Staff of the PUN for Transcarpathian Affairs operated on the territory of Carpatho-Ukraine in 1938–1939. It pursued the goals entailed in its program with the help of some officials. The Carpathian Sich was organized under the total influence of the PUN. As a result of such a bifurcation of functions— those of the Government on the one hand, and those of the Special Staff on the other—a kind of dual power was created over a period of time with the Supreme Sich Command arrogating to itself state functions that did not fall under its competence and which the population came to view as the formation of a second government. The situation that thus evolved was neither necessary nor advantageous. There was a national Government, which proved to be successful in coping with difficult problems under given conditions and which enjoyed the confidence of the people and of the Ukrainian world in general. Any manifestation of PUN's creative patriotism in Carpatho-Ukraine should have been made within the framework of the state represented by the Government and not outside of it. And even if such manifestations of dualism in the state had come to the fore, then it should have been PUN's duty to take appropriate measures to correct the situation to which appropriate party experts of PUN's Special Staff were obliged to pay attention.

As mentioned before, the Sich Supreme Command had not worked out any military contingency plan for an emergency situation. According to Sarvadiy, the Sich training instructor, the guardsmen were taken out to villages to engage in pre-elections campaigns, thereby creating chaos among them, undermining discipline, and causing them to lose interest in military training. These seem to be trivial matters, but if success is to be expected from such work then it is the ability to coordinate these very trivial matters and to form them into a great and useful whole on which success is dependent.

Special attention merits here the figure of Capt. Riko Yariy, who played a significant role in the PUN's Special Staff. We have already mentioned his name above, noting that Z. Knysh considered Riko Yariy to be a German agent. Accepting this premise, it may be safe to deduce that also his entire activity as member of the Special Staff in Carpatho-Ukraine was conducted in favor of Germany's political interests. It is, therefore, in the light of such facts that one is compelled to seek the cause for the clash between the army and the Sich and its pernicious influence on some members of the Sich's Supreme Command. To our knowledge, PUN, at whose behest Riko Yariy had operated as a member of the Special Staff, has so far not come out publicly to clarify its stance toward the role Riko Yariy had played in Carpatho-Ukraine in 1938–1939. By the same token, not a single member of the Sich Supreme Command or any person close to it has ever ventured to come out into the open with an appropriate clarification. Covering up the tracks of Riko Yariy's disruptive activities is not beneficial to the Ukrainian cause in general and to the Ukrainian nationalist movement, in particular, inasmuch as his pro-German covert operations, in fact, are wrongfully tied to the Ukrainian name.

Irrespective of what history will have to say about the clash, I can positively state at present that it was unnecessary and that it did not benefit either the Czechs or the Ukrainians. Aside from its lethal strike, the clash was also a moral blow to both peoples, so much so, in fact, that after a twenty-year span of free and common coexistence, culminating in a system of state federation, their separation was a tragic one which, surely, neither of them wished. The ruinous consequences and mutual distrust that the incident had engendered were soon to become evident. Already the day after the armed clash, some units of the retreating Czecho-Slovak army refused to turn over their weapons to our National Defense, which had taken over the defense of the land in the face of Hungary's aggression, a land considered a common enemy of both the Czechs and Ukrainians. In the past, there were many bright moments in the relationship between the two peoples which, I believe, cannot be blotted out because of an unfortunate incident that was the outcome of the reigning political circumstances enmeshing Central Europe.

According to Sarvadiy's information, the clash claimed some 120–150 lives of Sich guardsmen and 7 of soldiers of the Czecho-Slovak army, plus many wounded. The ratio of casualities in deaths was highly disproportionate. One of the victims was also Petro Lysiuk, the son of Kalenyk Lysiuk, a Ukrainian from the United States who was filming the battle.[24] In the following days, many more members of the National Defense laid down their lives in defense of their state independence. Among these were sons hailing from all corners of Ukraine. Also the head of the Carpathian Sich Staff, Mykhailo Huzar-Kolodzinsky and his deputy Zenon Kossak-Tarnavsky lost their lives.[25]

During the departure from Khust of the Carpatho-Ukrainian Government and the approach of the invading Hungarian army, there was no time to arrange a Christian burial for those who fell in the struggle. Only later, upon the petition of the faithful of the Greek-Catholic Church and local Germans did the Hungarian authorities give permission to bury them in a mass grave at the foothill under the ruins of the ancient castle in Khust—but without church ceremonies and without the public in attendance. In 1942, Sarvadiy commissioned some Khust carpenters to fashion a wooden oak cross, which was transported to the cemetery under the cover of a stormy night and buried into the ground of the mass grave. The Hungarians did not remove it. On November 1, All Saints Day, older and young people from Khust and elsewhere would come to the cemetery to light candles on the mass grave in reverence, memory, and hope. Perhaps someday a headstone or monument will be placed with the inscription: *To The Undefeated, Who Became Victors.*

Notes

[1] *See* V. P. Stakhiv's article in *Visti* (News), organ of the Fraternity of Former Combatants of I UD UNA (the 1st Ukrainian Division of the Ukrainian National Army), 5(11–12) [49–50] November-December 1954, p. 7.

[2] Letter from the Delegation to the UNO Executive Board, Saskatoon, Canada (Vienna, October 22, 1938).

[3] Ukrainian Press Service, *Karpats'ka Ukraïna v borot'bi* [A Collection of articles] (Vienna, 1939), pp. 27–32. *See also,* Dr. Yulian Chiminec, *Moï sposterezhennia iz Zakarpattia* (New York: 1984), pp. 60–81.

[4] Organization of Ukrainian Nationalists-Regional Executive Board of Transcarpathian Ukraine: "Vidozva," *Postii* August, 1938.

[5] Heinz Höhne, *Canaris: Patriot im Zwielicht* (Munich, 1978), pp. 302–306.

[6] *Visti* (Munich) 3–4 (89–90): 35.

[7] Ibid.

[8] From a letter of Dr. V. Komarynsky's to V. Kachurovsky, dated May 16, 1974.

[9] Ivan Rohach was editor of *Ukraïns'ke slovo* (Ukrainian Word) in Kyiv in 1941. In reacting to the conduct of the Germans in Ukraine, he wrote several critical articles which expressed approximately the view that "We tolerate the Germans, but we shall not tolerate them for long." At the beginning of December 1941, the Gestapo arrested him and kept him in jail for 12 days. On releasing him, they apologized to him, saying that the arrest was a mistake and, as related by him, told him: "You are a good editor, but we are in the midst of a war, and you should know what is permissable to write. We have, therefore, decided to drive you to Berlin and enroll you in a journalism course. Go home, pack your belongings, and our chauffer will pick you up." Ivan Rohach did just that, but before leaving he paid a visit the same day to his good acquaintance Yu. Komar (assumed name; real name is confidential) and related all about the incident. The latter instantly sensed danger in the whole affair and offered to help Rohach hide in a suburb of Kyiv. But Rohach declined the offer. When asked whether he was sure that the Germans would take him to Berlin, Rohach replied, "Yes, I am a hundred percent certain." Whereupon he bade farewell and left. Rohach took his sister along for the trip. Some four or five hours later, Komar's acquaintance, a Slovak German from Bratislava, stopped by and said in Czech, "Rohach, his sister, and other associates of his are no longer alive," adding that all of them were executed by gas in the "Black Raven," a black car so dubbed by the people. (From Yu. Komar's letter to this author, dated August 11, 1982.) It is hoped that this information will help to ascertain the exact cause of death of Rohach, our countryman and an avid patriot.

[10] Komarynsky's letter, ibid.

[11] Ibid.

[12] An aspirant was the non-commissioned officer rank in the Czechoslovak Army before promotion to the rank of officer.

[13] Hoensch, *Der ungarische Revisionismus und Zerschlagung der Tsechechoslovakei.* (Tübingen, 1967), p. 253. *See also,* Papée N 57 of March 8, 1939, No. PIII.119/26 Gn und Brief Papée von gleichem Datum, No. 11–b/C/14.

[14] Volodymyr Birchak, *Karpats'ka Ukraïna. Spomyny i perezhyvannia* (Prague, 1940), p. 39.

[15] Komarynsky's letter to V. Kachurovsky, *op. cit.*

[16] Birchak, *op. cit.,* p. 37

[17] Rosokha resided some 500 meters from the cathedral, the focal point of the armed clash. When this author asked Parčan whether Rosokha could not have heard anything, he replied: "Tell Rosokha that he probably had lead in his ears." Thus, the rank-and-file Sich members, bound by the order given to await a signal, were sent into the combat zone, while their commanders were absent, one hiding in the safest possible place—the apartment of the prime minister—while theother was sound asleep at home.

[18] Dr. Stepan Rosokha, "Narodzhennia derzhavy," in *Karpats'ka Ukraïna v borot'bi. Zbirnyk* (Vienna, 1939), p. 24.

[19] *Na stezhkakh istorychnykh podii. Karpats'ka Ukraïna i nastupni roky. Spohady i materialy* (New York: 1979), pp. 107–109.

[20] Ibid., p. 109.

[21] Ota Holub, "Drama pod poloninami," *Svĕt v obrazech* (Prague) 10 (7 March 1964).

[22] Dr. S. Suliatytsky, "Sribna zemlya mizh dvoma svitovymy viynamy," *Novy Shliakh Kalendar-Almanakh* (Toronto) 1984: 43–44.

[23] This conversation was related me by an army officer, a mutual friend of both myself and of Roman, who was present during the conversation.

[24] Ivan Sarvadiy, *Zmova proty uriadu Karpats'koï Ukraïny* (Chicago, 1984), p. 24.

[25] Mykhailo Huzar-Kolodzinsky arrived in Khust on January 19, 1939 and became chief of staff of Carpathian Sich. His adjutant was Zenon Kossak-Tarnavsky. Both hailed from Galicia. They were executed, together with a group of Sich guardsmen, by the Hungarians in the salt mines of Solotvyna village.

PART III

The World War II Years, 1939–1945

CHAPTER SEVEN

Invasion and Independence

The Hungarian Invasion

Once Hungary obtained Hitler's promise regarding Carpatho-Ukraine, it did not waste time waiting for Slovakia to proclaim its independence—by which act the Czecho-Slovak Republic would legally cease to exist—but immediately set out in the early hours of March 14 to attack the border of Carpatho-Ukraine. Col. Ján Heřman of the General Staff of the Czecho-Slovak Army was a liason officer in Carpatho-Ukraine during 1938–1939. In his military report, a copy of which is in my possession, he gives his account of the developments:

At 7 a.m. of March 14, I was summoned to the command post of the 12th Division where I was told that at 6 a.m. the Hungarians went into attack along the 172 km-long demarcation line in the direction of Uzhhorod, Perechyn, Mukachevo, Svaliava, and Berehovo-Sevliush. The Stráž Obrany Státu¹ retreated from the demarcation line but the Czecho-Slovak military units deployed in these vicinities repelled the attack and occupied defense positions. The Hungarians did not expect to run into such resistance and, as Col. Beldi of the General Staff was later to reveal to me, were convinced that they would reach the Polish border by the evening of the same day, namely March 14. In view of the fact that no declaration of war was made between Czecho-Slovakia and Hungary, it was the duty of liason officers to settle all border disputes with their respective counterparts of the other side. To this end, Col. Heřman and Lt. Melichar, together with a staff sergeant, crossed the border near Chinadiievo over to the Hungarian side, carrying a white flag and asked to be contacted by the Hungarian commander of the area. The Hungarians refused to negotiate. On the whole, our units managed to hold their defense positions at some of the sectors of the border, while the Hungarians were able to move ahead only at some points despite their numerical superiority. The

situation changed only when our Czecho-Slovak army was given an
order to withdraw. It was necessary to draw up a planned retreat of
the Czecho-Slovak units as well as to follow closely the advance of
the Hungarian formations lest it came to an armed confrontation
between them. I (Col. Heřman), therefore, remained in Chinadiievo
when the Hungarian army occupied the town. The Commander of the
Hungarian units occupying this sector was Col. Beldi of the General
Staff, my acquaintance from the time he served as a military attaché
in Berlin. Col. Beldi lamented the fact that during an exchange of fire
along the border the Hungarians suffered considerable losses, notably
near Velyki Luchky, amounting to 20 dead and many wounded. He
said that in the vicinity of Sárkágy the Sich guardsmen had lured
three Hungarian officers to negotiations, but then murdered them.
Col. Beldi dispatched a punitive expedition. In compliance with an
order received, one part of the Czecho-Slovak army was to cross into
Romania, the other into Slovakia via Perechyn. And, if it was to find
itself separated, it would then head for Poland.[2]

In executing the order to withdraw, the army thus weakened the defense possibilities of Carpatho-Ukraine. Its resistance lasted longest in
the sector Uzhhorod-Perechyn, where it had to protect its route of
retreat into Slovakia.

Such an unexpected withdrawal of the Czecho-Slovak 12th Division
from the territory of Carpatho-Ukraine shattered the entire defense
system of the land. Gen. Prchala, as the highest ranking general and
commander of the army, had the final say, especially since by
Slovakia's proclamation of independence the republic had ceased to
exist. The army was following the order to withdraw without reservation and, for its part, did not display any attempt to continue any further
organized resistance against the Hungarians. The brunt of the defense
now lay on the shoulders of the Carpatho-Ukrainian Government and
the militarily unprepared and ill-equiped Carpathian Sich, the Ukrainian Boy Scouts (*Plast*), students, and the general citizenry. There have
been instances when Carpatho-Ukrainian officers and enlisted men in
the Czecho-Slovak army had joined up with these defenders of the land
against the Hungarians.

Being pressed by time, I signed the document proclaiming the independence of Carpatho-Ukraine as it was and handed it over for translation to Oreletsky, who personally carried the copies thereof to the
embassies of the United States, Great Britain, Germany, France, Italy,
Yugoslavia, Poland, and Romania. In addition, I immediately notified

the Presidium of the Ministerial Council and the Ministry of Foreign Affairs of Czecho-Slovakia. The whole action took place between 12:30 and 2:30 p.m. For its part, the Khust government announced this news publicly from the Government Building around 6 p.m. The following day, March 15, the Soim approved the proclamation of independence.

Pursuant to the decisions of the Vienna Arbitration, Germany and Italy were the guarantors of Carpatho-Ukraine's borders. Based on such an international legal act, Prime Minister Msgr. Voloshyn's telegram appeal to the German Government on March 14 would then seem fully justified: "The Ukrainian Government asks the Reich's Government to intervene in Budapest so that the advance of Hungarian troops may be halted."[3]

In view of the change of the situation engendered by Slovakia's proclamation of independence, Msgr. Voloshyn was to dispatch another telegram to the German Foreign Ministry the same day: "In view of the declaration of independence by Slovakia, it was impossible for the Ukrainian people to remain within the federated union of the Czecho-Slovakia."[4]

The content of this telegram clearly demonstrates the obligation Germany had taken upon itself in Munich with regard to Czecho-Slovakia, which on this day ceased to exist. As a result, Carpatho-Ukraine was torn away from the federation. Although this telegram did not change anything in essence, it carries historical weight as a political document contradicting the arguments that Carpatho-Ukraine was responsible for the dismemberment of the Republic.

There followed, on the same day of March 14, a third telegram from Msgr. Voloshyn to the German Foreign Ministry in Berlin. It read: "In the name of the Government of Carpatho-Ukraine, I beg you to take cognizance of the declaration of our independence under the protection of the German Reich."[5]

The demand for protection of Carpatho-Ukraine's independence is a legitimate one, having its legal basis in the decision adopted by the Vienna Arbitration of which Germany was the chief partner. All three telegrams were restrained in both tone and content and did not go beyond the bounds of the land's political problems and the customary diplomatic politeness. It may be added here that neither the German nor the Slovak Government notified the Carpatho-Ukrainian Government of its political intentions. This fact also is most revealing about their attitudes. All these telegrams were addressed to the German Government not to Hitler, which, from the point of view of diplomatic protocol, was significant and reflected Voloshyn's distaste for Hitler and his views.

Dr. Hamilkar Hofmann, the German consul in Khust, was directed to convey to Msgr. Voloshyn a message from the German Ministry of Foreign Affairs no earlier than at 5 p.m. on March 15, that read as follows:

> Please inform the Carpatho-Ukrainian Government orally that Hungarian troops having advanced against Carpatho-Ukraine on a broad front, the German Government advises it to offer no resistance. As matters stand, the German Government regrets that is not in a position to assume the protectorate.[6]

The text of the notification of the proclamation of independence corresponded to the political exigencies of the times. Our contention was that with Slovakia's proclamation of independence the Czecho-Slovak Republic ceased to exist. We reached this conclusion because the Czecho-Slovak Republic had no juridical norms either in the Constitution of February 29, 1920 or in Constitutional Law 328 for establishing forms and methods of dissolving the Republic. In practice, Slovakia's declaration of independence had divided the Republic into two parts separated by great distance. On March 6, 1939, I had personally informed Minister Revay in Prague that in a few days, Slovakia would proclaim its independence and that we would have to do likewise, but only after Slovakia, so that responsibility for destroying the Republic would not fall on us.

Some authors, notably Dr. Hubert Ripka, who made a life-long specialty out of opposing the interest of Ukraine, have endeavored in their books to stigmatize Carpatho-Ukraine for the disintegration of the republic. The test cited above fully demonstrates that such arguments are without foundation. The question of the breaking up of the Republic was the central issue deliberated at the trial of Slovakia's President Msgr. Tiso in Bratislava in 1946–1947. This points to its fundamental political, moral, and legal weight.

On March 14, 1939, shortly before 3 p.m., I received a call from the Ministry of Foreign Affairs in Prague notifying me that it had refused to accept an ultimatum of the Hungarian Government concerning

Carpatho-Ukraine that had been presented by Hungary's Ambassador Count János Wettstein. It motivated its refusal by pointing out that Carpatho-Ukraine had already declared its independence and suggested to the Ambassador that he submit the ultimatum to the Carpatho-Ukrainian Government's Representation in Prague. A few minutes later, Ambassador Wettstein called me on the phone, stating that on behalf of Hungary's Government he was to present an ultimatum to the Government of Carpatho-Ukraine and requested the Representation to render this possible. My answer was that in view of the developments in the state I was not certain whether I could transmit the ultimatum at all in time to my Government in Khust, and would, therefore, suggest that the Hungarian government forward the ultimatum directly to Khust. The Ambassador concurred. It was my intention to gain time for us. The ultimatum was delivered the same evening at 7 o'clock in Khust by the Hungarian officer, Baron Wimsperg. The salient points entailed in the ultimatum, which the Carpatho-Ukrainian Government rejected, were as follows:

1. To free the Hungarian internees in Ruthenia.

2. To stop the persecution of Hungarians in Ruthenia and allow them to organize freely.

3. To give weapons to the Hungarian Home Guard.

4. To arrange that the Czech-Moravian troops evacuate Ruthenia within twenty-four hours.

5. To guarantee complete protection of life and liberty to Hungarians in Ruthenia.[7]

In accord with Germany's plans, Hungary endeavored to occupy Carpatho-Ukraine in a quiet, peaceful manner. In fact, Germany's Chargé d'Affaires in Prague, Andor von Henke, as Acting Ambassador, advised me that Carpatho-Ukraine "should not put up resistance to the Hungarians, since the German army was marching toward the borders of Carpatho-Ukraine and will take care of everything."[8] It was in the interests of Hungary, first and foremost, to obtain Carpatho-Ukraine without combat or the population's resistance in order to show the world that the process was indeed a "voluntary annexation of the land." Conversely, it was in the interest of Germany to allow the burial of the problem of Carpatho-Ukraine to be as unostentatious as possible since the land attracted great attention and gained importance on the international forum in 1938–1939 namely thanks to Germany, which now wanted to show Hungary its gratitude for having withdrawn from The League of Nations and joined the Berlin-Rome Axis.

The Carpatho-Ukrainian Government resolutely opposed these propositions and was in its decision historically justified. This decision was reflected in a telegram sent by the German ambassador in Budapest, Otto von Erdmannsdorff, at 9:35 a.m. on March 15:

> The Foreign Minister [of Hungary—V. Sh.] told me: "Voloshyn had demanded by telegram the independence of Carpatho-Ukraine in return for an offer of permanent friendship and close cooperation. He, for his part, had sent to him an ultimatum expiring at 8 p.m. today, demanding the transfer to the commander of the advancing Hungarian troops of the authority, hitherto exercised *de facto* by him, in order to avoid bloodshed.[9]

At 4 p.m. on March 14, President Hácha departed from Prague by train for Berlin, but by then Bohemia's fate had already been sealed. As before, Hitler now again strictly followed his predetermined timetable—the middle of March—to ultimately destroy Czecho-Slovakia. He proposed two alternatives to Hácha: either he "voluntarily" capitulates or else would have to see Prague destroyed by the German Luftwaffe. Hácha agreed to capitulate, and by 4:30 a.m. the following morning, March 15, he ordered Prague by phone not to put up any resistance against the occupying German troops, which at 6 a.m. moved to occupy Bohemia. This order was executed to its fullest extent.

Since the independence of Carpatho-Ukraine was proclaimed at 2 p.m. on March 14, which Hácha himself confirmed in Berlin where he arrived at 1:30 a.m. on March 15, Hácha's order did not apply to the army on the territory of Carpatho-Ukraine which Germany was not occupying. Hungary's attack against Carpatho-Ukraine took place at 6 a.m. on March 14, i.e., when Czecho-Slovakia still existed as a full-fledged federated state. In the given case, the army was defending the entire Czecho-Slovak territory, not merely that of Carpatho-Ukraine to which it was constitutionally obligated. Moreover, it was Hungary that had all the time harbored a hostile attitude toward the very existence of Czecho-Slovakia as a state and was much to blame for the latter's collapse. Even in September 1938, the Czechs could not or did not want to engage in an armed resistance against Hitler, this now was still the occasion to deliver a blow at his ally, particularly since it was Hungary that had attacked Czecho-Slovakia and then without a declaration of war.

On March 14, the Czecho-Slovak army units deployed along the borders were holding their defensive positions. The Division Command in Svaliava had pleaded with the 6th Corps command stationed in Spišská Nová Ves for some bombers to bomb the advanced Hungarian lines. However, the Corps failed to comply with the request. As a result, the Division Staff was left to its own devices to cope with the situation. That same evening, the Hungarians advanced north from Uzhhorod toward Perechyn, located 21 kilometers from Uzhhorod, apparently in an effort to cut off the Czecho-Slovak army's withdrawal to Slovakia.[10] The Hungarians were attacking along the Svaliava-Khust line. In command of the Czecho-Slovak army was Brig. Gen. Oleh Svátek. In the early hours of March 15, the army withdrew on the Uzhhorod sector of the front and in the afternoon from Chinadiievo toward Svaliava. Both these sectors of the front were holding their own well against the superior forces of the Hungarians, but less so on the sector of the Khust front.

In the afternoon of March 14, Non-Commissioned Officer Onderchanyn, a career soldier in the army, left Priashiv for Khust as a courier. He carried a sealed envelope containing important documents intended for Gen. Prchala from the 6th Corps. Among these documents was also an order for evacuation and withdrawal of the army from Carpatho-Ukraine.[11] On Gen. Prchala's orders, the Divisional Command issued an order to all military units to evacuate and withdraw. Although the Hungarians demanded that the Czecho-Slovak army capitulate, the latter rejected this demand and continued to withdraw in the direction of Slovakia, Poland, and Romania.[12] The National Defense of Carpatho-Ukraine demanded weapons from the retreating army. When the army refused, the National Defense members took them by force causing some exchange of fire to erupt between them.

With the Czecho-Slovak army on the retreat, the matter of defending the land was solely in the hands of our government. It was urgent to decide what position was to be taken. At first, opinions were divided regarding our armed resistance. Msgr. Voloshyn, as a priest and person of unusual gentleness, held the view that an armed resistance would cost us much bloodshed and that we alone could not hope to come out victorious against the Hungarian army. It was true, of course, but the sense of historical responsibility simultaneously dictated that we must put up resistance since our patriotic Carpathian Sich, Plast, the youth and citizenry in general would fight against the invading Hungarians with or without our Government's consent. This problem was also the subject of discussion among former politicians and members of the Directory of Ukraine who had gathered at the office of the Representation in Prague. As a result of the many telephone talks and deliberations between Khust, Prague, and Vienna, the Carpatho-Ukrainian Government decided to defend the country and declare the Carpathian Sich, Plast, and other organizations as constituting the military force of the land under the name of National Defense, to which Defense Minister Stepan Klochurak appointed Col. Serhiy Yefremov as its commander-in-chief. Col. Yefremov immediately formed his General Staff consisting of eleven persons.

The same evening, Roman reported in that "he was taken ill and asked to be relieved of his duties."[13] There were two other members of the Sich Supreme Command, the above-mentioned Rosokha and Rohach, who did not participate in any battle engagement and whom their superiors, commanders Yefremov and Fylonovych, regarded as deserters.

The Government proclaimed general mobilization, which under the circumstances was more of a symbolic nature, intended in its brief form to demonstrate the Government's attitude toward Hungary's aggression and its resolve to resist it with all possible means. Neither the Government, nor the National Defense nor the population was prepared for such a change of events. Admittedly, there was also no prospect of achieving military success. Yet, this was a correct answer to the call for capitulation, which the Government unanimously rejected. A capitulation would have entailed the danger that Hungary would take advantage of our hopeless situation and submit such clauses into the conditions of capitulation that would make it seem that the Government of the independent state, forced by the will of the people, had handed over the land to Hungary. Later on, Hungary might have used it against us politically.

In view of the controversy surrounding the figure of Gen. Prchala in Carpatho-Ukraine, it is of interest to cite his last talk with Msgr. Voloshyn over the phone as related by Col. of the General Staff of the Czecho-Slovak Army Ján Heřman:

It was about 21:00 hours when in Svaliava I was called to the telephone to receive a call from Perechyn. The call was from Army General Prchala, then a member of the Ukrainian Government, which throughout its tenure refused to recognize him. He directed me to transmit his order to all Czecho-Slovak commanders calling for an attack to drive the Hungarians out of the country. Astounded by such an order, I tried to explain to him that in view of the absolute Hungarian superiority and of our situation, the execution of such an order would be connected with great casualties inflicted upon our army and could hardly be successful. Gen. Prchala then ordered me to personally call on the Hungarian commanders to leave the country. I told him that such an intervention was bound to meet with failure and asked for the reason for these changed orders. Gen. Prchala pointed out that the German army was advancing toward Carpatho-Ukraine and wondered what would the Germans say if they would have to demand a territory from the Hungarians that we were relinquishing. I was stunned, but said that I did not know what to do in such a case.

A few moments later, Gen. Prchala asked me to connect him with Prime Minister Voloshyn in Khust and to listen in on the conversation. The connection was made without delay so that we were still able to intercept the talk between Voloshyn and a member of his cabinet, Klochurak, who cautioned the former against signing the capitulation demanded by Hungarians which he felt would be tantamount to treason committed on the Ukrainian people. Gen. Prchala asked Prime Minister Voloshyn whether he had any knowledge of the movement of German troops. Voloshyn replied that in response to his inquiry for help, Berlin declined the appeal in a telegram to the German consul in Khust and instead urged that the government of Carpatho-Ukraine surrender to the Hungarians. Upon hearing this, Gen. Prchala rescinded both orders he had issued to me.[14]

On the eastern front, namely the Khust sector, the:

> . . . soul of the defense of the demarcation line was Brig. Col. Antonin Zeman, commander of the Khust SOS Battalion who was more eager to retreat than to fight. Commanders of his companies engaged in battles on their own and on their own responsibility. The First Battalion stationed in the Khust barracks was constantly facing the threat of an attack by the National Defense, which has been attacking individual persons and small groups and seizing their weapons.

> The man, who had the real opportunity to conduct combat, coordinate the resistance and facilitate gradual evacuation, to hand over arms and defense positions to the Sich, the man who, admittedly, in these days was willing to fight against Hungarian aggression, the unrecog-

nized Minister Gen. Prchala, still capable of major decisions—was first to flee.

On March 15, after issuing orders relating to evacuation, Prchala left Khust for Svaliava [and then proceeded to Perechyn—V. Sh.] in the escort of armored cars and bodyguards. His conversation with Gen. Svátek will never be known as both are now deceased and, anyway, would have not revealed any new experience.[15]

Some of this information was culled from military reports on the role of Gen. Prchala as commander-in-chief of the Czecho-Slovak army formations in Carpatho-Ukraine during the battles with the Hungarians. Because of his sympathies for the Poles and Germans, Gen. Prchala was not interested in conducting a full-scale defense of the land. Yet, he had the possibility of transferring his command to Gen. Svátek but failed to do so. There were many Carpathian conscripts as well as reserve officers serving in the 12th Division, which fact would have constituted a positive balance in the event the land had to be defended. However, the order to withdraw and evacuate the army as well as the pressure of time did not make it possible to organize a combat-capable unit from the ranks of Carpathian officers and soldiers.

A curious situation evolved. An armed army is withdrawing, while an unarmed National Defense of Carpatho-Ukraine takes upon itself the defense of the state although it lacks adequate military training or weapons. Some army and SOS groups willingly handed over weapons to our National Defense, others refused. This forced our defenders to seize the weapons from the army, gendarmerie, and SOS by force. It was to our great dismay when in some cases units of the army would not give weapons to our national army but instead handed them over to the Hungarian populace. Officers of the retreating Czecho-Slovak army, however, admired the prowess and bravery of our National Defense that were displayed in combat against the vastly superior Hungary army and stood in awe of their heroic deaths. Many of these young people had never before held a rifle but demonstrated valor and devotion in defending their state and the rights of their people.

The main line of defense ran along the so-called Krasne Pole located between Velyka Kopanya and Khust, which forms a natural gateway to Khust seven kilometers in length and five in width. In charge of the defense operations before Sevliush was Prof. Yakiv Holota, a World War I officer, and the National Defense of Carpatho-Ukraine within whose ranks fought our brethren from Galicia, former members of the Ukrainian army, Ukrainian officers of the erstwhile Ukrainian National Republic, non-commissioned officers, and soldiers from the Czecho-Slovak army who also engaged in obtaining arms from the retreating troops. The bursts of artillery and tank fire from here could be heard in the hall in Khust when the Soim was in session. It was here in this sector of the front where greatest resistance was offered against the Hungarian army that rendered it possible for the Soim in Khust to convene on March 15.

The Hungarian army defied the 1907 Geneva Convention concerning prisoners-of-war and other rules governing the conduct of war. Members of the National Defense taken captive by the Hungarians were executed on the spot, the wounded were bayonetted to death. It should be noted here that by the decision of the Government of March 15, defenders of the land were formed into our army—the National Defense of Carpatho-Ukraine and as such the same military rules applied to them as to any other regular state army. But the Hungarians treated them as bandits. Yet, it was Hungary, which had until recently dispatched its officers and men disguised as civilians over the border into Carpatho-Ukraine to engage in terrorists acts, which, under the law, actually put them legally in the category of bandits. When these bandit-terrorists were captured, we did not shoot or bayonet them to death, but rather extradited them to Hungary. The explanation for such inhuman and cruel behavior on the part of Hungary toward our defenders may be sought in the fact that Hungary had Hitler's backing and, just like Hitler, did not feel obliged to adhere in the slightest to any international law or, for that matter, to the laws of humanity.

One such incident was related by Plast[16] Scoutmaster Stepan Pap-Puhach:

> In a shooting engagement, Mykhailo Kozychar, a student of the Teachers Seminary and commandant of the Plast companies in Vynohrady, was gravely wounded. As they withdrew, his Plast comrades Ivan Popovych, Yurko Pekar, and Osyp Shkiriak carried him away to the village of Veriatsi. The village, however, was surrounded by Hungarian troops, and the defenders were taken prisoners. They were manacled, including the gravely wounded one, whom his comrades-in-arms had to carry, and led to the river Tisa. At a spot on the steep bank undermined by the river's waters, a Hungarian officer untied their hands and ordered the strongest among them, Popovych,

"Take your leader [i.e., the gravely wounded Kozychar—V.Sh.] and hurl him into the Tisa!" When Popovych failed to move even upon repeated command, the enraged officer hit him in the face with all his might. His face covered with blood, Popovych straightened himself up and adroitly seized the officer by the throat. He made a step back and then plunged with the officer into the water. A volley of shots from a machine gun mowed down all three of them, including the wounded man. Popovych in the water still held the officer in his grip as both flowed down the river dead.[17]

American journalist Robert Parker gives the following eyewitness account of the events as he drove in a car with Col. Baron Unger, commander of a Hungarian army unit, toward Khust:

"These Ukrainians are fighting desperately," said the Baron. "I must say they show great courage. It's a pity to kill them because we could use them in the Hungarian army after this is over. Up to there our tanks will push them easily off the roads. But they have dug trenches this side of Khust and will fight like hell. I want to get into the town by four o'clock."[18]

In his further account, Parker relates having seen corpses of the Sich guardsmen, Boy Scouts, young students—"blue-eyed sons of Carpatho-Ukraine" scattered along the sides of the road.

The unforeseeable direction in which the development of events evolved was anything but conducive to putting up a resistance by the National Defense in terms of organized military strategy and tactics. The exemplary daring, courage, and patriotism of the National Defense and of the entire Ukrainian population were eminently demonstrated by their full devotion and their determined battle performance against the aggression by the invader. Special attention is merited by the fact that participating in the battles were sons of our people from all Ukrainian lands, such as Central Ukraine, Galicia, Bukovina, Volhynia, and the Kholm region. Many gave their lives in defense of Carpatho-Ukraine, among them Col. M. Huzar-Kolodzinsky and 2nd Lt. Zenon Kossak, both from Galicia. Together with other retreating comrades, they were arrested by the Hungarians in the village of Apsha and taken to Solotvyna, where all of them were executed. Another group of defenders, consisting of 373 men under the leadership of Col. Fylonovych, managed to cross the river Tisa into Romania only to be returned to the Hungarians and interned in the town of Velyky Bychkiv where they were subjected to unmerciful beatings and robbed of their belongings.

At the same time, the Hungarians arrested teacher M. Ostapchuk and Litvytsky in Bychkiv. On orders of the Hungarian officer Col. Makonyi, they were severely beaten, dragged into the street, and shot. Ostapchuk was the father of two young children.[19]

I do not known whether the Government of Carpatho-Ukraine had concluded an agreement with the Government of Romania that in such a critical situation the latter would receive our people as friends and not as enemies. Nevertheless, Romania's behavior toward us was all the more strikingly ill-intentioned since it was a member of the Little Entente together with Czecho-Slovakia and had always maintained unfriendly relations with Hungary.

It was on the battlefields of Carpatho-Ukraine that the first shots rang out against the march toward a "new Europe." At the time when the whole of Europe was submitting to the dictates of Germany's policies and receiving with trepidation every piece of news on further successes scored by Hitler, members of the National Defense were locked in a desperate struggle against Hitler's ally, Hungary. This resistance interdicted Germany's and Hungary's designs to arrange Carpatho-Ukraine's burial as "quietly" as possible. The free world reacted to this display of heroism on the part of the defenders of their statehood with expression of respect and recognition. All declarations by Hungarian statesmen, including those of regent Horthy, about the *Gens fidelissima* or the alleged fidelity and loyalty of Carpathian Ruthenians to Hungary, paled in the face of such reality. From the perspective of our common past within Hungary's realm and of the recurrent Hungarian occupation, the resistance of our population and the sacrifices it had made are historically fully justified. Hungary can neither deny nor erase from history such events of resistance. The people gave a resolute answer of "no" to Hungary.

Session of the Soim

In accordance with Article V of Constitutional Act No. 328 of Czecho-Slovakia, the President of the Republic was to convoke by separate decree the first session of the Carpatho-Ukrainian Soim within one month after the elections. The date for the convocation of the Soim was set for March 2, 1939, following an agreement reached between Msgr. Voloshyn and President Hácha. A special commission attached to the

Presidium of the Ministerial Council in Prague was created that was to work out a plan regarding the participation of Czech state officials at the ceremonial opening of the first Soim session in Khust. As the representative of the Carpatho-Ukrainian government, I got in touch with the commission as well as other leading civic and business circles of the Czech-Ukrainian Society.

When President Hácha postponed the convocation of the Soim from March 2 to March 9 and failed to sign a decree relative to the new date, I, upon the directive of Msgr. Voloshyn, paid a visit to the Office of the President where I met with Minister Havelka to ascertain the reason for the postponement. Speaking in guarded terms, Havelka blamed the reason for the postponment on internal state difficulties. The impression I got from the tone and mode of the discussion was that an important political game was being played behind the scenes that may have been responsible for altering the date of the Soym's convocation.

It was at this very moment that diplomatic dealings over Carpatho-Ukraine were being conducted behind the scenes and, at that, with the participation of the Czecho-Slovak Foreign Minister Dr. František Chvalkovský, The Poles offered advice to the Hungarian Government in an attempt to reach an agreement directly with the Czechs concerning the issue of Carpatho-Ukraine "whereby it would deprive Berlin of its most solid argument."[20] On March 6, the Hungarian Government sent Deputy Foreign Minister János Voernle to Prague who, together with the Hungarian ambassador in Prague, János Wettstein, conferred with Chvalkovský about incorporating Carpatho-Ukraine into Hungary. Wettstein promised Chvalkovský to compensate the Czechs for the loss of Carpatho-Ukraine, noting that [the Czecho-Slovak Government—V.Sh.] "can now receive something for Transcarpathia, while later nothing."[21]

Chvalkovský agreed to such a solution in principle and promised to take up the matter with President Hácha and obtain the German Government's sanction of it.[22] However, the German government's sanction was not received.

It is true that Czecho-Slovakia was undergoing a deep state crisis, but as it turns out this was not the only reason for the deferment of the Soym's convocation. What is striking is that those Czechs who were ill-disposed toward the Ukrainian cause should engage in bargaining with the Poles and even the Hungarians over Carpatho-Ukraine for the sake of retaining the integrity of what remained of their state. In the given situation, it was the intent of Hungary, Poland, and Germany to prevent the immensely successful elections in Carpatho-Ukraine from attaining confirmation in a Soim and simultaneously consolidating the constitutionally prevailing state of affairs. Granted, the lingering crisis in the country could have eventually had some influence on the scope and festive character of the opening of the Soim session in Khust itself, but could not have been the reason for a repeated postponement. On the contrary, the convocation of the Soim of the Carpatho-Ukrainian part of the federation was rather a manifestation of the stability and consolidation of the federation's unity that ran afoul of Hitler's policy.

On March 10, President Hácha issued a decree calling for the convocation of the Soim on March 21, but the further development of events preempted the date. As a result of Slovakia's proclamation of independence on March 14, we were geographically cut off from the Czech lands. In this situation, the Government of Carpatho-Ukraine saw itself compelled to also proclaim independence the very same day. At the same time, Prime Minister Msgr. Voloshyn convoked the first session of the Soim to be held at 3 p.m. on March 15.

At 3:00 that afternoon, Msgr. Voloshyn declared the first session of the Soim open. It was a historic event, for the first time in their long struggle Carpathian Ukrainians created their own legislative body and their own government. In his opening address, Msgr. Voloshyn, among other things, said:

> First of all, I express our profound gratitude to Almighty God for allowing us to see this day that is a holiday for our small land as well as for all territories inhabited by the Ukrainian people; to God's Providence for allowing us, the smallest part of the Ukrainian lands, to live to witness this historic moment.[23]

After the formal-legal procedure, Msgr. Voloshyn announced the act of the proclamation of independence of the day before which the Soim unanimously approved. In keeping with this, the Soim passed the following appropriate laws:

ACT No. 1 of the Diet of Carpatho-Ukraine of March 15, 1939.

Article 1: Carpatho-Ukraine is an independent State.

Article 2: The Name of the State is Carpatho-Ukraine.

Article 3: Carpatho-Ukraine is a Republic, headed by a President elected by the Diet of Carpatho-Ukraine.

Article 4: The official language in Carpatho-Ukraine is the Ukrainian language,

Article 5: The colors of the national flag of Carpatho-Ukraine are blue and yellow; the blue on top, and the yellow on the bottom.

Article 6: The State emblem of Carpatho-Ukraine is the present national emblem: a bear on a red field on the left hand, four blue and three yellow stripes on the right hand, as well as the Trident of St. Volodymyr the Great. This part of the Act shall be regulated by a special Act.

Article 7: The national Anthem of Carpatho-Ukraine is "Shche ne vmerla Ukraïna." [Ukraine still survives—V.Sh.]

Article 8: This Act becomes valid immediately after its passage.[24]

In accordance with the adopted laws and the decisions of the Soim, a new leadership of Carpatho-Ukraine was formed consisting of the following persons: Msgr. A. Voloshyn elected president of Carpatho-Ukraine; Prof. Avhustyn Shtefan—Speaker of the Soim, and Yulian Revay—prime minister and minister of Foreign Affairs.

Following the passage of these acts, the Soim adjourned, and President Msgr. A. Voloshyn later departed from Khust for Velyky Bychkiv.

The proclamation of full independence of Carpatho-Ukraine is an important act of state-political nature although it did not win international recognition. It is the highest expression of the will of the population in conformity with the principle of the right of self-determination, which belongs to the Ukrainian people on an equal basis with that of the contemporary ruling state nations. Such confirmation applies to all Ukrainian lands and the entire Ukrainian people. By force of historical circumstances, individual state territories of Ukraine have throughout the ages been separated from each other and from their maternal Kyivan center. Nontheless, the Soim of Carpatho-Ukraine, not unlike the Parliament of the Western Ukrainian National Republic in 1919 and the National Council of Bukovina and Bessarabia in 1918–1919, adopted political decisions declaring unification of the state with central Ukraine. Such manifestations of unification in all lands of Ukraine constitute a powerful juridical case in the international forum and a great moral force in their state-liberation struggle.

Each and every member of the Soim was aware of the fact that in the face of the Hungarian aggression, the days and perhaps even hours of the just ratified proclamation of independence of Carpatho-Ukraine by the Soim were counted. This general view from the perspective of history, was reflected in Soim Deputy Dr. Mykhailo Brashchayko's speech:

> No matter what course events may take, no matter what turn history may make, one thing is certain: this is our land and always will be our Ukrainian land, and our people will never allow anybody to take it away. Let our enemy know that he will come here as a guest but not as an overlord, for the overlord and master of this land will be us— the Ukrainian people. I am not to know whether our government's hours or days are numbered: but what I do know is that neither the days of Carpatho-Ukraine nor of the Carpathian people are numbered, for it has lived here for a thousand years and will live for another thousand.[25]

Hitler in Prague

The confusion that was caused by the news about the alleged movement of the German army in the direction of Carpatho-Ukraine and by the political machinations of the German Embassy in Prague was cleared up by Revay in Vienna. On the late evening of March 14, he made a direct telephone call to the Ministry of Foreign Affairs in Budapest, asking it to explain why Hungary's army was attacking Carpatho-Ukraine without a declaration of war. The answer he received was: "We are doing so with Germany's permission." All was made clear by this statement by the Hungarians.

No blow to the national pride of the Czechs could have been worse than the one they sustained when, after twenty years of a prosperous and well organized democratic statehood, they were to see Hitler in the Hradčany Castle in Prague. Hitler was driven through Prague in an open car and then settled in Hradčany—the palace of Czech kings and presidents. President Hácha, returning from Berlin by train, was prevented from arriving in Prague ahead of Hitler by numerous enforced stops along the way. What is more, he was not allowed to enter his quarters in Hradčany through the main entrance, only through a side entrance reserved for household personnel.

At about one o'clock in the afternoon of March 15, I received a telephone call from the Hungarian ambassador in Prague, János Wettstein, who inquired when he could take over the "Verkhovyna [i.e., "Highland"] Archives." I told him that I had no idea whatsoever as to what archives he was referring. He said that he had in mind the archives of my government. I explained that the country I had the honor of representing is called Carpatho-Ukraine and that I knew nothing about some "Verkhovyna" and its archives.

Wettstein apologized for his blunder and then explained that he meant the archives of the Representation Office of the Carpatho-Ukrainian Government. I then asked on what basis he was making this inquiry, to which he replied he was doing so on the historical-legal claims of Hungary to the territory of Carpatho-Ukraine. He added that the people were presently again voicing their desire to belong to Hungary and that their army in occupying the land was merely fulfilling the population's will and that as such the archives as property of the people now belonged to them.

The Ambassador raised a problem that required a more elaborate answer on my part. I noted that Hungary was never historically the owner of this territory, nor could it have been, for in relation to Carpatho-Ukraine it always figured as an aggressor and occupier. Both of these features denote violence and as such do not pass as historical claims. On the contrary, the people of Carpatho-Ukraine were fighting with arms in their hands against the new aggression and occupation of the land perpetrated by Hungary.

Ambassador Wettstein did not wish to end the conversation and continued further. He stated that, to his knowledge, I was a jurist by profession, (yes, was my answer) and as such that I ought to be familiar with such a juridical principle in Roman Law known as "Rei vindicatio," by virtue of which Hungary, having had Carpatho-Ukraine in its possession for centuries, became its owner and is now laying historical and legal claims to it. I replied that I did not know his profession, but that as an ambassador he also ought to know that to acquire the right of ownership on the basis of the Roman Law's juridical principle of "Rei vindicatio," five *bona fide* titles are needed as prerequisites, two of which Hungary lacked.

Thus, on this basis it could not have acquired the historical and legal title to the country. At this point in discussion I had the feeling that I was taking doctoral exams in Roman Law. Yet, I deemed it necessary to provide Wettstein with a more elaborate answer, once he touched on the subject of my profession and the principle of "Rei vindicatio" as Hungary's legitimate and historical claim to Carpatho-Ukraine.

Wettstein did not react, allowing me to continue. Moreover, I explained, Carpatho-Ukraine never was an integral part of Hungary, as the first Hungarian king, St. Stephen himself, had asserted by creating out of our land the "Marchia Ruthenorum" and appointing his son Imre as its prince. Likewise, the Hungarian government had enacted on its own initiative Law No. X in December 1918 endowing Carpatho-Ukraine with broad autonomy. Both these historical-legal acts of the Hungarian King and government supported my arguments. Wettstein did not produce any counterargument. He changed the subject to talk about the Hungarian army's campaign against Carpatho-Ukraine to "execute the will of the population."

In order to conclude the dispute, I remarked that by attacking Carpatho-Ukraine, the Hungarian army had committed a flagrant act of aggression and coercion which would meet with the Carpatho-Ukrainian population's resistance, the Free World's condemnation, and would not bring Hungary any honor. I told him that he would do well to spare both himself and me needless annoyance if he were to refrain from taking interest in the archives and talking on the subject of Carpatho-Ukraine. With this I terminated the discussion.

Those present in the office of our Representation were exhorting me to deliver a protest note on this issue to German Foreign Minister Ribbentrop, who was then visiting Prague. The editor of the Lviv newspaper *Dilo,* Roman Holian, was particularly insistent. I opposed the idea, arguing that all this would not help or change anything since it was clearly evident that Germany's Government had given its consent to the Hungarian invasion of Carpatho-Ukraine. In the end, they prevailed and prepared such a memorandum in German. When the protest note was drawn up, Holian, through his German journalist colleagues, made the necessary arrangements for the Representative of the Carpatho-Ukrainian government to deliver it to the German authorities at Hradčany Palace, the seat of the Czecho-Slovak goverment. I was reluctant to affix my signature to it because of its stylization and again voiced my objection to delivering any memorandum. A discussion ensued, the outcome of which was that I relented and finally signed it but with mental reservations.

Roman Holian, Vasyl Oreletsky and I took our official car and drove to Hradčany. Underway, I could not help noticing that every Czech policeman I saw was accompanied by an SS-man. As we were approaching Hradčany, German SS-men would halt us and not allow us to proceed. On each occasion, a Czech policeman would have to explain to his partner that ours was a ministerial vehicle and should be waved on. Once, we had to produce our official identity cards but finally we were able to reach the immediate vicinity of Hradčany. But we could not get any farther, for the entire area of Hradčany was swamped with German civilians and army men. However, at the spot prearranged by editor Holian, there awaited us an official of the Office of Protocol with an SS guard. We explained to him that the Representative of Carpatho-Ukraine wished to hand over to Ribbentrop a memorandum concerning Hungary's aggression against Carpatho-Ukraine. The official replied that an audience with Ribbentrop would be impossible as he was busy and soon to leave for Vienna, but that the memorandum could be turned over to one of his assistants.

I hastened to explain: "Carpatho-Ukraine has proclaimed its independence and according to diplomatic protocol, the first visit of a representative of a country is to be made to the minister of foreign affairs." Meanwhile, the situation around us became tense with the SS-men prodding us "*schnell, schnell*" (hurry, hurry). The crowd around us was like a beehive buzzing with activity. We were nervously discussing the subject of diplomatic protocol when suddenly Hitler appeared in the window, setting off a deafening shrill that gave me the shivers. All attention was directed toward him. The roar lasted a good two minutes and was so intense that it was impossible to conduct a conversation. I used the pause that followed to make my final stand in defending my argument. In such a surrounding it was no easy matter to engage in arguments and present certain demands for fear of making oneself a suspect in something else. The protocol official was getting impatient, but I continued to hold my ground. And so, after an exchange of views and arguments, we bade each other farewell and departed. My friends were not pleased with such an ending.

As we were returning from Hradčany, Holian urged me to go to the German Embassy and submit the memorandum there. I told him that we would go home and that I would attend to the matter myself. I never did hand over the memorandum and was right not to have done so. It was prepared in a specific atmosphere that was marked by Hitler's arrival in Prague and had a stipulation appropriate to the occasion. I viewed it as an official state document which, in my opinion, could possibly someday prove unfavorable for us. Hence it was this aspect that prompted me to take the decision I did.[26]

The High Command of the German Army wasted no time in hanging out signboards throughout Prague giving notice that it had taken over the government of the country and isuing instructions to the population. The placards bore the signature of Infantry General Blaskowitz. The text in the Czech language was incredibly faulty. It was beyond comprehension that the German army, being in such a center as Prague, would intoduce itself in such illiterate Czech. Prague now had a new overlord, the chief commanding general, Blaskowitz. Under international law and custom, on such occasions diplomatic representatives of foreign countries were obliged to pay a courtesy visit to the new ruler. The Protocol Bureau of the Czecho-Slovak Ministry of Foreign Affairs performed the technical and organizational work in the matter of the last one, having prepared a list of persons, set up a schedule of audiences, and other formalities relative to identifying personages, and the like. This was to be the last act performed by the Ministry of Foreign Affairs. The Protocol Bureau also approached the Representation office, since Carpatho-Ukraine was now an independent state and had a certain status enabling it to participate in such official affairs, and inquired whether it could do what is necessary also for the representative of Carpatho-Ukraine.

I welcomed the opportunity, for I was already trying to establish contact with the military headquarters, which under the circumstances was no easy or simple understanding. What I was interested in was following president Hácha's order issued from Berlin on dismantling the Czech Army, to secure the return to their homes of our conscripts from Carpatho-Ukraine who were drafted on March 1 as well as those who had served one year in the army in the Czech lands and Slovakia, which had declared its independence the day before. In these conditions, created by Slovakia's proclamation of independence and the Hungarian aggression, the situation for our soldiers in the Czech lands and Slovakia was especially complex. Hence, such a visit to a competent military authority was of great importance to me.

At the appointed hour, I announced myself to the officer on duty at the Regional Command Headquarters. He in turn reported my presence to his general and showed me into his office. After an exchange of the usual salutations, during which I could not help having a strange feeling emanating from the realization of Germany's role in the seizure of Carpatho-Ukraine by Hungary, I explained to the general the problems with our people in the Czech Army and asked him to help me in this matter. He instructed his adjutant, a major, to set an appointment for me with a general in charge the following day, which the major promptly attended to and told me what I was to prepare in writing for the meeting. At the Representation, we immediately set out to prepare the necessary memorandum which, following the customary introduction and explanation of the subject matter, entailed the following desiderata of ours:

> 1) That the soldiers from Carpatho-Ukraine serving in the army stationed on the territory of Bohemia, Moravia, Silesia, and Slovakia be gathered in barracks of the larger cities and that they be provided with military food supplies and care during their stay there.
>
> 2) Since our soldiers do not have civilian clothes and presently cannot obtain them from home, they should be allowed to go home in their military uniforms, having removed the rank and other military insignia from them.
>
> 3) To furnish them with appropriate documents for a free railroad ticket on the territory of Bohemia and Slovakia and up to their home destination and to arrange for Slovakia to allow them transit through its territory.
>
> 4) To furnish them with the necessary provisions and cash for the travel.

By 10:30 in the morning of the following day, I was already in the general's office located in the building of the former ministry of National Defense in Dejvice (one of Prague's districts) and handed over to the general our memorandum, giving him an oral explanation. The general showed an earnest interest in the matter and promised to make the necessary arrangements which he, indeed, did. Among the conscripts I found my own brother, whose whereabouts I had not been aware of. To be on the safe side, I also turned with the same request to the Representation of the Slovak Government (similar to ours), for our soldiers were stationed also in Slovakia or had to travel through Slovakia from Bohemia on their way home. The German Army had in the building of the Ministry of National Defense its own telephone exchange by now and did not use the old system.

As I was leaving the building, I noticed that German soldiers were hauling away from their military storage impressive Czech-manufactured anti-aircraft guns and loading them unto motorized convoys heading for Germany. The Czech onlookers on the street stared with saddened faces, some cried. I, too, was overcome with an unpleasant feeling watching this scene. It was not that long ago that I had been marching down these streets as a candidate for officers' school in the Czecho-Slovak Army.

Now all this had suddenly changed; the state ceased to exist without firing a single shot.

We were nearing the end of our official relations with the Czechs. Neither of us, however, anticipated such an ending. During my stay in Prague as representative of the Government of Carpatho-Ukraine, I had managed to win over for our cause many Czech sympathizers in prominent state, cultural, and business positions who accorded us significant help. But there were also those who were ill-disposed or even outright hostile toward our work, but such a phenomenon is quite normal in this line of work. During the era of the federation, Prague's attitude toward us was quite different than that over the preceding nineteen years. Much, of course, depended on us ourselves, on how we confronted the change and how we utilized it. I take pleasure in asserting that thanks to our mode of operations in cooperating with the Czechs in Prague, we were able to win their trust in Carpatho-Ukraine and the Ukrainian cause in general. This could come about only because of our understanding and respect for their national feelings and their tragic situation at the given moment as well as because of our stance toward their mortal enemy, Hitler's Germany. I was convinced that—from the point of view of our state interests, including the idea of preserving the unity of the federation—this was the only correct way of executing the tasks devolved upon me by the government of Carpatho-Ukraine.

On March 15, 1939, I announced myself for an appointment with Prof. Jan Kapras, minister of education, at the Presidium of the Ministerial Council, with whom I had maintained close official ties throughout my sojourn in Prague. The atmosphere at the Ministerial Council was one of dejection. One could feel the waft of death. The Professor welcomed me with the words, "My dear friend, it is the end of all things." "This is why I have come, to say goodbye to you and our other friends and to thank you and the Czech people on behalf of the Government of Carpatho-Ukraine for our life together for nineteen years." And I added, "In our relations, there were good and bad times, but in the face of what is taking place now we must remain strong in spirit and seek a common friendly trail." Minister Kapras thanked me for the kind consideration and noted that the Prague Government had also received a thank-you telegram from Msgr. Voloshyn. He was touched by the telegram and my expression of sympathy and remarked:

> I never expected you to act so nobly after all the wrongs we have caused you.[27] Your Government, by sending us the telegram, and you personally have made us very happy. By contrast, we have received nothing from the Slovaks. Please accept from me and the Czech people expression of our best wishes for Carpatho-Ukraine and the entire Ukrainian people.

The Professor had tears in his eyes. The official relations between our two governments came to an end.

With the arrival of the German armed forces and Germany assuming supreme power in the Czech lands, the legal correlation between the army in the Czech lands and in Carpatho-Ukraine was altered. Germany became master of the Czech lands and faced with this reality, I turned to the Acting German ambassador in Prague, Andor von Hencke, with the demand that, in view of the altered situation in the former Czecho-Slovak Republic, Germany issue a directive to the Czech military units, ordering them to join our National Defense in defending Carpatho-Ukraine against the Hungarian invasion, or if this was to prove impossible, to allow us to draw volunteers from the army and to divert the weapons of the former Czecho-Slovak Army to our National Army. The German Embassy communicated the message to Berlin the very same day, stating:

> Herr Hencke further stated that the Prague representative of the Carpatho-Ukraine Government had called at the Legation and asked that the Czechs be prevailed upon to send Czech troops in conjunction with the Sich to repel the advancing Hungarian troops. Herr Hencke refrained from giving any decision.[28]

The same day, I once again called von Hencke and told him that we had learned from Budapest that Hungary was occupying Carpatho-Ukraine with Germany's consent. I expressed my Government's deepest displeasure over the fact that Germany had the temerity and without our knowledge to sell us out to Hungary but not the courage to at least decently inform us about it. It may be noted in passing, that in his book *Augenzeuge einer Tragödie* (Witness of a Tragedy), Hencke mentioned the conversation but skipped this particular reference.

Notes

[1] SOS; special border guard units.

[2] Col. of the General Staff Jan Heřman's military report, pp. 16–17.

[3] DGFP, Series D, Vol. IV, 1951, p. 255.

[4] Ibid., p. 251.

[5] Ibid.

[6] Ibid., p. 276.

[7] Macartney, *A History of Hungary, 1929-1945*, part 2, (New York, 1956) p. 337.

[8] An American journalist in Budapest reported that Radio Berlin had broadcast the following news: "They [the German troops—V. Sh] were moving toward the Polish border and also toward Subcarpathian Ukraine . . . ." (Robert Parker, *Headquarters Budapest* (New York–Toronto, 1944), p. 30.) I did not regard von Hencke's information as reliable or politically logical and, therefore, immediately set out to call my source in Slovakia by telephone. My doubts were proven correct by the source, who told me that the German troops had moved as far as the city of Zilina but did not proceed any further eastward. From Priashiv, I was able to learn that "only one civilian car bearing a German standard was cruising the city but no German troops were in sight."

[9] DGFP, *op. cit.,* p. 280.

[10] Here the 36th Infantry Regiment suffered a loss of 9 dead and many wounded.

[11] Ota Holub, *Květy* (Prague) 8 February 1969.

[12] Ota Holub, *Květy* (Prague) 18 January 1969: 27–28.

[13] Serhiy Yefremov, "Kryvavyi Berezen' Karpats'koï Ukraïny," *Svoboda* (Jersey City) 4 March 1954.

[14] Colonel of the General Staff Ján Heřman, Military Report, p. 18; Ota Holub, *Květy* (Prague) 18 January 1969: 28 (from the memoirs of Chief of the General Staff Fischer recorded his last moments shortly before his departure from the command post in Svaliava at 22:00 hours on March 15, 1939).

[15] Ota Holub, ibid., p. 28.

[16] Remember that Plast was the organization of Ukrainian Boy Scouts. It was non-military in nature and became part of the National Defense force only because of the extraordinary nature of the attack on our homeland.

[17] Stepan Pap-Puhach, *Plastovy Almanakh. Z nahody 50 littia Ukraïns'koho Plastu na Zakarpattiu 1921–1971* (Rome, 1976), pp. 9–10. Rev. Pap-Puhach obtained this information from a fellow priest, who had chanced meeting a Hungarian soldier in the village of Dravtsi near Uzhhorod. The soldier admit-

ted having personally participated in the execution of those Plast Boy Scouts. Moreover, he showed the priest some personal documents belonging to the dead.

[18] Robert Parker, *op. cit.,* p. 40.; quotation by Parker.

[19] Col. V. Fylonovych in the journal *Visti* 3–4 (89–90) June 1958: 36, 38.

[20] Quoted from Akademia Nauk URSR. *Ukraïns'ko-uhors'ki istorychni zv'iazky* (Kyiv, 1964), p. 101. *See also,* Külmst. Hungary res. pol. 1939. 33/a t.195 a. sz.

[21] *Ukraïns'ko-uhors'ki,* p. 101. *See also,* Külmst. Hungary, No. o. 1939, B. Praga. No. 35. t.

[22] Külmst. Hungary, res. pol. 1939. 33/a t. No. 207 a.

[23] From the audio-tape recording taken by K. Lysiuk in Khust and later in the U.S. transcribed by Rev. A. Kist. Record 10, Reel 5, Tape 21, p. 15.

[24] Avhustyn Shtefan [Augustin Štefan], *From Carpatho-Ruthenia to Carpatho-Ukraine* (New York, 1954), pp. 42–43. *See also,* Peter G. Stercho, *Diplomacy of Double Morality* (Jersey City, 1971), pp. 408–409; *and* Stepan Rosokha, *Soim Karpats'koï Ukraïny. Za 10-littia proholoshennia samostiinosti* (Winnipeg, 1949), pp. 80–81.

[25] From the audio-tape recorded by K. Lysiuk in Khust and transcribed by Rev. A. Kist. Record 3, Reel 1, Tape 2, p. 7.

[26] Some 16 years later, editor P. Holian visited me in my office at the Secretariat of the Pan-American Ukrainian Conference in New York City. In the course of our conversation, I noticed that he wanted to tell me something, but hesitated in doing so. "I have the feeling that you would like to ask me something," I said to him. "Is it about the fate of the memorandum?" "Yes, yes! I have often thought what you may have done with it, for I could not locate it in any of the published German government documents," he explained. "I have kept the memorandum and have not shown or given it to anyone," I replied. "You handled the matter prudently, and I am glad that you have kept it," was his relieved reply.

[27] The idea to dispatch the telegram expressing thanks to the Czech government originated with M. Babota and was endorsed by President Voloshyn. The telegram was dispatched by Babota and V. Kachurovsky from the city of Satu Mare in Romania.

[28] DGFP, *op. cit.,* p. 275.

CHAPTER EIGHT

The Hungarian Army in Khust

At about 5 o'clock in the afternoon of March 16, 1939, as the Hungarian troops entered Khust, all churches began to toll their bells. Accompanying the army were special detachments that plundered and shot those Ukrainians whom they may have caught wearing a Sich or Ukrainian Plast (Boy Scout) uniform. They also shot those Ukrainians who were pointed out by Hungarian collaborators or by members of the fascistic "chornorubashniki" (Black Shirts),[1] the pro-Hungarian and pro-Russian group led by Stepan Fentsyk. After them came the Hungarian gendarmerie whose members covered up the traces of crimes committed by their predecessors, giving them, as it were, legal license for their acts. We cannot tell whether in the history of Khust there ever were as many prisoners as then. The prisons and other state buildings were overcrowded with people. The prisoners were not interrogated and no reports were taken from them, but they were repeatedly beaten. The beatings were administered to every part of the body and to every one, be they young or old, educated or uneducated. There was no need to ascertain guilt, because the "kangaroo courts" of the Hungarians considered legal due process as superfluous, guilt having already been decided in advance by higher authorities.

The practice of summary mass executions of uniformed and civilian people or even of clergymen by the Hungarian military authorities were in sharp contradiction to Hungary's own laws as well as International Law and without cause. The commanding general of the occupation army, Gen. Béla Novákovics, declared that Carpatho-Ukraine was taken *manu militari* (in the act of war) and, therefore, it was "natural and pursuant to the law of war: that a military administration was to be established.[2]

For the purpose of illustration, some concrete incidents are discussed below.

Prof. Yakiv Holata related that 26 students of the teacher's seminary fell in battles near Sevliush. On the other hand, Hungarian officers in Khust claimed to have killed 70 Sich guardsmen and Plast Scouts between Sevliush and Velyka Kopania. Twenty-three Sich guardsmen were shot in the backyard of the Khust courthouse and some 30 in the backyard of the Town Hall. Outside of the town shot to death were the teacher Mytrovych, storekeeper Vashchyshyn, and university student and Plast Scout Oleksa Blystiv. The Romanians extradited 373 refugees, part of whom the Hungarians executed and dumped their bodies into the Tisa river and interned others in a concentration camp near the Hungarian town of Varjulapos. Arrested was Col. Dr. Zarytsky, a Ukrainian physician serving in the 45th Infantry Regiment in Khust, who was severely beaten. According to testimony obtained from a priest, 36 persons were hanged in the village of Boroniava. In the village of Hrushovo, teacher Vasyl Nebola was shot to death and Father Aleksander Kupar, a Greek-Catholic priest, was imprisoned and subsequently taken to Solotvyna where he was shot. Dr. Figura, a Gymnasium (High-School) professor, Dr. Zavalnytsky, and 12 Boy Scouts and Sich guardsmen were executed in Volove. On the outskirts of Nyzhni Veretsky Ivan Gryga was executed as he was returning from the Soym's session in Khust; he had been a conscientious farmer and member of the Soim. A similar fate befell some 30 Sich guardsmen and civilians there. In Velyky Bychkiv, teacher Dmytro Ostapchuk and member of the cooperative Mykola Lytvytsky were gunned down in the street. In Tyachevo 16 persons were shot and hurled into the Tisa River, while 48 others were ordered into the nearby woods and shot, after having dug their own graves. In the town of Perechyn 18 were executed, among them Mykhailo Hranchak, I. Keretsman, the earlier mentioned M. Pekar, Dobey, Frantsko, Yuzkevych, and a farmer father of five children. The town's mayor, also a farmer, was severely beaten and was confined to bed for several months. The bodies of those shot were later unearthed in the woods. There is a mass grave in Iasinia with some 103 victims of the Hungarian terror. Peasants working on the Tisa River would cross themselves when asked about these atrocities and say, "Only God alone knows how many corpses flowed down the river."[3]

We are witnesses to what Hitler's officially nurtured policy of hatred had led to in his drive for a "New Europe" and how deep this policy had permeated the psychology of other peoples. A similar approach in instilling the spirit of hatred toward the subjugated peoples was taken by the Hungarians long before the Germans did, and with the same inevitable results. "They cultivated assidiusly a Magyar chauvinist spirit of astonishing intensity; and, under Koloman Tisza, who held the Premiership of Hungary from 1875 to 1890, governing for the greater part of that period alongside of Taaffe, they erected Chauvinism into a State policy."[4]

The Ukrainian Plast commander Stepan Pap-Puhach gives the following account of his imprisonment in Khust:

> I was beaten on my hands with rubber truncheons. They turned blue, numb, and then became swollen. Thereafter, I could not even feel my hands. The third from among the terrorists leaped at me like an infuriated wild animal, grabbed me by the hair and started banging my head against the wall. I immediately felt a sharp pain right under my eye caused by some hard object. I fell to the ground unconscious When I came to, they were rinsing my blood from the floor. I was carried and thrown into solitary confinement, where I lay for three days on boards and in fever. Every prisoner was subjected to such torture. Some several times over.[5]

The author goes on to describe the execution of Plast Scout A. Blystiv and the imprisonment of Prof. Rostyslava Birchak, daughter of Prof. Volodymyr Birchak.

Many Ukrainians were arrested in the village of Teresva, among them also Fedir Revay, director of the Teachers Seminary, Father Vasyl Lar, Prof. Ya. Holota, and Father Khrystofor Mysko of the Order of Basilian Fathers. Such arrests were carried out across the land. Some were arrested and shot on the spot, some were led into woods and shot there, others were taken to the hospital in Kryva near Khust and then deported to the concentration camp in Varjulapos near the city of Nyiregyház in Hungary proper.[6]

The overwhelming majority of the prisoners did not speak the Hungarian language. It was strange and painful for the prisoners to be allowed to have visitors but to converse only in the Hungarian language, which they did not master, so that the guard would understand them. Those who spoke the language were not allowed to say anything about their life in prison.

It would be impossible to set up an exact statistic of the number of casualties from the Hungarian occupation. Hungarians claim their casualties to be 72 dead, 144 wounded, and 3 missing in action.[7] According to Prof. Birchak, the Ukrainians suffered 1,000 to 1,500 dead.[8] These figures, however, refer to casualties in Khust and its vicinity that Prof. Birchak was able to garner since he stayed another six weeks in Khust after the invasion. On the other hand, Czecho-Slovak circles in Washington, who had researched this problem, have come out elsewhere with the figure of some 5,000 casualties from the time of the Vienna Arbitration in November 1938.[9]

Notwithstanding the fact that the Ukrainian populace had put up such a desperate resistance against the Hungarian aggression and occupation, Prime Minister Teleki had the temerity to tell the Hungarian Parliament in Budapest on March 16, 1939 that Carpatho-Ukraine had been taken by the Hungarian army "in response to the will of the Carpatho-Ruthenian population." He also declared that "We are incorporating the fraternal Ruthenian people into Hungary and granting them autonomy."[10] It is evident from the above that a subjugated people has few possibilities to fight against the allegations told to the world in its name.

By its military conduct against the defenders of Carpatho-Ukraine, Hungary flagrantly violated the provisions of the Hague Convention "IV. Respecting the Laws and Customs of War on Land," signed at the Hague, October 18, 1907, which contain the following sentence: "In countries where militia or volunteer corps constitute the army, or form part of it, they are included under the denomination 'army.'" The National Defense of Carpatho-Ukraine as an army was in consonance with the Geneva Convention; it had its own commanders, uniformed men, and combatants wearing distinguishable signs of the national blue-yellow insignia on the left arm. Furthermore, it complied with other requirements, namely: "to carry arms openly, and to conduct the operations in accordance with the laws and customs of war." Hungary was a participant to this Convention to which it subscribed in 1940.[11] We do not know whether any State-Participant to the Convention, save for Germany, may have drawn Hungary's attention to its irresponsible and inhumane conduct with regard to the defenders of Carpatho-Ukraine. During World War II, as is now well known, three of the major warring powers: Germany, the USSR, and Japan flagrantly defied this Convention and all concepts of human dignity, humaneness, and law in their behavior towards war prisoners.

Poland did not content itself with the liquidation of Carpatho-Ukraine and with a common border with Hungary. As mentioned before, many young Ukrainian activists from Galicia and other Ukrainian lands arrived in Carpatho-Ukraine for the purpose of taking part in the state life of the land and to contribute to its development. An overwhelming number of them joined the ranks of the Carpathian Sich, which clearly nettled Polish official circles. In the battles with the Hungarian army, many of them laid down their lives. The protest notes issued by Poland caused a great deal of concern in Prague and Khust. Obviously, it was not the danger of Carpatho-Ukraine militarily attacking Poland that the latter feared most, but rather the cultivation and strengthening of the idea of state unification of all Ukrainian lands. And therefore, after the fall of Carpatho-Ukraine, Poland demanded from Hungary the extradition of captured Sich guardsmen that hailed from Galicia. Hungary complied instantly by handing over 40 Sich guardsmen of Galician origin, who were imprisoned in Bereza Kartuzska until the arrival of German army units in September 1939.[12] Later on, it was learned from the Ukrainian prisoners that some of the extradited Sich guardsmen were shot on the border by the Polish military.

It was difficult to comprehend why the Western democracies would find no reason to intercede in defense of the Ukrainians when Hungary committed such brutal acts and thereby contravened all human rights with regard to the Ukrainian population. Such cooperation between Hungary and Poland regarding Carpatho-Ukrainians in general and Galician Ukrainians, in particular, prompted even the German authorities to intercede in their defense. On April 22, Gen. Sándor Homlók, chief of the 5th Department of the Hungarian General Staff, met with German Admiral Wilhelm Canaris. At this meeting, on Canaris's recommendation, the following points were agreed upon:

> 1. The Hungarians are obliged to refrain from extraditing to Poland any Sich guardsmen they might capture if such extradition were "tantamount to a death sentence for them," given that they were likely to be executed by Polish authorities.
>
> 2. They themselves are not to imprison them.

According to testimonies from the prisoners, their lot had somewhat improved and the harsh beatings had ceased, following this meeting between the parties.[13] On June 7, the remaining 242 Galician Sich members were released and transported to Vienna, thanks to the efforts of the Leadership of Ukrainian Nationalists (PUN).[14] Hirniak, quoting Gerald Reitlinger, also gives credit for the release of the Sich guardsmen to Admiral Canaris.[15] Another author, who was a prisoner in the Varjulapos concentration camp, asserts that the former Hetman of Ukraine, Pavlo Skoropadsky, was instrumental in the release of the Sich guardsmen.[16]

Acceding to the demands of the opposition parties in the Hungarian Parliament, the Hungarian Government dispatched in the summer of 1939 a special commission to Carpatho-Ukraine to investigate the arrest and cruel treatment of Ukrainian prisoners. The idea of an investigative commission came after the Greek-Catholic Bishop of Mukachevo, Aleksander Stoyka, had complained to the Hungarian Government about the mishandling of prisoners and asked for amnesty. The commission was headed by Béla Fábián, parliamentary deputy and head of the Committee of War Veterans. Fábián brought up the matter with regional administration leaders and Bishop Stoyka in Uzhhorod.[17] Soon after the return of the commission to Budapest, many Ukrainian prisoners were released and the brutality against many others diminished markedly. The letup, however, was to last only until the autumn of 1942, when the brutality erupted anew with full force. Even local Hungarians, who had lived together with the Ukrainians between the two world wars, were outraged at the behavior of their ethnic brothers. For instance, a Hungarian by the name of Zoltán Szábó voiced strong exception in the press to what he considered was the erroneous policy toward the Ukrainians, stating that Hungarians cannot overlook or dismiss out of hand or escape the fact that they have as their neighbor a great and strong Ukrainian nation.

Occupation

There exist among nations legal norms and well-established customs that govern their mutual cultural and political relations in times of both peace and war. Only on such foundations can they, especially neighbors, effect a viable and acceptable coexistence that will meet the necessary moral and legal requirements. In the interim between the two world wars and particularly since Hitler's ascension to power, Hungary carried on an intensive revisionist campaign, raising unjustifiable territorial demands with regard to the peoples once dominated by it, and in so doing grossly infringed on the aforementioned principles. Hitler, when giving his consent for the occupation of Carpatho-Ukraine, also put forward four conditions, the first three of which Hungary abided by, for they represented Germany's interest:

1. Take into account Germany's requirements as regard transportation, both during and after the occupation of Ruthenia.

2. Safeguard the economic interests of the Reich and of its citizens, in particular, recognizing as valid any economic agreements concluded by Ruthenia with the Government of the Reich, and with any German citizens.

3. Recognise the duly acquired rights [i.e., economic rights secured by treaty—V.Sh.] of the Volksdeutsche in Ruthenia.

4. Guarantee not to persecute members of the Ruthenian Government and other individuals, including leaders of the Sich [*original Ger.* "Sitsch"—V.Sh.] Guard for their political conduct.[18]

At 8 p.m. on March 16, 1939, the Hungarian Press Agency MTI, carried a report by the Chief of Staff of the Hungarian Army to the effect that the army had taken Khust, that one column had reached the Polish border by 2:15 p.m., and that another group starting out from Uzhhorod had taken the town of Perechyn after fighting.[19] In its resolve to meet with the Hungarian army, the Polish army crossed the border of Carpatho-Ukraine with tanks. The meeting was a jovial one with mutual embraces, drinks, and speeches. The commanding officer of the Polish units declared, "three cheers for the Hungarians who have settled the Ukrainian question."[20]

On the 18th of the month, Regent Miklós Horthy paid a visit to Mukachevo and Khust, and three days later issued a proclamation to the population of Carpatho-Ukraine in which he expressed the view that God had created mountains and plains that supplement each other and, therefore, no force can ever separate them. He then added, "The Ruthenian people will be granted their autonomy within the confines of the Hungarian state."[21]

And on March 20, Horthy made another proclamation in which he pathetically exclaimed: " . . . after the epoch of oppression, deprivation of rights, and backwardness, the dawn of freedom, right, and fraternal life together has appeared for the *Gens fidelissima,* the beloved people of our Prince Rákóczy."[22] These words of his were in gross contradiction to reality.

The "liberation" of the "beloved people"—i.e. the Ruthenians—by the *Honvéds* (Hungarian soldiers, literally "Home Guards") of which he spoke so magnanimously was soon to turn into prisons and concentration camps. The primary task of the *Honvéds* was "to give the terrain a thorough cleaning," to quote the Chief of the Hungarian Staff, Gen. Henrik Werth. To effect a more skillful cleaning up, the roles were divided. The army assumed supervision over concentration camps that "were fenced in with barbed wire," civilian authorities over camps "without barbed wire." The former camps were under the command of Gen. Novákovics. He supervised the camp Dumyn near Rakhiv and two or three more near the border of Galicia. The latter were under the supervision of Rev. Dr. Gyula [Yulius] Maryna and consisted of the camp at Varjulapos near Nyiregyház in Hungary proper, the Kovner prison in Mukachevo, the prison in the Commercial School building in Uzhhorod, and others, all in Carpatho-Ukraine. The Ukrainian intelligentsia were incarcerated here.[23]

The occupation of Carpatho-Ukraine spelled disaster for the Ukrainian population and its cultural institutions; it was an outright tragedy. The Poles, however, who were gleeful over the establishment of a common border with Hungary and over the "destruction of Ukraine," were not to cherish this joy themselves for too long. Signals of the disaster that was to befall Poland were becoming more and more evident. Within a month after Carpatho-Ukraine's tragedy, the Germans began to build roads in Slovakia leading in the direction of the Polish border. We doubt that in September 1939 the Poles had realized their historically recurrent error with regard to Ukraine in general and their blunder made with regard to Carpatho-Ukraine, in particular. As for Hungary, it was gripped with an unusually intensive enthusiasm over its successes in occupying the land. On March 16, Regent Horthy issued a battle appeal to the army, "*Honvéds*! For God and our homeland, forward! Forward to our thousand-year-old borders, to the Carpathian crests, so that we may shake the hands of our Polish comrades-in-arms!"[24] However, neither Horthy's exhortations nor the speeches of Prime Minister Teleki in Parliament could conceal the tragedy that befell the people of Carpatho-Ukraine. *The New York Times* of March 15 fittingly headlined its story on Carpatho-Ukraine on its front page: "Troops of Four Nations Contend for Ruthenia."

The whole of Hungary was in an extraordinary festive mood, marking the occupation of Carpatho-Ukraine with grandiose celebrations and pealing of church bells for half an hour.[25] In addition to his letter of thanks to Hitler, a grateful Horthy intended to give the latter a regiment of soldiers, noting that such an honor had been bestowed before only upon former German President Paul von Hindenburg and the Italian king, Victor Emmanuel III.[26]

The festive celebrations and manifestations of joy in Hungary overshadowed the bleeding of the victimized Ukrainian population. Those who had fallen into captivity, including 16- and 17-year-old students of the Ukrainian Teachers Seminary in Sevliush, were shot. The commander of the Beldi Brigade was supposed to have secretly told Miklós Kozma, the Regent's Commissioner for Carpatho-Ukraine, that to date 200 Ukrainians had been liquidated. Near the village of Kam'ianytsia, Hungarian *Honvéd*s shot a film of the execution of members of the resistance that took place on the banks of the river Uzh.[27]

Carried away by their achievments, the occupation authorities did not spare even church properties or the clergy. On March 23, Gendarmerie Captain Márton Zöldi, escorted by 15 gendarmes, appeared at the ancient monastery of Basilian monks on Chernecha Hora (Monks' Hill) on the outskirts of the city of Mukachevo to search the building. He had two monks manacled while his escort, who represented law and order, engaged in breaking household furniture and helped themselves to church money, watches, fountain pens, photo cameras, and personal belongings.[28] Because the news of this incident became too widespread, Zöldi was court-martialed. The judge, Maj. Babos, found him guilty of "improper" conduct and, as punishment, had him transferred to another gendarmerie station.

Special groups were formed in Carpatho-Ukraine, dubbed by the local people "Wild Magyars," whose members terrorized the population and intimidated individuals even when these sought to demand their natural national rights. Thus, for instance, after a stormy Hungarian demonstration in Uzhhorod during the night of April 22–23, 1939, they tore down the monument of the Ruthenian patriot Adolf

Dobriansky, smashed windows in houses occupied by non-Hungarians, and distributed threatening leaflets among the city's residents.[29]

By a stroke of its blunt bureaucratic pen, Hungary destroyed the well-functioning Ukrainian school system. In 1939, of the 420 grade schools, 320 were Magyarized; of the 18 "horozhanky" (middle schools of four years following four years of elementary schooling), 16 were Magyarized. In the entire territory, 113,000 Ukrainian children could attend only 114 schools in which the language of instruction was "Magyar-Orosz" Hungaro-Russian, the name that they used for Ukrainian. To cite another example: At the beginning of the school year in 1939, there were 1,868 pupils in 46 classes of the Mukachevo gymnasium, which had Russian as the language of instruction. By the end of 1939, the number of classes was reduced to 15 with only 570 attending.[30]

Of the 600 university students from Carpatho-Ukraine only 150 were admitted to Hungarian universities at Debrecen, Budapest, Pécs, Sopron. The majority of those not admitted escaped abroad—to Prague and Lviv.[31] The hopeless situation of the youth in general and that of the students, in particular, drove them to foreign countries—under the conditions of official terror, privation, and unavailability of studies for them, they were spiritually withering away.

In order to alter the correlation between the Ukrainian and Hungarian populations in favor of the latter, the Budapest Government instructed the Regental Commissioner, Miklós Kozma, to embark upon a campaign of Magyarizing non-Hungarian surnames.[32] The Government of Hungary tried every device known to it to effect a radical Magyarization, particularly of teachers. Significantly, when M. Köver, director of the Irshava elementary school, suggested to the local military commandant to organize courses of the Hungarian language for the teachers, not a single Ukrainian teacher came out to sign a petition to this effect.[33]

The lot of our teachers was unenviable. A great many of them found themselves immediately, in the wake of the ocupation process, in Hungarian concentration camps. And the so-called Justification Commissions set up by the Government, whose mode of operations was beneath human dignity, were to decide their future. Also, the exercise of their duties as teachers in villages was most ungratifying for them, since they were interfered in their work by notaries public, educators of the "Levente" organization,[34] gendarmes, and others who lacked knowledge of the local language. For instance, there were instances when armed Hungarian gendarmes would enter classrooms to ascertain whether the teacher was imparting anti-state ideas. On such occasions, and not infrequently, the gendarmes would cast aspersions at the teacher, or, in worst cases, even manhandle him.[35]

The Hungarian authorities saw in Ukrainianism or anything related to it a great danger to them and, therefore, declared a relentless war against it. In an anti-Ukrainian move that could only have been engendered by common agreement with Poland, the Hungarian authorities combatted any relations between Ukrainians living in the two states now that they occupied a common border.[36]

Immediately after the occupation, Hungary's Minister of Culture Homan Bálint sent Kozma, considered an "expert on the history and culture of Transcarpathia," to Poland to draw up a common anti-Ukrainian strategy. Kozma delivered several lectures in Poland on Transcarpathia, vindicating the "new regime." Among other things, he asserted that the Hungarian Government had never recognized the existence of a Ukrainian nation in Transcarpathia and suggested that such terms as "Carpathian Ruthenia" and "Carpatho-Ukraine" ought to be expunged from geographical dictionaries.[37] In taking exception to the terms applied to the land and its history, Kozma, in his capacity as Regental Commissioner for Carpatho-Ukraine, went so far as to prohibit the singing of the old national anthem "Podkarpats'kye Rusyny" (Subcarpathian Ruthenians) that had been used between the two world wars.

It ought to be clear to any researcher following the events of 1938–1939 that Hungary grabbed Carpatho-Ukraine after Hitler had willed it so and that Hungary was his most loyal ally—to quote Horthy. Horthy, however, disavowed what he had once said or wrote. In his memoirs he "hated from the bottom of his heart Hitler's methods and his national-socialist tenets."[38] If true, then Horthy's assertion is incongruous with his friendly relations with Hitler. As early as May 13, 1935, Horthy wrote a letter to Hitler regarding Germany's and Hungary's rearmament, consensus on the foreign policy of both states, and Marshal Göring's visit to Hungary. It follows from this letter that Horthy was in a confidential-secret contact with Hitler, which even Hungary's ambassador in Berlin Szilárd Masirevics knew nothing about. But when he finally learned about it and as ambassador began to take interest in it, he was recalled and replaced by Döme Sztojay, a devout and loyal supporter of Hitlerism.

Some Hungarian scholars and political circles in the free world have endeavored to propagate and introduce into political literature a new, amended thesis, namely that Hungary had occupied Carpatho-Ukraine against Hitler's will. To achieve this objective, they have avoided mentioning any official documents bearing on friendly relations with Hitler, particularly Horthy's letter of March 13, 1939 in which he expresses his thanks for Carpatho-Ukraine. Even Prime Minister Teleki's thesis advanced in 1939 alleging that Hungary had taken Carpatho-Ukraine as the *terra nullius* (no-man's land) by force of its own arms is simply one of the attempts to erase Carpatho-Ukraine from history, render it to a non-entity in politics, and to justify its occupation. The above-mentioned description (ch. 5, p. 154) by the American ambassador in Budapest, John F. Montgomery, indicates the ways in which experienced diplomats mistook this legend for truth.[39]

The Ukrainian population, and especially its intelligentsia, did not relinquish its national positions even when confronted with such illegal actions committed by the Hungarian authorities. It was able to find ways and means to make itself manifest and resist all attempts by the Hungarian authorities to involve it in activities harmful to its own national interests. The self-confident and steadfast resistance of the Ukrainians against the brutal behavior of the Hungarian government organs, especially that of the Justification Commission for teachers, could not go unnoticed in Budapest. In order to get to the bottom of the matter, the Hungarian Government entrusted its State Secretary Tibor Pataky with the task to go to Carpatho-Ukraine and open an investigation into the state of affairs there. After completing his assignment, Pataky reported back to Prime Minister Teleki on March 23. He drew Teleki's attention to the daily cases of brutality and asked that certain Hungarian groups known to be extremely chauvinistic be recalled from the territory, pointing out that the people of Carpatho-Ukraine could not be won over by violent means alone.[40]

Despite all the government's efforts and official proclamations that the occupation of Carpatho-Ukraine was an internal affair, the inhumane practice of the occupation authorities prompted the outside world to react. In May, during Teleki's and Csáky's visit in Berlin, Ribbentrop reproached them for the harsh treatment of the Carpatho-Ukrainian population. He advised them to grant the land its autonomy and allow Msgr. Voloshyn to participate in it, inasmuch as the German Government harbored certain moral commitments toward him. It is interesting and strange that the German Government should belatedly profess having moral obligations toward Msgr. Voloshyn. It will be recalled that Ribbentrop did not even notify Prime Minister Msgr. Voloshyn of his intentions when he was turning over Carpatho-Ukraine to the Hungarians. Csáky quickly replied that Msgr. Voloshyn would be allowed to return to Hungary but not to Carpatho-Ukraine, where he had not only followers but also enemies and therefore his safety could not be guaranteed.[41]

Ukrainians in America and the world at large launched a strong protest against the occupation of Carpatho-Ukraine by Hungary. Ninety Ukrainian organizations in Philadelphia " . . . urged President Roosevelt to make the same protest against invasion of Carpatho-Ukraine by Hungary as he has done against Hitler's recent seizures of Czechoslovakia." Dr. Walter Gallan, president of the United American-Ukrainian Organizations of Philadelphia, denounced the "libelous assertions" that Ukrainians are interested in furthering Hitler's ambitions. "The Ukrainians are fighting Hungary, which is the same as fighting Hitler," he said.[42]

The Soviet Union also reacted to the occupation of Carpatho-Ukraine by Hungary, but its gingerly-worded protest note betrayed its indifference to the problem. Despite the fact that at the time the Soviets had already begun negotiations with the Germans and that the occupation was in line with their political interests, they deemed it expedient not to remain silent altogether. According to a report communicated to Budapest by Hungarian Ambasador to Poland András Hory (No. 6570 of October 15, 1938), i.e., at the time of the formation of the Carpatho-Ukrainian federative state, Soviet diplomats already were on record as supporting the idea of a common Polish-Hungarian border. Hory then had this to add, "The Soviets are of the opinion that a Ukrainian Piedmont is being created in the Ruthenian land [read Carpatho-Ukraine—V. Sh.], but now suddenly there came into being a Polish-Hungarian border. Russian diplomats declared themselves in favor of it."[43] It appears that the "little mosquito," as Stalin dubbed Carpatho-Ukraine in his speech to the 18th Congress of the Communist Party of the Soviet Union in Moscow in March 1939, was not that small after all, for it carried the embryo of Ukrainian statehood, which even the great Stalin feared.

Civilian Administration

The military occupation administration of the land lasted from the latter half of March until July 7, 1939. The reason for the military administration and why the special formations associated with it persisted as long as they did lay in their determination to cleanse the territory of what they considered to be dangerous Ukrainian elements and to strike fear in the population. Thus, when the announcement came that a civilian administration was to be installed, it was wholeheartedly welcomed by the population. However, the joy was short-lived, for on the night of July 1 there appeared in Carpatho-Ukraine members of the Rongyos Gárda who went on a rampage of cutting down everything in sight and terrorizing people, especially in Mukachevo.[44] At the same time, Imre Egan happened to be staying in the village of Nyzhni Veretsky when the gendarmes arrested him and deported him handcuffed back to Hungary proper.[45] Imre Egan had authored the book entitled *Milyen legyen a Ruszin autonomia?* (Uzhhorod, 1939)—(What Should Ruthenian Autonomy Be Like?), in which he took a sympathetic stand toward the idea of an autonomy for the land. People who distributed leaflets on the issue of autonomy were brought to trial.[46] Statements made by Horthy and members of the Government promising autonomy for Carpatho-Ukraine turned out to be empty phrases bereft of substance. The promises of autonomy served merely as a device to cover up for the perpetrated illegal acts.

Acting on a proposal submitted by the Ministerial Council, Horthy appointed Zsigmond Perényi as regental commissioner for Carpatho-Ukraine. To this effect, an official Decree, No. 6200/1939 ME, was issued and published in the *Budapesti Közlöny* No. 140, 1939. One of the provisions of the Decree required of all ministries that they contact the Regental Commissioner when dealing with matters concerning Carpatho-Ukraine. To aid the commissioner, Rev. Yulius Maryna, professor of theology in Uzhhorod was appointed as chief advisor.[47]

On this occasion, speeches were delivered in the Hungarian Parliament emphasizing certain historical bounds with Carpatho-Ukraine which had given Hungary its greatest jurist and legislator István Verbóczy, whose real name was Kerepetsky, and recalling that Ferenc Rákóczi II and even Regent Horthy's ancestors had ties with this land.[48] Still, such "historical" arguments presented in Parliament do not constitute a legal title to the land Hungary claims to be its own by historical rights.

The issue of Carpatho-Ukraine, however, was not to be dealt with until a new Hungarian parliament was instituted, following the elections of May 28 and 29, 1939, from which the population of Carpatho-Ukraine as well as of the area annexed earlier after the Vienna Award were excluded. It is common knowledge that Hungary did not have a truly universal electoral law. According to existing laws and practice, only 6–7 percent of the population could participate in elections. The following table will demonstrate what the electoral law in Hungary looked like in practice prior to World War I:

Elections in Hungary[49]

Year	Total Number	Eligible Voters	Percentage
1870	13,654,964	890,416	6.73
1881	13,833,954	821,241	5.9
1890	15,201,947	846,202	5.5
1900	16,838,255	989,009	5.93
1910	18,264,533	1,162,241	6.4

Oszkár Jászi claims that the "so-called Nation accounts for only 6 percent of the voters and can be bought at will, pressured, or scattered by force."[50] It is obvious that the Hungarian occupation authorities were more than reluctant to allow a discontented people to participate in any elections, especially in secret and universal elections that they had experienced under the Czecho-Slovak regime. True, Carpatho-Ukraine was represented in the Parliament but only by government appointed persons. There were 10 delegates appointed to the Lower House and two (Rev. Aleksander Ilnytsky and Dr. Yosyf Kaminsky) to the Upper House.[51] Apparently, the former and the latter had earned their positions by serving Hungarian interests in Carpatho-Ukraine.

In order to carry out its denationalization policy more effectively with regard to the Ukrainian population, the Hungarian Government released a decree, No. 6200/1939 ME, under which the Ukrainians were to be henceforth referred to as *Magyar-Orosz* or "Magyar-Russians," thus creating a new nationality for the Ruthenians living in Hungary. Instead of enabling the people to continue their natural national development and growth, the Hungarians invented this denigrating appellation in order to obliterate their national identity and induce them to begin a supposedly "new" cultural life. The result was that all Ukrainian cultural institutions were liquidated, including Ukrainian-language newspapers. Although now the Ukrainians were renamed Magyar-Orosz, they were still not to enjoy the same educational rights and privileges they once had. The number of schools was drastically reduced. Thus:

> Instead of 7 Ukrainian Gymnasiums in 1939 only 3 were permitted; in their place 4 Hungarian Gymnasia were established in Carpatho-Ukraine; of the 25 community (lower middle) schools, only 12 were opened. On "Subcarpathian Territory" there were 692 elementary schools and they held 1387 Ukrainian and 297 Hungarian classes, i.e. there were 4.5 Ukrainian classes for 1 Hungarian while there were 25 Ukrainian children of school age for each Hungarian child.[52]

But even such drastic measures instituted by the military and civilian authorities could not erode the national consciousness of the population and could not divert its attention from its demands for its natural rights. To soothe the population's feelings, the Hungarian government circles raised the question of autonomy, which even during the Czecho-Slovak era aroused great interest and had become a sort of political program for 19 years.

Consideration of the problem of autonomy for Carpatho-Ukraine was given in speeches pronounced by Hungarian statesmen and even Regent Horthy. At first, the matter seemed to dovetail with Brody's Magyarophile policy, which he had espoused while deputy to the Prague Parliament. Brody and his followers were convinced that after the occupation Hungary would find a positive solution to this question.

Brody, having stocked his arsenal with promises and financial support over many years, propounded the issue of autonomy before the Hungarian Government in its full dimension. In an article Brody wrote, entitled "The Kind of Autonomy We Desire," that appeared in his party's mouthpiece *Russkii vestnik* in fifty thousand copies (normal circulation five thousand copies) on Easter April 2, 1939 (Julian Calendar) he called for "the broadest possible autonomy," which "in the main would correspond to the erstwhile Croatian autonomy" (i.e., Croatia's ability to choose its own leaders, maintain its own diet, and manage local affairs) with foreign affairs and national defense being commonly handled while internal matters, such as education and culture, transportation, and judicial matters were to belong to the competence of the autonomous land. The article ended with the words: "The Autonomist Agricultural Union has fought for such an autonomy for 20 years, and is still fighting for it today."[53]

To ingratiate himself with the Hungarians, Rev. Fentsyk presented on March 31 his plan for autonomy to government officials that carried the title "To Create a Carpatho-Russian Provincial Government."[54] Fentsyk, an implaccable adversary of Brody's, pointed out in his plan that the regained territory, i.e. Carpatho-Ukraine, "is an integral part of Hungary." Despite his attempts to curry the favor of Hungarian political circles, Fentsyk did not gain the confidence needed for them to install him as the leader of the land. The Hungarians apparently were mindful of the fact that for his anti-Ukrainian activities he had been receiving funds not only from Hungarian sources but at various times also from the Poles and Czechs.

To be sure, Brody's demand for autonomy lifted the spirits of the oppressed people, but at the same time aroused some misgivings in Hungarian political circles. However, the issue caused a split also among his close collaborators in his own party. Rev. Dr. Maryna, Rev. Canon Ilnytsky, Dr. Kaminsky, and Demko opposed Brody's project and demand for autonomy. The counsellor to the territory's comissioner, Dr. Maryna, stated that "unless he had anything to say in Ruthenia [read: Carpatho-Ukraine—V. Sh.] there would be no autonomy."[55] The Hungarian press as well as the Hungarian population of Carpatho-Ukraine expressed opposition to the idea of autonomy for fear that the influence of the local Ukrainian population would grow in strength.

Although Brody repeatedly professed his loyalty to Hungary in speeches and the press, and frequently reassured it that he would not act against it, the Hungarian Government looked askance at the idea of autonomy and interpreted it according to its own perception. As a result, Brody was no longer to perform the role of a player on the political chessboard; he became a figure, a stage extra. He was put under strict police supervision. His mail was opened and his telephone conversations were tapped. Outraged by such treatment, Brody complained to State Secretary for Minorities Tibor Pataki and to Minister of Internal Affairs Ferencz Keresztes-Fischer.[56] Brody also demanded a convocation of a Carpathian Soim, but the Government limited itself instead only to appointing "parliamentary" representatives of the territory in Budapest. In his conversation with the State Secretary, Brody brought up the subject of brutality perpetrated by the occupation authorities, claiming they had imprisoned a great number of innocent people whom they were subjecting to torture, had begun a forced Magyarization of the population, were supporting elements opposed to autonomy, and were holding the entire land in a state of fear.

In spite of all this, the issue of autonomy was gaining such momentum that Prime Minister Teleki felt compelled to visit Carpatho-Ukraine to survey the situation himself. What he had observed convinced him that his Government must take some action regarding autonomy and that this action could no longer be shelved or taken lightly. However, in order to paralyze Brody's influence, and over the opposition of the local Hungarians, Teleki submitted a bill on April 24, 1939 calling for a "Carpathian Province and its self-government," which voivodship (governorship) also conveyed to Horthy, since he technically continued to rule as the defender of the Crown of St. Stephen and in the stead of the King of the Magyars (whose return to power Horthy had actually blocked on at least two previous occasions).[57]

The concept of autonomy was merely a convenient maneuver of the Hungarian Government to pacify the population. Teleki hit the nail on the head when he declared in another speech, saying:

> Having acquired a new territory, whose population is predominantly non-Hungarian, we are witnessing the new tasks faced by the Hungarian-Danubian state of the Crown of St. Stephen, which we are to resolve in the spirit of the old Hungarian constitutionality, of the old St. Stephen patriarchal traditions, in the spirit of the given time and its demands understandably, in such forms that are in agreement with our constitutionality, but not those that would correspond to the constitution of Czechoslovakia.[58]

Just as the idea of a "Greater Hungary" and the state's constitution were the source in the past on which the denationalization policy regarding non-Hungarian peoples was based, so now the same ideas of denationalization were to be incorporated, in essence, into the government-envisaged, so-called autonomy.

The basic idea contained in Teleki's project of voivodship, with which also the well known Hungarian politician Count István Bethlen was in full accord, called for the retention of the centralist system in Carpatho-Ukraine as well. The system was to be applied to branches of public life. Subcarpathia (*Kárpátalja* in Hungarian), as Voloshyn's Carpatho-Ukraine was renamed, was not intended as a self-ruling territory but rather as the policy of an ancillary body. Its administration consisted of the following organs: *Voivoda,* head of the provincial government; his deputy; and the Great Assembly. Organizationally, the administration was a copy of the Hungarian district (*zhupa*) system with its appointed organs. Half of those elected by secret balloting to the Great Assembly were to represent the population at large, one-fourth the local great estate owners and owners of large enterprises, and, one-fourth the clergy, teachers, trade and engineering establishment, and others.[59] Teleki's plan regarding an autonomy for the territory, however, was of no significance, for it did not offer much, was greatly restrictive, and did not correspond to the demands of time. That the Ukrainian population's national and political consciousness had developed between the two wars came as a great surprise to Budapest. The rights that the Ukrainians had acquired particularly during the period of their federative statehood served as a point of departure for their similar demands on Hungary. It would seem that Brody had correctly understood the juridicial and factual basis on which he was to lean in demanding autonomy for the territory.

On June 5, 1939, the Russophile leader of the American Carpatho-Russian Union, Alexander [Aleksei] Gerovsky, arrived in Uzhhorod from the United States, to lend support to Brody's demand for autonomy in the name of Ruthenian Americans. At the same time there arrived Vasyl Karaman, secretary of the Ruthenian National Council of the Priashiv (Prešov) region, who declared his support for Brody's demands in the name of the Priashiv Ruthenians. On June 6, a congress of the Society of Ruthenian Teachers was to take place at which Brody was scheduled to raise the question of autonomy. However, in order to prevent the passing of any resolution regarding autonomy, the Government dissolved the Society shortly before the congress could take place.[60]

The autonomy question had picked up such momentum that even representatives of Carpatho-Ukrainians from Msgr. Voloshyn's camp ventured to raise their demands. In their memorandum, dated June 18, they backed the demand for territorial autonomy and the introduction of the Ukrainian language in schools as was the case "under Voloshyn's Government."[61] This was the first public and official appearance, coupled with political demands, of persons who in the past were connected with Msgr. Voloshyn and independent Carpatho-Ukraine. Given the prevailing conditions, theirs was a courageous step. They ventured for the first time to come out into the open from their forced isolation and silence.

Faced with such a manifestation of a near-unanimous will of the population of the territory on the issue of autonomy, the Hungarian ruling circles began to interpret it as a peril to the security of the state. Voices were to be heard to the effect that "the Ruthenian land we had obtained from the Czechs is a veritable hornet's nest. Let us defend ourselves lest their strings turn out to be fatal to the Hungarian nation."[62] The situation was such that it ultimately forced the Hungarian Government to take some drastic action regarding the autonomy question. Four members of Brody's party's Presidium, whom he termed renegades, came out in support of the Government's view as did the majority of the Carpathian deputies. As a result, Brody's party was disintegrating. Such a division was also to affect the entire organizational structure of the party down to its lowest echelons. The controversial issue had by now reached the ears of Horthy, who summoned Rev. Maryna for a briefing on the matter. In referring to Brody and his supporters, Maryna explained that "there are those who lay themselves down across the road to hamper the consolidation and to create confusion." Horthy was supposed to have responded, "either they remove themselves from the road or we shall carry them away or kick them away."[63]

In reply to such a resolute and not very diplomatic declaration by Horthy, Brody turned to Teleki, telling him that he and his collaborators had lost confidence in Commissioner Perényi and therefore were no longer inclined to support the Government's policy but forced to go into opposition.

He also added that "he is refusing to take any responsibility for events in Subcarpathia, for he knows that the people are discontent."[64]

The Government made a settlement with him and paid him off. It also canceled all subsidies given him, but allowed him the right to continue publishing his newspaper *Russkii vestnik*, which, however, because of frequent state censorship, experienced difficulties and appeared only irregularly.

Having cooperated with Brody over a period of many years and under different conditions, Hungary was vexed at Brody's persistent and resolute demand for autonomy. It, therefore, decided to drop him and engage Fentsyk in his stead although, it was aware that the latter was politically unreliable and that he was receiving money from whomever offered it to him. Yet it was convinced that he would play his "role" according to its wishes. The initial salary it allotted him was 2,830 *pengö* per month.[65]

Such was the inglorious end of Brody's service to Hungary. Even as a deputy to the Czecho-Slovak Parliament in Prague and as first prime-minister of the Government of Carpatho-Ukraine, he faithfully served the interests of Hungary. But eventually, under changed circumstances, he did recognize Hungary's deceitful game and his role in it. Having made this discovery, he still had the courage to defend his political concept up to the very end and, as his conduct had shown, he apparently believed in it sincerely.

The occupation of Carpatho-Ukraine whetted all the more the territorial expansionist appetites of Hungarian politicians. They turned their sights toward further possible occupations, namely toward Yugoslavia and Romania. Teleki, however, warned that first they should learn how to administer an annexed territory. To make his point, he recalled an incident that occurred in the village of Ublia in Carpatho-Ukraine on January 20, 1940 where because of the unprovoked attack by the Hungarian gendarmerie one man and two women were killed, triggering widespread unrest throughout the territory and provoking even greater hatred toward the Hungarians.

Recurrent Magyarization

With Brody's demise and removal from the political scene, the voices of those who advocated autonomy and propogated it as a concrete political solution, which found great resonance among the people, also fell silent. The manner in which Brody was deposed was well prepared in advance by the Government in conjunction with his close party members. With the occupation of Carpatho-Ukraine, Hungary deemed Brody's role terminated and did not feel any obligation toward him, not even a moral one.

After the installation of the civilian administration, the local Magyar-Orosz, the "Hungaro-Russians," appeared on the scene. The administration's chief consultant became the Very Rev. Ilnytsky, and head of the school system the Very Rev. Dr. Yulius Maryna. Brody branded both of them as "renegades," who would do anything to be allowed to climb into the Hungarian bandwagon.

The aforementioned twosome, through their activities, were responsible for the period of a rather dismal state of affairs in the territory's cultural life. They fastidiously conducted a Hungarian assimilation policy by creating a distinct, separate "Hungaro-Russian" nationality and language negating anything that carried the people's national name or was in someway or other related with Ukrainianism. As early as March 24, 1939, a directive was issued by Gen. Géza Császár, chief military commandant, Dr. István Buday, head of the National Council, and Nikolai Dragula, head of the Department of Education that appeared in the circular of the Department of Education of the Civil Administration of Carpatho-Russia in Khust under point 11: "Communication with parties is to be conducted, first and foremost, in their language with the exception of Ukrainian and Czech."[66]

It is difficult to imagine a more chauvinistic absurdity than to prohibit, in the 20th century, communication with the local population in its own native Ukrainian language, particularly since these people did not speak the Hungarian language. And yet, the so-called Russophiles, or Russian-oriented, were actually legal and had their own newspapers, such as *Russkoe slovo* (Russian Word) and *Karpatorusskii golos* (Carpatho-Russian Voice).

Shortly after the occupation, over 1,000 elementary school teachers were dismissed from their jobs. Many of them found themselves detained in prisons and concentration camps. Special "Justification Commissions" were set up to grill the teachers about their alleged "sins" committed against Hungary during the Czecho-Slovak era. A transgression included the use by the teachers during the Czecho-Slovak era of the school administration-approved textbooks in which figured such statements as, for instance, that in Czecho-Slovakia the Ruthenian-Ukrainians enjoyed greater rights than during the Hungarian era prior to World War I. Any rabble-rouser could anonymously point a finger at a teacher. One can only imagine the moral and personal degredation the teachers suffered.

The Hungarian administration and its Magyar-Russian servants knew no bounds in their unfettered hatred. In fact, it progressed to such limits that even Rev. Maryna felt compelled—but not until his immigration to the U.S.A. in June 1949—to recognize the baleful consequences of the Justification Commissions as being "very pernicious, degrading, and harmful."[67] In this book, he claims to have been in opposition to these Commissions. And yet in several instances he is known to have denied help to teachers, whom the Commissions had not acquitted, because they spoke Ukrainian.[68] Moreover, he caused those students to fail their Graduation Exam (Maturity Exam) who professed their nationality to be Ukrainian. Rev. Maryna used to attend these Gymnasium (High School) exams as a representative of the school authorities.

These arrangements were not the last the Hungarian Government was to contrive regarding Carpatho-Ukraine. Its Ministry of Internal Affairs issued a circular adressed to all other ministries demanding that as many as possible "public officials bearing foreign [read non-Hungarian—V. Sh] surnames change them to appropriate Hungarian names."

It is an age-old tested device to produce "Hungarians" by changing surnames, place-names, and the like. Not too long before, in December 1897, during the administration of Prime Minister Dezsö Bánffy, the Hungarian Parliament had even passed a law to this effect, "for the compulsory Magyarization of all place-names of Hungary."[69] Such artifice enabled Hungarian politicians participating in international peace conference to prove the alleged ethnic Hungarian character of the country and population.[70]

The animosity harbored toward the Ukrainian population also extended to include public officials. In the Department of Finances in Khust, ten Ukrainian officials were fired for not having properly mastered the Hungarian language. In their place were hired 45 persons from Hungary proper, but it did not seem to bother anyone that they did not speak or ever would want to learn the language of the local Ukrainian population.[71]

The primary thrust of the radical Magyarization campaign conducted by the state machinery was directed toward teachers, who were to be "re-educated." Special courses were set up for Ukrainian teachers, followed by required examinations in Hungarian language and literature. Because of the highly exacting demands, 60 percent of teachers would fail their exams. At the same time, the place of these teachers was taken by Hungarian teachers brought into the land who had no command of the language spoken in Carpatho-Ukraine and had to teach through interpreters. Only Prime Minister Teleki opposed such a mode of Magyarization, viewing it as premature and damaging. But the gendarmerie and local authorities thought otherwise. They would force purely Ukrainian villages to demand the introduction of Hungarian-language schools, at times even under the convincing argument of bayonets.

Even after liquidating Ukrainian cultural institutions, the Hungarian Government was not to be fully appeased. It then turned to deal with the Muscophile orientation, represented by the A. Dukhnovych Cultural Society, which it once so unfailingly supported. In accord with Horthy's wish, Kozma showed his iron hand by prohibiting any mention of Dukhnovych's poem at the Russian Cultural Evening held in Budapest.[72] But the ultimate blow delivered by the "iron hand" was when the singing of the land's former national anthem "Podkarpatskye Rusyny" (Subcarpathian Ruthenians), after Dukhnovych' poem and Stepan Fentsyk's music was banned.[73] This ban caused many sympathizers of the Muscophile orientation, who once welcomed the Hungarian Government's anti-Ukrainian campaign, to see the stark reality. This was particularly true of the Muscophile youth, who felt nationally humiliated and began to grow antagonistic to the Hungarian occupation and its system.

Commissioner Perényi proved unsuccessful, "too soft," in resolving the problems of the land. He was relieved of his post upon "his own request" and replaced by Miklós Kozma, a stern and firm man, appointed by Regent Horthy on September 21. Kozma was the prime moving force behind the ordering of the Rongyos Gárda into Carpatho-Ukraine during and after the Vienna Arbitration to terrorize the population and provoke unrest. He was equally resolved, and often stressed the need, to take a merciless stand toward the Brodyites as well as all pro-Russians of whatever hue and color and to squash them just the same as the Ukrainians and Communists. He had Horthy's support and coaxing to keep order "with a firm hand."[74]

In order to steer further the cultural and thereby national development of the land in the direction of a policy supportive of the Government, Kozma set out to organize a "Subcarpathian Society of Sciences,"[75] which was to be a champion of these very pro-Hungarian sentiments. And to disseminate these ideas, he founded the scientific quarterly *Zoria* (Star) and the bi-weekly *Literaturna nedilia* (Literary Sunday). The goal the society pursued was to create on a scientific basis in Carpatho-Ukraine a separate nationality distinct from the Ukrainians and favorably disposed toward the Hungarians, and leaning toward Hungary.[76]

Furthermore, two grammars were published. The first was written by Yulius Maryna and entitled *Hrammatyka uhro-russkoho iazyka dlia serednykh uchebnykh zavedenii* (Uzhhorod: Izdanie RK, 1940; Grammar of the Hungaro-Russian Language for Secondary Schools of Learning), containing a welter of Russian-language elements and, in general, very confusing. The other was written by Dr. Ivan Harayda, *Hrammatyka rus'koho iazyka* (Uzhhorod: Vydania PON, 1941; Grammar of the Ruthenian Language). This was a grammar of mutilated Ukrainian language with an etymological orthography. At first, Ukrainian cultural workers tended to accept with reservations Harayda's work, but later came around to realizing that there was still room in the language field for a positive national Ukrainian cultural activity which they, indeed, took advantage of.[77] We have related a few instances from the various domains of cultural life in Carpatho-Ukraine that pointed to the cultural genocide conducted by the Hungarian Government.

Economic Poverty and the Policy of Detention

Even during the Czecho-Slovak era, the Highland inhabitants of Carpatho-Ukraine lived in perpetual poverty, but during the Hungarian occupation they lived in even greater want. In its revisionist propaganda between the two world wars, Hungary repeatedly stressed the great benefits the Carpathian Ukrainians would have that would extricate them from their unenviable situation if their land were to be joined to Hungary. The propaganda was directed primarily at farm workers and referred to seasonal summer work, such as grain and hay harvesting. It was generally estimated that some 60,000 to 80,000 such farm workers from Carpatho-Ukraine could be employed in Hungary. In reality, however, during the occupation only two to three thousand found jobs on Hungarian fields and then at wages so low that they at times barely covered their travel expenses. Living conditions there, as well as the debasing treatment they suffered at the hands of their employers, were in stark contrast to the promises held out to them. Because of their privations and lack of knowledge of the Hungarian language, they were forced to accept wages lower than their local Hungarian counterparts, a situation that led to frequent fist-fighting.[78] Count János Batthyány, a large estate owner in Sopronynémeti suggested that children between the ages of 10 and 14 be brought in from Carpatho-Ukraine to be employed as shepherds or cowhands.[79]

During the occupation, the prices of industrial products rose by 200 to 300 percent as did the prices of foodstuffs, especially corn. What outraged the people most was that the price of salt also rose, despite the fact that the salt was being produced in Carpatho-Ukraine at 40–50 rail carloads a day. The people were also robbed of their savings when they had to exchange their Czecho-Slovak *koruny* at a rate of 7:1 when the official rate of exchange was 5:1.

The Government of Hungary imposed restrictions upon other areas of the land's economic life, including even that of the high plains. For instance, the "Ministerial Council had set up two hunting grounds comprising a total of 58,000 cadastral yokes (143,260 acres) which it immediately offered to Regent Horthy."[80] Consequently, people were not allowed to pick the fruits of the woods lest they disturb wildlife and were required to move their flocks of sheep off the pasture clearances on time. What is more, the population was not given sufficient pasture acreage to rent so that the possibility to keep sheep and cows, which provided the population's main source of livelihood, was considerably limited.[81] The description and examples presented above do afford, if only in a general way, a picture of the economic situation in Carpatho-Ukraine under Hungarian occupation, reflecting Hungary's economic policy in regard to the land and its population. As the war dragged on, the situation became even worse up and until the end of the occupation in October 1944.

The territory's occupation by Hungary began and ended with prisons and terror. The suppression of Ukrainian national culture temporarily hampered its development but could not completely eradicate it from the lives of the intelligentsia and of the ethnically conscious segment of the population. Though given only minimal possibilities, which the state system could not well prohibit or refuse, it continued to develop and grow. Group get-togethers among the intelligentsia and the youth, secret literary circles and private meetings were outlets that allowed the national consciousness to avoid withering away. Feeling insecure and threatened, Hungary reacted to these persistent manifestations of national consciousness on the part of these groups by unleashing a new wave of mass arrests in 1942.

Armed with the necessary documents, Rev. Maryna visited the Varjulapos concentration camp. He stated that interned in the camp were over 100 persons, among whom he had found many acquaintances from Uzhhorod, including priests. One of the inmates was supposed to have cried out after Maryna, "We know you, you are a traitor to our homeland."[82] Spyrydon Dovhal, another inmate, states that the number of prisoners was as high as one thousand. In one single hall which Maryna visited, over eight hundred persons slept in four rows on the floor in terrible filth.[83]

The prisoners were beaten unmercifully. For instance, an Orthodox priest by the name of Mardak was beaten into unconsciousness several times. During a visit of the Varjulapos camp by a Hungarian general, poet Vasyl Grendzha-Donsky, also an inmate, complained about the severe beatings and torture inflicted upon the prisoners. The camp administration immediately denied the accusations. However, after the general's departure, the poet suffered such beatings that he could not walk.[84]

The prison in the Kovner building in Mukachevo was under Gen. Novákovics' jurisdiction. Most of its inmates were young intelligentsia, nationalists, members of the Carpathian Sich, Plast Scouts, teachers, and students. Among them were Rev. Dr. Bohdan Voloshyn, Margaret Shandor-Babosa, V. Markus, Yu. Kostiuk, Yu. Hrytsiuk, and others. The methods of punishment here were equally barbarous. Prisoners would be beaten on their feet with rubber truncheons causing wounds and swelling that did not allow them to put on their shoes or prisoners would be driven out onto a path covered with sharp shards of crushed stone and forced to walk or even run over them. The many who were barefoot left traces of blood behind them.

In Uzhhorod, the building of the Commercial School had been transformed into a prison and placed under the supervision of Rev. Maryna. One of the modes of punishment here was to force the prisoners to sit on the floor against a wall and not make the slightest movement while staring at a fixed point in the room. If a prisoner moved, he would be hit with the butt of a rifle. Prisoners were subjected to Medieval modes of torture. To illustrate: a young woman teacher was tied on her hands and feet, with the rope attached to a roller equipped with wheels. When the wheels were turned, the rope stretched the woman's limbs, causing excrutiating pain. Simultaneously she was beaten on her toes with rubber truncheons and sat upon. On top of it all, the tormentors lit their cigarettes and poked fun at her. The victim, Margaret, was my sister. Among the other prisoners were Dr. Yuliy Brashchayko, Dr. Mykola Bandusiak and his two brothers, Fedir Revay, Andriy Voron, Pavlo Czapovczy, Vasyl Sverenyak, Stepan Pap, and others. Seventy-two year-old retired teacher Petro Bokshay and my brother Mykhailo were repeatedly beaten on their heels. The latter, with his hands tied behind his back, was held by his head and banged against the wall until, covered with blood, he was dropped to the floor and left there overnight still fettered and choking on his own blood. The incidents recounted here were not exceptions but rather the rule, and there were many more and even worse such excesses.

It is understandable that such a description of the conduct of public officials with regard to helpless prisoners may evoke in the reader disbelief. Unfortunately, this is but only one part of the whole truth. The brutal handling of prisoners was applied to the intelligentsia as well as to nationally conscious peasants. These brutally abused people did not violate any penal or other laws. Their guilt lay only in the fact that they loved their people and worked to enhance their cultural standards. Patriotism for one's own people cannot be considered a crime.[85]

It should come as no surprise to anyone that the Carpatho-Ukrainian youth began to escape in droves from the state-organized terror across the Carpathian Mountains into Galicia, then occupied by the Soviet Union, and to a lesser extent to Slovakia, Yugoslavia, and Germany.

The young people did not stop to consider what was in store for them in a foreign country, as not a characteristic trait of young people to dwell on the dangers looming ahead. Their only goal was to escape at all cost.

Another factor that induced them to escape was that they, as recruits in the Hungarian army, were subjected to a variety of physical punishments and indignities, a phenomenon quite common in the Hungarian military and a carryover from pre-World War I times. Even Ukrainian recruits with university backgrounds were not spared the humiliation. According to the officers' honor code, no officer or officer candidate was to be dishonored or manhandled in any way. In fact, he was allowed to defend his honor by resorting to a duel with the offender. Although officially banned by law, dueling was still practised in the military in secrecy, although such incidents occurred rather seldom. The officer candidate, for instance, was given a manual governing the procedure of a duel—how to select his seconds, what weapons he was allowed to choose, where the place of the duel would take place, and the like. But this right of officers and officer candidates could seldom be exercised, for higher ranking officers would always find a way to thwart such intentions against them particularly if the challenger was a non-Hungarian and did not master the Hungarian language. Such was the case of I. Kardashinetz, a university student and officer candidate, whose complaints for mistreatment and indignities incurred for not knowing the language merely led to his being subjected to further physical punishments in the form of unbearable exercises and drills. One can imagine how difficult it must have been for a Ukrainian recruited into the Hungarian army who did not speak the language. He was expected to understand not only his superiors, the commands, the terms for a variety of weapons, but also his Hungarian comrades recruits and thus expose himself to constant ridicule and derision. Only a supercilious Hungarian bureaucracy could label such people as stupid and punish them for it. This was thus the other reason why many "Carpathian young fellows were running away *en masse* and crossing into the Soviet territory upon receiving their conscription papers."[86]

Rev. Maryna, as head of the school system in Carpatho-Ukraine, admits that the youth fled from their schools and crossed the border over to the Soviets by the hundreds. It is difficult to ascertain the number of people who had fled the land. Nevertheless, it is interesting to observe that these young people, instead of being sent to schools in the Ukrainian Soviet Republic, were immediately arrested and sentenced to 3 to 10 years of internal exile "for espionage, diversion, and enemy propaganda." This provides evidence that very few of them were Communists.[87]

This tragedy that befell the Carpatho-Ukrainian youth is described in the Soviet literature thus: "One of the forms of protest against the Fascist [i.e., Hungarian—V.Sh.] regime was the illegal mass exodus of Transcarpathians, particularly of military conscript age, and of young girls into the Soviet Union. In 1939–1941 alone, approximately 18 thousand persons emigrated from the territory to the USSR. The majority of the refugees eventually joined up with the Soviet Army and the Czecho-Slovak Corps under the command of Gen. Ludvík Svoboda, fighting "heroically on the fronts of the Great Fatherland War." On the occupied territory of Carpatho-Ukraine, young people were forcibly impressed into the Red Army.[88] Significantly, Soviet sources make no mention of the fact that these young people were sent to Siberia after crossing the border into the then Soviet occupied territory of Galicia.

With German military failures on the front becoming more and more frequent, particularly after the German loss at Stalingrad in February 1943, the self-confidence of Hungarian leaders began to wither away correspondingly. Moreover, they were beginning to show signs of feelings of guilt. This situation prompted Horthy to announce publicly for the consumption of Western democracies, an appropriate clarification regarding Hungary's policy stance and refute the irrelevant accusations leveled against them. One of the three principal accusations was that "Hungary had subjugated non-Hungarians and seized territories of its neighbors."[89]

In an effort to justify Hungary's position, Horthy postulated, "We have never harbored any aspirations toward foreign territories, we have never infringed upon the rights of other peoples, and we have never been guided by any design of conquest. What we have always insisted upon, and still do, is to have what is and has been ours and nobody else's in the eyes of God and the people for a thousand years.[90] Obviously, what Horthy was alluding to was the territories that once had belonged to Hungary and seceded from it after World War I. Even in this instance, Horthy's claims are legally and historically groundless.

Another case also deserves attention. During Horthy's visit with Hitler near Rastenburg on September 7, 1941—his fifth visit and one at which he was to have received highest honors from Hitler and embraced him—the Regent raised the question of Hungary's territorial demands. He contended that it was indispensable to push the crest of the Carpathian Mountains farther north and, therefore, would demand the annexation of part of Galicia. Hitler, being in high spirits, was supposed to have promised to join the coveted territory to Hungary.[91]

These kinds of territorial demands were not the only ones, nor were they exceptional. In a letter, dated August 19, 1941, Gen. Henrik Werth, Chief of Hungarian Staff, submitted a number of concrete proposals to this effect, namely:

1. To recover our thousand-year borders.

2. To evacuate the Slavic and Romanian elements living in these areas.

3. To resettle the Jews.

4. To secure Hungary's participation in the distribution of Soviet raw materials.

In his letter, the Chief of Staff referred to

... information, according to which the Germans were toying with the idea of creating individual national states after the war. Hence, one had to reckon with the possibility of Slavs (Serbs, Slovaks, Ruthenians) earlier evacuated from the territories of historical Hungary. Romania would be given, east of the Dneister River, a territory of such great dimension that all Transylvanian Wallachians could be settled there. As a result, the entire Carpathian Basin would belong exclusively to Hungary's lebensraum, filled with the Hungarian race.[92]

Of course, in order to carry out such a large-scale plan of resettlement of non-Hungarian peoples—in all, some 8 million—it was necessary first to secure possession of the relevant territories. Hitler's military and political designs on the East and the Balkans caused Horthy to entertain sanguine hopes that he could resolve the problem of resettlement in a similar manner. The Hungarian chief of the General Staff's Counter-Intelligence Services, Gen. István Ujszászy, echoed the same line when he testified at the Nuremberg Trials, stating that, in accordance with an agreement with the German General Staff, Hungary was to receive for participating in the war against the Soviet Union the territory extending eastward from the Carpathian Mountains.[93] It would thus follow from the above that Horthy had indeed aspired to foreign territories, if the opportunity presented itself.

The relentless campaign for the revision of Hungary's borders poisoned the atmosphere and rendered impossible the cultivation of good-neighborly relations. However, on Mussolini's advice, Hungary did enter into negotiations with Yugoslavia that culminated in an agreement of eternal friendship concluded on December 12, 1940. The pact was ratified and signed by Horthy on February 27, 1941. As a result of a *coup d'état* in Yugoslavia, which led to Yugoslavia pulling away from the Axis and declaring neutrality, Hitler decided to punish Yugoslavia by invading it, but for this move he needed Hungary's cooperation.

In his preceding secret negotiations with Horthy dealing with the idea of a military attack against Yugoslavia, Hitler promised Hungary the return of all the lands it had lost to Yugoslavia in 1918 if it participated in the attack. Ignoring the pact of eternal friendship with Yugoslavia, Horthy welcomed Hitler's proposition with satisfaction. A month to the day after the ratification of the Pact of Eternal Friendship, i.e., on March 27, Ambassador Sztojay brought from Berlin a letter from Hitler conveying the message that the time was ripe for an onslaught on Yugoslavia and that he "fully recognizes Hungary's revisionist demands toward Yugoslavia and that in dimensions Horthy himself would set."[94] The news was greeted with joviality in the official Hungarian circles, much the same as had greeted Hitler's consent to the occupation of Carpatho-Ukraine just two years before.

Hungary was to attack the part of Yugoslavia that had once belonged to it. Prime Minister Teleki refused to sign an order for general mobilization, considering that Horthy's move and that of his government to be a dishonest one and politically an egregious mistake. However, upon Horthy's insistence, Teleki did sign the order after all.

On April 11, 1941, Horthy issued orders to the Hungarian Army to cross the Hungarian-Yugoslav border in what seemed clearly to be an act of aggression. This act occurred only four months after the solemn signing of the pact of eternal friendship with Yugoslavia in Belgrade. The behavior of the Hungarian troops on Yugoslav soil was no different than on Carpatho-Ukrainian soil in 1938–1939. During the proceedings of the International Tribunal in Nuremberg, Gen. Feketehalmi-Czeidner, the Hungarian commander in occupied Bácska province in Yugoslavia, was accused of atrocities committed there. "You have brought the greatest possible dishonor upon the nation when you had ordered the slaughter of four thousand innocent people, among them four-year-old children." Feketehalmi-Czeidner tried to justify his action by accusing the civilian population for having attacked his army.[95] However, to quote an American author, "in the winter of 1941–1942 Hungarian troops occupying the Serb town Subotica went berserk and murdered more than a thousand Serbian men, women, and children."[96]

For these deeds perpetrated by the Hungarian troops, the government of Yugoslavia declared Horthy a war criminal and requested that he be extradited to Yugoslavia. This, however, did not happen, for allegedly the request was not accompanied by proper documentation. The American military authorities in Germany did not interrogate Horthy since "the government of Hungary, upon Stalin's advice, did not demand his arrest."[97]

On the other hand, Prime Minister Miklós Kállay argued that it was the Yugoslav partisans who had provoked the Hungarian troops to such acts, "admitting that there had been excesses, he gave a figure, which he swore to be correct, of 2,250 Serb victims (he seems to have omitted the victims of other nationalities)."[98]

Some Hungarians, however, were also appalled upon hearing about the massacre in Yugoslavia. Most vehemently opposed to the invasion of Yugoslavia by the Hungary troops was Prime Minister Teleki, an honorable statesman who did not wish to see Germany playing one nation against the other. A few days before the first Hungarian soldier crossed the border into Yugoslavia, Teleki shot himself to death.

In protest against the political course now taken and the breaking of Hungary's word given to Yugoslavia, Teleki had written two letters to Horthy in which he explained what had driven him to this decision.

The first letter read in part:

> We have committed perfidy—out of cowardice—with regard to the Pact of Eternal Friendship based on the speech delivered at Mohács.[99] Our people sense this, and we have sacrificed its honor. We have allied ourselves with scoundrels, for there is not a kernel of truth in the alleged atrocities. Neither against the Hungarians, nor against the Germans! We shall become robbers of corpses. A most miserable nation. I have not forsaken you. I am to blame.

And an excerpt from the second letter—"If my act should fail and I should remain alive, I would herewith tender my resignation."[100] Indeed, a sad but implicit incident. And the finale of the whole affair was even sadder, for in protest against the violation of the agreement with Yugoslavia, Teleki ended his life with a bullet.

Of all the Hungarian statesmen during the occupation of Carpatho-Ukraine, Teleki was the one to show the most benevolent interest in the hapless lot of the Ukrainian population. Frequently, his sincere intentions were blocked by ruthless actions of his countrymen who were appointed commissioners to the territory.

For obtaining the Yugoslav territory of Bácska, Horthy sent Hitler a letter expressing his heartfelt thanks, as he had done on the occasion of occupying Carpatho-Ukraine. Among other things, he stated that, "in the past, Hungary had always stood by Germany's side as it does today, is firmly convinced and conscious of our common destiny, pursues the same political line, and stands with immutable devotion to the best of its ability on the side of the German Reich."[101]

But hardly a year elapsed after Hungary had broken the eternal friendship pact with Yugoslavia, ratified on February 27, 1941, when Horthy dispatched another letter to Hitler, dated January 10, 1942, in which he assured the German leader that "throughout our history there is not a single case of our ever having conducted an equivocal policy or deceived our friend. We do not raise any claims even to a single square meter of foreign territory, but with time wish to restore our old borders."[102] It is also a fact of history, however, that Hungary had not won a single war in the previous 200 years, but had always had a military alliance with the losing side.

Notes

[1] A Fascist organization under Dr. S. Fentsyk's leadership. Fentsyk was a Carpathian civic worker of the pro-Russian, Muscophile orientation and a Hungarian sympathizer and collaborator.

[2] Quotation by Tilkovszky, *Revizió és nemzetiségpolitika Magyarországon 1938-1941* (Budapest, 1967), pp. 164, 218. *See also,* OL ME Nemzetiségi o. 77. cs. L 17029/1940; *and* Maciej Kozmiński, *Polska i Węgry przed drugą Wojną światową (Pazdziernik 1938-Wrzesień 1939). Z dziejów dyplomacji i irredenty* (Wrocław, 1970), p. 303.

[3] Volodymyr Birchak, *Karpats'ka Ukraïna. Spomyny i perezhyvannia* (Prague, 1940), pp. 81–86. Dr. Volodymyr Birchak, a Gymnasium professor, was a member of the Ukrainian Evacuation Commission attached to the German Consulate in Khust. In that capacity, he was in a singular position to collect these data and on occasion personally witness some of these incidents. The Commission departed from Khust in April 1939.

[4] H. W. Steed, *The Hapsburg Monarchy* (London, 1914), pp. 28–29.

[5] Stepan Pap-Puhach, *U madiars'kii tiurmi. Spomyny molodoho v'iaznia* (New York, 1978), p. 8.

[6] The means and methods of the inhuman brutality administered by the Hungarian authorities during the transportation of prisoners from Kryva to Nyiregyház was graphically recounted in Mykola Chyrsky's article "Prisons and Camps" that appeared in *Karpats'ka Ukraïna v borot'bi* (Vienna: Ukrainian Press Service, 1939).

[7] Macartney, *op. cit.,* part 1, p. 339.

[8] Birchak, *op. cit.,* p. 86.

[9] Czechoslovak Ministry of Foreign Affairs. *Czechoslovakia Fights Back,* introduction by Jan Masaryk, (Washington, D.C., 1943), pp. 170–71.

[10] Eduard Táborský, *Naše věc: Československo ve světle mezinárodního práva za druhé světové války* (Prague, 1946), p. 60. *See also, Lidové Noviny* 17 March 1939.

[11] Herbert W. Briggs, ed., *The Law of Nations,* 2nd ed. (New York, 1952), pp. 1004–1005.

[12] Hirniak, *op. cit.,* p. 220.

[13] Quotation by Kozmiński, *op. cit.,* p. 295.

[14] Ibid., p. 238.

[15] Ibid., p. 212. *See also,* Gerald Reitlinger, The House Built on Sand. *The Conflicts of German Policy in Russia 1939–1945* (New York, 1960).

[16] Antin Kuschchynskyj, *Zakarpattia v borot'bi. Spohady* (Buenos Aires, 1981), p. 156.

[17] Béla Fábián volunteered this information to one of our compatriots now residing in the United States. He also revealed to him a practically unknown incident that had apparently not been recorded anywhere because of its secretive nature. Sometime in 1940, Béla Fábián was sent on a secret mission to Carpatho-Ukraine, during the Hungarian occupation, to meet with the then First Secretary of the Communist Party of the Ukrainian SSR, Nikita Khrushchev, in or near the town of Uzhok bordering on the Soviet Union. The USSR had occupied Galicia following the collapse of Poland and thus became Hungary's immediate neighbor. Béla Fábián did not divulge the circumstances of the arrangement for the meeting, as he was planning to mention it in his memoirs, but revealed that his mission was to inquire about the fate of some 30,000 Carpatho–Ukrainians who had fled across the border into the Soviet Union, were reportedly promptly arrested, and sent into concentration camps. According to Fábián, Khrushchev denied reports about the arrests, but conceded that people had fled to the Soviet Union from Hungary. Fábián was also to have endeavored to persuade Khrushchev to return the refugees, but met with Khrushchev's stern rebuttal. In the 1950s, in New York, Fábián frequently figured in front-page news reports for his organized anti-Soviet demonstrations in front of the United Nations or theaters, whenever and wherever a Soviet delegation or theatrical group visited the city.

[18] A. C. Macartney, *op. cit.*, p. 332. *See also,* Jörg K. Hoensch, *Der ungarische Revisionismus and die Zerschlagung der Tschechoslovakei* (Tübingen, 1967), p. 257.

[19] *Pester Lloyd* 17 March 1939. *See also, Květy* (Prague) January–February 1969: 26.

[20] Parker, *op. cit.*, p. 48. *See also,* Macartney, *op. cit.*, p. 339.

[21] *Pesti Hirlap* 21 March 1939.

[22] As quoted by Hoensch *op. cit.*, p. 277.

[23] As quoted by Yulius Maryna [Gyula Marina], *Ruténsors-Kárpátalja végzete* (Toronto, 1977), p. 127.

[24] *Pesti Hirlap* 17 March 1939.

[25] Tilkovszky, *op. cit.*, p. 162. *See also,* OL ME Társadalompolitikai o.2. cs. Rádió Ügyek.]

[26] Tilkovszky, ibid. *See also,* Note for Ribbentrop, Berlin, March 25, 1939, OL Filmtár, 11586, doboz 51804.

[27] Tilkovszky, ibid., p. 162. *See also,* Kozma Miklós naplója (Miklós Kozma's Diary), March 22–24, 1939, OL Kozma-iratok (Kozma's papers) No. 27.

[28] Tilkovszky, ibid., p. 163. *See also,* OL ME Nemzetiségi o. 58. cs.L 16630/ 1939.

[29] Tilkovszky, ibid., p. 175. *See also,* OL ME Nemzetiségi o.67.cs.T 16788/ 1939.

[30] Z. A. Pashkui, "Polityka madiarizatsiï ukrains'koho naselennia na Zakarpatti v 1939–1944 rr.," *Ukraïns'kyi istorychnyi zhurnal* (Kyiv) 1972 (4): p. 100. *See also*, A. D. Bondar, "Iz istorii shkoly v Zakarpatskoi Ukrainy do vozsoedineniia s Sovetskoi Ukrainoi," *Dukla* 1954 (3–4): 160.

[31] Tilkovszky, *op. cit.*, p. 248. *See also*, Andrij Monajlo, *Küzalapotaink a Kárpatalján c. beadványa* (Budapest, 1939); *and* November 29, OL ME Nemzetiségi o. 61. cs.L 20528/1939.

[32] Pashkui, *op.cit..* *See also*, 01 K 429, Kozma iratok, 32 csomó, pp. 196–99 and 200–210.

[33] Pashkui, ibid. *See also*, Zakarpats'kyi oblasnyi derzhavnyi arkhyv (ZODA)—(Transcarpathian Regional State Archives), f. 7/47, op. I, p. 101, od.zb.49, ark.8–8a.

[34] Levente was the official Hungarian nationalist paramilitary youth organization.

[35] Tilkovszky, *op. cit.*, p. 246.

[36] Ibid., p. 164. *See also*, Ferencz Farkas ezredes jelentése Csáky külügyminiszterhez (Budapest, April 12) [Col. Ferencz Farkas' Report to Foreign Minister Csáky]; OL ME Nemzetiségi o.58.cs. L 16474/1939.

[37] Pashkui, *op. cit.*, p. 101. *See also*, OL k-429, Kozma iratok, 10 cs. II, kötet, p. 137.

[38] Horthy, *Emlékirataim*, 2nd ed. (Toronto, 1974), p. 203.

[39] Montgomery, *Hungary—the Unwilling Satellite* (New York, 1947), pp. 122–23.

[40] Quotation by Tilkovszky, *op. cit.*, p. 164. *See also*, "Kárpát Ukrajnára vonatkozó iratok" (Materials Relating to Carpatho-Ukraine), March 24, 1939, OL Küm. Béke elökészitö o. XXVI-2.

[41] Tilkovszky, ibid., p. 176. *See also*, "Erdmannsdorf feljegyzése Ribbentrop második megbeszélésröl Telekivel és Csákyval" (Erdmannsdorf's Notes on Ribbentrop's Second Discussion with Teleki and Csáky), Berlin, May 1, TTI Filmtár 222/I./25603–11.

[42] Volodymyr Gallan, *Bateriia smerty* (New York, 1968). *See also, Philadelphia Record* 20 March 1939.

[43] Ádám Magda, *A Müncheni egyezmóny létrejösse és Magyarország Külpolitikája 1936–1938* (Budapest, 1965), pp. 802–803.

[44] As mentioned above, the "Rongyos Gárda" [*literally*, the Ragtag Guards], officially called "Szabadcsapatok" or Voluntary Legions, were terrorist groups organized for the express purpose of infiltrating Carpatho–Ukraine during the period of the Czecho–Slovak Federation, carrying out subversive activities, and fomenting unrest.

[45] Imre Egan was the son of Edward Egan, who sympathized with our people. The Hungarian government had directed the father, in 1897, to investigate and find a solution to the problem of deplorable poverty in Carpatho-Ukraine.

[46] Tilkovszky, *op. cit.*, p. 184. *See also,* OL ME Nemzetiségi o.78.cs. L 18276/1940.

[47] Kozmiński, *op. cit.*, p. 310. *See also,* Vasyl Markus, "Carpatho-Ukraine under Hungarian Occupation (1939–1944)" *Ukrainian Quarterly* (New York) 10(3) 1954: 253.

[48] Tilkovszky, *op.cit.*, p. 182.

[49] Fedor Houdek, "Kapitulácia Maďárov v roku 1918," reprint of articles from *Prúdy* 12(1, 2, 3) with an appendix (Bratislava, 1928), p. 50. *See also, Indokolás az országos képviselök választásának szóló törvényjavaslathoz* (Budapest, 1919), p. 22; *and, A Magyar sztatisztikai évkönyv,* new 12th ed. (Budapest, 1916), p. 314.

[50] Oskár Jászi, *Die Krise der ungarischen Verfassung* (Budapest, 1912), pp. 11–12.

[51] Tilkovszky, *op. cit.*, p. 183.

[52] *Ukrainian Quarterly* (New York) 10(3) 1954: 255.

[53] Tilkovszky, *op. cit.*, p. 171.

[54] Ibid., p. 169. *See also,* OL ME Nemzetiségi o.56. cs. K 16563/1939.

[55] As quoted by Kozmiński, *op. cit.*, p. 312. *See also,* "Raport konzulatu v Ungvarze, July 22, 1939." AAN MSz, P III, W 118, t.12 (Polish Consulate's Report from Uzhhorod to Warsaw).

[56] Tilkovszky, *op. cit.*, p. 177. *See also,* "Pataky Tibor levele Keresztes-Fischer Ferenczhev, Budapest, May 11, 1939, OL Küm Bekeelökészitö o.XXVI-2"—(Tibor Pataky's Letter to Ferencz Keresztes-Fischer).

[57] Tilkovszky, *op. cit.*, p. 217. *See also,* "Kárpátalja Vajdaság iktatmányai" OL ME Nemzetiségi o. 74. cs.H 19167/1940 (Voivodship Records). Note that in his project, Teleki used the word "Ruthenian" and not "Magyar-Orosz" (Hungaro–Russian) as used in the official decree.

[58] As quoted by Tilkovszky, *op. cit.*, p. 182.

[59] Ibid., p. 168.

[60] Tilkovszky, ibid., p. 179. *See also,* OL ME Nemzetiségi o.59.cs L 17660/ 1939.

[61] Tilkovszky, ibid., p. 181. *See also,* OL ME Nemzetiségi o.60.cs. L 18582/ 1939.

[62] Tilkovszky, ibid., p. 181. *See also,* OL ME Nemzetiségi o.65.cs. P 17935/ 1939.

[63] Tilkovszky, ibid., p. 201. *See also,* "Szilágyi Pál jelentése, Ungvár, October 16, 1939" OL Kozma iratok lo. cs. Adatgyüjtemény II.1939 (Pál Szilágyi's Report, Uzhhorod, October 16, 1939).

[64] Quoted by Tilkovszky, ibid., p. 202. *See also,* "Szilágyi Pal jelentése, Ungvár, October 22, 1939" OL Kozma iratok 10.cs. Adatgyüjtemény II.1939 (Pál Szilágyi's Report, Uzhhorod, October 22, 1939).

[65] Ibid.

[66] Directive No. 3/1939. From the personal archives of Prof. A. Shtefan.

[67] Maryna, *op. cit.,* p. 141.

[68] The author's youngest brother fell into this category, when Rev. Maryna reminded him that "this you got coming because of your brother."

[69] R. W. Seton-Watson, *Racial Problems in Hungary* (London, 1908), p. 188.

[70] In his book entitled *Térkép az 1906 évi Országgyülés képviselöválasztások eredményéröl* (Budapest, 1906), Count Béla Kreith enumerates 26 deputies whose names had been changed. To mention only some of them: Secretary of State Szterényi (formerly Stern), former Minister of Justice Polonyi (formerly Pollatschek), Farkasházy (formerly Fischer), Fényvesi (formerly Veikelsbert), Földes (formerly Weiss), Hoitsy (formerly Hojča), Kálosi (formerly Grünfeld), etc. Out of a total number of 453 members only 261 could rightly claim to be true Magyars by heritage. *See also* Seton-Watson, *op. cit.,* p. 188.

[71] Tilkovszky, *op. cit.,* p. 245. *See also,* "Flachbart Ernö feljegyzése, August 16, 1939" OL ME Nemzetiségi o.65. cs. P 18623/1939 (Ernö Flachbart's Notes, August 16, 1939).

[72] Tilkovszky, ibid., p. 250, fn. 86. *See also,* OL Kozma iratok, 34, cs. 769 sz.

[73] Tilkovszky, ibid. *See also,* OL Kozma iratok, 33 cz. 728 sz.

[74] Although Perényi's hand was not light, Kozma's was by far much heavier. It struck out not only against Ukrainians, but, in part, also against followers of the Muscovite cultural orientation, such as the Duknovych Society, despite the fact that the Hungarians had supported them during the era of the Czechoslovak Republic and stll tolerated them during the occupation. Significantly, the younger generation of Muscophiles raised and educated during the Czechoslovak era were not willing to follow blindly the Magyarization policy of their leaders Brody, Fentsyk, Maryna, Ilnytsky, and others. For them, the breaking point, and with it the signal to reawakening, came when the Hungarians tore down the Adolf Dobriansky monument in Uzhhorod, the monument of their 19th century Ruthenian national and political activist.

[75] It was founded on January 26, 1941. Prof. Antal Hodynka, president; Rev. Iriney Kondratovych, vice-president; Prof. Ivan Harayda, secretary.

[76] Tilkovszky, *op. cit.,* pp. 232–33. *See also,* "Kozma Miklós levele Kozma Györgyhöz, Budapest" December 14, 1940, OL Kozma iratok 31.cs.vegyes

politikus tartalmu levelezés (Miklós Kozma's letter to György Kozma 31.cs. mixed correspondence of political nature).

[77] *See* the remarks by Vasyl Markus in *Visnyk* (New York) April-June, 1952: 18.

[78] Tilkovszky, *op. cit.*, pp. 238–39. *See also,* "Ruszin munkások ügye" OL FM Alt.ir..62.tétel, 130147/1939.sz. (The Case of the Ruthenian Workers).

[79] Tilkovszky, ibid., p. 239. *See also,* "Elöterjesztés Teleki gróf miniszterelnök részére a magyarorósz kérdés szociális és demografiai megoldás ügyében," n.d. (at the end of 1939), OL ME Társadalompolitikai o.4.cs.sz.n. (A Proposal Submitted to Prime Minister Count Teleki with Regard to the Solution of the Magyar-Russian Social and Demographic Problem).

[80] Tilkovszky, ibid., p. 242. *See also,* OL Minisztertanácsi jegyzökönyvek, August 4, 1939.

[81] Tilkovszky, ibid., p. 242. *See also,* Kozma Miklós levele Bárdossy László miniszterelnökhöz, September 22, 1941, OL Kozma-iratok 31.cs.sz.n. (Miklós Kozma's letter to Prime Minister László Bárdossy).

[82] Maryna, *op. cit.*, pp. 128–29.

[83] Personal communication from S. Dovhal and recorded on tape, now in the author's possession.

[84] For an account of his beatings, see the report of an eyewitness in V. Grendzha-Donsky's article in *Shliakhom ternovym* (Bratislava-Pryashiv, 1964), pp. 383–85.

[85] For that matter, Hungary itself had experienced the sad fate of being under a military occupation after its defeat in 1849, when in the city of Arad, nine Hungarian insurgent generals were hanged and four executed by a firing squad. In the same city, of another 475 accused, 231 were sentenced to death. (R. Averbakh, *Tsarskaia interventsiia v bor'be s vengerskoi revolutsiei, 1848–1849* [Moscow: Gosudarstvennoe sotsialno-ekonomicheskoe izdatelstvo, 1935], p. 182). The key role in these verdicts and executions was played by Field Marshal of the Austrian Army Yu. Haynau, whose brutality did not earn him a place of honor in Hungarian history. The offenses of Carpatho-Ukrainian patriots toward Hungary were of the same national content as were those of Hungarian patriots with regard to Austria. By analogy, the Hungarians cannot expect Carpatho-Ukrainians to characterize them any differently for their atrocities than they had the Austrians.

    Yet there is a difference between the two incidents, namely that Hungarian officials Count Dezsöfy and Majláth had presented a memorandum to Austria suggesting how best to stamp out the Hungarian revolution and its participants and listing 50 names of active revolutionaries. Count Ferencz Zichy sent a letter, dated August 20, 1849, to Felix Fürst von Schwarzenberg, Austria's prime minister at the time, stating in it that the accused Hungarian patriots

Minister László Csányi and Zsigmund Perényi were not deserving of a clemency. Both were hanged. [Ibid., p. 186. *See also,* Steiner, *Haynau és Paskewits,* vol. 2, p. 233.] By comparison there were no similar reports submitted on the part of the Carpatho-Ukrainians to the Hungarian occupation authorities in 1939–1944. The stark reality was in utter contrast to the magnanimous declarations of Regent Horthy and other Hungarian statesmen professing to take the Ruthenians into their "brotherly embrace" as the *Gens fidelissima.*

86 As quoted by Tilkovsky, *op. cit.,* p. 215. *See also,* "Bereg-Ugocsa megye foispánja jelentése. Beregszáz, July 5, 1940," OL ME Nemzetiségi o.74.cs. H 15028/1940.

87 As quoted in *The Ukrainian Quarterly* (New York) 10(3) 1954: 256.

88 S. M. Bilak, *A narod za nymy ne pishov* (Uzhhorod, 1981), p. 192. *See also, Shliakhom Zhovtnia. Zbirnyk dokumentiv,* vol. 5 (Uzhhorod, 1967), pp. 350 and 447; *and* Ludvik Svoboda, *Cestami života,* vol. 1 (Prague, 1971).

89 Miklós Szinai and László Szücs, ed. *Horthy Miklós titkos iratai,* 3rd ed., (Budapest, 1965), p. 411.

90 Ibid., p. 413.

91 István Pintér, *Ki volt Horthy Miklós?* (Budapest, 1968), pp. 177–78.

92 As quoted by Szinai and Szücs, *op. cit.,* p. 306.

93 Elek Karsai, *Stálo sa v Budíne v Šándorovskom paláci 1919-1941* (Bratislava, 1966), pp. 508–509.

94 Pintér, *op. cit.,* p. 158.

95 Márton Himler, *Igy néztek ki a magyar nemzet sirásói* (New York, 1958), p. 185.

96 Parker, *op. cit.,* p. 316.

97 Himler, *op. cit.,* p. 26.

98 Macartney, *op. cit.,* vol. 2, p. 108.

99 The reference is to Horthy's great political speech on August 29, 1926 elucidating the need for a Hungarian-Yugoslav rapproachment.

100 Pintér, *op. cit.,* pp. 161–62.

101 Szinai and Szücs, *op. cit.,* pp. 289–90.

102 Ibid., p. 319.

CHAPTER NINE

Unification with the Ukrainian Soviet Socialist Republic

The legal-political development of Carpatho-Ukraine within the system of the Czecho-Slovak Republic passed through several stages, culminating with the status of a federative state. As a component part of the state federation, Carpatho-Ukraine disengaged itself from foreign spokesmen and representatives, most of whom were adversely disposed toward its national and political interests, and substituted representatives from among its own people. Carpatho-Ukraine's transition into a federative system had its constitutional and internationally legal basis since 1920 and, therefore, in no way can it be construed as an act that came into being due to the then political maneuvers of Germany.

With its proclamation of independence on March 14, 1938, Carpatho-Ukraine's previous legal status in relation to Czecho-Slovakia had changed fundamentally. The result was:

1. Nullification of the provisions of the St. Germain Treaty applying to the territory of Podkarpatská Rus. However, the provisions relating to the Priashiv (Prešov) region (i.e. Eastern Slovakia) remained in force.

2. Nullification of existing state-legal acts concluded between the Czecho-Slovak Republic and Carpatho-Ukraine.

3. Creation of new foundations for international relations.

The military occupation of Carpatho-Ukraine by Hungary with Hitler's approval, from March 1939 until October 1944, did not and could not legally alter what had become a reality. Analogously, the restoration of the Czecho-Slovak Republic after World War II did not restore the *status quo ante,* as it came about in a situation involving new partners and was based on an entirely new international-legal foundation and without Carpatho-Ukraine, which was instead incorporated into the Ukrainian SSR. The latter occurrence came about as a result of the Treaty between the Czecho-Slovak Republic and the Union of Soviet Socialist Republics Concerning Carpatho-Ukraine signed on June 29, 1945. As shall be seen, this treaty was not enacted under duress but rather in cooperation between the competent Czecho-Slovak and Soviet authorities. Article I of the Treaty reads as follows:

> Transcarpathian Ukraine (referred to as Subcarpathian Ruthenia in the Czecho-Slovak Constitution), which was incorporated as an autonomous unit into the frame of the Czecho-Slovak Republic pursuant to the St. Germain-en-Laye Treaty of September 10, 1919, is being united with its age-old fatherland Ukraine in concurrence with the wishes manifested by the population of Transcarpathian Ukraine and on the basis of a friendly understanding between the two High Contracting Parties and enters the frame of the Ukrainian Soviet Socialist Republic."
>
> The border between Slovakia and Transcarpathian Ukraine that existed prior to September 29, 1938 remains, with introduced changes, the border between Czecho-Slovakia and the Union of Soviet Socialist Republics as depicted on the appended map."

In his state policy while in exile, Beneš used as his point of departure the demand for the nullification of the consequences of the Munich *Diktat* regarding the new structural form of the future restored republic as well as its legal status in the international forum. The resolution he and his government-in-exile adopted reflected this stance: "All that happened since September 19, 1938 had happened illegally, unconstitutionally, and had been forced upon us by threats, terror and violence. We would never recognize it."[1] It was on this political basis that Beneš and his exile government perceived Czecho-Slovakia's continuity with its pre-Munich borders.

Thus, the resolution as cited, which was adopted by Beneš' government-in-exile, would also formally invalidate the most important political act that was completed in Czecho-Slovakia after Munich, namely the introduction of a federative state system by virtue of constitutional Law No. 328 of November 22, 1938 (*Sb. zák. a n.*). In keeping with the said resolution, this law, too, was proclaimed unconstitutional. As far as Carpatho-Ukraine is concerned, Beneš' declaration was groundless, for Carpatho-Ukraine's autonomy rights were guaranteed by both the Constitution of the Czecho-Slovak Republic and the St. Germain Peace Treaty and, therefore, the realization of the autonomy, even if in a broader federative form, was executed as a constitutional requirement and not as an unconstitutional act.

It may be noted that Beneš was never favorably disposed toward granting autonomy to Carpatho-Ukraine although he frequently talked about it and promised it. Even during the critical days of his liberation policy, Beneš was not able to muster enough courage to stand up for the truth and constitution of his own country, which he once himself accepted and under which he became minister of foreign affairs and subsequently president of the Czecho-Slovak Republic.

Beneš and Masaryk's pro-Muscovite, and to a certain extent also pro-Soviet, political conceptions may be traced back to the historical development of the Czech people, who were constantly exposed to the Austro-German menace and sought security from Russia. This became apparent immediately following the Bolshevik October Revolution in 1917 toward which both statesmen had taken a positive stance. By 1935, Beneš' pro-Soviet policy became even more pronounced, when Hitler's intentions were becoming more obvious with regard to Czecho-Slovakia, and ultimately led to the signing of a defense pact with the Soviet Union. But Beneš' pro-Soviet policy gained even greater momentum during and after World War II, when it became the cornerstone of his foreign and internal policies.

At the time of his exile (1938–1945), the problem of Carpatho-Ukraine was frequently the subject of deliberations between him and representatives of the Soviet Union. As early as September 19, 1939, Beneš, in a conversation with Soviet Ambassador Ivan Maisky in London, declared that "After this new war we must be neighbors of the Soviet Union directly and permanently. For us, this is one of the lessons of Munich! The question of Subcarpathian Ruthenia will be solved between us later and we surely will agree."[2]

On the occasion of the signing of the Friendship Pact in Moscow in 1943, the issue of Carpatho-Ukraine was broached anew in a discussion with Stalin. The latter silently listened to Beneš' political prognoses, which led Beneš to believe that Stalin fully supported Czecho-Slovakia's restoration in its original borders. Armed with this impression, Beneš conveyed the same in his broadcasts to the Czechs at home and in his instructions to the Czecho-Slovak underground. Both Beneš and his government-in-exile believed in the good will and sincerity of the Soviet Union and Stalin. Such faith and rapture best characterize

Beneš' words pronounced over the Moscow radio to his countrymen after the signing of the said pact of friendship: "For me this moment is one of the greatest in my political activity and my political life."[3]

No doubt, Stalin was aware of the fact that Carpatho-Ukraine within the confines of Czecho-Slovakia would continue to be a place where the idea of Ukrainian statehood would be cultivated and a source of aspirations toward the independence and unification of a Ukrainian state. Consequently, the Soviet Union welcomed with secret joy the occupation of Carpatho-Ukraine, as may be deduced from the amorphous text of the Soviet protest note to Hungary.

If in Beneš' concept Carpatho-Ukraine constituted a bridge to the countries of the Little Entente during the first republic and, after the war, to the USSR, then in Stalin's opinion it was to serve him (Stalin) as a bridge to Central Europe. Carpatho-Ukraine's strategic location would provide him with access to the Hungarian plain and to Czecho-Slovakia, making it possible to maintain them as satellites.

There was no doubt in Stalin's mind that certain conditions would have to be met first before Carpatho-Ukraine could be torn away from Czecho-Slovakia, among them, the actual occupation of the land by his army and Beneš' transformation from an exile president to a constitutional one backed by the state's parliament. He, therefore, deemed it premature to discuss the matter of Carpatho-Ukraine with Beneš in 1943.

As early as the beginning of 1942, Stalin had a talk with Britain's Foreign Minister Anthony Eden during which he outlined his territorial claims once the war was over. Aside from some other territorial claims, Stalin intended "to incorporate parts of Hungary [i.e., Carpatho-Ukraine—V. Sh.] into the Soviet Union."[4]

It may be safe to assume that finally, in 1944, Beneš came around to grasp what Stalin's silence during the conversation on Carpatho-Ukraine was to mean and what danger it boded, for he then decided to establish contact with Carpathian Ukrainians in exile in the hope of enlisting their support in the event of a plebiscite in their country.

In January 1944, President Beneš ordered the leaders of the Czecho-Slovak underground organization in Czecho-Slovakia (the Protectorate and Slovakia) to make contact with Carpathian Ukrainians. According to his instructions from London, a representative of "Flora" visited me and transmitted information to me in written and oral form.[5] The gist of it was that President Beneš and the Czecho-Slovak government-in-exile wished to enter into contact with the Carpatho-Ukrainians, that they had had a sad experience with the local Russophiles, and that the Ukrainian national movement had proved itself strong and sound, was well organized, backed by the people, and was resisting the Hungarian occupation. After a prompt verification through Radio London and after three talks with the representative of the underground, I consented to cooperate. In April 1944, I submitted a memorandum specifying among others the following demands:

> United by fate and the will of the Ukrainian people in Carpatho-Ukraine in 1919 and in bringing at this time our mutual national interests together, we in principle agree with your appeal for cooperation, provided you honor the following demands:
>
> 1. The Constitutional Law of November 22, 1938, No. 328 on the autonomy of Subcarpathian Ruthenia to remain valid in all its ramifications and in the future to serve as a basis for the state and juridical relations of Carpatho-Ukraine.
>
> 2. The juridical relations of Carpatho-Ukraine in economic and social matters to be analogous with those of Slovakia, especially in the matter of national resources.
>
> 3. As soon as the power in the liberated territory of Carpatho-Ukraine is turned over to a representative of the Allied armies, he shall have an advisor, proposed by us, from the local population.
>
> 4. An announcement of the principle that the present-day Czecho-Slovak government-in-exile now and in the future cease supporting the so-called Russophile trend, which is hostile to the state and to our common interests, and that the government rely on the Ukrainian population exclusively.

The memorandum was prepared in the Ukrainian and Slovak languages. It was transmitted to London, where it was acknowledged.[6] Unfortunately, no further concrete action was to follow, inasmuch as soon thereafter an anti-German uprising broke out in Slovakia severing all contact with the leading figures of the Czecho-Slovak underground. It should be pointed out that this was the first time ever that President Beneš and his government in-exile established contact with Carpathian Ukrainians.

Stalin changed his tactic only when the Soviet Army in October 1944 entered the territory of Carpatho-Ukraine and reached Khust. At the same time, Beneš dispatched a delegation of the Czecho-Slovak government headed by Dr. František Němec to organize the land's administration. It was only then that Beneš saw through Stalin's strategy, which enabled Stalin to stage a demonstration of the population's will once the land was fully occupied by his army.

In conformity with the decision of the national committees, installed by the Soviets and convened in Mukachevo, the following resolution was adopted on November 26, 1944:

> The First Congress of the National Committees of All Transcarpathian Ukraine Resolves:
>
> 1. To reunite Transcarpathian Ukraine with its great mother, the Soviet Ukraine and to secede from Czechoslovakia.
>
> 2. To ask the Supreme Soviet of the Ukrainian Soviet Socialist Republic and the Supreme Soviet of the Union of the Soviet Socialist Republics to include Transcarpathian Ukraine as part of the Ukrainian Soviet Socialist Republic.
>
> 3. To elect a National Council of Transcarpathian Ukraine as the only central authority executing the will of the people in the territory of Transcarpathian Ukraine.
>
> 4. To empower and obligate the National Council of Transcarpathian Ukraine to put into effect the decisions of the Congress regarding the reunion of Transcarpathian Ukraine with the Soviet Ukraine.[7]

The Manifesto, which promulgated this decision, also refers to the All-National Congress held in Khust on January 21, 1919, which at that time resolved to join the territory to the Ukrainian National Republic. By its act, the Congress of the National Councils in Mukachevo deftly used the political-juridical argument of a quarter of a century before to reinforce its resolution and create for itself a historical and juridical continuity. As a result, Dr. Němec' delegation, which had issued one proclamation in Khust, had to leave the territory of Carpatho-Ukraine.

By the decision of the National Committees, Stalin placed before Beneš a *fait accompli* which left the latter with very limited room for diplomatic maneuvering. Under the pretext of the right of self-determination—which the peoples of the USSR were not permitted to exercise—Stalin had thus exploited the age-old aspirations of the Ukrainian nation to a national and state unity. Given the situation, Beneš and his exile government had to reconcile themselves to the fact that they had preserved the territorial integrity of the remainder of the republic, even if at the expense of Carpatho-Ukraine, for the Communist representatives of Slovakia were calling for a proclamation of an independent Soviet Slovakia. In order to bring the act of ceding Carpatho-Ukraine to its completion and demonstrate it as an expression of Czecho-Slovakia's good will, Beneš decided to cast it in the form of an international agreement, which was then concluded between Czecho-Slovakia and the Soviet Union on June 29, 1945.

Czechs in the free world endeavor with every means possible to impair the legitimacy of the annexation of the territory to Ukraine and at the same time deny its Ukrainian national character. It would be appropriate in this connection to refer to an article by Beneš in which he explained that:

> ... as far back as 1918 both I and President Masaryk regarded Czechoslovakia as a trustee of Ruthenia and were willing to relinquish this trusteeship when the Ukrainian people became nationally united. This occurred when Eastern Galicia was absorbed into the Soviet Ukraine.[8]

If Beneš felt that the Soviet Union had breached the agreement concerning Carpatho-Ukraine that stipulated that the pre-Munich boundaries of Czecho-Slovakia were to be retained, i.e., the *status quo ante,* he had the possibility of submitting the matter for consideration to two other members of the coalition, namely the U.S. and Britain. However, Beneš failed to pursue this course. In a letter to Stalin, dated February 1, 1945, Beneš writes: "This question [i.e., of Carpatho-Ukraine—V. Sh.] will not become a subject of discussion on our part or, for that matter, a subject of intervention on the part of other powers, but we shall come to an eventually held peace conference, for this problem has already been solved between us in full friendship."[9]

As the development of further political events in Czecho-Slovaia was to show, the problem of Carpatho-Ukraine did not shake the confidence of Beneš and other Czech politicians in the USSR. In 1945 and 1946, members of Parliament in Prague sought to outdo one another in professing fidelity, loyalty, and gratitude to the Soviet Union and its politics, shunting, at the same time, the merits of the Western democracies for the liberation of their country unto the sidetracks. As Prof. Masaryk was recognized in Western democracies as an expert on Russia during World War I, so now was Beneš recognized as an expert on Eastern Europe, meaning the Soviet Union. The positive, pro-Soviet political opinion thus created among the allied powers was bound to have an impact in spawning a similar stance in other countries of the western world. Beneš' deliberations with President Roosevelt in Washington in 1943 also played a role in this direction.

Beneš failed to disclose to the Allies Stalin's breach of the agreement regarding the boundaries of pre-Munich Czecho-Slovakia. It is doubtful if such a disclosure would have changed the course of events to come, for otherwise Churchill would have had no reason to declare to Parliament on February 27, 1945 that he "knows of no other government that would adhere to the contract terms taken upon itself, even when these proved to be burdensome, than the government of the Soviet Union."[10] If the world today is trying to find out what the objectional features of the Yalta agreement were, then they are not to be found in the agreement's stipulations but rather in the all too optimistic interpretation given it by the Allies, as by Churchill. But it was Stalin who gave the agreement his own imprint, implementing the agreement accordingly.

The agreement regarding Carpatho-Ukraine was signed by authorized representatives of the contracting states, properly ratified, and followed by an exchange of the ratification papers in Prague on January 30, 1946 at a time when there were no Soviet soldiers on the territory of Czecho-Slovakia. The agreement was endorsed by President Beneš and Foreign Minister Jan Masaryk and was published *in toto* in the official Collection of Laws and Decrees (*Sb. zák. a n.*), thereby also assuming juridical validity within the country. When the agreement was put to vote in the Prague Parliament, there was not a single vote cast against it. In fact, there was not a single abstention. From the constitutional and juridical arguments presented here the conclusion may be drawn that Czecho-Slovakia had voluntarily and legitimately renounced Carpatho-Ukraine and ceded it to Ukraine. This action was fully in keeping with the attitude among Muscophile Czechs and Slovaks during the postwar period, when the Soviets were given complete credit for liberating the country from the Nazis and many pro-Soviet policies were enacted.

The cardinal point that delineates the president's competency in concluding such agreements, embodied in Article 64 of the Czecho-Slovak Constitution, No. 121, of February 29, 1920, states that the president: "shall represent the State in its relations with other States, shall negotiate and ratify international treaties. Commercial treaties, and treaties which for the State or its citizens entail financial or personal burdens, especially military burdens, as well as treaties affecting the territories of the State require the affirmation of Parliament." Hence, in order to surrender part of the state territory the affirmation by a 3/5 majority of qualified votes of both Chambers was needed. Beneš could legally act on this matter only when his status of exile president changed to constitutional president and could have received the required affirmation of the Lower and Upper Chambers in Prague—which he as president in exile did not possess.

In the case of Carpatho-Ukraine's annexation to Ukraine, it is important to establish, from the point of view of International Law since 1938, what was Beneš' and the Czecho-Slovak government's stand with regard to the territory in view of the situation created as a result of the Vienna Arbitration and the Hungarian occupation of the territory. In this respect, Beneš assumed an explicit stand and also directed attention to the struggle waged by the Carpathian Ukrainians against Hitler in the services of the British and Soviet armies. We quote relevant passages from his book:

> Carpathian Ruthenia has never ceased to be legally part of the Republic, for the Hungarian seizure was an act of pillage, and all the more heinous, because shortly before they occupied that whole territory the Hungarians had voluntarily admitted for the first time since Trianon that the greater part of it belonged to the Czechoslovak Republic. Nor do we, of course, recognize the German-Italian arbitration of November 1938 either, and so the whole of Carpathian Ruthenia belongs to us as just it did before Munich.
>
> I should like to emphasize that the vast majority of the Carpathian people remained true to the Republic also after the Hungarian occupation, when thousands upon thousands of the inhabitants of that country fled to the Soviet Union, where all those who were fit then volunteered for the Czechoslovak Army and were placed under our authorities by agreement with the Soviet Government and are now serving as Czechoslovak citizens in our units on the Eastern front. The position is similar with regard to the Carpathian Ruthenians in our military unit in Great Britain.[11]

We consider Beneš' quotation here as a sufficient answer to the generalized reproaches made by uninformed, or disinformed, or ill-intentioned quarters about alleged sympathies of Carpatho-Ukrainians for Hitler. Such a position taken by Beneš and his government, from the point of view of the law of the land, secured for them the constitutionality of the act of ceding Carpatho-Ukraine, which, in their opinion, was considered a part of the Czecho-Slovak state territory.

Beneš felt so convinced that he was justified in making such political decisions that he deemed it redundant to consult with parliamentary representatives of Carpatho-Ukraine on the matter—persons who represented their land in the Prague Parliament under his presidency. A change of heart among the Czecho-Slovak political circles set in only when, after having successfully carried out the tasks assigned to them by the Communist Party of Czecho-Slovakia, they by their irresolution helped the Communists seize power in February 1948. Only then did they realize the danger that was in store for them personally as people to be dispensed with in political life and triggered the exodus of refugees to the West. Here, in the West, they tended to portray their former activity in quite a different light. To mention just a few examples:

Dr. Peter Zenkl, at home head of the National Socialist Party (Beneš' party), member of the Parliament, and prominent politician, said in a speech delivered to the Provisional National Assembly in Prague on November 14, 1945: "Czecho-Slovakia's basic policy must rest on the principle of never being without, never against the Soviet Union, but always in league with and alongside it."[12] However, the *Bulletin* of the Council of Free Czecho-Slovakia in Washington, D.C., of which Zenkl was president, published in its January 1950 issue, no. 3, on page 4 the following:

> The territorial changes in 1938–1945 affecting Subcarpathian Ruthenia that were occasioned by the Munich Agreement of 1938, the factual occupation by Hungary in 1939 and by the USSR in 1944, and the Czecho-Slovak-Soviet agreement of 1945, came about without asking the Subcarpathian Ruthenians and without a freely expressed approval by the competent constitutional institutions of the Czecho-Slovak Republic. All these acts were executed under coercion and thus run counter to International Law and the legalistic Czecho-Slovak internal norms. In this sense, all these acts are illegal, void, and not binding.

A similar dichotomy of opinion is manifest in a communiqué issued by the Council of Free Czecho-Slovakia in Washington, D.C., on the occasion of the 20th anniversary of Carpatho-Ukraine's incorporation into the Ukrainian SSR (not Union of Soviet Socialist Republics, as the Council stated). It said:

> It is twenty years this year, when the Soviet Union took away from
> Czechoslovakia this autonomous Subcarpathian Ruthenia and incor-
> porated the Carpatho-Russian people against their will into the
> USSR, thereby posing a menace to the entire Balkans and entire
> Western Europe.[13]

To familiarize the reader more in detail with the political reasons
behind the Czecho-Slovak-Soviet agreement concerning the annexation of Carpatho-Ukraine to the Ukrainian SSR, it is necessary to
scrutinize the aforementioned agreement of December 1943 somewhat
closer. Beneš' statements dealing with this agreement afford the opportunity to recognize how deeply imbedded were these reasons in the
minds and plans of Czecho-Slovak political leaders. The following
factors laid the groundwork for the friendship treaty:

1. Beneš and his Czecho-Slovak government-in-exile, headed by Prime
Minister Msgr. Jan Šrámeek, had their headquarters in London, not in
Moscow. On the occasion of the second anniversary of the Munich
Diktat, Winston Churchill, in his appeal to the Czecho-Slovak people
on September 30, 1940, outlined Great Britain's Government's basic
position with regard to the Munich events, stating:

> It is for this reason that we have welcomed the Provisional Czecho-
> slovak government in this country and, therefore, we set the restora-
> tion of Czechoslovak freedom as one of our primary military goals.
> With the confidence and resoluteness in which both of our peoples
> commonly and equally excel, these goals have been achieved. Be of
> good cheer, the hour of your liberation shall come. The spirit of
> freedom is immortal.[14]

2. The Communists were not in the government, which signed the
Friendship Agreement; they merely cooperated with it.

3. Before his departure for Moscow in December 1943, Beneš had met
with Britain's Foreign Secretary Eden on three occasions, during which
all aspects of this policy were scrutinized. Beneš comments on the
meetings thus:

> Eden, without opposing either the treaty or my visiting Moscow, was
> inclined to think that in view of British public opinion, I might indeed
> go to Moscow at once and agree on the treaty but that I should only
> sign it later, preferably after the conclusion of the armistice with
> Germany, when the position with regard to the Soviet Union and
> Poland and the Soviet Union's post-war policy would be quite clear
> to all the Allies.[15]

Beneš did not pay heed to Eden's practical advice, nor did he take notice of Churchill's earnest opinion, for he decided to go to Moscow nonetheless and sign the agreement. In his radio speech from Moscow to his countrymen at home, he clearly articulated his stance and that of the entire government-in-exile—a fact which contemporary Czecho-Slovak figures in the free world, including the Council of Free Czecho-Slovakia, tend to gloss over in their protests. He said:

> . . . this direction is the natural result and the logical conclusion to the development of our politics in the course of the century that was made possible thanks to the Russian revolution of the last war, to the remarkable consolidation of the Soviet state, and to its present great military successes in union with Great Britain and the United States of America.[16]

Beneš further asserted that the Friendship Agreement respected the sovereignty of both countries and guaranteed non-interference in the internal affairs of Czecho-Slovakia. He said:

> With this agreement, both of us, Czechoslovakia and the USSR, wish to make a most resolute protest before the whole world against that insane and boundlessly mendacious propaganda of the Germans as well as of our own Czech and Slovak treacherous Quislings and to point out what had already been underscored at the Moscow conference of the three great powers, namely that these powers and especially the Soviet Union, fully respect the independence of small nations and states and wish a strong Czecho-Slovakia, a strong Poland, a strong Yugoslavia, and, of course, an independent Austria, Romania, Bulgaria, Hungary, and Finland."[17]

Beneš' efforts in exile were aimed at securing from the Western countries recognition for Czecho-Slovakia in its pre-Munich boundaries. In July 1940, Great Britain recognized Beneš as president of the pre-Munich Czecho-Slovak Republic with the proviso that "it has no intention of committing itself in advance as to whether it will recognize or will support the delineation of whatever future boundaries in Central Europe."[18]

In 1941, the United States also established diplomatic relations with Beneš' government, but withheld recognition or proviso concerning the future boundaries of Czecho-Slovakia. Following the signing of the Molotov-Ribbentrop pact in August 1939, the USSR denied the then representative Dr. Zdeněk Fierlinger the status of a diplomat. After June 1941, i.e., after the German attack on the Soviet Union, the USSR recognized Czecho-Slovakia in its pre-Munich boundaries, a move designed to preempt Great Britain and the United States. Beneš became victim of his own boundless trust in Stalin and the Soviet Union by ignoring the experience of other peoples, which, as he had done, also believed in Soviet protestations of good will and in their agreements only to fall victim to their own credulity. Beneš, in his statements, depicted the USSR as a country that respects and is faithful to its own agreements and, therefore, saw it fit to prefer the Soviet Union to the Western democracies.

It was no coincidence that Prof. Tomáš G. Masaryk, acting on the wishes of France and Great Britain, journeyed to Russia and Ukraine in 1917 and, on returning via Japan, communicated a secret report to the governments of these countries in which he echoed the same political concept with regard to the East, i.e., Russia and other peoples. As an example, we shall cite a relevant part of the report:

1. The Allies should recognize the Bolsheviks (*de facto;* as for *de jure* there is no need to discuss it).

2. All small peoples in the East (the Finns, Poles, Estonians, Latvians, Lithuanians, Czechs with the Slovaks, Romanians, etc.) need a strong Russia, for else they will be at the mercy or mercilessness of the Germans and Austrians; the Allies must lend their support to Russia at whatever cost and with all means available to them.

3. An apt government could induce the Ukrainians to content themselves with an autonomous republic constituting a part of Russia; originally, the Ukrainians themselves wanted it and only later had proclaimed their independence. However, an independent Ukraine would in actual fact become a German or Austrian province. The Germans and Austrians pursue the same policy toward Ukraine as they do toward Poland.[19]

In an article dealing with the Bolsheviks, Masaryk states: "The enemies of democracy know that the Russian revolution is the surest pledge of the Allies' victory."[20] The same issue of the journal carried a map projecting the future boundaries of a Czecho-Slovak state on which Carpatho-Ukraine is still marked as belonging to Hungary. The area north of the Priashiv region on the map features a stripe indicating where Ruthenians live.[21]

The question arises whether and to what extent Ukraine's destiny was affected as a state by Masaryk's confidential report from Tokyo to the Allies regarding the importance and role of an independent Ukraine by characterizing it as a "province of the Germans and Austrians." The Allies regarded Masaryk as an expert on Russian reality and as such he was sent to Russia after the fall of the monarchy. Masaryk visited Kyiv where he met with a very friendly welcome from the Ukrainian Central Rada. The Czech Legions, which were under Masaryk's command, were armed by and received the necessary funds from the Rada. Years later, when Ukrainian émigrés, among them some members of the Ukrainian government and the Ukrainian Central Rada, found themselves in Czecho-Slovakia, Masaryk reciprocated with a likewise very friendly welcome. Of all European countries, the newly established Czecho-Slovak Republic treated the Ukrainian émigrés after World War I best. Ukrainian scientific institutions, such as the Ukrainian Free University, the Ukrainian Pedagogical Institute, the Ukrainian Academy of Economics, the Ukrainian Gymnasium (High-School), and others were constituted in Czecho-Slovakia and funded by the state, while Ukrainian émigré students from eastern Ukraine, Galicia, and Bukovina were granted full scholarships to study at Czech schools of higher learning, which created a sound foundation for Czech-Ukrainian friendship.

Since access to the state archives of that time is not available, it is certainly difficult to assert there was some decisively negative influence the confidential Masaryk report may have had on the Allies' attitude regarding the matter of a Ukrainian statehood. However, taking into account Masaryk's role as an expert sent by the Allies, his positive evaluation of Bolshevism may have had a certain modicum of influence upon them. Masaryk would time and time again find a kind word to say about the Bolsheviks and justify their policies, including the signing of the Brest-Litovsk Treaty. He also went to lengths to assure the Allies that there was nothing to fear of the Bolshevik Revolution and that they would do well to support Lenin. In a conversation with a Romanian journalist in Kyiv on September 1, 1917, Masaryk declared: "A separate peace is out of the question. I do not believe that Russia [read: Bolshevik Russia—V. Sh.] is capable of perfidy."[22] And when the Brest-Litovsk Treaty became an accomplished fact, Masaryk wrote:

> I know that the Bolsheviks are accused of one-sided Germano-philism because they had concluded peace with the Germans. I beg to differ with this viewpoint. There was no alternative for the Bolsheviks. What were they to do? The negotiations at Brest-Litovsk, the coercive manner in which the Germans tried to enforce peace, and

especially the so-called supplementary condition, adduce to the fact that the Bolsheviks reluctantly signed the peace.[23]

The Legionnaire publication *Československý Denik* carried in its No. 24, 1918 issue appearing in Kyiv another statement made by Masaryk regarding the Bolsheviks: "They recognize our armed neutrality. I told the Allies openly that I am not afraid of a Bolshevik victory. The Bolshevik government is a democratic, socialist one."[24]

Masaryk came to Russia, as he himself admitted, with the intention of staying only for a few weeks, but remained there an entire year. He left Kyiv for Moscow on February 22, 1918, and on March 7 left Moscow for Vladivostok by the Siberian railroad. After the arrival of the Bolshevik army in Kyiv under the command of Mikhail Muravyov, Masaryk elicited from him permission for a free passage of 50,000 armed Czecho-Slovak legionnaires through Siberia. Masaryk dubbed this arrangement an "armed neutrality." This is but a small part of the political balance that reveals the pro-Russian and pro-Soviet policies of the Czechs and Slovaks frequently operating in the name of Slavdom. It was not until the end of World War II that they and other smaller nations came around to realizing the true nature of this policy, but once confronted with this reality, they became terrified.

In view of the above-cited facts, such statements are puzzling indeed if we take into consideration that after the end of the war, almost all members of the Council of Free Czechoslovakia were at that time (i.e., January 1946) members of the Prague Parliament, and had voted for the incorporation of Carpatho-Ukraine into the Ukrainian SSR. Beneš and the Czechs firmly believed in Moscow, signed solemn treaties with it, and refused to countenance even theoretically any possibility of their violation by Moscow.

The Czechoslovak-Soviet Agreement regarding Carpatho-Ukraine was ignored by Ukrainian political representatives residing in the Free World. Even former members of the Carpatho-Ukrainian government, for whom this matter should have been at heart, had not taken a stand on it. At long last, Carpatho-Ukrainians of the United States and Canada, at a gathering convoked by the Carpathian Alliance in Glen Spey, N. Y. in September 1972 and in the presence of members of the former government and Soim as well as of the Government Representation in Prague, and of a large audience of countrymen, adopted an appropriate resolution clarifying their stand toward Czecho-Slovak and

Hungarian territorial aspirations as well as toward the annexation of the land to Ukraine. The Declaration, which I wrote, reads in part:

> In the process of the historical development of the Ukrainian people, whose national identity was partitioned and occupied by neighboring states over a period of many centuries, the unification of Carpatho-Ukraine with Ukraine is considered by us to be an accomplished historical fact, which corresponds to the age-old aspirations of the Ukrainian people to achieve their national and sovereign state unity. Therefore, we reject all claims to the territory of Carpatho-Ukraine raised by Czecho-Slovak and Hungarian quarters as juridically and historically unfounded, notwithstanding the fact that Carpatho-Ukraine has been incorporated in a state system imposed upon Ukraine by Muscovite military aggression against which the Ukrainian people have been waging a struggle for over more than half a century in defense of their national and state rights.

This declared intention of the Carpathian Ukrainians in favor of unification of Ukrainian lands has its roots in the thousand-year history of the territory, which, despite Hungarian occupation and persecution, has always striven to the national and political union with Kyiv.

The foes of Ukrainian statehood have always done their best to prevent Ukraine from developing politically. Stalin and Russia were conscious of the fact that after every war, nations strive for their historical and national rights, and that Ukrainians would do so after World War II. Throughout this period, we recognized that while under the domination of Moscow, Ukraine would not be able to achieve its full national rights or restore its statehood. Nevertheless, we felt it was essential to strengthen the position of Ukraine as a member state of the United Nations and in other international forums in order to reinforce the sovereignity of Ukraine.

Masaryk, as a member of the Vienna Parliament, cooperated with Ukrainian deputies and stood up in defense of the Ukrainian cause. For instance, on April 25, 1908, upon an unexpected motion made by Ukrainian deputies (E. Petrushevych, S. Vityk, and Ya. Ostapchuk, and a number of others) on the floor of the Parliament to discuss some irregularities during the regional elections in Galicia, Masaryk took the floor to say among other things:

> " . . . the Czechs, who have no nobility of their own, are sympathetic to the Ruthenians as a democratic nation of peasants without a large industry and without a nobility." He recalled that the first Slavophile

and Ukrainophile was [Johann Gottfried von] Herder, who transferred the Eldorado of culture [i.e., the ideal land of prosperity and
well-being—V.Sh.] to Ukraine, where earlier the Greeks had established their settlements and where the first Ruthenian city of Kyiv
was founded, and who extolled the superb abilities of the southern
Ruthenian people.[25]

"Ukraine," wrote Herder, "will become a new Greece. This people's
marvelous climate, their cheerful disposition, their musical talent, fer-
tile soil, etc. will suddenly awaken."[26]

Masaryk as well as other Slavic and European political workers
were sympathetic to the cultural promotion of the Ukrainian people,
but at the same time they passed in silence, were indifferent to, and
frequently even inimical to Ukrainian aspirations to statehood and
liberation. All Slavic peoples, even the smallest ones, have been striving toward their own state independence, but when it comes to the 50
million-strong Ukrainian people, then they are, as a rule, accused of
breaking up Slavic unity, i.e., meaning the Russian empire. Critical
though he was of the Russian tsarist police-state system in principle,
Masaryk had to admit that "We grew up with illusions about Russia;
we are Russophiles by education."[27] And it is because of these illusions
about Russia, nurtured for centuries by many generations and insidi-
ously instilled in the consciousness of European political and cultural
workers, that they have not, when tackling the problems of Central-
Eastern Europe, disabused themselves of these illusions, particularly
not during the period of the Soviet occupation. Russian and Soviet
diplomats expended huge sums and spared no effort to create these
illusions and to divert the attention of the world from the Ukrainian
state-liberation issue.

I have dwelt here at length on the activities and role of Masaryk in
Ukraine because of the fact that at that time, as well as today, the state-
liberation issue concerning Ukraine was a key problem in Central-
Eastern Europe. Had the Allies then resolved the problem in favor of
independent statehood, the further political course and development of
Europe would have been altered. Masaryk was the principal representative of the liberation struggle of the Czechs and Slovaks; thus, it was
natural for him to channel all his political and military efforts toward
this goal. Yet, his well-meaning utterances in favor of the Bolsheviks
and his unfavorable attitude toward the Ukrainian state aspirations

went far beyond the purview of what the liberation struggle of the Czechs and Slovaks needed. Ukraine also was engaged in a liberation struggle for independence and also was making necessary political moves on the same juridical and moral basis for the benefit of the Ukrainian people as did Masaryk for the Czech and Slovak peoples and Ukrainian military units were holding the front against the Germans and Austrians, as the Russian units were disintegrating under Bolshevik agitation and propaganda. In the end, life itself was to prove the fallacy the pro-Russian political and cultural concept cultivated and adopted in practice by leading Czechs and Slovaks, as well as many European political figures over many years. Only a half a century later were they to experience the baleful results of this concept for Europe.

Notes

[1] Eduard Beneš, *Memoir of Dr. Eduard Beneš. From Munich to New War and New Victory* (Boston, 1953), p. 106.

[2] Ibid., p. 139.

[3] As quoted by J. Miroslav Brouček, *Československá Tragedie. Jak byla bolševisována Československá republika* (Germany-New York, 1956), p. 151.

[4] Jim Bishop, *FDR's Last Year, April 1944–April 1945* (New York, 1974), p. 288.

[5] "Flora" was the conspiratorial name for a resistance group that was formed in Czecho-Slovakia immediately after Beneš and General Rudolf Viest escaped. The group was formed around the wife of Viest's brother, Dušan, Flora. The group included social democrats of Dr. Ivan Derer's group—Dr. Derer himself was the previous minister of justice of Czecho-Slovakia—the group further included Messrs. Pocysk, Bečko, Benda, and Kapinaj. Another group within Flora centered around the dean of Blumenthal Church, Avgustin Pozdecha, and this included a certain Blaha, an engineer, Hurta, a teacher, and the two most important of the group, Dr. Jurčo and Dr. Maksian from the Central Administration for State Security. These latter two served as a guarantee that when the time came for the uprising, there would be no hesitation. Resistance packages and all micro-photographs from Slovakia and the Protectorate passed through "Flora" to Switzerland through R. Fraštacký.

Other important figures belonged to this group as well, including the head of the Slovak National Bank, Imrich Karvaš, the minister of national security, General Čatloš, General Gustav Maliar (a good acquaintance of mine) and other noted political and military figures.

[6] The memorandum and other materials are in my possession. The action that I undertook was in full knowledge and agreement with four leading citizens of Carpatho-Ukraine.

[7] Extract from the Manifesto issued at the Congress of Peoples' Committee of Transcarpathian Ukraine concerning the reunification of Transcarpathian Ukraine with Soviet Ukraine.

[8] Eduard Beneš, "Post-War Czecho-Slovakia," *Foreign Affairs* 24 (1945–46): 397–98.

[9] Dr. J. W. Brügel, *Případ Podkarpatské Rusi, doklady a rozpravy* (London, 1954), p. 22. [=Dr. E. Beneš Institute, London, England, publications, vol. 14.].

[10] Quotation by Brügel, *op.cit.,* p. 28.

[11] Eduard Beneš, "Czecho-Slovak Policy for Victory and Peace." The Fourth Message of the President of the Republic to the State Council on February 3, 1944, (London, 1944,) p. 49.

[12] Quoted in *Rozpravy* (Letter for Christian Democracy; Bruxelles, Belgium) 4(3–4) 1953: 13.

[13] *Denní Hlasatel* (Chicago, Ill.) 14 April 1965. For more details on the subject, see author's article in *Svoboda* (Jersey City, NJ) 21 August 1965.

[14] Eduard Beneš, *Šest lět v exilu a druhé světové války. Řěči, projevy a dokumenty z r. 1938-1945* (Prague: Orbis, 1947), p. 444.

[15] Eduard Beneš, *Memoirs of Dr. Eduard Beneš. From Munich to New War and New Victory* (Boston, 1953), p. 244.

[16] Beneš, *Šest lět,* p. 225.

[17] Ibid, p. 227.

[18] Brügel, *op. cit.,* p. 2. The original reading of Lord Halifax' note appears in the *Czecho-Slovak Yearbook of International Law* (London, 1942), p. 231 and in Beneš' *Šest lět ,* in its Czech translation, pp. 284–85.

[19] Thomas Garrique Masaryk, *Svitova revoliutsiia za viiny i u viini, 1914–1918* (Lviv, 1930), pp. 199–200.

[20] Tomáš Garrigue Masaryk, "Russia: From Theocracy to Democracy," *The New Europe, A Weekly Review of Foreign Politics* (London) 2(23) 28 March 1917. The journal, which appeared in 211 issues and was published from October 19, 1916 until October 28, 1920, contained articles of foreign sympathizers of the Czecho-Slovak liberation.

[21] Ibid., 2(18) 15 February 1917.

[22] *Čechoslovan,* No. 36, as quoted by Janik-Horak in *Vondrák contra Masaryk,* vol. 1 (Köln n.R., 1958), p. 7.

[23] Masaryk, *Svitova revoliutsiia,* p. 191.

[24] As quoted by František Janík-Horák in *Vondrák contra Masaryk,* vol. 1 (Köln n/R, 1958), p. 6.

[25] Quotation by editors Halagan, Hryhoriyiv, and others in Prof. T. G. Masaryk. *Dobirni dumky Profesora T. Garika Masaryka. Z nahody 75 littiazhyttia 1850–1925.* (Prague, 1925), p. 52.

[26] Ibid.

[27] Ibid., p. 57.

Afterword

Nature recognizes neither dominating nor subjugated peoples—only free peoples. If the development of jurisprudence in the modern age proceeds from the tenets of Natural Law, then this law should apply equally to all peoples, including the Ukrainian people, who do not wish to constitute an exception to the rule. Denial of these natural rights to Ukrainians has been a gross infringement on these tenets. The Ukrainian people have been fighting for their natural right to their own statehood for almost three hundred years, thereby demonstrating cogent proof of their striving to be not only liberated but also free.

By the end of World War II, free world statesmen were beginning to have an awareness of the struggle Ukrainians were waging for liberation and independent statehood. President Harry Truman, in his review of historical events, arrived at an interesting conclusion. He declared that " . . . his study of history convinced him that all major wars of the previous two centuries had originated in the area from the Black Sea to the Baltic, and from the eastern frontier of France to the western frontier of Russia."[1]

President Truman's observation is correct and corresponds to the actual development of historical events. In the area between the Danube and Volga rivers, Ukraine is of paramount importance in the concept of two aggressors: the German *Drang nach Osten* and the Imperial and Soviet Russian *Drang nach Westen*. Their imperialist interests have intersected directly in Ukraine. Because of its exceptionally important strategic and economic location, Ukraine has been paying a high price to this day. As a truly "Mediterranean" land, Ukraine is at the same time the gateway to the Middle East and even India. It is, therefore, no coincidence that both world wars were fought to a large extent on the territory of Ukraine, and for it. The victor became the one who was able to hold and keep Ukraine in its possession. A sound and correct solution to the historical "Ukrainian problem" has been possible only if a strong and independent Ukrainian state could be formed that would ensure peace in this area and preclude the need for conquest, aggression, and conflict.

When Tsarist Russia was expanding its influence to the Balkans, it prompted Britain's Foreign Minister Lord John Russell (1782–1878) on the eve of the 1853–1856 Crimean War to declare that if Britain were not to fight the Russians on the Danube, it would be forced to fight them on the Indus. In response to his declaration, there appeared critical voices in the press alleging the Minister's knowledge of geography left much to be desired. However, not only was Lord Russell well versed in geography but he also correctly sensed and envisaged the course of history as well as evaluated the strategic importance of some of the geopolitical factors, such as undoubtedly are the Danube, Dnipro, Volga, and Indus rivers.

Not to accord Ukraine the status of statehood at the Paris Peace Conference in 1918–1920 was perhaps the greatest political mistake of the first half of the 20th century. Clemenceau's brainchild, the so-called *Cordon Sanitaire*, forming a chain of states extending from Finland to Bulgaria and intended as a buffer zone against young Soviet Russia's influence to the west and possible German aggression to the east, proved to be militarily and politically unrealistic and far too vulnerable. If the rule holds true that a chain is only strong as its weakest link, then the *Cordon Sanitaire*'s weakest link was to be found on the road leading to Ukraine, namely in Poland. Had an independent Ukrainian state existed, Germany's invasion of the East in 1941 would have not taken place and a possible Soviet aggression against the West would have been thwarted. Hence, it was no accident that the chain of the *Cordon Sanitaire* states broke up in the area of Ukraine.

Instead of lending Ukraine support in its stuggle against Soviet Russia in 1919–1920 and against Poland, the Entente countries set up a blockade against it so that even drugs to combat the typhoid that had been decimating the Ukrainian civilian population and army could not be supplied. Even defeated Germany and Austro-Hungary—adjudged guilty and responsible for the outbreak of World War I—were never treated in such an inhumane manner by the victors. Not to be overlooked is the fact that Ukrainians fought in the ranks of the Russian Army, the Entente's ally, against the Central Powers, and perished by the thousands on the fronts. By leaving the state territory of Ukraine divided, the Entente had thereby forged for it a bleak and tragic fate and also laid the foundation for a pending second world war.

The political situation of the Cold War after World War II, as it evolved from the crises engendered by the problems of Korea, Vietnam, Afghanistan, the Middle East, etc., can be seen as a direct result of the historical error committed by the Entente and its anti-Ukrainian decision. In the case of Ukraine, the Entente infringed from the very outset its own principle on the right of self-determination for all peoples. Future generations had to suffer the consequences of that historical error.

In the world of the 1990s it is clear to this author that under no circumstances and at no price will the Carpathian Ukrainians ever be willing to live again under occupation of another country. Carpatho-Ukraine is a state territory of Ukraine and is its integral component part of it. The fact that it had belonged to Hungary or Czechoslovakia does by no means detract from this circumstance. In both cases, as has already been pointed out, Carpatho-Ukraine constituted a foreign unit unrelated with them nationally, culturally, or religiously. Consequently, the sheer fact of territorial possession cannot constitute historical or legal claims. Any future encroachment on the territory of Carpatho-Ukraine would be an unlawful act, contravention of International Law and the principle of self-determination, and negation of the will of the population to belong to a Ukrainian state as expressed in 1919, 1939, and 1991.

Another change that had set in the wake of World War II was that the historical Franco-German antagonism has faded away, thereby rendering Bismarck's political concept no longer feasible that "Germany must be in a close touch with either England or Russia."[2] Bismarck's strategy was aimed at isolating France which was emulated in reverse—and in revenge—by Clemenceau to isolate Germany after World War I. Given the present relationship between France and Germany and the circumstances in today's free Europe, such concepts are mere remnants of the past.

The two world wars did not furnish a solution to the problem of Ukraine's struggle for liberation and statehood, for in both events Russia—the USSR in World War II—happened to be an ally of the Western democratic world, which shaped the political image of Europe and opposed the interests of Ukraine toward an independent statehood.

As matters stand today, due to the contemporary constellation of forces, the problem of Ukraine's struggle for liberation and statehood and of other peoples of the former Soviet Union is to a large extent a decisive political force. It is evident that today, as in the past, Moscow, regardless of the political system it embraces, is availing itself of every possible means to divert the attention of the Western world from a resolution of the problem of Ukraine's statehood. Moscow's avid opposition to the natural rights of the Ukrainian people to statehood is the best indication of the force and importance of the Ukrainian liberation problem that has worried Tsarist Russia and the Soviet Union in the past, and the Russian Federation today. The Western world must enshrine in the international consciousness, once and for all, a denunciation of the age-old nurtured formula of Russian national and state imperialism that preaches "Never, never will it happen that Russia— whether totalitarian or democratic republican or monarchic—allow Ukraine to be torn away."[3]

As a powerful economic partner, Ukraine will be a constructive factor in the family of free states. Through Carpatho-Ukraine, as its component part, Ukraine will secure a peaceful coexistence of the peoples of the Danubian Basin whence the aggression against the East has always originated. Such an arrangement of the Ukrainian problem brings to naught the German *Drang nach Osten* as well as the Soviet Russian and now Russian *Drang Nach Westen,* because without Ukraine Russia does not have a strategic base for its aggression against Europe.

Notes

[1]   Robert Murphy, *Diplomat among Warriors* (New York, 1965), p. 310.

[2]   *See* Count Julius Andrássy, *Bismarck, Andrássy, and Their Successors* (Boston-New York, 1927), p. 137.

[3]   General Anton Ivanovich Denikin, *World Events and the Russian Problem* (Paris, 1939), p. 30.

Selected Bibliography

Unpublished sources

Dovhal, Sprydon. Tape-recorded recollections on his imprisonment in Varjulapos camp.

Klochurak, Stepan. Letters. To the author. Dated June 22, 1971; September 1, 1975; November 17, 1979

Komarynsky, Volodymyr, Letters. To the author. Dated January 28, 1978. To V. Kachurovsky, dated May 16, 1974

Lysiuk, Kalenyk. Discussion recorded on sound tape in Ontario, California; tape-recorded proceedings of the Soim and proclamation of Carpatho-Ukraine's independence

Parčan, Jozef. Letters. To the author. Dated January 30, 1975; March 31, 1975

Shandor, Vincent. Diary excerpts on talks with Yulian Revay on January 25, 1974.

Published sources

Ádám, Magda. *Allianz Hitler-Horthy-Mussolini. Dokumente zur ungarischen Aussenpolitik (1933-1944)*. Budapest: Magyar Tudományos Akadémia, 1966. [The Hitler-Horthy-Mussolini Alliance. Documents on Hungary's Foreign Policy.]

——. *Magyarország és a második világháboru. Titkos diplomáciai okmányok a háboru elözményeihez és történetéhez*. Budapest: Magyar Tudományos Történettudományi Intézete, 1961. [Hungary and the Second World War. Secret Diplomatic Documents on the Antecedents and the Course of the War.]

——. *A Müncheni egyezmény létrejötte és Magyarország külpolitikája 1936-1938*. Budapest: Akadémiai Kiadó, 1965. [The Establishment of the Munich Agreement and Hungary's Foreign Policy.]

Akademia Nauk URSR. *Ukraïns'ko-uhors'ki istorychni zv'iazky*. Kyiv: Naukova dumka, 1964. [Ukrainian-Hungarian Historical Ties.]

American Legation, Budapest. *Despatches*. Reports of Ambassadors Montgomery and Kennan to the State Department. National Archives. File No. 760F 64/224, pp. 2 and 5.

————. *Despatch* No. 1351 of January 11, 1939; file No. 762.64/132.

Andrássy, Julius. *Bismarck, Andrássy and Their Successors.* Boston-New York: Houghton, Mifflin Co., 1927.

Appeal of the Organization of Ukrainian Nationalists—The Land's Executive Board of Transcarpathian Ukraine, *Postii* August 1938.

Apponyi, Albert. *A Brief Sketch of the Hungarian Constitution and of the Relations Between Austria and Hungary.* Budapest, 1908.

Arató, Endre. *A magyar-cseh-szlovák viszony ötven éve. Történeti áttekintés.* Budapest, 1969. [Fifty Years of Relations Between the Hungarians-Czechs-Slovaks. A Review of History.]

Averbukh, Rebeka. *Tsarskaia interventsiia v bor'be s vengerskoi revolutsiei 1848-1849.* Moscow: Gosudarstvennoe sotsial'no-ekonomicheskoe izdatel'stvo, 1935. [The Tsarist Intervention in the Struggle Against the Hungarian Revolution of 1848-1849.]

Baitsura, Ivan (Bajcura). *Rozvytok ta stanovyshche natsional'nykh menshostei v ChSSR.* Priashiv: Naukovo-populiarna biblioteka TsK KSUT, No. 9, 1976. [The Development and Staus of the National Minorities in CzSSR.]

————. *Ukrajinská otázka v ČSSR.* Košice: Vychodoslovenské vydavatelstvo, 1967. [The Ukrainian Question in CzSSR.]

Ballreich, Hans. *Karpathenrussland. Ein Kapitel tschechischen Nationalitätenrechts und tschechischen Nationalitätenpolitik.* Heidelberg, 1938. [Carpathian Russia. A Chapter on the Czech Nationality Rights and the Czech Nationality Policy.]

Balogh, Béry László. *A rutén autonomia.* Pécs, 1937. [The Ruthenian Autonomy.]

Beneš, Eduard, "Czechoslovak Policy for Victory and Peace." The Fourth Message of the President of the Republic to the State Council on February 3, 1944. Czechoslovak Ministry of Foreign Affairs. London: Information Service, 1944.

————. *Šest let exilu a druhé světové války. Řeči, projevy a dokumenty z r. 1938–1945.* Prague: Orbis, 1947. [Six Years of Exile and of the Second World War; Speeches, statements, and documents from the years of 1938–1945.]

————. *Memoirs of Eduard Beneš. From Munich to New War and New Victory.* Boston: Houghton Mifflin Co., 1953.

————. "Post-War Czechoslovakia." *Foreign Affairs* 24 (1945–46): 397–98.

Bilak, S. M. *A Narod za nymy ne pishov.* Uzhhorod: Vydavnytstvo "Karpaty," 1981. [The People Did Not Follow Them.]

Birchak, Volodymyr. *Karpats'ka Ukraïna. Spomyny i perezhyvannia.* Prague: Natsia v pokhodi, 1940. [Carpathian Ukraine: Reminiscences and Experiences.]

Bishop, Jim. *FDR's Last Year. April 1944-April 1945.* New York: William Morrow and Co., 1974.

Bondar, A. D. "Iz istorii shkoly v Zakarpatskoi Ukraine do vozsoedineniia s Sovetskoi Ukrainoi," *Dukla* 1954 (3–4). [From the History of the School System in Transcarpathian Ukraine before its Reunification with Soviet Ukraine.]

Bonsal, Stephen. *Suitors and Suppliants. The Little National Versailles.* Port Washington, New York: Kennikat Press, 1946.

Briggs, Herbert W. *The Law of Nations.* New York: Appleton-Century-Crofts, 1952.

Brouček, Miroslav J. *Československá Tragedie. Jak byla bolševisována Československá republika.* Germany-New York, 1956. [The Czechoslovak Tragedy. How the Czechoslovak Republic Was Bolshevized.]

Brügel, J. W. *Případ Podkarpatské Rusi, doklady a rozpravy.* London: Beneš Institute, 1954. [The Case of Subcarpathian Ruthenia, Documents and Treatises;=Eduard Beneš Institute, London, England, publications, vol. 14.]

Bullock, Alan. *Hitler, A Study in Tyranny.* New York and Evanston: Harper and Row, 1964.

Cecil, Robert. *Hitler's Decision to Invade Russia in 1941.* U.S. National Archives. EAP 99/110. London: Davis-Poynter, 1975.

Chamberlin, William H. *The Ukraine: A Submerged Nation.* New York: The Macmillan Co., 1944.

Chiminec, Yulian [Khymynets]. *Moï sposterezhennia iz Zakarpattia.* New York: Carpathian Alliance, 1984. [My Observations of Transcarpathia.]

Chmelář, Josef; Klíma, Stanislav; Nečas, Jaromír, eds. *Podkarpatská Rus: obraz poměrů přírodních, hospodářských, politických, církeních, jazykových a osvětových.* Prague: Orbis, 1923. [Subcarpathian Ruthenia: A Description of Natural, Economic, Political, Religious, Language and Educational Conditions.]

Ciano, Count Galeazzo. *The Ciano Diaries 1939-1943.* New York: Doubleday and Co., 1946.

Clementis, Vlado. *Slováci a Slovanstvo.* London, 1943. [The Slovaks and Slavdom.]

Crankshaw, Edward. *Bismarck.* New York: Viking Press, 1981.

———. *Maria Theresa.* New York, 1969.

Čulen, Konstantin. *Po Svátoplukovi druhá naša hlava. Život Jozefa Tisu.* Cleveland, Ohio: Prvá Katolická Slovenská Jednota, 1947. [After Sviatopluk Our Second Head of State.]

Czecho-Slovakia. *Czecho-Slovak Memoirs 1-6.* Their History and Civilization, 1919.

Czechoslovak Ministry of Foreign Affairs. *Czechoslovakia Fights Back.* Washington, D.C.: American Council on Public Affairs, 1943. Introduction by Jan Masaryk.

Czechoslovak Socialist Republic. *The Constitution of the Czechoslovak Socialist Republic.* Prague: Orbis, 1960.

Dánás, Jozef. *Ludacký separatismus a Hitlerovské Německo.* Bratislava: Vydavatelstvo politické literatury, 1963. [Ludacká Movement Separatism and Hitlerite Germany.]

Danko, Joseph, *Plebiscite of Carpatho-Ruthenians in the United States.* Reprinted from *the Annals of the Ukrainian Academy of Arts and Sciences in the United States* 11(1–2) 31-32. New York, 1964–1968.

Darás, Gábor. *A rutén kérdés tegnap és ma.* Budapest, 1938. [The Ruthenian Question Yesterday and Today.]

Delegation of Carpatho-Ukraine. A Letter to the Executive of the UNO (Ukrainian National Unity), Saskatoon, Canada, of October 22, 1938.

Denikin, A. J., Gen. *World Events and the Russian Problem.* Paris: Imprimerie Rapide C-T, 1939.

Department of State. *Nazi-Soviet Relations 1939–1941. Documents from the Archives of the German Foreign Office.* Ed. Raymond James Sontag and J. S. Beddie. Washington, D.C., 1948.

—————. *Documents on German Foreign Policy 1918-1945. From the Archives of the German Foreign Ministry.* U.S. Government Printing Office, Series D (1937-1945). The Aftermath of Munich October 1938-March 1939. Washington, D.C., 1951.

Dérer, Ivan. *Češi a Slováci ve střední Evropě.* Prague, 1938. [The Czechs and Slovaks in Central Europe.]

Documents on the Eve of World War II. Prague, n.d. No. 23.

Doroshenko, Dmytro. *Istoriia Ukraïny 1917–1923*, vol. 2, *Doba Tsentral'noï Rady.* Uzhhorod, 1930. New York: Bulava, 1954. [History of Ukraine 1917-1923. The Period of the Central Rada (Central Council.]

Ďurčanský, Ferdinand, *Biela kniha. Svázok Prvý. Právo Slovákov na samostatnosí vo svetle dokumentov.* Buenos Aires: Slovenský Oslobodzovací Výbor, 1954. [The White Book. The Right of the Slovaks to Independence in the Light of Documents.]

Egán, Imre. *Milyen legyen a ruszin automonia?* Uzhhorod: Husvét havában, 1939. [What Is the Ruthenian Autonomy Like?]

Fajták, Ladislav. *Narodno-demokratická revolúcia na Východnom Slovensku roku 1918.* Monograph 6. *Historica.* Bratislava: Acta Facultatis Philosophicae Universitatis Safarikonea, 1973. [The People's Democratic Revolution in Eastern Slovakia in 1918.]

Faro, Stefan. "Zakarpatská Ukrajina v politických kalkuláciach ústredných štátov v období od Mnichova po marec 1939." *Slovanské študia* (Bratislava) 9 Historia 1971: 68. [Transcarpathian Ukraine in the Calculations of Central States during the Period from Munich to March 1939.]

Feierabend, Ladislav, *Ve vládách Druhé republiky.* New York: Universum Press, Co., 1961. [In the Governments of the Second Republic.]

Fényes, Alexius. *Ungarn in Vormärz. Nach Grundkraften, Verfassung, Verwaltung und Kultur.* Leipzig: Verlag von Friedrich Ludwig Herbig, 1851. [Hungary Before the March. Its Main Strength, Constitution, Administration, and Culture.]

Fierlinger, Zdeněk. *Ve službách ČSR. Paměti z druhého zahraničního odboje,* vol. 1. Prague: Dělnické nakladatelstvi, 1951. [In the Services of the Czechoslovak Republic. Reminiscences from the Second Resistance Abroad.]

Foerster, F. W. *Evropa a německá otázka.* Prague. Date unknown. [=*Europe and the German Question.* Translated into English. New York: Sheed and Wand, 1940.]

Friedrichs, Axel. *Deutschlands Aufstieg zur Grossmacht.* Berlin: Junker und Dünnhaupt Verlag, 1937. [Germany's Rise to a Great Power.]

Gafencu, Grigor. *Vorspiel zum Krieg im Osten.* Zürich: C. J. Bucker A. G. Luzern, 1944. [The Prelude to the War in the East.]

Gallan, Volodymyr. *Bateriia smerty.* New York: Vydavnytstvo "Chervona Kalyna," 1968. [The Battery of Death.]

Halagan, Hryhoriyiv, et al. eds. *Dobirni dumky Profesora T. Garika Masaryka. Z nahody 75-littia zhyttia 1850–1925.* Prague: Ukraïnskyi hromadianskyi komitet, 1925. [Selected Views of Prof. Thomas Garrigue Masaryk.]

Hencke, Andor von. *Augenzeuge einer Tragödie. Diplomatenjahre in Prag 1936-1939.* Munich: Fides Verlagsgesellschaft, 1977. [Eyewitness of a Tragedy. Years of a Diplomat in Prague 1936=1939.]

Henderson, Alexander. *Eyewitness in Czechoslovakia.* London: George G. Harrap and Co., 1939.

Col. Heřman, Ján. Military Report by Commander of SOS, March 1939. [Copy of original in the author's possession.]

Hilger, Gustav. *The Incompatible Allies. A Memoir-History of German-Soviet Relations 1918–1941.* New York: The Macmillan Co., 1953.

Hillgruber, Andreas. *Germany and the Two World Wars.* Translated from German by William C. Kirby. Cambridge, Massachusetts: Harvard University Press, 1981.

Himler, Marton. *Igy néztek ki a magyar nemzet sirásoi.* New York: The Hungarian Department Head Himler of the Office of Strategic Services, 1958. [This Is What the Hungarian Nation's Gravediggers Looked Like.]

Hirniak, Liubomyr. *Na stezhkakh istorychnykh podii. Karpats'ka Ukraïna i nastupni roky. Spohady i materialy.* New York, 1979. [On the Paths of Historical Events. Carpatho-Ukraine and the Years Following. Reminiscences and Materials.]

Hoensch, Jörg K. *Die Slovakei und Hitlers Ostpolitik. Hlinkas slovakische Volkspartei zwischen Autonomie und Separation 1938–1939.* Köln-Graz: Böhlan Verlag, 1965. [Slovakia and Hitler's East Policy. Hlinka's Slovak Populist Party Between Autonomy and Separation.]

——————. *Der ungarische Revisionismus und Zerschlagung der Tschechoslovakei.* Tübingen J. C. B. Mohr (Paul Siebeck), 1967. [The Hungarian Revisionism and the Destruction of Czechoslovakia.

Hoettl, Wilhelm. *The Second Front. The Story of Nazi Political Espionage.* New York: Frederick A. Praeger, 1954.

Höhne, Heinz. *Canaris: Patriot im Zwielicht.* Munich: Wilhelm Goldman Verlag, 1978. [Canaris: A Patriot in the Twilight.]

Holub, Ota. "Drama pod poloninami." *Svět v obrazech* (Prague) 10 (7 March 1964).

Hora, Alois. *Karpatská Rus a hranice našeho státu.* Prague: Československý cizinecký uřad, 1919. [Carpathian Ruthenia and the Borders of Our State.]

Horthy, Miklós. *Emlékirataim.* 2nd ed. Toronto, 1974. [My Memoirs.]

Horváth, Jenö. *A magyar kérdés a XX században. Felelöség a világháboruért és a békeszerzödésért.* Budapest, 1939. [The Hungarian Question in the 20th Century. Responsibility for the World War and the Peace Treaty).

Horváth, Mihály. *A kereszténység elsö században Magyarországon.* Budapest, 1878. [Christianity's First Century in Hungary.]

Houdek, Fedor. *Kapitulácia Maďárov v roku 1918, Prúdy* (Bratislava) 12(1), 12(2), 12(3) 1928. [The Capitulation of the Hungarians in 1918.]

Hungary Exposed. Secret Document Reveals the plotting of that Government in the United States. American Slovaks and Ruthenians. New York, 1907.

Húsek, Jan, *Národopisná hranice mezi slovaký a karpatorusy.* Bratislava: Knižnica "Prúdov," 1925. [Ethnographic Frontier Between the Slovaks and the Carpatho-Ruthenians.]

Indokolás az országos képviselok választásának szóló törvényjavaslathoz. Budapest, 1919. [Motives Behind the Bill Relating to the Elections of State Representatives.]

Institute of Jewish Affairs. *Hitler's Ten-Year War on Jews.* New York: International Press, September 1943.

Ipolyi, Arnold, et al. *History and Description of the Holy Hungarian Crown and the Insignia* (in Hungarian). Budapest, 1886.

Jaminsky, Borys. *Viden' 1683. Kozaky i Kulchyts'kyi.* Vienna: Union of Ukrainian Philatelists in Austria, 1983. [Vienna 1683. The Cossacks and Kultchytsky.]

Janík-Horák, František. *Vondrák contra Masaryk,* vol. 1. Köln n/R: Knižnice Bohemia, 1958.

Jászi, Oszkár *Die Kriese der ungarischen Verfassung.* Budapest, 1912. [The Crisis of the Hungarian Constitution.]

————. *The Dissolution of the Habsburg Monarchy.* Chicago: University of Chicago Press, 1929.

Jehlicska, František, *Father Hlinka's Struggle for Slovak Freedom.* London: Slovak Council, 1938.

Kann, Robert A. *History of the Habsburg Empire 1526–1918.* Los Angeles: University of California Press, 1974.

Karácsonyi, János. *Szent István király Oklevelei és a Szilveszter Bulla.* Budapest: Diplomatikai tudomány, 1891. [King St. Stephen's Documents and the Sylvester Edict.]

Károlyi, Mihály. *Memoirs of Michael Károlyi. Faith Without Illusion.* London, 1956.

Karsai, Elek. *Stálo sa v Budíne v Šándorovskom paláci 1919-1941.* Bratislava: Vydavatelstvo politické literatúry, 1966. Translated from Hungarian. [It Happened at the Sandor Palace in Buda.]

Kennan, George. *From Prague after Munich. Diplomatic Papers 1938–1940.* Princeton: Princeton University Press, 1968.

Kertész, Stephen D. *Diplomacy in a Whirlpool. Hungary Between Nazi Germany and Soviet Russia.* Notre Dame: University of Notre Dame Press, 1953.

Khrushchev, Nikita S. *Khrushchev Remembers. The Last Testament.* Boston-Toronto: Little, Brown and Co., 1970. Transl. and ed. by Strobe Talbott.

Klochurak, Stepan. *Do Voli.* New York: Carpathian Alliance, Inc., 1978. [Toward Freedom.]

Knysh, Zynovii. *Rozbrat. Spohady i materialy do rozkolu OUN u 1940–1941 rokakh.* Toronto: Sribna Surma, 1960. [The Falling Out. Memoires and Materials Relating to the Split of the OUN in 1940–1941.]

Kolarz, Walter. *Myth and Realities in Eastern Europe*. London, n.d.

Kordt, Erich. *Wahn und Wirklichkeit. Die Aussenpolitik des Dritten Reiches. Versuch einer Darstellung*. Stuggart, 1948. [Illusion and Reality. The Foreign Policy of the Third Reich. An Attempt at a Description.]

Kosarenko-Kosarevych, V. *Moskovs'kyi Sfinks. Mit i syla v obrazi Skhodu Evropy*. New York: R. Krupka and A. Bilan, 1957. [The Muscovite Sphinx. Myth and Strength in the Image of Eastern Europe.]

Kováč, Andrej. "K politike Slovenskej Republiky voči Rusinom na základe štátobezpečnostných spisov Šarišsko-Zemplinskej župy. Materialova študia." *Acta Facultatis Philosophicae Universitatis Safarikanae Presovensis*, vol. 1 (Bratislava, 1970). [Regarding the Slovak Republic's Policy Toward the Ruthenians on the Basis of State Security Documents of the Saris-Zemplin District: A study of Materials.]

Kozmiński, Maciej. *Polska i Węgry przed drugą Wojną światową (Pazdziernik 1938-Wrzesień 1939). Z dziejów dyplomacji i irredenty*. Wrocław: Zaklad Narodowy im. Ossolińskich, 1970. [Poland and Hungary before World War II (October 1938-September 1939). On the Basis of Diplomatic and Irredentist Actions and Events.]

Kramer, Juraj. *Slovenské autonomistické hnutie v rokoch 1918–1929*. Bratislava: Vydavatelstvo Slovenskej Akademie Vied, 1962. [The Slovak Autonomist Movement in 1918–1929.]

Kreith, Count Béla. *Térkép az 1906 évi Országgyülés képviselöválasztások eredményéröl*. Budapest, 1906. [An Atlas of the Results of the 1906 Parliamentary Elections.]

Krempa, Ivan. *Za internacionálnu jednotu revolúčneho hnutia v Československu*. Bratislava: Nakladatelstvo "Pravda," 1975. Ústav marxismu a leninizmu. [For International Unity of the Revolutionary Movement in Czechoslovakia.]

Kren, Jan. *Do emigrace: buržoazni zahranicni odboj, 1938–1939*. Prague: Naše vojsko, 1963.

Krofta, Kamil. *The Substance of Hungarian Revisionism*. Prague: Orbis, 1937.

Kushchynsky, Antin. *Zakarpattia v borot'bi. Spohady*. Buenos Aires: Vydavnytstvo Iuliana Seredniaka, 1981. [Transcarpathia in Struggle.]

Lang, Jochen von. *The Secretary: Martin Bormann. The Man Who Manipulated Hitler*. New York: Random House, 1979.

Lansing, Robert. *The Peace Negotiations. A Personal Narrative*. Boston-New York: Houghton-Mifflin Co., 1921.

Latham, R.G. *The Nationalities of Europe*, vol. II. London: Wm. H. Allen & Co., 1863.

Légrády, Otto. *Justice for Hungary. The Cruel Errors of Trianon.* 3d rev. ed. Budapest, 1931.

Lelekach, Mykola. "Pro prynalezhnist Zakarpattia do Kyivskoi Rusi v X-XI st." *Naukovi zapysky Uzhorodskoho Derzhavno Univesitetu,* vol. 2 (Uzhhorod, 1949), pp. 28–38. ["On Transcarpathia's Belonging to Kyivan Rus' in the 10th and 11th centuries."]

Lipski, Jozef. *Diplomat in Berlin 1933–1939.* New York: Columbia University Press, 1968.

Lockhart, Robert Bruce, Sir. *What Happened to the Czechs?* London: The Batchwood Press, 1953.

Lottick, Kennet V. "Soviet Russia's First Victim." *Sudeten Bulletin* (Munich) 8(10) October 1960.

Lukács, George, ed. *La Hungrie et la civilization.* Paris, 1929.

Lukeš, František. *Podivný mír.* Prague: Svoboda, 1968. [Strange Peace.]

Macartney, Carlisle A. *A History of Hungary, 1929-1945,* part 1. New York: Praeger, 1956.

————. *A History of Hungary, 1929-1945,* part 2. New York: Praeger, 1957.

Macůrek, Josef. *Dějiny Madarů a uherského státu.* Prague: Melantrich, 1934. [History of the Hungarians and of the Hungarian State.]

Magosci, Paul Robert. *The Shaping of a National Identity. Sub-Carpathian Rus, 1848–1948.* Cambridge, Massachusetts: Harvard University Press, 1978.

A Magyar sztatisztikai évkönyv. New, 12th ed. Budapest, 1916. [Hungarian Statistical Yearbook.]

Malaniuk, Evhen. *Do problemy bolshevyzmu.* New York: Spilka Ukrains'koï Molodi Ameryky, 1956. [About the Problem of Bolshevism.]

Marczali, Heinrich. *Ungarns Geshichtsquellen in Zeitaltern der Arpaden.* Berlin, 1882. [Hungary's Historical Sources During the Era of the Arpads.]

Maryna, Yulius [Gyula Marina]. *Ruténsors—Kárpátalja végzete.* Toronto: Patria Publishing Co., 1977. [The Fate of the Ruthenians—Subcarpathia's Ruin.]

Markus, Vasyl. "Carpatho-Ukraine under Hungarian Occupation (1939–1944)" *Ukrainian Quarterly* (New York) 10(3) 1954.

————. *L'incorporation de l'Ukraine subcarpathique à l'Ukraine sovietique 1944–1945.* Louvain: Centre d'études ukrainiens en Belgique, 1956.

Masaryk, Tomáš [Thomas] Garrigue. *Svitova revoliutsia za viiny i u viini, 1914–1918.* Lviv: Chervona Kalyna, 1930. [Translated from the 11th

Czech Edition by Mykola Sayevych.] [World Revolution During and in the War of 1914–1918.]

————. *Dobirni dumky Profesora T. Garika Masaryka. Z nahody 75-littia zhyttia 1850–1925.* Ed. Halagan, Hryhoriyiv, et al. Prague: Ukraïns'kyi hromadians'kyi komitet, 1925. [Selected Views of Prof. Thomas Garrigue Masaryk.]

Mayer, Mária, *Kárpátukrán/Ruszin/politikai és társadalmi törekvések 1860–1910.* Budapest: Akadémiai kiadó,1977. [Carpatho-Ukraine/the Rusyns/ Politics and . . . 1860–1910]

Mikúš, Jozef A. *Slovakia: A Political History 1918–1950.* Milwaukee: The Marquette University Press, 1963.

Miller, David Hunter. *My Diary at the Conference of Paris, with Documents.* 21 vols. New York: 1924.

Mindszenty, József Cardinal. *Memoirs.* New York: Macmillan Publishing Co., Inc. 1974. [Translation from German.]

Molnar, Mykhailo. *Slovaky i ukraïntsi.* Bratislava and Pryashiv: Slovats'ke pedahohychne tovarystvo v Bratyslavi, Viddil ukraïns'koï literatury, 1965. [Slovaks and Ukrainians.]

Monajlo, Andrij. *Közalapotaink a Kárpátaljón c. beadványa* (Budapest, 1939). [Written Statement on the State of Affairs in Subcarpathia.]

Montgomery, John Flournoy. *Hungary—the Unwilling Satellite.* New York, 1947.

Morávcsik, Gyula. *Bizánc és Magyarorország.* Budapest: A Magyar Tudományos Akadémia kiadása, 1953. [Byzantium and Hungary.]

Mosley, Leonard. *On Borrowed Time. How World War II Began.* New York: Random House, 1969.

Murphy, Robert. *Diplomat among Warriors. Secret Decisions That Changed the World.* New York, 1965.

Museum of Ukrainian Culture in Svydnyk, Slovakia. *Shliakh do voli. Zbirnyk spohadiv i dokumentiv pro natsional'no-vizvol'nu borot'bu ukraïns'koho naselennia proty fashyzmu u 1939–1945 rr,* vol. 2. Ed. Ivan Vanat. Bratislava and Pryashiv: Slovats'ke pedahohychne tovarystvo v Bratyslavi, Viddil ukraïns'koï literatury, 1966). [The Road to Freedom: A collection of reminiscences and documents on the national-liberation struggle of the Ukrainian population of Czechoslovakia against Fascism in 1939–1945.]

Narodní Shromáždění Republiky Československé. Prague: Předsednictvo Poslanecké Sněmovny a Předsednictvo Senátu, 1928. [National Assemblies of the Czecho-Slovak Republic.]

Naukove Tovarystvo imeny Shevchenka. *Entsyklopedia Ukraïnoznavstva, Slovnykova chastyna*. Munich, 1955. [Encyclopedia of Ukrainian Studies, Dictionary Section.]

New Hungarian Quarterly. Vol. 4, no. 11 Budapest, July-September 1963.

Nicolson, Harold George, Sir. *Peacemaking, 1919*. New York: The Universal Library. Grosset & Dunlap, 1965.

Niederle, Lubor. *Slovanský svět. Zeměpisný a statistický obraz současného Slovanstva*. Prague: Nakladem Jana Laichtera na Králových Vinohradech, 1909. [The Slavic World. Geographical and Statistical Portrait of Contemporary Slavdom.]

Nové dokumenty k historii Mníchova. Bratislava: Štátní nakl. politické literatury, 1958.

OUN-KE Zakarpats'koï Ukraïny [Organization of Ukrainian Nationalists-Regional Executive Board of Transcarpathian Ukraine]. "Vidozva" *Postii* August 1938. [Appeal.]

Ortoskop (Mykhailo Tvorydlo). *Derzhavni zmahannia Prykarpats'koï Ukraïny*. Vienna: Nova Hromoda, 1924. [Aspirations of Carpathian Ukraine toward Statehood.]

Pap-Puhach, Stepan. *Plastovyi Almanakh. Z nahody 50 littia Ukraïns'koho Plastu na Zakarpattiu 1921–1971*. Rome, 1976. [Scouting Almanac. On the 50th Anniversary of the Founding of the Ukrainian Scouting in Transcarpathia, 1921–1971.]

——— [Rev. Stepan Pap]. *Pochatky Khrystianstva na Zakarpatti*. Philadelphia, PA.: Metropolis of the Ukrainian Catholic Church, 1983. [The Inception of Christianity in Transcarpathia.]

——— [Stepan Puhach]. *U madiars'kii tiurmi. Spomyny molodoho v'iaznia*. New York: Carpathian Alliance, Inc., 1978. [In a Hungarian Prison.]

Parker, Robert. *Headquarters Budapest*. New York-Toronto: Farrar and Rinehart, 1944.

Parker, Štefan. *Protifašistický odboj na Východnom Slovensku*. Košice, 1974.

Pashkui, Z. A. "Polityka madiarizatsiï ukrains'koho naselennia na Zakarpatti v 1939–1944 rr." *Ukraïns'kyi istorychnyi zhurnal* (Kyiv) 1972 (4): p. 100. ["The Policy of Magyarization of the Ukrainian Population in Transcarpathia, 1939–1944."]

Pekar, Athanasius OSBM, Rev. *The Bishops of the Eparchy of Mukachevo with Historical Outlines*. Pittsburgh: Byzantine Seminary Press, 1979.

——— *Narysy istoriï tserkvy Zakarpattia*, vol. 1. Hierarchial Structure. Rome: Analecta OSBM, 1967. [Outline of the History of the Church in Transcarpathia.]

Peroutka, Ferdinand. *Budování státu. Československa politika v letech popřevratových,* vols. 1–4. Prague, 1936. [The Formation of the State. Czechoslovak politics during the pre-revolutionary years.]

Pintér, István. *Ki volt Horthy Miklós?* Budapest: Zrinyi katonai kiadó, 1968. [Who was Miklós Horthy?]

Pop, I. I. *Chekhoslovatsko-Vengerskie otnosheniia 1935–1939.* Moscow: Izdatel'stvo Nauka, 1972. [Czechoslovak-Hungarian Relations 1935–1939.]

Popovych, Mikhal. *Revolutsiino-demokratychne iednannia slovian u XIX st.* Bratislava and Pryashiv: Slovats'ke Pedahohychne Vyd-vo v Bratislavi. Viddil ukraïns'koï literatury v Pryashevi, 1973. [Revolutionary-Democratic Unification of the Slavs.]

Ránki, György. *A Wilhelmstrasse és Magyarország. Német diplomáciai iratok Magyarországból 1933–44.* Budapest: Kossuth Kiadó, 1968. [Wilhelmstrasse and Hungary. German Diplomatic Papers on Hungary 1933-44.]

————. *Emlékiratok és valóság Magyarország második világháborus szerepéröl.* Budapest, 1964. [Memoirs and the Truth about Hungary's Role in the Second World War.]

Rauschning, Herman. *Hitler Wants the World.* London, 1941.

————. *Hitler Speaks. A Series of Political Conversations with Adolf Hitler on His Real Aims.* London, 1940.

Reiners, Ludwig. *The Lamps Went Out in Europe.* New York: Pantheon, 1955.

Reitlinger, Gerald. *The House Built on Sand. The Conflicts of German Policy in Russia 1939–1945.* New York: Viking Press, 1960.

Ribbentrop, Joachim von. *The Ribbentrop Memoirs.* Introduction by Alan Bulock, Werdenfeld, and Nicolson. London, 1954.

Ripka, Hubert, *Munich: Before and After.* London: Victor Gollanz, 1939.

————. *East and West.* London: Lincoln-Prager, 1944.

Rosenberg, Alfred. *Memoirs of Alfred Rosenberg.* With commentaries by S. Lang and E. von Schenk. Edited by Serge Lang & Ernest von Schenk. New York-Chicago: Ziff-Davis, 1949.

Rosokha, Stepan. "Narodzhennya derzhavy." In *Karpats'ka Ukraïna v borot'bi. Zbirnyk.* Vienna: Ukrainian Press Service, 1939. ["Birth of the State" in Collection: Carpatho-Ukraine in Struggle).

————. *Soim Karpats'koï Ukraïny. Za 10-littia proholoshennia samostiinosti.*Winnipeg: Ukrainian National Publishing Co., Ltd., 1949. [The *Soim* of Carpatho-Ukraine. On the Occasion of the 10th Anniversary of the Proclamation of Independence.]

Russell of Liverpool, Edward Frederick Langley Russell, Baron. *The Scourge of the Swastika. A Short History of Nazi War Crimes.* New York: Philosophical Library, 1954.

Sarvadiy, Ivan. *Zmova proty uriadu Karpats'koï Ukraïny.* Chicago: Carpathian Alliance, 1984. [Conspiracy Against the Government of Carpatho-Ukraine.]

Schellenberg, Walter. *The Schellenberg Memoirs.* Ed. and trans. Louis Hagen. London: Andre Deutsch, 1956.

Schuman, Friedrich L. *Soviet Politics at Home and Abroad.* New York: Alfred A. Knopf, 1953.

Scotus Viator (Seton-Watson, R.W.). *Racial Problems in Hungary.* London: Archibald Constable, 1908.

Seton-Watson, R. W. *Racial Problems in Hungary.* London: A. Constable, 1908.

―――. *Treaty Revision and the Hungarian Frontiers.* London: Eyre and Spottiswoode, 1934.

―――. *Twenty-Five Years of Czechoslovakia.* London: The New Europe Publishing Co., 1945.

Shandor, Vincent [Vikentii]. *Spomyny,* vol. 1, *Karpats'ka Ukraïna, 1938–1939.* Uzhhorod-New York: Grazhda-Carpathian Alliance, 1996.

―――. *Zakarpattia. Istorichno-pravnyi narys IX st.–1920.* New York: Carpathian Alliance, 1992.

Shirer, William L. *The Rise and Fall of the Third Reich. A History of Nazi Germany.* New York: Third Crest Printing, June 1962.

Shtefan, Avhustyn. *Avhustyn Voloshyn. Spomyny.* Toronto, Canada: Carpathian Research Center, 1977. [Avhustyn Voloshyn. Recollections.]

―――― [Augustin Štefan]. *From Carpatho-Ruthenia to Carpatho-Ukraine.* New York: Carpathian Star, 1954.

Sichynsky, Volodymyr. *Roksoliana.* Monograph. London: Ukrainian Publishing Co., 1957. [Roxalana.]

Sidor, Karol. *Slovenská politika na póde pražského snemu 1918–1938,* vols. I and II. Bratislava, 1943. [Slovak Politics on the Floor of the Prague Parliament 1918–1938.]

―――. *Moje poznámky k historickým dňom.* Middletown, Pa., 1971. [My Notes on Historic Days.]

Slovatska Akademiya Nauk. *Z istoriï chekhoslovats'ko-ukraïns'kykh zv'iazkiv.* Bratislava: Slovatske vydavnytstvo khudozn'oï literatury, 1959. [From the History of Czechoslovak-Ukrainian Relations.]

Snyder, Louis L. *The War. A Concise History 1939–1945.* New York: Simon and Schuster, 1960.

Speer, Albert. *Infiltration.* Transl. Joachim Neugroschel. New York: Macmillan Publishing Co., 1981.

—————. *Memoirs. Inside the Third Reich.* Transl. Richard and Clara Winston. New York: Macmillan Co., Inc., 1970.

Staško, Joseph. *Slovensko po druhej svetovej vojne. Aprilova dohoda r. 1946–1947.* Cambridge, Ont., Canada, 1977. [Slovakia after World War II.]

Steed, Henry Wickham. *The Hapsburg Monarchy.* 2nd ed. London, 1914.

—————. *A Short History of Austro-Hungary and Poland.* London, 1914.

Stercho, Peter G. *Diplomacy of Double Morality. Europe's Crossroads in Carpatho-Ukraine 1919–1939.* New York: Carpathian Research Center, 1971.

Street, C. J. C. *Slovakia Past and Present.* London: Czech Society of Great Britain, 1928.

Suliatytsky, S. "Sribna zemlya mizh dvoma svitovymy viynamy." *Novyi Shliakh Kalendar-Almanakh.* Toronto, 1984. [The Silver Land Between the Two World Wars. *Silver Land* is reference to Carpatho-Ukraine—V.Sh.]

Svoboda, Ludvík. *Cestami života,* vol. 1. *Prague: Naše věc. Československo ve světle mezinárodního práva za druhé světové války.* Prague, 1946. [Along the Roads of Life. Vol. 1, Our Cause. Czechoslovakia in the Light of International Law During World War II.]

Szinai, Miklós and Szücs, László. *Horthy Miklós titkos iratai,* 3rd ed. Budapest: Kossuth Könyvkiadó, 1965. [Miklos Horthy's Secret Papers.]

Táborský, Eduard. *Naše věc. Československo ve světle mezinárodního práva za druhé světové války.* Prague, 1946. [Our Cause. Czechoslovakia in the Light of International Law During World War II.]

Thomson, S. Harrison. *Czechoslovakia in European History.* Hamden, Conn., 1965.

Tilkovszky, Loránt. *Revizió és nemzetiségpolitika Magyarországon 1938-1941.* Budapest: Akademiai kiadó, 1967. [Revisionism and Nationality Policy in Hungary.]

Toland, John. *Adolf Hitler,* vol. II. Garden City, N.Y.: Doubleday and Co., 1976.

Tomashivsky, Stepan. *Halychyna.* 2nd ed. Lviv, 1915. [Galicia.]

Trevor-Roper, H. R. *Hitler's Secret Conversations 1941–1944.* New York: Farrar, Strauss, and Young, 1953.

Tsehelsky, Lonhyn. *Vid legendy do pravdy. Spomyn pro podiï v Ukraïni zv'iazani z Pershym Lystopadom 1918.* New York-Philadelphia: "Bulava," 1960. [From Legend to Truth. Remembering the Events in Ukraine Connected with November 1, 1918. *November 1, 1918 was the taking of Lviv by Western Ukrainian forces and the proclamation of Western Ukraine's independence*—V.Sh.]

Turlejska, Maria. *Rok przed kleską - l. Wrzesnia 1938 - 1. Wrzesnia 1939.* 3rd ed. Warsaw: Biblioteka Wiedzy Historycznej, 1965. [A Year Before the Collapse September 1, 1938 –September 1, 1939.]

Ukrainian Press Service. *Karpats'ka Ukraïna v borot'bi* [A Collection of articles]. Vienna, 1939. [Carpatho-Ukraine in Struggle.]

Urban, Rudolf, *Tajné fondy III sekce. Z archivu Ministerstva Zahraničních Věcí Republiky Československé.* Prague, 1943. [Secret Fonds of the 3rd Section. From the Archives of the Ministry of Foreign Affairs of the Czechoslovak Republic.]

Vacovský, Dr. [Milán Hlinká]. *Slováci a Maďari. Politicko-historická úvaha.* Pittsburgh: Vyd. Slovacká liga v Amerike/Tlačou slovenského hlasnika N.S., 1914. [The Slovaks and Hungarians. A Political-Historical Essay.]

Vámbéry, Ármin. *A magyarság keletkezése és gyarapodása.* Budapest: Franklin Társulat, 1895. [The Rise and Growth of the Hungarian Nation.]

Vanat, Ivan. *Narysy novitnoï istoriï ukraïntsiv Skhidnoï Slovachchyny,* vol. 1 *(1918–1938).* Pryashiv-Bratislava: Slovats'ke pedahohychne vydavnytstvo v Bratislavi, Viddil Ukraïns'koï literatury v Priashevi, 1979. [An Outline of the History of Ukrainians of Eastern Slovakia.]

————. *Narysy novitnoï istoriï Skhidnoï Slovachchyny,* vol. 2. Pryashiv: Slovats'ke pedahohychne vydavnytstvo v Bratislavi, Viddil Ukraïns'koï literatury v Priashevi, 1985. [An Outline of the History of Ukrainians of Eastern Slovakia.]

Voloshyn, Augustyn, Msgr. *Spomyny. Relyhiyno-natsional'na borot'ba Karpats'kykh rusyniv proty madiars'koho shovynyzmu.* Philadelphia, 1959. [Memoirs. The Religious-National Struggle of Carpathian Ruthenians Against Hungarian Chauvinism.]

Welles, Sumner. *Roosevelt zachranuje mír. Paměti amerického diplomata.* Prague, 1947. [Roosevelt Saving Peace. Memoirs of an American Diplomat.]

Wiskemann, Elizabeth. *Undeclared War.* 2nd ed. New York: St. Martin's Press, 1967.

Wright, Gordon. *The Ordeal of Total War, 1939-1945.* New York: Harper and Row, 1968.

Yefremov, Serhiy. "Kryvavyi Berezen′ Karpats′koï Ukraïny." *Svoboda* (Jersey City) 4 March 1954. [Carpatho-Ukraine's Bloody Month of March.]

Zhatkovich, G. I. *Otkrytoe-Exposé*. Homestead, Pa.: Rusin Information Bureau, n.d.

Zawadowski, Zygmund. *Rús Podkarpacka i jej stanowisko prawno-polityczne*. Warsaw, 1931. [Subcarpathian Ruthenian and its Juridical-Political Status.]

Zbirnyk (Collection of Articles). *Karpats′ka Ukraïna v borotbi*. Vienna: Presova Sluzhba, 1939. [Carpatho-Ukraine in Struggle.]

Žeguc, Ivan. *Die nationalpolitischen Bestrebungen der Karpato-Ruthenen 1848–1914*. Wiesbaden: Otto Harrassowitz, 1965. [The National-Political Aspirations of Carpatho-Ukrainians, 1848–1914.]

Index

 Ukrainian Research Institute
HARVARD UNIVERSITY
Selected Publications

The Great Soviet Peasant War. Bolsheviks and Peasants, 1917–1933.
Andrea Graziosi. Harvard Papers in Ukrainian Studies. Booklet,
ISBN 0-916458-83-0.

*The Ukrainian Language in the First Half of the Twentieth Century
(1900–1914). Its State and Status.* George Shevelov. Harvard Series in
Ukrainian Studies. Clothbound, ISBN 0-916458-30-X.

The Poet as Mythmaker. A Study of Symbolic Meaning in Taras Ševčenko.
George Grabowicz. Harvard Series in Ukrainian Studies. Clothbound,
ISBN 0-674-67852-4.

*Alexander A. Potebnja's Psycholinguistic Theory of Literature. A
Metacritical Inquiry.* John Fizer. Harvard Series in Ukrainian Studies
Clothbound, ISBN 0-916458-16-4.

To receive a free catalogue of all Ukrainian Research Institute
publications (including the journal *Harvard Ukrainian Studies*) please
write, fax, or call to:

URI Publications
1583 Massachusetts Avenue
Cambridge, MA 02138
USA
tel. 617-495-3692 *fax.* 617-495-8097

e-mail:
huri@fas.harvard.edu
on-line catalog:
http://www.sabre.org/huri (follow the publications path)